THE AMERICAN INDIAN AS
SLAVEHOLDER AND SECESSIONIST

The American Indian as Slaveholder and Secessionist

BY

ANNIE HELOISE ABEL

Introduction to the Bison Book Edition
by Theda Perdue and Michael D. Green

University of Nebraska Press
Lincoln and London

Introduction copyright © 1992 by the University of Nebraska Press
Manufactured in the United States of America

First Bison Book printing: 1992
Most recent printing indicated by the last digit below:
10   9   8   7   6   5   4   3   2   1

Library of Congress Cataloging-in-Publication Data
Abel, Annie Heloise, 1873–
The American Indian as slaveholder and secessionist / by Annie Heloise
Abel: introduction to the Bison book edition by Theda Perdue and
Michael D. Green.
p.   cm.
Originally published: Cleveland: Arthur H. Clarke Co., 1915, in series:
The slaveholding Indians: v. 1.
Includes bibliographical references and index.
ISBN 0-8032-5920-4 (pa)
1. Indians of North America—Slaves, Ownership of.   2. Indians of
North America—History—Civil War, 1861–1865.   3. Indians of North
America—Indian Territory—History.   4. United States—History—
Civil War, 1861–1865—Participation, Indian.   I. Title.
E98.S6A24   1992
973'.0497—dc20
92-13971   CIP

Reprinted from the original 1915 edition published by the Arthur H.
Clark Company, Cleveland, which carried the subtitle *An Omitted Chapter
in the Diplomatic History of the Southern Confederacy*

TO
MY FATHER AND MOTHER

CONTENTS

ILLUSTRATIONS

INTRODUCTION
By Theda Perdue and Michael D. Green

The secession of southern states in the winter and spring of 1861–62 created a crisis for the Cherokees, Chickasaws, Choctaws, Creeks, and Seminoles who lived west of the Mississippi in Indian Territory. Forced out of the South in the 1830s, these nations relocated in what is today the state of Oklahoma. Governed by their own laws, they maintained a relationship with the United States through treaties and resident agents. Now civil war threatened and called into question both the Union and its relationship to the southern Indians. In this first volume of *The Slaveholding Indians*, Annie Abel explores the diplomatic maneuvers of the Confederacy to secure alliances with these nations.

The strategic location of the southern Indians meant that neutrality would be difficult. Indian Territory lay at a crossroads between East and West, North and South. Slaveholding southerners had led immigration from the United States into Mexico south of Indian Territory, and when Mexico threatened their rights as slaveholders, they fought for an independent Texas. They welcomed annexation by the United States, but the Lone Star state's constitution protected the institution of slavery.[1] Arkansas also was a slaveholding state settled largely by southerners. Commercial, social, and intellectual ties bound many residents of Indian Territory to Arkansas: Native peoples traded with Arkansas merchants, attended Arkansas schools, and sometimes even took up residence in the state.[2] With Texas to the south and Arkansas to the east, geography seemed to dictate a Confederate alliance, but Kansas lay to the north. Since 1854, when the United States Congress adopted the principle of popular sovereignty, Kansas had been a battleground between proslavery and antislavery settlers. The inability of warring sides to agree on a state constitution delayed the admission of Kansas into the Union until after the Civil War had begun.[3] If the southern Indians needed reminding, "bleeding" Kansas illustrated just how violent the conflict over slavery could become.

Slavery linked the five nations to the South.[4] Long familiar with the "peculiar institution" in their homeland, southern Indians began to acquire significant numbers of African-American slaves in the late eighteenth and early nineteenth centuries.[5] The acquisition of slaves enabled Native peoples to distance themselves from African-Americans in an increasingly racist white society, and they adopted many of the racial attitudes of the dominant Anglo-American culture.[6]

Furthermore, the "civilization" program encouraged Indians to adopt the lifestyle of Anglo-Americans, and in the South that lifestyle included plantation slavery. Some of those committed to "civilization" grew wealthy from the labor of their slaves. They took them to Indian territory where they renewed their dependence on slave labor. By the eve of the Civil War over four thousand slaves lived in the southern Indian nations west of the Mississippi. Laws protected the rights of masters to their slave property and regulated the behavior of slaves.[7] Slaveholding, however, was limited to a very small minority: only 2.3 percent of Native southerners owned slaves. Although they were a minority, these slaveholders tended to dominate political and economic life, particularly among the Cherokees, Chickasaws, and Choctaws.[8]

Yet slavery was not an uncontested issue in Indian territory. Creeks and Cherokees harbored considerable animosity toward the Seminoles who did not regard most African-Americans among them as chattel. The Seminoles had seized slaves from the Creeks during the Creek Civil War of 1813–14 and had taken them to Florida where they developed a tributary relationship. Joined by escaped slaves, these black Seminoles fought against the United States in the Seminole War and endured removal along with other captured Seminoles.[9] The United States expected the Seminoles to share a nation with the Creeks, but the Seminoles refused because they feared Creek enslavement of the black Seminoles. Instead, many Seminoles and African-Americans took refuge in the Cherokee Nation where slaveholders charged them with contributing to a slave rebellion.[10] Final resolution came in 1855 with the creation of a separate Seminole Nation.[11]

Many Indians other than the Seminoles had misgiv-

ings about the institution of slavery. Within the Cherokee and Creek nations, in particular, traditionalists
saw slavery as a foreign institution that had no place in
Native life. The individuals who profited from it were
those who had abandoned their Native heritage. Consequently, slavery became a symbol of "civilization"
and a target for those who sought to revitalize traditional culture. The Kee-too-wah society among the
Cherokees, for example, was both an abolitionist and
revitalization movement.[12] And Opothle Yoholo, who
led thousands of Creeks and Cherokees to Union lines
in Kansas after the war began, was a cultural conservative with distinct anti-southern opinions.[13] Debates
over slavery, therefore, often had far deeper roots
within Native societies. The Cherokees held ambiva-
lent feelings about slavery largely because of the presence of anti-slavery missionaries, particularly those of
the Baptists and the American Board of Commissioners for Foreign missions.[14] Their defense of Native
rights during the removal crisis endeared them to the
Cherokees and permitted them considerable latitude
on the subject of slavery. Although the Cherokees at
the insistence of their agent ultimately expelled one of
the Baptists, the missionaries continued to enjoy a
large following, particularly among non-slaveholding
traditionalists. But even prominent slaveholders dem-
onstrated gratitude and respect.

Other southern Indians also recalled their recent
histories. Land-hungry southerners had been responsible for their removal west of the Mississippi. They
had denounced Native peoples as "savages" who had
no claim to their land, and they had moved onto Indian land in droves.[15] The state governments now
forming the Confederacy had done nothing to protect
the Native title and had demanded that the federal

government remove the Indians immediately.[16] Many
people could remember the hardship and suffering
that accompanied the journey west and the difficulties
involved in rebuilding their lives. They also remembered the defense of Native rights that came almost exclusively from the Northeast, the same region that had
given birth to abolition.[17] How could they so easily turn
on those who had befriended them and unite with
their former oppressors?

Furthermore, all the nations of Indian Territory
had enjoyed treaty relations with the United States
that extended back to the 1780s. These treaties were
important statements of the rights of each nation, they
defined the protective obligations of the United States,
and they had become central to the emerging national-
ist thinking of many Native leaders. The treaties also
bound each nation to the United States financially in
the form of stipulated payments for land sold and for
services such as the subsidies paid by Congress to support public schools. By 1861 these treaties had assumed an importance in the public and private affairs
of most southern Indians that could be abandoned, or
rejected, only with the greatest difficulty.

Annie Abel chronicles the process by which the
southern Indians arrived at a Confederate alliance.
They defected, she suggests, because the United States
paid so little attention to them. The Confederacy, on
the other hand, relied on the skill of southerners who
had served these Indians as agents and advisers and
who were authorized to offer them extremely favorable terms. Abel regards the negotiations as an important chapter in American diplomatic history.[18] In doing
so, she takes the notion of Indian sovereignty seriously.
The southern Indians whom she describes acted as nations, and the Union and Confederacy treated them as

such. These Indians were not faceless victims: their leaders made hard and perhaps unwise choices, but they understood the issues, considered the consequences, and made reasoned decisions.

Abel lived long before the advent of ethnohistory and she pays little attention to the domestic politics of Native nations. The tensions between highly acculturated slaveholders and pro-Union traditionalists receives only cursory treatment. Native peoples, in her work, act within the same cultural parameters as non-Indians: "They were moved to fight, not by instincts of savagery, but by identically the same motives and impulses as the white men" (p. 17). She is concerned about Indian-white relations, not the internal dynamics of Native societies. She has little interest in the political economy of slavery, the changes in cultural values and social structure that slavery engendered, or the distinctive African-Indian slave culture that developed. These topics had to await the social and political awareness born of the civil rights movement, and the theoretical constructs and methodology of the new social history.

She uses language that is ethnocentric and sometimes racist. She employs the offensive term *half-breed* and concludes that all Indians "have an aversion to work" (p. 46). Without condoning her language or attitudes, we must remember that Abel lived in a racist age. She was a contemporary of Ulrich B. Phillips, who portrayed the antebellum South as a land where slavery protected intellectually and morally deficient Africans.[19] Like Phillips, however, her broader conclusions hit the mark. Modern historians, who denounce Phillips's racism, concur with his assertion that slavery made the South unique. Similarly, we recognize that Abel was right to point out that the southern Indians' long association with slavery shaped their history.

Abel based her work on extensive research in the records of the Indian office, some of which she recovered from an attic. The first historian to use many of these sources, she demonstrates, as one reviewer phrased it, "a tendency towards over-documentation."[20] Footnotes often print complete letters, and an appendix contains selections from the recovered documents. In this sense, Abel's book is documentary as well as narrative history. Her work also represents the respect that historians of her generation had for evidence. Historians had embraced the scientific method and self-consciously moved their discipline from literature to social science. Readers may wish that Abel had paid somewhat more attention to literary style: one reviewer accurately described it as "unusually dry."[21]

Annie Heloise Abel was born in England in 1873.[22] At the age of twelve, she emigrated with her family to Kansas. She received her undergraduate and master's degrees from the University of Kansas and studied for a year to Cornell. In 1893 she became the first woman to receive Yale's Bulkley Fellowship; Yale awarded her Ph.D. in 1905. Her dissertation, "The History of Events Resulting in Indian Consolidation West of the Mississippi," appeared in the Annual Report of the American Historical Association in 1906 and remains a standard work on Federal removal policy.[23] In that year, she moved from her first job at Wells College to Women's College of Baltimore, now Goucher College, where she remained until 1915. While she was living in Baltimore, Abel had easy access to Indian Bureau records in Washington. She began to investigate the role of Indians in the Civil War, and published an article on the subject in 1910.[24] In 1915, the year the first volume in *The Slaveholding Indians* appeared, Abel moved to

Smith College. There she developed an interest in British policy towards Native peoples and in 1921 she went to Australia on her sabbatical to research aboriginal policy. Abel married while she was in Australia and resigned her position at Smith. She used her husband's name, Henderson, but after they separated permanently in 1927, she adopted a hyphenated surname, Abel-Henderson. She taught briefly at Sweetbriar College and the University of Kansas before retiring in 1930 and moving to Aberdeen, Washington, to live with her sister. When she died in 1947, Abel left a substantial body of work on Native peoples. In addition to her studies of southern Indians, she meticulously edited the records of travelers, fur traders, and Indian agents.[25]

Abel's major legacy, however, is her work on slaveholding Indians. In this work, she charts the diplomatic maneuvers that led to the Confederate alliances, the participation of Native soldiers in military operations that brought devastation to Indian Territory, and the impact of Confederate defeat on the nations that had repudiated their treaties with the United States. The story is a tragic one, but leaving it untold would be a greater tragedy. Native southerners shared the experience of the Civil War with other Americans, and their involvement in that upheaval had as profound an effect on their subsequent history. Abel's was the first serious telling of that story.

NOTES

1. Randolph B. Campbell, *An Empire for Slavery: The Peculiar Institution in Texas, 1821–1865* (Baton Rouge: Louisiana State University Press, 1989).

2. Edward Everett Dale, "Arkansas and the Cherokees," *Arkansas Historical Quarterly* 8 (1949): 95–114; James M. Woods, *Rebellion and Realign-*

ment: Arkansas's Road to Secession (Fayetteville: University of Arkansas Press, 1987).

3. Don E. Fehrenbacher, *The South in Three Sectional Crises* (Baton Rouge: Louisiana State University Press, 1980), pp. 45–65; Gerald W. Wolff, *The Kansas-Nebraska Bill: Party, Section, and the Coming of the Civil War* (New York: Revisionist Press, 1977); James A. Rawley, *Race and Politics: "Bleeding Kansas" and the Coming of the Civil War* (Philadelphia: Lippincott, 1969); Alice Nichols, *Bleeding Kansas* (New York: Oxford University Press, 1954).

4. See Theda Perdue, "Indians in Southern History," in *Indians in American History,* ed. Frederick E. Hoxie (Arlington Heights, Ill.: Forum Press, Inc., 1988), pp. 137–57.

5. There has been considerable scholarly interest in slaveholding among the southern Indians. See Wyatt F. Jeltz, "The Relations of Negroes and Choctaw and Chickasaw Indians," *Journal of Negro History* 33 (1948): 24–37; C. Calvin Smith, "The Oppressed Oppressors: Negro Slavery among the Choctaw Indians of Oklahoma," *Red River Valley Historical Review* 2 (1975): 240–53; Perdue, *Slavery and the Evolution of Cherokee Society, 1540–1866* (Knoxville: University of Tennessee Press, 1979); Daniel F. Littlefield, *Africans and Creeks: From the Colonial Period to the Civil War* (Westport, Conn.: Greenwood Press, 1979); Martha Condray Searcy, "The Introduction of African Slavery into the Creek Nation," *Georgia Historical Quarterly* 66 (1982): 24; William G. McLoughlin, *The Cherokee Ghost Dance: Essays on the Southeastern Indians, 1789–1861* (Macon, Ga.: Mercer University Press, 1984); Daniel H. Usner, Jr., "American Indians on the Cotton Frontier: Changing Economic Relations with Citizens and Slaves in the Mississippi Territory," *Journal of American History* 72 (1985): 297–317; Kathryn E. Braund, "The Creek Indians, Blacks, and Slavery," *Journal of Southern History* 57 (1991): 602–36.

6. William S. Willis, Jr., "Divide and Rule: Red, White, and Black in the Southeast," *Journal of Negro History* 48 (1963); James H. Merrell, "The Racial Education of the Catawba Indians," *Journal of Southern History* 50 (1984): 363–84.

7. The law codes of the Cherokees, Chickasaws, Choctaws and Creeks have been published in *The Constitutions and Laws of the American Indian Tribes* (Series I and II, Wilmington, Del.: 1973, 1975).

8. Michael F. Doran, "Negro Slaves of the Five Civilized Tribes," *Annals of the Association of American Geographers* 68 (1978): 335–50.

9. Kenneth W. Porter, "Negroes on the Southern Frontier," *Journal of Negro History* 33 (1948): 53–78; J. Leitch Wright, Jr., *Creeks and Seminoles: The Destruction and Regeneration of the Muscogulge People* (Lincoln: University of Nebraska Press, 1986).

10. Daniel F. Littlefield, Jr., and Lonnie E. Underhill, "Slave 'Revolt' in the Cherokee Nation, 1842," *American Indian Quarterly* 3 (1977): 121–31.

11. Littlefield, *Africans and Seminoles: From Removal to Emancipation* (Westport, Conn.: Greenwood Press, Inc., 1977).

12. James Duncan, "The Keetoowah Society," *Chronicles of Oklahoma* 4 (1926): 251–55; Howard Q. Tyner, "The Keetoowah Society in Cherokee History," M.A. Thesis, University of Tulsa, 1949; Janey E. Hendrix, "Redbird Smith and the Nighthawk Keetoowahs," *Journal of Cherokee Studies* 8 (1983): 22–39, 73–86.

13. Edwin C. Bearss, "The Civil War Comes to Indian Territory, 1861: The Flight of Opothleyoholo," *Journal of the West* 11 (1972): 9–42; Carter Blue Clark, "Opothleyohola and the Creeks during the Civil War," in *Indian Leaders: Oklahoma's First Statesmen*, ed. H. Glen Jordan and Thomas M. Holm (Oklahoma City: Oklahoma Historical Society, 1979), pp. 49–63.

14. Robert Lewit, "Indian Missions and Antislavery Sentiments: A Conflict of Evangelical and Humanitarian Ideals," *Mississippi Valley Historical Review* 50 (1963–64): 39–55; William G. McLoughlin, *Champions of the Cherokees: Evan and John B. Jones* (Princeton: Princeton University Press, 1990).

15. For an example of this kind of rhetoric, see Wilson Lumpkin, *The Removal of the Cherokee Indians from Georgia* (New York: Dodd Mead & Co., 1907).

16. For the development and implementation of the removal policy, see Ronald N. Satz, *American Indian Policy in the Jacksonian Era* (Lincoln: University of Nebraska Press, 1975). For the response of one Native group, see Michael D. Green, *The Politics of Indian Removal: Creek Government and Society in Crisis* (Lincoln: University of Nebraska Press, 1981).

17. For an example of this defense, see Jeremiah Evarts, *Cherokee Removal: The "William Penn" Essays and Other Writings* (Knoxville: University of Tennessee Press, 1981).

18. The most recent history of the Confederacy described relations with southern Indians as "the ultimate reality of the Southern diplomatic circumstance." Emory M. Thomas, *The Confederate Nation, 1861–1865* (New York: Harper & Row, 1979), pp. 188–89.

19. Ulrich B. Phillips, *American Negro Slavery* (New York: D. Appleton and Co., 1918).

20. *American Historical Review* 21 (1916): 359.

21. *Journal of Negro History* 1 (1916): 339.

22. This biographical sketch is condensed from Harry Kelsey, "A Dedication to the Memory of Annie Heloise Abel Henderson, 1873–1947," *Arizona and the West* 15 (1973): 1–4.

23. "The History of Events Resulting in Indian Consolidation West of the Mississippi," *Annual Report of the American Historical Association* 1 (1906) 235–450.

24. "The Indians in the Civil War," *American Historical Review* 15 (1910): 281–96.

25. *The Official Correspondence of James S. Calhoun While Indian Agent at Santa Fe and Superintendent of Indians Affairs in New Mexico* (Washington: U.S. Government Printing Office, 1915); "The Journal of John Greiner," *Old Santa Fe* 3 (1916): 189–243; *A Report from Natchitoches in 1807 by Dr. John Sibley* (New York: Museum of the American Indian, 1922); *Chardon's Journal at Fort Clark, 1834–1839* (Pierre: South Dakota Department of History, 1932); *Tabeau's Narrative of Loisel's Expedition to the Upper Missouri* (Norman: University of Oklahoma Press, 1939); "Indian Affairs in New Mexico under the Administration of William Carr Lane; from the Journal of John Ward," *New Mexico Historical Review* 16 (1941): 106–32, 328–58.

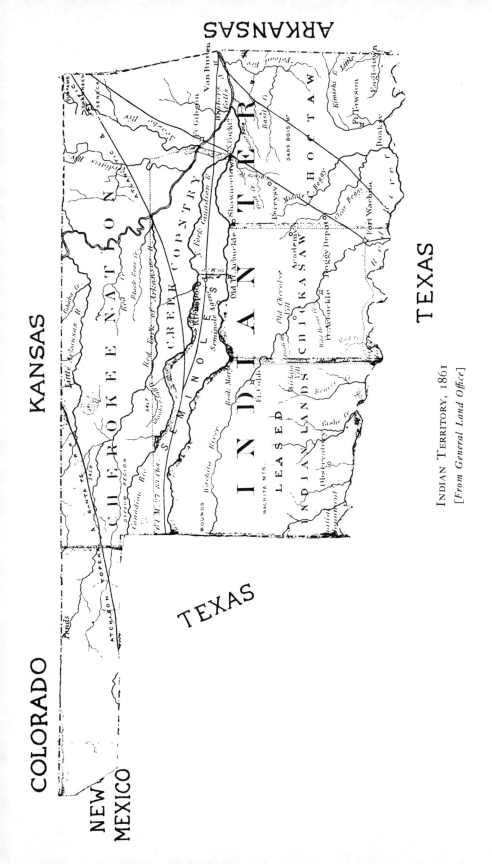

Indian Territory, 1861

[From General Land Office]

THE AMERICAN INDIAN AS
SLAVEHOLDER AND SECESSIONIST

I. THE GENERAL SITUATION IN THE INDIAN COUNTRY, 1830-1860

Veterans of the Confederate service who saw action along the Missouri-Arkansas frontier have frequently complained, in recent years, that military operations in and around Virginia during the War between the States receive historically so much attention that, as a consequence, the steady, stubborn fighting west of the Mississippi River is either totally ignored or, at best, cast into dim obscurity. There is much of truth in the criticism but it applies in fullest measure only when the Indians are taken into account; for no accredited history of the American Civil War that has yet appeared has adequately recognized certain rather interesting facts connected with that period of frontier development; viz., that Indians fought on both sides in the great sectional struggle, that they were moved to fight, not by instincts of savagery, but by identically the same motives and impulses as the white men, and that, in the final outcome, they suffered even more terribly than did the whites. Moreover, the Indians fought as solicited allies, some as nations, diplomatically approached. Treaties were made with them as with foreign powers and not in the farcical, fraudulent way that had been customary in times past. They promised alliance and were given in return political position – a fair exchange. The southern white man, embarrassed, conceded much, far more than he really believed in, more than he ever could or would have conceded, had he not himself been so fearfully hard pressed. His own predicament, the exigencies of the moment, made him give to the Indian a justice, the like of which neither one of them had dared even to dream. It was quite otherwise with the northern white man, however; for he, self-confident and self-reliant, negotiated with the Indian in the traditional way, took base advantage of the straits in which he found him, asked him to help him fight his battles, and, in the selfsame moment, plotted to dispossess him of his lands, the very lands that had, less than five and twenty years before, been pledged as an Indian possession "as long as the grass should grow and the waters run."

From what has just been said, it can be easily inferred that two distinct groups of Indians will have to be dealt with, a northern and a southern; but, for the present, it will be best to take them all together. Collectively, they occupied a vast extent of country in the so-called great American desert. Their situation was peculiar. Their participation in the war, in some capacity, was absolutely inevitable; but, preparatory to any right understanding of the reasons, geographical, institutional, political, financial, and military, that made it so, a rapid survey of conditions ante-dating the war must be considered.

It will be remembered that for some time prior to 1860 the policy[1] of the United States government had been to relieve the eastern states of their Indian inhabitants and that this it had done, since the first years of

---

[1] Confessedly much to its discredit, the United States government has never had, for any appreciable length of time, a well-developed and well-defined Indian policy, one that has made the welfare of the aborigines its sole concern. Legislation for the subject race has almost invariably been dictated by the needs of the hour, by the selfish and exorbitant demands of pioneers, and by the greed and caprice of politicians.

Andrew Jackson's presidency, by a more or less compulsory removal to the country lying immediately west of Arkansas and Missouri. As a result, the situation there created was as follows: In the territory comprehended in the present state of Kansas, alongside of indigenous tribes, like the Kansa and the Osage,[2] had been placed various tribes or portions of tribes from the old Northwest[3] – the Shawnees and Munsees from Ohio,[4] the Delawares, Kickapoos, Potawatomies, and Miamies from Indiana, the Ottawas and Chippewas from Michigan, the Wyandots from Ohio and Michigan, the Weas, Peorias, Kaskaskias, and Piankashaws from Illinois, and a few New York Indians from Wisconsin. To the southward of all of those northern tribal immigrants and chiefly beyond the later Kansas boundary, or in the present state of Oklahoma, had been similarly placed the great[5] tribes from the South[6] – the Creeks from

---

[2] There were, of course, other indigenous tribes to the westward, in the direction of Colorado and Texas, and to the northward, in southern Nebraska; but only the latter were more than remotely affected, as far as local habitation was concerned, by the coming of the eastern emigrants and the consequent introduction of the reservation system.

[3] Kansas Historical Society *Collections*, vol. viii, 72-109.

[4] In scarcely a single case here cited was the old home of the tribe limited by the boundaries of a single state nor is it to be understood that the state here mentioned was necessarily the original habitat of the tribe. It was only the territorial headquarters of the tribe at the time of removal or at the time when the policy of removal was first insisted upon as a *sine qua non*. Some of the Indians emigrated independently of treaty arrangements with the United States government and some did not immediately direct their steps towards Kansas or Oklahoma; but made, through choice or through necessity, an intervening point a stopping-place. The Kickapoos, the Shawnees, and the Delawares tarried in Missouri, the Choctaws and the Cherokees, many of them, in Arkansas but that was before 1830, the date of the removal law. After 1830, there was no possible resting-place for weary Indians this side of the Ozark Mountains.

[5] Some of the more insignificant southern Indians eventually found their way also to Oklahoma. In 1860 there were a few Louisiana Caddoes in the northwestern part of the Chickasaw country, most likely the same that, in 1866, were reported to have been driven out of Texas in 1859 by bushwhackers and then out of the Washita country at the opening of the Civil War. They

Georgia and Alabama, the Cherokees from Tennessee
and Georgia, the Seminoles from Florida, and the Choctaws and Chickasaws from Alabama and Mississippi.[7]
The population of the whole country thus colonized

continued throughout the war loyal to the United States. In 1853 the Choctaw
General Council passed an act admitting to the rights of citizenship several
Catawba Indians; and, from that circumstance, the Office of Indian Affairs
surmised that the Choctaws would be willing to incorporate Catawbas yet in
the Carolinas. In 1857 there were about seventy Catawbas in South Carolina on
a tiny reservation. They expressed an ardent wish to go among the Choctaws.
In 1860 the Catawbas were in possession of the northeastern part of the Choctaw country.

   [6] For the detailed history of events leading up to Indian removals, particularly the southern, see American Historical Association, *Report*, 1906, 241-450.

   [7] Not all of the southern Indians had emigrated in the thirties and forties.
A considerable number of Cherokees removed themselves from the country east
of the Mississippi to Texas. This was immediately subsequent to and induced
by the American Revolution [Texas Historical Association, *Quarterly*, July,
1897, 38-46 and October, 1903, 95-165]. Many Cherokees, likewise, took the
suggestion of President Jefferson and moved to the Arkansas country prior to
1820. Moreover, there were "Eastern Cherokees" in controversy with the
"Western Cherokees" for many years after the Civil War. Their endless
quarrels over property proved the occasion of much litigation. In the late
fifties active measures were taken by the Office of Indian Affairs to complete
the removal of the Seminoles and to accomplish by intrigue and diplomacy
what the long and expensive Second Seminole War had utterly failed to do.
Elias Rector of Arkansas superintended the matter and the Seminole chief,
John Jumper, gave valuable assistance, as did also the Creeks, who generously
granted to the Seminoles a home within the Creek country west [Creek Treaty,
1856, Kappler's *Indian Laws and Treaties*, vol. ii, 757]. Billy Bowlegs was
the last Seminole chief of prominence to leave Florida [Coe's *Red Patriots*,
198]. In 1853 there were still some four hundred Choctaws reported as living
in Alabama and there must have been even more than that in Mississippi. In
1854 steps were taken, but unsuccessfully, for their removal. In 1859 Representative John J. McRae presented a petition from citizens of various Mississippi counties asking that the Choctaws be removed altogether from the
state because of their intimacy and intercourse with the negroes. The Office
of Indian Affairs refused to act. Perchance, it considered the moment inopportune or the means at hand insufficient. It may even have considered the
charge against the Choctaws a mere pretext and quite unfounded since it was
commonly reported that the Choctaws had a decided aversion to that particular
kind of race mixture. In that respect they differed very considerably from
the Creeks who to-day are said to present a very curious spectacle of an almost complete mixture. Choctaws from Mississippi and Cherokees from North
Carolina and Catawbas from South Carolina fought with the South in the
Civil War.

and, in a sense, reduced to the reservation system, amounted approximately to seventy-four thousand souls, less than seven thousand of whom were north of the Missouri-Compromise line. The others were all south of it and, therefore, within a possible slave belt.

This circumstance is not without significance; for it is the colonized, or reservation, Indians [8] exclusively that are to figure in these pages and, since this story is a chapter in the struggle between the North and the South, the proportion of southerners to northerners among the Indian immigrants must, in the very nature of things, have weight. The relative location of northern and southern tribes seems to have been determined with a very careful regard to the restrictions of the Missouri Compromise and the interdicted line of thirty-six degrees and thirty minutes was pretty nearly the boundary between them. [9] That it was so by accident may or may not be subject for conjecture. Fortunately for the disinterested motives of politicians but most unfortunately for the defenceless Indians, the Cherokee land obtruded itself just a little above the thirty-seventh parallel and formed a "Cherokee Strip" eagerly coveted by Kansans in later days. One objection, be it remembered, that had been offered to the original plan of removal was that, unless the slaveholding southern Indians were moved directly westward along parallel

[8] Other Indians made trouble during the progress of the Civil War, as, for instance, the Sioux in the summer of 1862. The Sioux, however, were not fighting for or against the issues of the white man's war. They were simply taking advantage of a favorable occasion, when the United States government was preoccupied, to avenge their own wrongs.

[9] The existence of the "Cherokee Neutral Land" out of which the southeastern counties of Kansas were illegitimately formed was not exactly an exception to this. The Neutral Land, eight hundred thousand acres in extent, was an independent purchase, made by the Cherokees, and was not included in the exchange or in the original scheme that forced their removal from Georgia. It was a subsequent concession to outraged justice.

lines of latitude, northern rights under the Missouri
Compromise would be encroached upon. Yet slavery
was not conscientiously excluded from Kansas in the
days antecedent to its organization as a territory. Within the Indian country, and it was all Indian country
then, slavery was allowed, at least on sufferance, both
north and south of the interdicted line. It was even encouraged by many white men who made their homes or
their living there, by interlopers, licensed traders, and
missionaries;[10] but it flourished as a legitimate institution only among the great tribes planted south of the
line. With them it had been a familiar institution long
before the time of their exile. In their native haunts
they had had negro slaves as had had the whites and
removal had made no difference to them in that particular. Since the beginning of the century refuge to fugitives and confusion of ownership had been occasions for
frequent quarrel between them and the citizens of the
Southern States. Later, when questions came up touching the status of slavery on strictly federal soil, the Indian country and the District of Columbia often found
themselves listed together.[11] Moreover, after 1850, it
became a matter of serious import whether or no the
Fugitive Slave Law was operative within the Indian
country; and, when influenced apparently by Jefferson
Davis, Attorney-general Cushing gave as his opinion
that it was, new controversies arose. Slaves belonging

---

[10] By far the best instance of missionary activity in behalf of slavery among
the northern Indian immigrants is to be found in the case of the Reverend
Thomas Johnson's work at the Shawnee Mission [Ray's *Repeal of the Missouri
Compromise*, footnote 207]. Johnson, like William Walker, head chief of the
Wyandots, was an ardent pro-slavery advocate [*ibid.*, footnote 205] and took a
rather disgracefully prominent part in the notorious election frauds of early
Kansas territorial days [House *Report*, 34th congress, first session, no. 200, pp.
14, 18, 94, 425].

[11] Buchanan's *Works*, vol. iii, 348, 350, 353.

to the Indians were often enticed away by the abolitionists [12] and still more often were seized by southern men
under pretense of their being fugitives.[13]   In cases of
the latter sort, the Indian owners had little or no re-
dress in the federal courts of law.[14]

[12] Siebert's *Underground Railroad from Slavery to Freedom*, 284.

[13] The most interesting case that came up in this connection was that of the
so-called Beams' Negroes, resident in the Choctaw country and illegally
claimed as refugees by John B. Davis of Mississippi [Indian Office, *Special
Files*, no. 277]. The Reverend S. A. Worcester interested himself in their behalf [Jefferson Davis to Worcester, October 7, 1854] and a decision was finally
rendered in their favor. Another interesting case of similar nature was, "In
re negroes taken from Overton Love and David Wall of the Chickasaw Nation
by Citizens of Texas, 1848-'57" [*ibid.*, no. 278].

[14] Under the Intercourse Law of 1834, the Indian Territory had been annexed for judicial purposes to the western district of Arkansas. The Indians
were much dissatisfied. They felt themselves entitled to a federal court of
their own, a privilege the United States government persistently denied to
them but one that the Confederate government readily granted. As matters
stood, prior to the Civil War, the red men seemed always at the mercy of the
white man's distorted conception of justice and were, perforce, quite beyond
the reach of the boasted guaranties of theoretical Anglo-Saxon justice since
the very location of the court precluded a trial by their peers of the vicinage.
The journey to Arkansas, in those early days, was long and tiresome and expensive. Complications frequently arose and matters, difficult of adjustment,
even under the best of circumstances. Among the Creeks and Seminoles, the
status of the free negro was exceptionally high, partly due, with respect to the
latter, to conditions growing out of the Second Seminole War. As already intimated, the Creeks had no aversion whatsoever to race mixtures and inter-
marriage between negroes and Indians was rather common. The half-breeds
resulting from such unions were accepted as bona fide members of the tribe by
the Indians in the distribution of annuities, but not by the United States
courts — another source of difficulty and a very instructive one as well, particularly from the standpoint of reconstructionist exactions.

Occasionally the presence of the free negro within the Indian country was
a source of grave danger. The accompanying letters outline a case in point:

HEAD QUARTERS 7TH. MIL: DEPT. FORT SMITH, March 5th. 1852.

SIR: By direction of the Colonel commanding the Department I
transmit herewith copies of a communication from George Folsom,
Chief of the Pushmataha District, to Colonel Wilson Choctaw Agent and
one from Colonel William Wilson Choctaw Agent to Brevet Major
Holmes commanding Fort Washita asking aid from the Military force.

As the letter from the Choctaw Agent is not sufficiently explicit as to
what he wishes done by the Military authority the subject is referred to
you, and if on investigation it be found that Military interference is

In point of fact, during all the years between the various dates of Indian removal and the breaking out of the Civil War, the Indian country was constantly

necessary to enforce the intercourse law, prompt assistance will be rendered for the purposes therein specified, under the direction and in presence of the Choctaw Agent. Respectfully Yr Obt. Servt.,

FRANCIS N PAGE, Asst. Adjt. Genl.

Colonel John Drennen, Superintendent W. T.

Inclosure

CHOCTAW AGENCY, February 9th 1852

SIR: The enclosed copy of a letter from Colonel George Folsom Chief of Pushmataha District of the Choctaw Nation will put you in possession of the facts and reasons why I address you at this time.

As the position of the free Negros and Indians alluded to in the Chief's letter seems to be of rather a hostile character, having built themselves a Fort doubtless for the purpose of defending themselves if interupted in their present location, it seems to me necessary that they should be driven away if necessary by Military authority; and, as your post is the most convenient to the place where the Negroes and Indians are Forted I have thought that a command could be sent with less trouble and at less expense to the government by you than any one else. I would therefore most respectfully call upon you to take such steps as you may think most advisable to remove from the Choctaw country the persons complained of by the Chief, and if necessary call upon Chief Folsom to aid you with his light horse, who may be of much service to you in the way of Guides. Very Respectfully Yr. Obt Servt.

(Signed)   WILLIAM WILSON, Choctaw Agent

[Endorsement]   A true Copy, Francis N Page, Asst. Adjt. Genl.

Inclosure

PUSHMATAHA DISTRICT, January 23. 1852.

DEAR SIR: I spoke to you about those free negroes upon the head waters of Boggy, when I last saw you, requesting to have something done with them. I have just learned that the negroes and some Indians are banded together and have built themselves a little Fort. There is no doubt but that they will be a great trouble to us. One of our country judges sent for the light-horse-men to go and seize the negroes, but I have forbid them going, and many of our people wish to go and see them. I have forbid any body to go there with intentions to take them. It will no doubt be hard to break them up. You have probably just returned home, and it may seem tresspassing upon you to write you about those negroes and Indians, but you are our agent, and we have the right to look to you for help. It seems to me this affair wants an immediate action on it.

I have simply stated to you how these negroes and Indians are Forted up that you may better know how to deal with them. In pur-

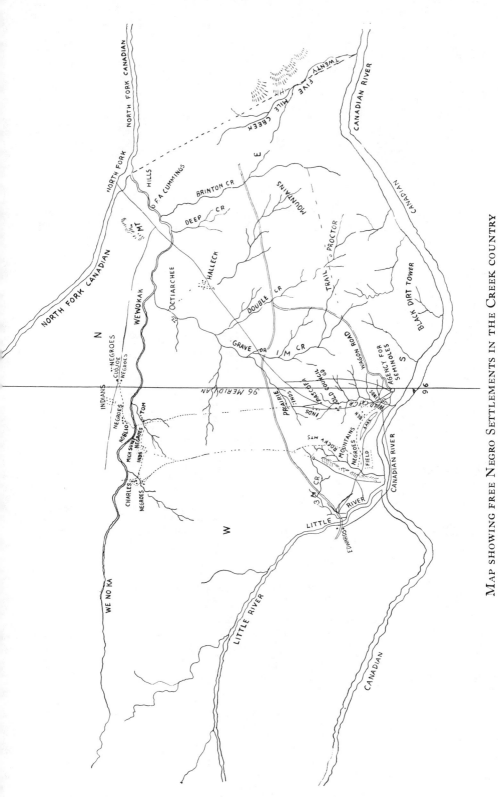

MAP SHOWING FREE NEGRO SETTLEMENTS IN THE CREEK COUNTRY

[From Office of Indian Affairs]

beset by difficulties. Some of the difficulties were incident to removal or to disturbances within the tribes but most of them were incident to changes and to political complications in the white man's country. Scarcely had the removal project been fairly launched and the first Indian emigrants started upon their journey westward than events were in train for the overthrow of the whole scheme.

When Calhoun mapped out the Indian country in his elaborate report of 1825, the selection of the trans-Missouri region might well have been regarded as judicious. Had the plan of general removal been adopted then, before sectional interests had wholly vitiated it, the United States government might have gained and, in a measure, would have richly deserved the credit of doing at least one thing for the protection and preservation of the aborigines from motives, not self-interested, but purely humanitarian. The moment was opportune. The territory of the United States was then limited by the confines of the Louisiana Purchase and its settlements by the great American desert. Traders only had penetrated to any considerable extent to the base of the Rockies; but experience already gained might have taught that their presence was portentous and significant of the need of haste; that is, if Calhoun's selection were to continue judicious; for traders, as has been amply proved in both British and American history, have ever been but the advance agents of settlers.

Unfortunately for the cause of pure philanthropy, the United States government was exceedingly slow in

forming your duties if I can in any way render you any assistance I shall always be happy to do so. Very respectfully Your friend
(Signed) GEORGE FOLSOM, Chief Push: Dist:
Col: William Wilson, Choctaw Agent
[Endorsement] a true Copy, Francis N Page, Asst. Adjt. Genl.

adopting the plan of Indian removal; but its citizens were by no means equally slow in developing the spirit of territorial expansion. Their successful seizure of West Florida had fired their ambition and their cupidity. With Texas annexed and lower Oregon occupied, the selection of the trans-Missouri region had ceased to be judicious. How could the Indians expect to be secure in a country that was the natural highway to a magnificent country beyond, invitingly open to settlement! But this very pertinent and patent fact the officials at Washington singularly failed to realize and they went on calmly assuring the Indians that they should never be disturbed again, that the federal government would protect them in their rights and against all enemies, that no white man should be allowed to intrude upon them, that they should hold their lands undiminished forever, and that no state or territorial lines should ever again circumscribe them. Such promises were decidedly fatuous, dead letters long before the ink that recorded them had had time to dry. The Mexican War followed the annexation of Texas and its conquests necessitated a further use of the Indian highway. Soldiers that fought in that war saw the Indian land and straightway coveted it. Forty-niners saw it and coveted it also. Prospectors and adventurers of all sorts laid plans for exploiting it. It entered as a determining factor into Benton's great scheme for building a national road that should connect the Atlantic and Pacific shores and with the inception of that came a very sudden and a very real danger; for the same great scheme precipitated, although in an indirect sort of way, the agitation for the opening up of Kansas and Nebraska to white settlement, which, of course, meant that the recent Indian colonists, in spite of all the solemn governmental guaranties that had been given to them, would have to be ousted, for would not the "sovereign" people of America demand it? Then, too, the Dred Scott decision, the result of a dishonorable political collusion as it was,[15] militated indirectly against Indian interests. It is true that it was only in its extralegal aspect that it did this but it did it none the less; for, if the authority of the federal government was not supreme in the territories and not supreme in any part of the country not yet organized into states, then the Indian landed property rights in the West that rested exclusively upon federal grant, under the Removal Act of 1830, were virtually nil. It is rather interesting to observe, in this connection, how inconsistent human nature is when political expediency is the thing at stake; for it happened that the same people and the same party, identically, that, in the second and third decades of the nineteenth century, had tried to convince the Indians, and against their better judgment too, that the red man would be forever unmolested in the western country because the federal government owned it absolutely and could give a title in perpetuity, argued, in the fourth and fifth decades, that the states were the sole proprietors, that they were, in fact, the joint owners of everything heretofore considered as national. Inferentially, therefore, Indians, like negroes, had no rights that white men were bound to respect.

The crucial point has now been reached in this discussion. From the date of the Kansas-Nebraska Bill, the sectional affiliation of the Indian country became a thing of more than passing moment. Whatever may have been John C. Calhoun's ulterior and real motive

---

[15] Buchanan's *Works*, vol. x, "the Catron letter," 106; "the Grier letter," 106-107.

in urging that the trans-Missouri region be closed to white settlement forever, whether he did, as some of his abolitionist enemies have charged, plan thus to block free-state expansion and so frustrate the natural operations of the Missouri Compromise, certain it is, that southern politicians, after his time, became the chief advocates of Indian territorial integrity, the ones that pleaded most often and most noisily that guaranties to Indians be faithfully respected. They had in mind the northern part of the Indian country and that alone; but, no doubt, the circumstance was purely accidental, since at that time, the early fifties, the northern [16] was the only part likely to be encroached upon.[17] Their interest in the southern part took an entirely different direction

[16] This was as it appeared to N. G. Taylor, Commissioner of Indian Affairs, as he looked back, in 1867, upon events of the past few years. He was then of the opinion that the very existence of slavery among the southern tribes had most probably saved their country from being coveted by emigrants going westward.

[17] One agency under the Southern Superintendency, the Neosho River Agency, was, however, included in the scheme preliminary to the organization of Kansas and Nebraska. See the following letters found in Thomas S. Drew's *Letter Press Book*:

(a)   OFFICE SUPT. IND. AFFAIRS FORT SMITH, ARKS. Dec. 21, 1853.
    SIR: Inclosed herewith you will receive letters from Agent Dorn, dated the 1st and 2nd instant; the former in relation to the disposition of the Indians within his agency to meet Commissioners on the subject of selling their lands, or having a Territorial form of Government extend over them by the United States: and the latter nominating John Finch as Blacksmith to the Great and Little Osages. Very respectfully Your obt. servt.   A. H. RUTHERFORD, Clerk for Supt.
Hon. Geo. W. Manypenny, Comʳ Ind. Affairs
    Washington City.

(b)   OFFICE SUPT. INDIAN AFFAIRS FORT SMITH, ARKS. Dec. 29, 1853.
    SIR: . . . I have also to acknowledge the receipt of letters from you of the 2nd instant to the Commissioner of Ind. Affrs. upon the subject of the Indians within your Agency being willing to meet Commissioners on the part of the U.S. preparatory to selling their lands, or to take into consideration the propriety of admitting a Territorial form of Government extended over them & . . .
                         A. H. RUTHERFORD, Clerk for Supt.
A. J. Dorn, U.S. Indian Agt., Crawford Seminary.

and that also may have been accidental or occasioned by conditions quite local and present. For this southern part, by the way, they recommended American citizenship and the creation of American states [18] in the Union,

[18] In this connection, the following are of interest:

(a) The Choctaws, it is understood, are prepared to receive and assent to the provisions of a bill introduced three years since into the Senate by Senator Johnson of Arkansas, for the creation of the Territories of Chah-la-kee, Chah-ta, and Muscokee, and it is greatly to be hoped that that or some similar bill may be speedily enacted. . . Their country, a far finer one than Kansas. . . The Choctaws have adopted a new constitution, vesting the supreme executive power in a governor. . . It is understood that this change has been made preparatory to the acceptance of the bill already mentioned.

The foregoing is taken from the *Annual Report* of the southern superintendent for 1857 and in that report, Elias Rector who was then the superintendent, having taken office that very year, argued that all the five great tribes ought to be allowed to have delegates on the floor of Congress and to be made citizens of the United States; for the constitutions of the Cherokees, Choctaws, and Chickasaws would compare favorably, said he, with those of any of the southwestern states [Senate *Documents*, 35th congress, first session, vol. ii, 485].

(b) The Fort Smith *Times* of February 3, 1859 printed the following:

SAM HOUSTON AND THE PRESIDENCY

The following we take from a printed slip sent to us by our Doaksville correspondent, who informs us that it was sent to that office just as he sends it. We presume that it is the programme laid down by some of the Texas papers, friendly to the election of Sam Houston to the Presidency. . .

Re-organization of the Territories

1. The organization of the Aboriginal Territory of Decotah, from that part of the late Territory of Minnesota, lying west of the State of Minnesota.

2. To fix the western boundaries of Kansas and Nebraska, at the Meridian 99 or 100; and to establish in those Territories, Aboriginal counties, for the exclusive and permanent occupation of the Aboriginal tribes now located east of that line and within those Territories; also to provide, that said Territories shall not be admitted into the Union as States unless their several Constitutions provide for the continuation of the Federal regulations adopted for better government and welfare of the Aboriginal tribes inhabiting the same.

3. To organize the Indian territory lying west of Arkansas, as "the Aboriginal Territory of Neosho," under regulation similar to those proposed by Hon. Robert W. Johnson of Arkansas in 1854 for the organization of the Indian territory of Neosho.

4. To purchase from the State of Texas all that portion of the State

also a territorial organization immediately that should look towards that end.   Such advice came as early as 1853, at least, and was more natural than would at first glance appear; for the southern tribes were huge in population, in land, and in resources.   They were civilized, had governments and laws modelled upon the

lying north of the Red river and include the same in the Aboriginal territory of Comanche or Ouachita.

5. The territory of New Mexico.

6. From the western portion of New Mexico to take the Aboriginal territory of Navajoe.

7. From the western portion of Utah, to take the Aboriginal territory of Shoshone.

Re-organize the eastern part of Utah, (the Mormon country), as an Aboriginal territory.

Organize the western territory of Osage.

From Nebraska, west of the M.100, and south of the 45th parallel take the Aboriginal territory of Mandan.

Organize the eastern half of Oregon, as the Aboriginal territory of Umatilla.

Washington east of the M.118 to be the Aboriginal territory of Okanagan.

Nebraska, north of the 45th parallel to be the Aboriginal territory of Assinneboin.   Emigration into these territories to be prohibited by law of Congress, until the same shall have been admitted into the Union as States.

In each territory, a resident Military Police to preserve order. . .

(c)   Henry Wilson, in the *Rise and Fall of the Slave Power*, vol. ii, 634-635 says,

In the Indian Territory there were four tribes of Indians — Cherokees, Choctaws, Chickasaws, and Creeks.   Under the fostering care of their governments slavery had become so firmly established that slaveholders thought them worthy of political fellowship, and articles in favor of their admission began to appear in the southern press.   "The progress of civilization," said the New Orleans "Picayune," "in several of the Indian tribes west of the States will soon bring up a new question for the decision of Congress. . . It cannot fail to give interest to this question that each of the Indian tribes has adopted the social institutions of the South."   To concentrate and give direction to such efforts, a secret organization was formed to encourage Southern emigration, and to discourage and prevent the entrance into the Territory of all who were hostile to slaveholding institutions.   It was hoped thus to guard against adverse fortune which had defeated their purposes and plans for Kansas. . .

American, and more than all else, they were southern in origin, in characteristics, and in institutions.

The project for organizing[19] the territories of Kansas and Nebraska caused much excitement, as well it might,

[19] With reference to the proposed organization the subjoined documents are of interest:

MR. MIX,   C. STREET, July 2.

Dear Sir, Please have the western boundary of Mis. laid down on this map, and the *outline* of the Pawnee, Kanzas & Osage purchases, and the reservations, as they now stand within that *outline*. You need not show each purchase, but the *outline* of the whole. Yours truly

THOMAS H. BENTON.

Letter of July 2, 1853, Indian Office *Miscellaneous Files, 1851-1854.*

WASHINGTON CITY, August 5th, 1854.

HON. G. W. MANYPENNY Esq., Com Indian Department, Washington City.

Dear Sir, Many people of Ohio, as well as of the states west of it, have for a long time been most anxious to learn through your Department, the nature of the several treaties made by yourself in behalf of the Government, with the several tribes of Indians occupying the Territories of Nebraska & Kansas: particularly as to the *reservation* of *land* made by such Tribes, *its extent, where, when,* & how to be *located,* & *within what time,* — and also what lands in both of said Territories by virtue of said treaties *are now subject* to *location?*

I regret to inform you that much censure has attached to your Department, in consequence of the delay which has attended the promulgation of the above information, but which from my long knowledge of you personally, and of the very prompt manner in which you have invariably discharged your public duties, I believe to be most unjust.

I seek the above information, not only for myself (contemplating a removal to Kansas) but also in behalf of many persons in the western states, who have solicited my intervention in that matter on my visit to this City. Very respectfully your friend   S. W. WHITE

Indian Office *Miscellaneous Files, 1851-1854.*

C. STREET, Aug. 19, '53.

TO GEO. W. MANYPENNY ESQ., Com. of Indian Affairs,

Sir, I have the honor to acknowledge the receipt of your note of yesterday with the accompanying copy of a letter to the Hon. Mr. Atchison, and make my thanks to you for this mark of your attention. The reply will be immediately forwarded to Meas Ami, to be published in the same paper in which your note to me covering the map on which the Indian's cessions & reserves west of Missouri, was published, Very respectfully, Sir, Yr. obt. servant,   THOMAS H. BENTON.

Indian Office *Miscellaneous Files, 1851-1854.*

among the Indian immigrants, even though the Wyandots, in 1852, had, in a measure, anticipated it by initiat-
ing a somewhat similar movement in their own restricted locality.[20]   Most of the tribes comprehended to the
full the ominous import of territorial organization; for,
obviously, it could not be undertaken except at a sacri-
fice of Indian guaranties.   At the moment some of the
tribes, notably the Choctaw and Chickasaw,[21] were having domestic troubles that threatened a neighborhood
war and the new fear of the white man's further aggrandizement threw them into despair.   The southern
Indians, generally, were much more exercised and
much more alarmed than were the northern.[22]   Being
more highly civilized, they were better able to compre-
hend the drift of events.   Experience had made them
unduly sagacious where their territorial and treaty
rights were concerned, and well they knew that, although the Douglas measure did not in itself directly
affect them or their country, it might easily become the
forerunner of one that would.

The border strife, following upon the passage of the

---

[20] Ray, *op. cit.*, 86; Connelley, in Kansas Historical Society, *Collections*, vol.
vi, 102; Connelley, *Provincial Government of Nebraska Territory*, pp. 24, 30
et seq.

The Wyandots took an active part in the Kansas election troubles.   For
some evidence of that, see, House *Reports*, 34th congress, first session, no. 200,
pp. 22, 266.

[21] By the treaty of 1837 [Kappler, *op. cit.*, vol. ii, 486], the Choctaws, for a
money consideration as was natural, agreed to let the Chickasaws occupy their
country jointly with themselves and form a Chickasaw District within it that
should be on a par with the other districts (Moo-sho-le-tubbee, Apucks-hu-
nubbe, and Push-ma-ta-ha), or political units, of the Choctaw Nation.   The
arrangement meant political consolidation, one General Council serving for
the two tribes, but each tribe retaining control of its own annuities.   The
boundaries of the Chickasaw District proved the subject of a contention, constant and bitter.   Civil war was almost precipitated more than once.   Finally,
in 1855, the political connection was brought to an end by the terms of the
Treaty of Washington [Kappler, *op. cit.*, vol. ii, 706], negotiated in that year.

[22] See Report of C. C. Copeland to Cooper, August 27, 1855.

Kansas-Nebraska Bill, disturbed in no slight degree the Indians on the Kansas reservations, which, by-the-by, had been very greatly reduced in area by the Manypenny treaties of 1853-1854. Some of the reserves lay right in the heart of the contested territory, free-state men intrenching themselves among the Delawares and pro-slavery men among the Shawnees,[23] the former north and the latter south of the Kansas River. But even remoteness of situation constituted no safeguard against encroachment. All along the Missouri line the squatters took possession. The distant Cherokee Neutral Lands[24] and the Osage and New York Indian reservations[25] were all invaded.[26] The Territorial Act had expressly excluded Indian land from local governmental control; but the Kansas authorities of both parties utterly ignored, in their administration of affairs, this provision. The first districting of the territory for election purposes comprehended, for instance, the Indian lands, yet little criticism has ever been passed

[23] A secret society is said to have been formed in Missouri for the express purpose of gaining the Shawnee land for slavery.

[24] Dean wrote to Butler, November 29, 1855 [*Letter Press Book*] saying that the disturbed state of things in Kansas was having a very serious effect upon the Cherokee Neutral Land. Early in 1857, Butler reported that he had given notice that if intruders had not removed themselves by spring he would have them removed by the military [Butler to Dean, January 9, 1857]. Manypenny approved Butler's course of action which is quite significant, considering that the federal administration was supposed to be unreservedly committed to the pro-slavery cause and the intruders were pro-slavery men from across the border.

[25] Andrew Dorn took charge of the Neosho Agency, to which these reservations as well as the Quapaw, Seneca, and Seneca and Shawnee belonged, in 1855 and regularly had occasion to complain of intruders. White people seem to have felt that they could with impunity encroach upon the New York Indian lands because they were only sparsely settled and because the Indian title was in dispute.

[26] Apart from any sectional desire to obtain the Indian country, would-be settlers seem to have been attracted thither from a mistaken notion that there were mines of precious metals west of Missouri [Commissioner of Indian Affairs, *Report*, 1858].

upon that grossly illegal act.   Needless to say, the controversy between slavocracy and freedom obscured and obliterated, in those years, all other considerations.

As the year 1860 approached, appearances assumed an even more serious aspect.   Kansas settlers and would-be settlers demanded that the Indians, so recently the only legal occupants of the territory, vacate it altogether.   So soon had the policy of granting them peace and undisturbed repose on diminished reserves proved futile.   The only place for the Indian to go, were he indeed to be driven out of Kansas, was present Oklahoma; but his going there would, perforce, mean an invasion of the property rights of the southern tribes, a matter of great moment to them but seemingly of no moment whatsoever to the white man.   Some of the Kansas Indians saw in removal southward a temporary refuge – they surely could not have supposed it would be other than temporary – and were glad to go, making their arrangements accordingly.[27]   Some, however, had to be cajoled into promising to go and some had to be forced.   A few held out determinedly against all thought of going.   Among the especially obstinate ones were the Osages,[28] natives of the soil.   The Buchanan

[27] As early as 1857, the Sacs and Foxes of Missouri were reported as looking for a new home to the southward, in a less rigorous climate, and, with that purpose in mind, they visited the Cherokees.   When the Delaware treaty of 1860 was being negotiated, the Delawares expressed themselves as very anxious to get away from white interference, to leave Kansas.   The Ottawas thought and thought rightly, forsooth, judging from the experience of the past, that removal would do no good.   They declared a preference for United States citizenship and tribal allotment [Jotham Meeker, Baptist missionary, to Agent James, September 4, 1854, also Agent James's *Report*, 1857].   At this same period, Agent Dorn reported that the Kansas River Shawnees were desirous of joining those of the Neosho Agency.   Greenwood replied, January 18, 1860, that the subject of allowing the northern Indians to go south was then under consideration by the department [Letter to Superintendent Rector].

[28] The evidence of this is to be found in a letter from W. G. Coffin to Dole, June 17, 1861 [*Neosho Files, 1838-1865*, C1223].

government failed utterly to convince them of the wisdom of going and was, thereupon, charged by the free-state Kansans with bad faith, with not being sincere and sufficiently persistent in its endeavors to treat, its secret purpose being to keep the free-state line as far north as possible. The breaking out of the Civil War prevented the immediate removal of any of the tribes but did not put a stop to negotiations looking towards that end.

All this time there was another influence within the Indian country, north and south, that boded good or ill as the case might be. This influence emanated from the religious denominations represented on the various reserves. Nowhere in the United States, perhaps, was the rivalry among churches that had divided along sectional lines in the forties and fifties stronger than within the Indian country. There the churches contended with each other at close range. The Indian country was free and open to all faiths, while, in the states, the different churches kept strictly to their own sections, the southern contingent of each denomination staying close to the institution it supported. Of course the United States government, through its civilization fund, was in a position to show very pointedly its sectional predilections. It will probably never be known, because so difficult of determination, just how much the churches aided or retarded the spread of slavery.[29]

Among the tribes of Kansas, denominational strength was distributed as follows: The Kickapoos[30] and

---

[29] For information on this subject, see Carroll's *American Church History*, 19, 93, 253-254, 302.

[30] Feeling that, under the treaty of 1854, they were free to choose whatever denomination they pleased to reside among them, the Kickapoos expressed a preference for the Methodist Episcopal Church South, but the Presbyterian Board of Foreign Missions was already established among their neighbors of

Wyandots[31] were Methodists; but, while the former were a unit in their adherence to the Methodist Episcopal Church South, the latter were divided and among them the older church continued strong. The American Baptist Missionary Union had a school on the Delaware reservation and, previous to 1855, had had one also on the Shawnee, which the political uproar in Kansas had obliged to close its doors. These same Northern Baptists were established also among the Ottawas, as the Moravians were among the Munsees and the Roman Catholics[32] among the Osages and the Potawatomies. The Southern Baptists were likewise to be found among the Potawatomies[33] and the Southern Methodists among the Shawnees. The Shawnee Manual Labor School, under the Southern Methodists, was, however, only very grudgingly patronized by the Indians. Its situation near the Missouri border was partly accountable for this as it was for the selection of the school as the meeting-place of the pro-slavery legislature in 1855. The management of the institution was from time to time severely criticized and the super-

the Otoe and Missouria and Great Nemaha Agencies, their own agent, Mr. Baldwin, was a Presbyterian, and so, before long, in some almost unaccountable way, they found that the Presbyterians (Old School) had obtained an entry upon their reserve and had established a mission school there. The Kickapoos were indignant, as well they had a right to be, and made as much trouble as they possibly could for the Presbyterians. In 1860, the Presbyterian Board vacated the premises and the Methodist Episcopal Church South took possession, Agent Badger favoring the change. The change was of but short duration, however; for, in 1861, the Southern Methodists, finding the sympathy of the Kickapoos was mainly with the federal element, took their departure.

[31] Ray, *op. cit.*, 86, footnote 107.

[32] The most flourishing schools seem to have been the Roman Catholic. The Roman Catholics did not greatly concern themselves, as a church organization, with the slavery agitation, and St. Mary's Mission and the Osage Manual Labor School were scarcely affected by the war and not at all by the troubles that presaged its approach.

[33] The Baptist school among the Potawatomies closed in 1861. See Appendix.

intendent, the Reverend Thomas Johnson, an intense pro-slavery agitator,[34] was strongly suspected of malfeasance,[35] of enriching himself, forsooth, at the expense of the Indians. The school found a formidable rival, from this and many another cause, in a Quaker establishment, which likewise existed on the Shawnee Reserve but independently of either tribal or governmental aid.

If church influences and church quarrels were discernible among the northern tribes, they were certainly very much more so among the southern. The American Board of Commissioners for Foreign Missions (Congregational) that had labored so zealously for the Cherokees, when they were east of the Mississippi, extended its interest to them undiminished in the west; and, in the period just before the Civil War,[36] was the strongest religious force in their country. There it had no less than four mission stations[37] and a flourishing school in connection with each. The same organization was similarly influential among the Choctaws[38] or, in the light of what eventually happened, it might better be said its missionaries were. Both Southern and Northern Baptists and Southern Methodists likewise were to be found among the Cherokees;[39] Presbyterians[40] and

[34] House *Report*, 34th congress, first session, no. 200, pp. 14, 18, 94, 425.

[35] See Indian Office, *Special File, no. 220.*

[36] The work of the American Board among the Cherokees was discontinued just before the war [*Missionary Herald*, 1861, p. 11; American Board *Report*, 1860, p. 137].

[37] The four were: "Park hill, five miles south from Tahlequah; Dwight, forty-two miles south-southwest from Tahlequah; Fairfield, twenty-five miles southeast from Tahlequah; Lee's creek, forty-three miles southeast from Tahlequah" — Commissioner of Indian Affairs [*Report*, 1859, p. 173]. There had been a fifth, an out station.

[38] The Congregational schools among the Choctaws were: Iyanubbi, near the Arkansas line; Wheelock, eighteen miles east of Doaksville; and Chuahla, one mile from Doaksville.

[39] The Southern Baptist Convention had not been long in the country prior

Southern Methodists among the Chickasaws and Choctaws; and Presbyterians only among the Creeks and
Seminoles.   In every Indian nation south, except the
Creek and Seminole,[41] the work of denominational
schools was supplemented, or maybe neutralized, by
that of public and neighborhood schools.

True to the traditions and to the practices of the old
Puritans and of the Plymouth church, the missionaries
of the American Board,[42] so strongly installed among
the Choctaws and the Cherokees, took an active interest
in passing political affairs, particularly in connection
with the slavery agitation.   On that question, they
early divided themselves into two camps; those among
the Choctaws, led by the Reverend Cyrus Kingsbury,[43]

to the Civil War. The Methodist Episcopal Church South had no schools but
several missionaries. The American Baptist Missionary Union had a number
of meeting-houses.

[40] The Presbyterians (Old School) established Wah-pa-nuc-ka Institute for
young women, forty miles north of Red River and one and one-eighth miles
west of the Choctaw and Chickasaw line; but differences arose between the
Presbyterian Board of Foreign Missions and the Chickasaw authorities, neither
institutional nor sectional, but purely financial, which caused the Presbyterians
to abandon the school in 1860 [C. H. Wilson, attorney for the Presbyterian
Board of Foreign Missions, to Cooper, April 16, 1860]. The Presbyterian
schools among the Choctaws were: Spencer Academy, "located on the old military road leading from Fort Towson to Fort Smith, about ten miles north of
Fort Towson," and Koonsha Female Seminary. Both of them were under the
Presbyterian Board. A third institution, Armstrong Academy, belonged to the
Cumberland Presbyterians. The Southern Methodists had Bloomfield Acad-
emy, Colbert Institute, and the Chickasaw Manual Labor School among the
Chickasaws; and the Fort Coffee and New Hope academies, for boys and
girls respectively, among the Choctaws.

[41] The Seminoles were late in manifesting an interest in education, and, when
interest did arise among them, John Jumper, the chief, declared for boarding-
schools and asked that such be established under the Presbyterian Board, the
same that had influence among their near neighbors, the Creeks.

[42] The American Board itself was inclined to be non-committal and temporizing [Garrison, *op. cit.*, vol. iii, 30]. The *Missionary Herald*, so valuable
an historical source as it proved itself to be for Indian removals, is strangely
silent on the great subject of negro slavery among the Indians. Its references
to it are only very occasional and never more than incidental.

[43] Kingsbury was superintendent of the Chuahla Female Seminary.

supporting slavery; and those among the Cherokees, led by the Reverend S. A. Worcester,[44] opposing it. The actions of the former led to a controversy with the American Board and, in 1855, the malcontents, or proslavery sympathizers, expressed a desire to separate themselves and their charges from its patronage.[45] When, eventually, this separation did occur, 1859-1860, the Presbyterian Board of Foreign Missions (Old School) stepped into the breach.[46]

The rebellious conduct of the Congregational missionaries met with the undisguised approval of the Choctaw agent, Douglas H. Cooper,[47] formerly of Mississippi. It was he who had already voiced a nervous apprehension, as exhibited in the following document,[48] that the Indian country was in grave danger of being abolitionized:

☞ If things go on as they are now doing, in 5 years slavery will be abolished in the whole of your superintendency.

(*Private*) I am convinced that something must be done speedily to arrest the systematic efforts of the Missionaries to abolitionize the Indian Country

Otherwise we shall have a great run-away harbor, a sort of

[44] Worcester died, April, 1859 [*Missionary Herald*, 1859, p. 187; 1860, p. 12].

[45] *Missionary Herald*, 1859, pp. 335-336; 1860, p. 12; The American Board of Commissioners for Foreign Missions, *Report*, 1856, p. 195.

[46] Report of C. C. Copeland, 1860.

[47] Cooper was also Chickasaw agent. On the fifth of October, 1854, some of the principal men of the Chickasaw Nation, Cyrus Harris, James Gamble, Sampson Folsom, Jackson Frazier, and D. Colbert, petitioned President Pierce for the removal of Agent Andrew J. Smith on charges of official irregularity and gross immorality. A year later, Superintendent Dean reiterated the charges. Smith's commission was revoked, November 9, 1855; and, in March, 1856, Cooper was assigned the Chickasaws as an additional charge. Henceforth, the two tribes had an agent in common.

[48] This note itself bore no date but there is documentary proof that it was received at Fort Smith, November 27, 1854. It is to be found in the Indian Office among the *Fort Smith Papers*.

Canada – with "underground rail-roads" leading to & through it – adjoining Arkansas and Texas.

It is of no use to look to the General Government – its arm is paralized by the abolition strength of the North.

I see no way except secretly to induce the Choctaws & Cherokees & Creeks to allow slave-holders to settle among their people & control the movement now going on to abolish slavery among them.   C—

Cooper sent this note, in 1854, as a private memorandum to the southern superintendent, who at the time was Charles W. Dean. In 1859, it was possible for him to write to Dean's successor, Elias Rector, in a very different tone. The missionaries had then taken the stand he himself advocated and there was reason for congratulation. Under such circumstances, Cooper wrote,

I cannot close this report without calling your attention to the admirable tone and feeling pervading the reports of superintendents of schools and missionaries among the Choctaws, and particularly to that of the Rev. Ebenezer Hotchkin, one of the oldest missionaries among the Choctaws, who, in referring to past political disturbances, says: "We have looked upon our rulers as the 'powers that be, are ordained of God,' and have respected them for this reason. 'Whomsoever, therefore, resisteth the power resisteth the ordinance of God' (Romans, xiii, 2). This has been our rule of action during the political excitement. We believe that the Bible is the best guide for us to follow. Our best citizens are those most influenced by Bible truth."

I rejoice to believe the above sentiments are entertained by most, if not all, the missionaries now among the Choctaws and Chickasaws, and that they entirely repudiate the higher-law doctrine [49] of northern and religious fanatics. It is but lately, as I learn, that the Choctaw mission, for many years under the control of the American Board of Commissioners for Foreign Missions (whose headquarters are at Boston) has been cut off, be-

---

[49] The allusion is, of course, to the "higher law" doctrine expressed in Seward's Senate Speech of March 11, 1850.

cause they preferred to follow the teachings of the Bible, as understood by them, rather than obey the dogmas contained in Dr. Treat's letter and the edicts of the parent board.

It is a matter of congratulation among the friends of the old Choctaw missionaries, who have labored for thirty years among them, and intend to die with armor on, that all connection with the Boston board has been dissolved. If it had been done years ago, when their freedom of conscience and of missionary action was attempted to be controlled by the parent board, much of suspicion, of ill-feeling, and diminished usefulness, which attached to the Choctaw missionaries in consequence of their connection with and sustenance by a board avowedly and openly hostile to southern institutions, would have been prevented.[50]

[50] Commissioner of Indian Affairs, *Report*, 1859, pp. 190-191.

The letter of Dr. Treat referred to by Agent Cooper is herewith given. It is accompanied by the letter that covered it and that letter, as it is found among the *Fort Smith Papers* in the United States Indian Office, bears a record to the effect that the copy of it was transmitted by the southern superintendent to Washington, November 28, 1855.

FORT TOWSON Nov. 16, 1855

SIR: I have the pleasure to forward a copy of letter, addressed to the Revd S. B. Treat, Corresponding Secretary of the American Board of Commissioners for Foreign Missions, by C. Kingsbury and others – Missionaries among the Choctaws – and request the same may be transmitted to the Hon Comr of Indian Affairs for the information of the Government of the United States.

The letter as you will perceive refers to an exciting and highly important subject – in which the States adjoining the Indian Territory are deeply & directly interested, as well as the Choctaw People.

I cannot refrain from the expression of my gratification at the position assured in this letter by the old and valued Missionaries among the Choctaws. The copy was handed to me by Revd Cyrus Kingsbury, one of the signers to the original letter. Respectfully

DOUGLAS H COOPER, U. S. Agent for Choctaws

Hon. C. M. Dean, Supt. Indian Affairs,

Ft Smith.

[*Inclosure*] – *Copy*

PINE RIDGE, CHOC. NA. Nov. 15, 1855.

REV. S. B. TREAT, Cor. Secretary of the A.B.C.F.M.

Rev. & Dear Brother, When the Rev. G. W. Wood visited us as a deputation from the Prudential Committee, he treated us, our views, and *our practice* so kindly, and spoke to us so many encouraging words, that we were constrained to meet him in a similar spirit of concilliation. We were willing to re-examine the difference in views on the subject of slavery, which for a long time had existed between the Committee

In the next year, 1860, Cooper was still sanguine as
to affairs among the Indians of his agency and he could

and ourselves, and to see if there was not common ground on which
we could stand together.

At the opening of the meeting at Good Water, Mr. Wood laid aside
the letter of June 22nd '/48. This was a subject we were not to dis-
cuss. He then introduced, by way of compromise, as we understood
it, certain articles to show that there were principles, or modes of expression, in relation to slavery, in which there was substantial agreement. To these articles, though not expressed in every particular as we
could have wished, (and after some of them had been modified by oral
explanations,) we gave our assent, for the sake of peace. We
hoped it would put an end to agitation on a subject which had so long
troubled us, and hindered us in our work. We took it for granted that
the Committee had yielded certain important points, insisted on in the
letter of June 22nd '/48. This gladdened our hearts, and disposed us to
meet Mr. Wood's proposal in a spirit of concilliation and confidence.
We are not skilled in diplomacy, and had no thought that we were
assenting to articles which would be considered as covering the whole
ground of the letter of June 22nd. The first intimation that we had
been mistaken, was from a statement made by Mr. Wood, in New York,
that the result of the meeting at Good Water *"involved no change of
views or action* on the part of the Prudential Committee and Secretaries."

In Mr. Wood's report to the Pru. Com. which was read at Utica,
the Good Water document was placed in such a relation to other statements, as to make the impression that we had given our full and willing
assent to the entire letter of June 22d. The Com. on that Report, of
which Dr. Beman was chairman, say, "The great end aimed at by the
Pru. Com. in their correspondence with these missions for several years;
and by the Board at their last annual meeting; has been substantially
accomplished."

This is a result we had not anticipated. We can not consent to be
thus made to sanction principles and sentiments which are contrary to
our known, deliberate, and settled convictions of right, and to what we
understand to be the teachings of the word of God. We are fully convinced that we can not go with the Committee and the Board, as to the
manner in which as Ministers of the Gospel and Missionaries we are
to deal with slavery. We believe the instructions of the Apostles, in
relation to this subject, are a sufficient guide, and that if followed the
best interests of society, as well as of the Church, will be secured.

We have no wish to give the Com. or the Board farther trouble on
this subject. As there is no prospect that our views can be brought to
harmonize, we must request that our relations to the A.B.C.F.M. may be
dissolved in a way that will do the least harm to the Board, and to our
Mission.

We have endeavored to seek Divine guidance in this difficult matter,

report to Rector, unhesitatingly, as if confident of official endorsement both at Forth Smith and at Washington,[51]

> Great excitement has prevailed along the Texas border, in consequence of the incendiary course pursued in that State by horse thieves and religious fanatics; but I am glad to say, as yet, so far as I am informed, no necessity has existed in this agency for the organization of "vigilance committees" . . . No doubt we have among us *free-soilers*; perhaps abolitionists in sentiment; but, so far as I am informed, persons from the North, residing among the Choctaws and Chickasaws, who entertain opinions unfriendly to our system of domestic slavery, keep their opinions to themselves and attend to their legitimate business.[52]

George Butler, the United States agent for the Cherokees, seems to have been, no less than Cooper, an adherent of the State Rights Party and an upholder of the

> and we desire to do that which shall be most for the glory of our Divine Master, and the best interests of his cause among this people. We regret the course we feel compelled to take, but we can see no other relief from our present embarassment.   Fraternally and truly yours,
>
> (Signed)   C. KINGSBURY   C. C. COPELAND
>   C. BYINGTON   O. P. STARK
>   E. HOTCHKIN

[51] That the Buchanan administration did endorse pro-slavery policy and actions requires no proof today. The findings of the Covode committee of investigation, 1860, are in themselves sufficient evidence, were other evidence lacking, of the intensely partisan and corrupt character of the Democratic régime just prior to the Civil War. Of the officials, having Indian concerns in charge, the Secretary of the Interior and the Commissioner of Indian Affairs are, for present purposes, alone important. Buchanan's Secretary of the Interior was Jacob Thompson, who had formerly been a representative in Congress from Mississippi and had thrown all the weight of his influence in favor of the Lecompton constitution for Kansas [Rhodes, J. F. *History of the United States*, vol. ii, 277]. After his retirement from Buchanan's cabinet, Thompson served as commissioner from Mississippi, working in North Carolina for the accomplishment of secession [Moore's *Rebellion Record*, vol. i, 5]. A. B. Greenwood of Arkansas was Commissioner of Indian Affairs in Buchanan's time. He also had been in Congress and, while there, had served on the House Committee of Investigation into Brooks's attack upon Sumner. He formed with Howell Cobb of Georgia the minority element [Von Holst, vol. v, 324].

[52] Commissioner of Indian Affairs, *Report*, 1860, p. 129.

institution of slavery. In 1859, he ascribed the very
great material progress of the Cherokees to the fact that
they were slaveholders.[53]   Slavery, in Butler's opinion,
had operated as an incentive to all industrial pursuits.
To an extent this may have been true, since all Indians,
no matter how high their type, have an aversion for
work. As Professor Shaler once said, they are the
truest aristocrats the world has ever known. But the
slaveholders among the great tribes of the South were,
for the most part, the half-breeds, the cleverest and
often, much as we may regret to have to admit it, the
most unscrupulous men of the community.

Butler's commission as Indian agent expired in
March, 1860, and he was not reappointed, Robert J.
Cowart of Georgia[54] being preferred. This man, illiterate and unprincipled, immediately set to work to
perform a task to which his predecessor had proved
unequal. The task was the removal of white intruders
from the Cherokee country. For some time past, the
southern superintendent and the agents under him, to
say nothing of Commissioner Greenwood and Secretary
Thompson, the one a citizen of Arkansas and the other
of Mississippi, had resented most bitterly the invasion
of the Cherokee Neutral Lands by Kansas free-soilers
and the division of it into counties by the unlawfully
assumed authority of the Kansas legislature. The re-
sentment was thoroughly justifiable; for the whole proceeding of the legislature was contrary to the express
enactment of Congress; but no doubt, enthusiasm for
the strict enforcement of the federal law came largely
from political predilections, precisely as the Kansan's

---

[53] Commissioner of Indian Affairs, *Report*, 1859, p. 172.

[54] Greenwood to Rector, March 14, 1860 [Indian Office, *Letter Book*, no. 63,
p. 128]; Greenwood to Cowart, March 14, 1860 [*ibid.*, 125].

outrageous defiance of it came from a deep-rooted distrust of the Buchanan administration.

There were, however, other intruders that Cowart and Rector and Greenwood designed to remove and they wanted to remove them on the ground that they were making mischief within the tribe and interfering with its institutions, or, more specifically, with slavery. The intruders meant were principally the missionaries against whom Greenwood had even the audacity to lay the charge of inciting to murder.   Newspapers of bordering slave states were full of criticism,[55] just before the war, of these same men and, notably, of the Reverend Evan [56] and John Jones, the reputed ringleaders.

---

[55] Commissioner of Indian Affairs, *Report*, 1860.   See also additional documents in Appendix B.

[56] The following extract from the *Fort Smith Times* of February 3, 1859 makes particular mention of the Reverend Evan Jones:

> In the *True Democrat* of the 19th inst., we find an article credited to the *Fort Smith Times*, in which the Rev. Evan Jones, a Baptist Missionary, residing near the State line, Washington county, is handled rather roughly so far as words are concerned.   He is said to be an abolitionist, and a very dangerous man, meddling with the affairs of the Cherokees, and teaching them abolition principles.
>
> "As such reports will be circulated to the prejudice of the Southern Baptists, we hereby request some of our Brethren in the northwest part of the State to write us the grounds for such reports.
>
> "Is the 'Rev. Evan Jones' connected with any Missionary Society and if so, what one?
>
> "We hope shortly to hear more concerning this matter."
>
> The above notice is from the first number of the *Arkansas Baptist*, a new paper just published in Little Rock, P. S. G. Watson, Editor.   It was not our intention to cast any reflections on the Baptist Church by noticing the Rev. gentleman named above, as we have great respect for the Church.   We deny, however, that Mr. Jones "is handled roughly so far as words are concerned," for there are no harsh words or epithets in the article referred to; but he is *handled roughly* so far as *facts* are concerned.   He is a Missionary Baptist, and the society by which he is supported, has, we believe, its headquarters in Boston, Mass.   Mr. Jones' conduct has been fully reported to the Indian office, at Washington, by a number of the Cherokees, and by their Agent, Mr. George Butler, to whom we refer the editor of the *Baptist*, for the truth of the

The official excuse for removing them is rather interesting because it is so similar to that given, some thirty years earlier, in connection with the removal from Georgia. Ulterior motives can so easily be hidden under cold official phrase.

That the cause of slavery within the Cherokee country was in jeopardy in the spring and summer of 1860 can not well be denied. To the men of the time the evidence was easily obtainable. Almost as if by magic, a "search organization" started up among the full-bloods, an organization profoundly secret in its membership and in its purposes, but believed to be for no other object than the overthrow of the "peculiar institution." Its existence was promptly reported to the United States government and, as was to be expected, the missionaries were held responsible for both its inception and its continuance. It was then that Greenwood made [57] his most serious charge against these men and prepared, under color of law, to have them removed. Later, in this same year of 1860, Quantrill, the Hagerstown, Maryland man of Pennsylvania Dutch origin, who afterwards became such a notorious frontier guerrilla in the interests of the Confederate cause, leagued himself with some abolitionists for the sake of

charges we have made against him; and, if they are not satisfactory we can give a full history of Evan Jones' conduct for a number of years, well known among the Cherokees.

In connection with the foregoing newspaper extract, it is well to note that Richard Johnson was the editor of the *True Democrat*. Richard was a brother of Robert W. Johnson who represented one faction of the Democratic party in Arkansas while Thomas C. Hindman represented another. This was before their devotion to the Confederate cause had made them friends. Robert W. Johnson served in the United States Congress, first as representative, then as senator. He was later a senator in the Confederate States Congress. The Johnson family, although not so numerous as the Rector family, was, like it, strongly secessionistic.

[57] Greenwood to Thompson, June 4, 1860 [Indian Office, *Report Book*, no. 12, pp. 323-324].

making an expedition to the Cherokee country and rescuing negroes, there held in bondage.[58]   The timely distrust of Quantrill, however, caused the enterprise to be abandoned even before its preliminaries had been thoroughly well arranged; yet, had the rescue been carried to completion, it would not have been entirely without precedent[59] and its very contrivance indicated an uncertainty and a precariousness of situation south of the Kansas line.

Ever since their compulsory removal from Georgia under circumstances truly tragic, the Cherokees had been much given to factional strife.   This was largely in consequence of the underhand means taken by the state and federal authorities to accomplish removal. The Cherokees had, under the necessities of the situation, divided themselves into the Ross, or Anti-removal Party, and the Ridge, or Treaty Party.[60]   Removal took place in spite of the steady opposition of the Rossites and the Cherokees went west, piloted by the United States army.   Once in the west a new division arose in their ranks; for, as newcomers, they came into jealous contact with members of their tribe who had emigrated many years previously and who came to figure, in subsequent Cherokee history, as the Old Settlers' Party.[61] In 1846, the United States government attempted to assume the role of mediator in a settlement of Cherokee tribal differences but without much success.[62]   The old wrongs were unredressed, so the old divisions remained

---

[58] Connelley, *Quantrill and the Border Wars*, 147-149, 152.

[59] Siebert, *Underground Railroad from Slavery to Freedom*, 284.

[60] This party came to be known, almost exclusively, as the Treaty Party. After the murder of John Ridge, from whom the party took its name, his nephew, Stand Watie, became its leader.   Stand Watie figured conspicuously on the southern side in the Civil War.

[61] A good general account of these Cherokee factional disputes may be found in Thomas Valentine Parker's *Cherokee Indians*.

[62] Kappler, *op. cit.*, vol. ii, 561; Polk's *Diary* (Quaife's edition), vol. ii, 80.

and formed nuclei for new disintegrating issues. Thus, in 1857, there were no less than three factions created in consequence of a project for selling the Cherokee Neutral Lands.[63] Each faction had its own opinion how best to dispose of the proceeds, should a sale take place. In 1860, there were two factions, the selling and the non-selling.[64] This tendency of the Cherokees perpetually to quarrel among themselves and to bear long-standing grudges against each other is most important; inasmuch as that marked peculiarity of internal politics very largely determined the unique position of the tribe with reference to the Civil War.

The other great tribes had also occasions for quarrel in these same critical years. The disgraceful circumstances of their removal had widened the gulf, once simply geographical, between the Upper and the Lower Creeks. They were now almost two distinct political entities, in each of which there were a principal and a second chief. In 1833, provision had been made for the accommodation of the Seminoles within a certain definite part of the Creek country[65]—just such an arrangement, forsooth, as worked so ill when applied to the Choctaws and Chickasaws; but it took several years for the Seminoles to be suited. At length, when their numbers had been considerably augmented by the coming of the new immigrants from Florida, they took up

---

[63] George Butler to Dean, January 9, 1857.

[64] ". . . The Cherokee Council is in session, tho they do not seem to be doing much. It will hold about four weeks yet. I will stay till it breaks. I think the Councilmen seem to be split on some questions. It seems as if there are two parties. one is called the land selling party & those opposed to selling the land (that is Neutral lands). They passed a bill last council to sell it. Congress would not have anything to do with it & in fact they got up a protest against selling it & sent it to Washington City & they did not sell the land."—Extract from J. C. Dickinson to Captain Mark T. Tatum, dated Tahlequah, October 16, 1860 [*Fort Smith Papers*].

[65] Kappler, *op. cit.*, vol. ii, 388.

their position, for good and all, in the southwestern corner of the Creek Reserve, a politically distinct community.   By that time, the Creeks seem to have repented of their generosity,[66] so, perhaps, it was well that the United States government had not yielded to their importunity and consented to a like settlement of the southern Comanches.[67]   It had taken the Chickasaws a long time to reconstruct their government after the political separation from the Choctaws; but now they had a constitution,[68] all their own, a legislature, and a governor.   The Choctaws had attempted a constitution, likewise, first the Scullyville, then the Doaksville, set up by a minority party; but they had retained some semblance of the old order of things in the persons of their chiefs.[69]

There were other Indians within the southern division of the Indian country that were to have their part in the Civil War and in events leading up to it or resulting from it.   In the extreme northeastern corner, were the Quapaws, the Senecas, and the confederated Senecas and Shawnees, all members, with the Osages and the New York Indians of Kansas, of the Neosho River Agency which was under the care of Andrew J. Dorn. In the far western part, at the base of the Wichita Mountains, were the Indians of the Leased District,

---

[66] Rector to Greenwood, June 14, 1860.

[67] Tuckabatche Micco and other Creek chiefs wished the southern Comanches to be located somewhere between the Red and Arkansas Rivers.   That might or might not have meant a settlement upon the actual Creek reservation. Manypenny promised to look into the matter and find out whether there were any vacant lands in the region designated [Manypenny to Dean, May 25, 1855, Indian Office, *Letter Book*, no. 51, pp. 444-445].

[68] Dean to Manypenny, November 24, 1856, and related documents [General Files, *Chickasaw, 1854-1858*, D304, I400].

[69] For Choctaw political disturbances in 1858, see General Files, *Choctaw, 1859-1866*, I933 and R1004.

Wichitas, Tonkawas,[70] Euchees, and others, collectively
called the "Reserve Indians." Most of them had been
brought from Texas,[71] because of Texan intolerance of
their presence, and placed within the Leased District,
a tract of land west of the ninety-eighth meridian,
which, under the treaty of 1855, the United States had
rented from the Choctaws and Chickasaws. It was a
part of the old Chickasaw District of the Choctaw Nation. Outside of the Wichita Reserve and still wandering at large over the plains were the hostile Kiowas and
Comanches, against whom and the inoffensive Reserve
Indians, the Texans nourished a bitter, undying hatred.
They charged them with crimes that were never committed and with some crimes that white men, disguised
as Indians, had committed. They were also suspected
of manufacturing evidence that would incriminate the
red men and of plotting, in regularly-organized meetings, their overthrow.[72]

Although the plan for colonizing some of the Texas
Indians had been completed in 1855, the Indian Office
found it impossible to execute it until the summer of
1859. This was principally because the War Department could not be induced to make the necessary military arrangements.[73] In point of fact, the southern In-

---

[70] Some of the Tonkawas most probably went back to their old Texan hunting-grounds upon the breaking out of the war and were found encamped, in
1866, around San Antonio [Cooley to Sells, February 15, 1866, Indian Office,
Letter Book, no. 79, p. 293].

[71] The Leased District was designed to accommodate any Indians that the
United States government might see fit to place there, exclusive of New Mexican Indians, who had caused the Wichitas a great deal of trouble, and those
tribes "whose usual ranges at present are north of the Arkansas River, and
whose permanent locations are north of the Canadian. . ." [Kappler, *op.
cit.*, vol. ii, 708].

[72] The treatment of the Indians by Texas will be made the subject of a later
publication. The story is too long a one to be told here.

[73] Mix to Rector, March 30, 1859 [Indian Office, *Letter Book*, no. 60, pp.
386-388].

dian country was, at the time, practically without a force of United States troops, quite regardless of the promise that had been made to all the tribes upon the occasion of their removal that they should *always be protected* in their new quarters and, inferentially, by the regular army. Even Fort Gibson had been virtually abandoned as a military post on the plea that its site was unhealthful; and all of Superintendent Rector's recommendations that Frozen Rock, on the south side of the Arkansas a few miles away, be substituted [74] had been ignored, not so much by the Interior Department, as by the War. Secretary Thompson thought that enough troops should be at his disposal to enable him to carry out the United States Indian policy, but Secretary Floyd demurred. He was rather disposed to dismantle such forts as there were and to withdraw all troops from the Indian frontier, [75] a course of action that would leave it exposed, so the dissenting Thompson prognosticated, to "the most unhappy results." [76]

It happened thus that, when the United States surveyors started in 1858 to establish the line of the ninety-eighth meridian west longitude and to run other boundary lines under the treaty of 1855, [77] they found the country entirely unpatrolled. Troops had been ordered from Texas to protect the surveyors; but, pending their arrival, Agent Cooper, who had gone out to witness the

[74] *Annual Report,* 1857.

[75] Samuel Cooper, the New York man, who was now in United States employ but later became adjutant-general of the Confederacy [Crawford, *Genesis of the Civil War,* 310], made, about this time, a very significant inquiry as to how many Indian warriors there were in the vicinity of the various settlements [Cooper to Mix, January 29, 1856, Indian Office, *Miscellaneous Files, 1858-1863*].

[76] J. Thompson to J. B. Floyd, March 12, 1858 [Indian Office, *Miscellaneous Files*].

[77] By this treaty, the Choctaws had surrendered to the United States all their claims to land beyond the one hundredth degree of west longitude.

determination of the initial point on the line between his agency and the Leased District, himself took post at Fort Arbuckle and called upon the Indians for patrol and garrison duty.[78]   It would seem that Secretary Thompson had verbally authorized[79] Cooper to make this use of the Indians; but they proved in the sequel very inefficient as garrison troops.   On the thirtieth of June, Lieutenant Powell, commanding Company E, First United States Infantry, arrived at Fort Arbuckle from Texas and relieved Cooper of his self-imposed task.   The day following, Cooper set out upon a sixteen day scout of the Washita country, taking with him his Indian volunteers, Chickasaws[80] and a few Cherokees;[81] and for this act of using Indian after the arrival of white troops, he was severely criticized by the department.   One thing he accomplished: he selected a site for the prospective Wichita Agency with the recommendation that it be also made the site[82] of the much-needed military post on the Leased District.   The site had originally been occupied by a Kechie village and was admirably well adapted for the double purpose Cooper intended.   It lay near the center of the Leased

[78] Cooper to Rector, June 23, 1858.

[79] Cooper to Rector, June 30, 1858.

[80] Some of the Chickasaws came to Cooper under the lead of the United States interpreter, James Gamble, later Chickasaw delegate in the Confederate Congress.

[81] The Cherokees soon deserted Cooper, no cause assigned. Why they were with him at all can not very easily be explained unless they were looking out for the interests of the "Cherokee Outlet." They may, indeed, have been some refugee Cherokees who, in 1854, were reported as living in the Chickasaw country and consorting with horse thieves and other desperadoes. Under ordinary circumstances, Cooper had no authority to command the actions of Cherokees and his call was to Choctaws and Chickasaws whose agent he was and whose interests were directly involved in the survey then being made.

[82] On the question of the proposed site, see Rector's *Report*, 1859, pp. 307, 309. For Emory's familiarity with the region, note his report of a military reconnaissance undertaken by him in 1846 and 1847 [Pacific Railroad *Surveys*, vol. ii].

District and near the sources of Cache and Beaver Creeks. It was also, so reported Cooper, "not very distant from the Washita, & Canadian" (and commanded) "the Mountain passes through the Wichita Mountains to the Antelope Hills – to the North branch of Red River and also the road on the South side of the Wichita Mountains up Red River."

The colonization of the Wichitas and other Indians took place in the summer of 1859 under the excitement of new disputes with Texas, largely growing out of an unwarranted and brutal attack[83] by white men upon Indians of the Brazos Agency. That event following so closely upon the heels of Van Dorn's[84] equally brutal attack upon a defenceless Comanche camp brought matters to a crisis and the government was forced to be expeditious where it had previously been dilatory. The Comanches had come in, under a flag of truce, to confer in a friendly way with the Wichitas. Van Dorn, ignorant of their purpose but supposing it hostile, made a forced march, surprised them, and mercilessly took summary vengeance for all the Comanches had been charged with, whether justly or unjustly, for some time past. After it was all over, the Comanches, with about sixty of their number slain, accused the Wichitas of having betrayed them. Frightened, yet innocent, the

---

[83] Commissioner of Indian Affairs, *Report*, 1859, and accompanying documents.

[84] It would seem that Van Dorn had been ordered by General Twiggs, commanding in Texas, to explore the country between the one hundredth and the one hundred and fourth meridians as far north as the Canadian River. He was to do it quite irrespective of department jurisdictional lines. Van Dorn had the Texan's unrelenting hatred for all Indians and, as was to have been expected, considering the latitude of his orders, soon got himself into trouble. It is interesting to note in connection with this affair and in view of all that followed when Van Dorn and Albert Pike were both serving under the Confederacy, that their dislike of each other dated from Pike's condemnation of Van Dorn's cruel treatment of the Comanches.

Wichitas begged that there be no further delay in their removal, so the order was given and arrangements made. Unfortunately, by the time everything was ready, the season was pretty far advanced and the Indians reached their new home to find it too late to put in crops for that year's harvest. Subsistence rations had, therefore, to be doled out to them, the occasion affording, as always, a rare opportunity for graft. Instead of calling for bids, as was customary, Superintendent Rector entered into a private contract[85] with a friend and relative of his own, the consequence being that the government was charged an exorbitant price for the rations. Soon other troubles[86] came. The Leased District proved to be already occupied by some northern Indian refugees[87] and became, as time went on, a handy ren-

[85] The contractor was Charles B. Johnson of Fort Smith. Under the firm name of Johnson & Grimes, this man and Marshal Grimes, also of Arkansas, were able again and again to secure subsistence contracts from Rector and always with the suspicion of fraud attaching. Whenever possible, Rector and his friends eliminated entirely the element of competition. Abram G. Mayers of Fort Smith seems to have been the chief informer against Rector. As a matter of fact, and this must be admitted in extenuation of Rector's conduct, the Indian field service was so grossly mismanaged, officials from the highest to the lowest were so corrupt, that it is not at all surprising that each one [unless by the merest chance he were strong enough morally to resist temptation] took every opportunity he could get to enrich himself at the Indian's expense; for, of course, all such ill-gotten gains came sooner or later out of the Indian fund. Very few Indian officials seem to have been able to pass muster in matters of probity during these troublous times. Secretary Thompson and even Ex-president Pierce were not above suspicion in the Indian's estimation [Article, signed by "Screw Fly" in the *Chickasaw and Choctaw Herald*, February 11, 1859]. Mix was accused of dishonesty, so were Commissioner Dole, Commissioner Cooley, and Secretary Usher, to say nothing of a host of lesser officials.

[86] Supervising agent, Robert S. Neighbors, who had always befriended the Indians when he conveniently could against unfounded charges, was killed soon after the removal by vindictive Texans. S. A. Blain was then given charge of the Texas superintendency in addition to his own Wichita Agency. The consolidation of duties gave the Texans, apparently, a fresh opportunity to lodge complaints against the Wichitas.

[87] These refugees were mostly Delawares and Kickapoos. There were oth-

dezvous for free negroes; but, as soon as Matthew Leeper[88] of Texas became agent, the stay of such was extremely short.[89]

Such were the conditions obtaining among the Indians west of Missouri and Arkansas in the years immediately antedating the American Civil War; and, from such conditions, it may readily be inferred that the Indians were anything but satisfied with the treatment that had been and was being accorded them. They owed no great debt of gratitude to anybody. They were restless and unhappy among themselves. Their old way of living had been completely disorganized. They had nothing to go upon, so far as their relations with the white men were concerned, to make them hopeful of anything better in the future, rather the reverse. Indeed at the very opening of the year 1860, a year so full of distress to them because of the great drouth[90] that ravaged Ne-

---

er "strays," or "absentees," scattered here and there over the Indian country. There were Shawnees near the Canadian, Delawares among the Cherokees, and Shawnees and Kickapoos on the southwestern border of the Creek lands.

[88] Matthew Leeper was appointed to succeed S. A. Blain as agent, July, 1860. He had previously been special Indian agent in Texas.

[89] Among the *Leeper Papers* is found the following:

> Notice: All free negroes are notified to leave the Wichita Reserve or Leased District forthwith, except an old negro who is in charge of Messrs. Grimes & Rector, who will be permitted to remain a few days.

Wichita Agency, L.D. Sept. 26, 1860.   [M. Leeper], U. S. Ind. Agt.

[90] The suffering among the Indians must have been very great. There was a complete failure of crops everywhere. Subsistence had to be continued to the Wichitas, the Seminoles were reported absolutely destitute, and even the provident Choctaws were obliged to memorialize Congress for relief on the basis of the Senate award under their treaty of 1855 [General Files, *Choctaw, 1859-1866*]. Out of this application of Choctaw funds to the circumstances of their own pressing needs, came the great scandal of the Choctaw Corn Contract, in which Agent Cooper and many prominent men of the tribe were implicated. In some way Albert Pike was concerned in it also; but it must have been practically the only time a specific charge of anything like peculation could possibly have been brought against any of his transactions. His character for honesty seems to have been impeccable.

braska, Kansas, and Oklahoma, the worst that had been
known in thirty years, there came occasion for a new
distrust.   Proposals were made to the Creeks,[91] to the
Choctaws,[92] and to the Chickasaws to allot their lands in
severalty, notwithstanding the fact that one of the inducements offered by President Jackson to get them
originally to remove had been, that they should be permitted to hold their land, as they had always held it, in
common, forever.   The Creeks now replied to the proposals of the Indian Office that they had had experience
with individual reservations in their old eastern homes
and had good reason to be prejudiced against them.
The Indians, one and all, met the proposals with a
downright refusal but they did not forget that they had
been made, particularly when there came additional
cause for apprehension.

The cause for apprehension came with the presidential campaign of 1860 and from a passage in Seward's
Chicago speech,[93] "The National Idea; Its Perils and
Triumphs," expressive of opinions, false to the national
trust but favorable to expansion in the direction of the
Indian territory, most inopportune, to say the least, and
foolish.   Seward probably spoke in the enthusiasm of
a heated moment; for the obnoxious sentiment, "The
Indian territory, also, south of Kansas, must be vacated
by the Indians," was very different in its tenor from
equally strong expressions in his great Senate speech[94]

---

[91] In January, 1860, Agent Garrett asked the Creeks in their National
Council to consent to the apportionment of the tribal lands.   Motty Cunard
[Motey Kennard] and Echo Mayo [Echo Harjo] sent the reply of the Council
to Garrett, January 19, 1860.   It was an unqualified and absolute refusal.

[92] Cooper to Greenwood, March 31, 1860 [General Files, *Choctaw, 1859-
1866,* C445].

[93] George E. Baker, *Works of W. H. Seward* (edition of 1884), vol. iv,
363; Bancroft's *Seward,* vol. ii, 460-470.

[94] *Congressional Globe,* 33rd congress, first session, Appendix, p. 155.

on the Kansas-Nebraska Bill, February 17, 1854. It soon proved, however, easy of quotation by the secessionists in their arguments with the Indians, it being offered by them as incontestable proof that the designs of the incoming administration were, in the highest degree, inimical to Indian treaty rights. At the time of its utterance, the Indians were intensely excited. The poor things had had so many and such bitter experiences with the bad faith of the white people that it took very little to arouse their suspicion. They had been told to contract their domain or to move on so often that they had become quite super-sensitive on the subject of land cessions and removals. Seward's speech was but another instance of idle words proving exceedingly fateful.

Two facts thus far omitted from the general survey and reserved for special emphasis may now be remarked upon. They will show conclusively that there were personal and economic reasons why the Indians, some of them at least, were drawn irresistibly towards the South. The patronage of the Indian Office has always been more or less of a local thing. Communities adjoining Indian reservations usually consider, and with just cause because of long-established practice, that all positions in the field service, as for example, agencies and traderships, are the perquisites, so to speak, of the locality. It was certainly true before the war that Texas and Arkansas had some such understanding as to Indian Territory, for only southerners held office there and, from among the southerners, Texans and Arkansans received the preference always. It happened too that the higher officials in Washington were almost invariably southern men.

The granting of licenses to traders rested with the

superintendent and everything goes to show that, in the
fifties and sixties, applications for license were scrutin-
ized very closely by the southern superintendents with
a view to letting no objectionable person, from the
standpoint of southern rights, get into the territory.
The Holy See itself could never have been more vigilant in protecting colonial domains against the introduction of heresy. The same vigilance was exercised
in the hiring of agency employees, blacksmiths, wheelwrights, and the like. Having full discretionary power
in the premises, the superintendents could easily inter-
pret the law to suit themselves. They could also evade
it in their own interests and frequently did so. One
notorious case[95] of this sort came up in connection with
Superintendent Drew, who gave permits to his friends
to "peddle" in the Indian country without requiring of
them the necessary preliminary of a bond. Traders once
in the country had tremendous influence with the Indians, especially with those of a certain class whom ordinarily the missionaries could not reach. Then, as before and since, Indian traders were not men of the highest moral character by any means. Too often, on the contrary, they were of degraded character, thoroughly unscrupulous, proverbial for their defiance of the law, general illiteracy, and corrupt business practices. It stands to
reason that such men, if they had themselves been selected with an eye single to the cause of a particular section
and knew that solicitude in its interests would mean
great latitude to themselves and favorable reports of
themselves to the department at Washington, would
spare no efforts and hesitate at no means to make it their
first concern, provided, of course, that it did not interfere with their own monetary schemes.

95 Dean to Manypenny, October 24, 1855 [Dean's *Letter Book*].

To cap the climax, the last and greatest circumstance to be noted, if only because of the great weight it carried with the Indians when it was brought into the argument by the secessionists, is that practically all of the Indian money held in trust for the individual tribes by the United States government was invested in southern stocks;[96] in Florida 7's, in Georgia, Kentucky, Louisiana, Maryland, South Carolina, Missouri, Virginia, and Tennessee 6's, in North Carolina and Tennessee 5's, and the like. To tell the truth, only the merest minimum of it was secured by northern bonds. The southerners asserted for the Indians' benefit, that all these securities would be forfeited[97] by the war. Sufficient

---

[96]   INDIAN TRUST FUND

List of stocks held by the Secretary of the Interior in trust for Indian tribes

STATE	PER CENT	AMOUNT
Arkansas	5	$ 3,000.00
Florida	7	132,000.00
Georgia	6	3,500.00
Indiana	5	70,000.00
Kentucky	5	183,000.00
Louisiana	6	37,000.00
Maryland*	6	131,611.82
Missouri	5½	63,000.00
Missouri	6	484,000.00
North Carolina	6	562,000.00
Ohio	6	150,000.00
Pennsylvania*	5	96,000.00
South Carolina	6	125,000.00
Tennessee	5	218,000.00
Tennessee	6	143,000.00
United States	6	251,330.00
Virginia	6	796,800.00

3,449,241.82

* Taxed by the State.

Commissioner of Indian Affairs, *Report*, 1859, p. 452.

[97] David Hubbard to Ross and McCulloch, June 12, 1861 [*Official Records*, first ser., vol. xiii, 497].

is the fact, that the position of the Indians [98] was unquestionably difficult. With so much to draw them
southward, our only wonder is, that so many of them
stayed with the North.

---

[98] The position of the tribes in the northern part of the Indian country, in
Kansas, was considerably different from that of the tribes in the southern part,
in Oklahoma. Each of the great tribes to the southward had a government
of its own that was modelled very largely upon that of the various states.
The tribes to the northward had retained, unchanged in essentials, their old
tribal community government. Moreover, they had already been obliged to
allow themselves to be circumscribed by territorial lines, soon to be state lines;
their integrity had been broken in upon; and now they were not of sufficient
importance to have, either individually or collectively, anything to say about
the sectional affiliation of Kansas. As a matter of fact, they never so much
as attempted to take general tribal action in the premises. Neither their situation nor their political organization permitted it.

II. INDIAN TERRITORY IN ITS RELA-TIONS WITH TEXAS AND ARKANSAS

For the participation of the southern Indians in the American Civil War, the states of Texas and Arkansas were more than measurably responsible. Indian Territory, or that part of the Indian country that was historically known as such, lay between them. Its southern frontage was along the Red River; and that stream, flowing with only slight sinuosity downward to its junction with the Mississippi, gave to Indian Territory a long diagonal, controlled, as far as situation went, entirely by Texas. Texas lay on the other side of the river and she lay also on almost the whole western border of Indian Territory.[99] She was, consequently, in possession of a rare opportunity, geographically, for exercising influence, should need for such ever arise. Running parallel with the Red River and northward about one hundred miles, was the Canadian. Between the two rivers were three huge Indian reservations, the most western was the Leased District of the Wichitas and allied bands, the middle one was the Chickasaw, and the eastern, the Choctaw.[100] The Indian occupants of these three reservations were, therefore, and sometimes to their sorrow, be it said, the very next door neighbors

[99] An interruption to this came in the shape of the indefinitely defined "Cherokee Outlet," which lay north of Texas and in addition occupied the northern part of Indian Territory.

[100] The subjoined map will illustrate the relative position of the individual Indian reservations. Although published in 1867, it is not correct for that date but is fairly correct for 1861. The "reconstruction treaties" of 1866 made various changes in the Indian boundaries but the map takes no account of them.

of the Texans. The Choctaws were, likewise, the next
door neighbors of the Arkansans who joined them on
the east; but the relations between Arkansans and Choctaws seem not to have been so close or so constant during the period before the war as were the relations between the Choctaws and the Texans on the one hand and
the Cherokees and the Arkansans on the other.

The Cherokees dwelt, like the Choctaws, over against
Arkansas but north of the Canadian River and in close
proximity to Fort Smith, the headquarters of the Southern Superintendency.[101] Their territory was not so compactly placed as was the territory of the other tribes;
and, in its various parts, it passes, necessarily, under
various designations. There was the "Cherokee Outlet," a narrow tract south of Kansas that had no definite
western limit. It was supposed to be a passage way to
the hunting grounds of the great plains beyond. Then
there was the "Cherokee Strip," the Kansas extension
of the outlet, and for most of its extent originally and
legally a part of it. The territorial organization of
Kansas had made the two distinct. Finally, as respects
the more insignificant portions of the Cherokee domain,
there were the "Cherokee Neutral Lands," already sufficiently well commented upon. They were insignificant, not in point of acreage but of tribal authority operating within them. They lay in the southeastern corner
of Kansas and constituted, against their will and against
the law, her southeastern counties. They were separated, to their own discomfiture and disadvantage, from
the Cherokee Nation proper by the reservation of the
Quapaws, of the Senecas, and of the confederated Senecas and Shawnees. This Cherokee Nation lay, as has

---

[101] Van Buren had a short time previously been the headquarters of the
Southern Superintendency.

COLONEL DOWNING, CHEROKEE
[*From Smithsonian Institution, Bureau of American Ethnology*]

already been indicated, over against Arkansas and north of the northeastern section of the Choctaw country. The Arkansas River formed part of the boundary between the two tribal domains. So much then for the location of the really great tribes, but where were the lesser?

The Quapaws, the Senecas, and the confederated Senecas and Shawnees, the most insignificant of the lesser, occupied the extreme northeastern corner of Indian Territory and, therefore, bordered upon the southwestern corner of Missouri. The Creeks lived between the Arkansas River, inclusive of its Red Fork, and the Canadian River, having the Cherokees to the east and north of them, the Choctaws and Chickasaws to the south, and the Seminoles to the southwest, between the Canadian and its North Fork. The Indians of the Leased District have already been located.

In the years preceding the Civil War, the interest of Texas and of Arkansas in Indian Territory manifested itself, not in a covetous desire to dispossess the Indians of their lands, as was, unfortunately for national honor, the case in Kansas, but in an effort to keep the actual country true to the South, settled by slaveholders, Indian or white, as occasion required or opportunity offered. When sectional affairs became really tense after the formation of the Republican Party, they redoubled their energies in that direction, working always through the rich, influential, and intelligent half-breeds, some of whom had property interests and family connections in the states operating upon them.[102] The half-breeds were essentially a planter class, institutionally more

---

[102] We find that this intimate intercourse extended even to things scholastic; for, though there were plenty of female seminaries, so-called, within Indian Territory, Indian girls regularly attended similar institutions in Fayetteville [Bishop, A. W., *Loyalty on the Frontier*, 143].

truly so than were the inhabitants of the border slave states. It is therefore not surprising that, during the excitement following Abraham Lincoln's nomination and election, identically the same political agencies worked among them as among their white neighbors and events in Indian Territory kept perfect pace with events in adjoining states.

The first of these that showed strong sectional tendencies came in January, 1861, when the Chickasaws, quite on their own initiative apparently, met in a called session of their legislature to consider how best the great tribes might conduct themselves with reference to the serious political situation then shaping itself in the United States.   There is some evidence that the Knights of the Golden Circle had been active among the Indians as they had been in Arkansas[103] during the course of the late presidential campaign.   At all events, the red men knew full well of passing occurrences among their neighbors and they certainly knew how matters were progressing in Texas.   There the State Rights Party was asserting itself in no doubtful terms.   For the time being, however, the Chickasaws contented themselves with simply passing an act,[104] January 5, suggesting

---

[103] Bishop [*Loyalty on the Frontier*, 20] says that to the zeal of the Knights of the Golden Circle, or "Knaves of the Godless Communion," was mainly attributable "the treasonable complexion" of the Arkansas legislature that organized in November of 1860.

[104] The following documents include the act of the Chickasaw Legislature and related correspondence:

> Be it enacted by the Legislature of the Chickasaw Nation, That the Governor of the Chickasaw Nation, be and he is hereby authorized to appoint four Commissioners, one from each county, namely: – Panola, Pickens, Tishomingo, and Pontotoc County, on the part of the Chickasaw Nation, to meet a like set of Commissioners appointed respectively by the Choctaw, Creek, Cherokee, and Seminole Nations, to meet in General Convention at such time and place That the Chief of the Creek Nation, may set, for the purpose of entering into some compact, not inconsistent with the Laws and Treaties of the United States, for

an inter-tribal conference and arranging for the executive appointment of a Chickasaw delegation to it.   The

the future security and protection of the rights and Citizens of said
nations, in the event of a change in the United States, and to renew
the harmony and good feeling already established between said Nations by a compact concluded & entered into on the 14th of Nov. 1859,
at Asbury Mission Creek Nation.

Be it further enacted That said Commissioners shall receive for their
services the sum of One hundred dollars each, and shall report the proceedings of said Convention to the next session of the Chickasaw Legislature for its approval or disapproval. . .

Passed the House Repts as amended Jany 5th 1861.

Passed Senate Jan. 5, 1861.

Approved Jan. 5, 1861.

Indian Office General Files – *Cherokee 1859-1865*, C515.

Enclosed please find an Act of the called Session of the Chickasaw
Legislature, the object of which you will readily understand. Your
coöperation, and union of action of the Cherokee people in effecting the
object therein expressed is hereby respectfully solicited.

It will be left to the Principal Chiefs of the Creek Nation to appoint
the time and place of meeting, of which you will have timely notice. –
CYRUS HARRIS, governor of the Chickasaw Nation, to John Ross, principal chief of the Cherokees, dated Tishomingo, C.N. January 5th, 1861
[*ibid.*].

You will please find enclosed a communication from the Govr of
the Chickasaw Nation & an Act of the Chickasaw Legislature calling
upon their Brethren the Creeks to appoint a time & place for a General Convention of the Chickasaws, Choctaws, Cherokees, and Creeks.
We therefore appoint the 17th inst. to meet at the General Council
Ground of the Creek Nation – At which time & place we will (be)
happy to meet our Brethren the Cherokees. – JACOB DERRYSAW, acting
chief of the Creek Nation, to John Ross, dated Cowetah, Creek Nation,
February 4, 1861 [*ibid.*].

I was much surprised to receive a proposition for taking action so
formal on a matter so important, without having any previous notice or
understanding about the business, which might have afforded opportunity to confer with our respective Councils and People.

Although I regret most deeply, the excitement which has arisen
among our White brethren: yet *by us* it can only be regarded as a family misunderstanding among themselves. And it behooves us to be careful, in any movement of ours, to refrain from adopting any measures
liable to be misconstrued or misrepresented: – and in which (at present
at least) we have no direct and proper concern.

I cannot but confidently believe, however, that there is wisdom and
virtue and moderation enough among the people of the United States,

authorities of the other tribes were duly notified [105] and to the Creek was given the privilege of naming time and place.

The Inter-tribal Council assembled at the Creek

to bring about a peaceable and satisfactory adjustment of their differences. And I do not think we have the right to anticipate any contingency adverse to the stability and permanence of the Federal Union.

Our relations to the United States, as defined by our treaties, are clear and definite. And the obligations growing out of them easily ascertained. And it will ever be our wisdom and our interest to adhere strictly to those obligations, and carefully to guard against being drawn into any complications which may prove prejudicial to the interests of our people, or imperil the security we now enjoy under the protection of the Government of the United States as guaranteed by our Treaties. In the very worst contingency that can be thought of, the great National Responsibilities of the United States must and will be provided for. And should a catastrophe as that referred to in (your) communication, unhappily occur, then will be the time for us to take proper steps for securing the rights and interests of our people.

Out of respect to the Chiefs of neighboring Nations, and from the deep interest I feel for the peace and welfare of our red brethren, I have deemed it proper to appoint a Delegation to attend the Council appointed by the Creek Chiefs at your request, on the 17th inst. at the Genl Council Ground of the Creek Nation, for the purpose of a friendly interchange of the views & sentiments on the general interests of our respective Nations.

In the language of our Fathers, I am your
   "Elder Friend and Brother"
      JOHN ROSS, Principal Chief, Cherokee Nation.

Extract from letter to Cyrus Harris, February 9, 1861 [*ibid.*].

Previous to the receipt of your Communication enclosing the proceedings of the Chickasaw Authorities, I had received similar papers from the "Governor of the Chickasaw Nation."

And I herewith enclose for the information of yourself & people a copy of my reply. I will appoint a Delegation to attend your Council for the purpose therein stated. – Ross to Derrysaw, February 9, 1861 [*ibid.*].

I have received a communication from the Gov. of the Chickasaw Nation, with a copy of an Act of their Legislature. And I presume a similar communication has been received by you. Deeming it important that much prudence and caution should be exercised by us in regard to the object of the Governor's communication, I have thought it proper to address him a letter, giving a brief expression of my views on the subject, a copy of which I enclose for your information. – Ross to the principal chief of the Choctaw Nation, February 11, 1861 [*ibid.*].

[105] See preceding note.

Agency,[106] February 17, but comparatively few delegates were in attendance. William P. Ross, a graduate [107] of Princeton and a nephew of John Ross, the principal chief of the Cherokees, went as the head of the Cherokee delegation. It was he who reported the scanty attendance,[108] saying that there were no Chickasaws present, no Choctaws, but only Creeks, Seminoles, and Cherokees. Why it happened so can not now be exactly determined but to it may undoubtedly be ascribed the outcome; for the council did nothing that was not perfectly compatible with existing friendly relations between the great tribes and the United States government. John Ross, in instructing his delegates, had strictly enjoined caution and discretion.[109] William P. Ross and his associates seem to have managed to secure

---

[106] The Creek Agency was probably chosen because of its convenient situation. It was at the junction of the North Fork and the Canadian and, consequently, in close proximity to three of the reservations and not far distant from the other two.

[107] See Mrs. W. P. Ross, *Life and Times of William P. Ross.*

[108] *American Historical Review*, vol. xv, 282.

[109] . . . On your deliberations it will [be] proper for you to advise discretion, and to guard against any premature movement on our part, which might produce excitement or be liable to misrepresentation. Our duty is very plain. We have only to adhere firmly to our respective Treaties. By them we have placed ourselves under the protection of the United States, and of no other sovereign whatever. We are bound to hold no treaty with any foreign Power, or with any individual State or combination of States nor with Citizens of any State. Nor even with one another without the interposition and participation of the United States. . .

Should any action of the Council be thought desirable, a resolution might be adopted, to the effect, that we will in all contingencies rest our interests on the pledged faith of the United States, for the fulfilment of their obligations. We ought to entertain no apprehension of any change, that will endanger our interests. The parties holding the responsibilities of the Federal Government will always be bound to us. And no measures we have it in our power to adopt can add anything to the security we now possess. Relying on your intelligence & discretion I will add no more. – CHIEF ROSS'S instructions to the Cherokee Delegation, February 12, 1861 [Indian Office General Files, *Cherokee 1859-1865*, C515].

the observance of both. Perchance it was Chief Ross's [110] known aversion to an interference in matters that did not concern the Indians, except very indirectly, and the consciousness that his influence in the council would be immense, probably all-powerful, that caused the Chickasaws to draw back from a thing they had themselves so ill-advisedly planned. It is, however, just possible that, between the time of issuing the call and of assembling the council, they crossed on their own responsibility the boundary of indecision and resolved, as most certainly had the Choctaws, that their sympathies and their interests were with the South. It might well be supposed that in this perilous hour their thoughts would have travelled back some thirty years and they would have remembered what havoc the same state-rights doctrine, now presented so earnestly for their acceptance, although it scarcely fitted their case, had then wrought in their concerns. Strangely enough none of the tribes seems to have charged the gross injustice of the thirties exclusively to the account of the South. On the contrary, they one and all charged it against the federal government, against the states as a whole, and so, rightly or wrongly, the nation had to pay for the inconsistency of Jackson's procedure, a procedure that could so illogically recognize the supremacy of federal law in one matter and the supremacy of state law in another matter that was precisely its parallel.

The decision of the Choctaws had found expression in a series of resolutions under date of February 7. They are worthy of being quoted entire.

---

[110] The Indian Office files are full of testimony proving John Ross's wisdom, foresight, sterling worth generally, and absolute devotion to his people. Indeed, his whole biography is written large in the records. His character was impeccable. Judged by any standard whatsoever, he would easily rank as one of the greatest of Indian half-breeds.

February 7, 1861.

RESOLUTIONS *expressing the feelings and sentiments of the General Council of the Choctaw Nation in reference to the political disagreement existing between the Northern and Southern States of the American Union.*

Resolved by the General Council of the Choctaw Nation assembled, That we view with deep regret and great solicitude the present unhappy political disagreement between the Northern and Southern States of the American Union, tending to a permanent dissolution of the Union and the disturbance of the various important relations existing with that Government by treaty stipulations and international laws, and portending much injury to the Choctaw government and people.

Resolved further, That we must express the earnest desire and ready hope entertained by the entire Choctaw people, that any and all political disturbances agitating and dividing the people of the various States may be honorably and speedily adjusted; and the example and blessing, and fostering care of their General Government, and the many and friendly social ties existing with their people, continue for the enlightenment in moral and good government and prosperity in the material concerns of life to our whole population.

Resolved further, That in the event a permanent dissolution of the American Union takes place, our many relations with the General Government must cease, and we shall be left to follow the natural affections, education, institutions, and interests of our people, which indissolubly bind us in every way to the destiny of our neighbors and brethren of the Southern States upon whom we are confident we can rely for the preservation of our rights of life, liberty, and property, and the continuance of many acts of friendship, general counsel, and material support.

Resolved further, That we desire to assure our immediate neighbors, the people of Arkansas and Texas, of our determination to observe the amicable relations in every way so long existing between us, and the firm reliance we have, amid any disturbance with other States, the rights and feelings so sacred to us will remain respected by them and be protected from the encroachments of others.

Resolved further, That his excellency the principal chief be requested to inclose, with an appropriate communication from himself, a copy of these resolutions to the governors of the Southern States, with the request that they be laid before the State convention of each State, as many as have assembled at the date of their reception, and that in such as have not they be published in the newspapers of the State.

Resolved, That these resolutions take effect and be in force from and after their passage.

Approved February 7, 1861.[111]

These resolutions of the Choctaw Council are in the highest degree interesting in the matter both of their substance and of their time of issue. The information is not forthcoming as to how the Choctaws received the invitation of the Chickasaw legislature to attend an inter-tribal council; but, later on, in April, 1861, the Choctaw delegation in Washington, made up of P. P. Pitchlynn, Samuel Garland, Israel Folsom, and Peter Folsom, assured the Commissioner of Indian Affairs that the Choctaw Nation intended to remain neutral,[112]

---

[111] *Official Records*, first ser., vol. i, 682.

[112] The evidence of this is to be found in an official letter from Commissioner W. P. Dole to Secretary Caleb B. Smith, under date of April 30, 1861, which reads as follows:

I have the honor to enclose herewith a copy of a letter, dated 17th. Inst. from Elias Rector, Esq., Supt. Indian Affairs . . . together with copy of its enclosure, being one addressed to *Col. W. H. Emory* by *M. Leeper*, Agent for the Indians within the "Leased District," having reference to the removal of the troops from Fort Cobb.

The Government being bound by treaty obligations to protect the Indians from the incursions of all enemies, I would respectfully ask to be informed, if it is not its intention to keep in the country a sufficient force for the purpose.

The Choctaw and Chickasaw delegation – composed of the principal men of those Nations – while recently in this City expressed great apprehensions of attack upon their people, by Citizens of Texas and Arkansas; and these delegations having assured me of their determination to maintain a neutral position in the anticipated difficulties throughout our Country, I would recommend that a depot for arms be established within the Southern Superintendency in order that the Indians there may be placed in the possession of the means to defend themselves against any attack. . . – Indian Office *Report Book*, no. 12, p. 152.

which assurance was interpreted to mean simply that the Choctaws would be inactive spectators of events, expressing no opinion, in word or deed, one way or the other. The Chickasaw delegation gave the same assurance and at about the same time and place. Now what is to be concluded? Is it to be supposed that the Act of January 5, 1861 in no wise reflected the sentiments of a tribe as a whole and similarly the Resolutions of February 7, 1861, or that the tribal delegations were, in April, utterly ignorant of the real attitude of their respective constituents? The answer is to be found in the following most interesting and instructive letter, written by S. Orlando Lee to Commissioner Dole from Huntingdon, Long Island, March 15, 1862:[113]

> Thinking you and the government would like to hear something about the state of affairs among the Choctaws last summer and the influences which induced them to take their present position I will write you what I know. I was a missionary teacher at Spencer Academy for two years and refer you to Hon. Walter Lowrie Gen. Sec. of the Pres. Board of Foreign Missions for information as to my character &c. I left Spencer June 13th & the nation June 24th but have heard directly from there twice since, the last time as late as Sept 6th. So that I can speak of occurrences as late as that.
>
> After South Carolina passed her secession ordinance in Dec. 1860 there was a public attempt to excite the Choctaws and Chickasaws as a beginning hoping to bring in the other tribes afterwards. Many of the larger slaveholders (who are nearly all half breeds) had been gained before and Capt. R. M. Jones was the leader of the secessionists. The country was full of lies about the intentions of the new administration. The border papers in Arkansas & Texas republished from the New York & St. Louis papers a part of a sentence from Hon. W. H. Seward's speech at Chicago during the election campaign of 1860 to this effect "And Indian Territory south of Kansas must be vacated by the Indian" (These words do occur in the report of Mr. Seward's Chicago

[113] General Files, *Southern Superintendency, 1859-1862*, L632.

speech as published in New York Evening Post Weekly for I read it myself). This produced intense excitement of course and to add to the effect the Secessionist Journals charged that another prominent republican had proposed to drive the indians out of Indian Ter. in a speech in congress. "This" they were told "is the policy of the new administration. The abolitionists want your lands — we will protect you. Your only safety is to join the South." Again they were told "that the South must succeed in gaining their independence and the money of the indians being invested in the stocks of Southern states the stocks would be cancelled & the indians would lose their money unless they joined the south, if they did that the stocks would be reissued to the Confederate States for them." Their special commissioners Peter Folsom &c, who came to Washington to get the half million of dollars for claims, reported that they got along very well until they were asked if they had slaves after that they said they could do nothing. Sampson Folsom said however that he thought they would have succeeded had it not been for the attack on Sumpter — He said President Lincoln then told them "He would not give them a dollar until the close of the war" An interesting fact in relation to these commissioners is that they came to Washington by way of *Montgomery* & were when they reached Washington probably all, except Judge Garland, secessionists. Thus all influences were in favor of the rebels — Where could the indians go for light — The former indian agent Cooper was a Col. in the rebel service. The oldest missionary who has undoubtedly more influence with the Choctaws than any other white man is an ardent secessionist believing firmly both in the right & in the final success of the rebel cause — He (Dr. Kingsbury) prays as earnestly & fervently for the success of the rebels as any one among us does for the success of the Union cause. The son of another, Mr. Hodgkin, is a captain in the rebel service — another Mr. Stark actively assisted in organizing a company acted as sec. of secessionist meetings &c. Even Mr. Reid superintendant of Spencer was confident the rebels could never be subdued and thought when the treaty should be made they ought in justice to have Ind. Territory. Again when Fort Smith was evacuated the rebel forces were on the way up the Ark. river to attack it & the garrison evacuated it in the night which

looked to the Indians (if not to the white men) as if the northerners were afraid. The same was true of Fort Washitaw where
our forces left in the night and were actually pursued for several days by the Texans. Thus matters stood when Col. Pitchlynn the resident Com. of the Choctaws at Washington returned
home. He gave all his influence to have the Choctaws take a
neutral position. The chief had called the council to meet June
1st. & Col. P. so far succeeded as to induce him to prepare a
message recommending neutrality. Col. P. was promptly reported as an *abolitionist* and *visited* & *threatened* by a Texas
Vigilance committee.

The Council met at Doaksville seven miles from Red River
& of course from Texas. It was largely attended by white men
from Texas our Choctaw neighbors who attended said the place
was full of white men.

The Council did not organize until June 4th or 5th (I forget
which) In the meanwhile the white men & half bloods had a secession meeting when it leaked out through Col. Cooper that the
Chief Hudson had prepared a message recommending neutrality
at which Robert M. Jones was so indignant that he made a fu-
rious speech in which he declared that "any one who opposed secession ought to be hung" "and any suspicious persons ought to
be hung." Hudson was frightened and when the Council was
organized sent in a message recommending that commissioners
be appointed to negotiate a treaty with the Confederates and that
in the meantime a regiment be organized under Col. Cooper for
the Confed. army.

This was finally done but not for a week for the Choctaws
were reluctant. They feared that their action would result in
the destruction of the nation. Said Joseph P. Folsom, a member
of the council & a graduate of Dartmouth College New Hamp-
shire, "We are choosing in what way we shall die" Judge Wade
said to me, "We expect that the Choctaws will be buried. That
is what we think will be the end of this." Judge W. is a member of the Senate (for the Choctaw Council is composed of a
Senate & lower house chosen by the people in districts & the constitution is modeled very much after those of the states.) & he
has been a chief. Others said to me "If the north was here so
we could be protected we would stand up for the north but now

if we do not go in for the south the Texans will come over here and kill us." Mr. Reid told me a day or two before we left that he had become convinced during a trip for two or three days through the country that the *full bloods* were strongly for the north. I am sure it *was* so *then* & it was the opinion of the missionaries that if we had all taken the position, that we would not leave, some of us had been warned to do so by Texan vigilance committees, we could have raised a thousand men who would have armed in our defence – Our older brethren told us that this would hasten the destruction of the indians as they would be crushed before any help could come. – We thought this would probably be the case and the missionaries who were most strongly union in sentiment left.

One of the number Rev. John Edwards had been hiding for his life from Texan & half blood ruffians for two weeks & we at Spencer had had the *honor* to be visited by a Texas committee searching for arms.

I continue my narrative from a letter from one of our teachers who was detained when we left by the illness of his wife & who left Spencer Sept 5th & the Nation Sept. 9th. He says Col. Coopers regiment was filled up with Texans "The half breeds after involving the full bloods in the war have rather drawn back themselves and but few of them have enlisted & gone to the war." This indicates that the full bloods have at last yielded to the pressure and joined the rebels. The missionaries who remained would generally advise them to do this.

The Choctaw commissioners met Albert Pike rebel commissioner & made a treaty with him, with reference to this he says "The Choctaws rec'd quite a bundle of promises from the rebel government. Their treaty gives their representative a seat in the rebel congress, acknowledges the right of the Choctaws to give testimony in all courts in the C. S., exempts them from the expences of the war, their soldiers are to be paid 20$ a month by the C. S. during the war, the C. S. assume the debts due the Choctaws by the U. S., they have the privilege of coming in as a state into the Confederacy with equal rights if they wish it, or remain as they are, the C. S. to sustain their schools *after the war*, they guarantee them against all intrusion on their lands by white men, allow them to garrison the forts in their territory

with their own troops if they wish it said troops to be paid by
the C. S." – Here is a list of promises and when I think of these,
of the belief of their oldest missionaries in the final success of
the rebels, of the fact that all the old Officers of the U. S. government were in the service of the rebels, of the occupation of
the forts there by rebels, of the activity of a knot of bitter dis-
unionists led by Capt. Jones, who has long been a very influential
man, of the Texas mob law which considered it a crime for a
young man to refuse to volunteer, of the fact that there was no
way for them to hear the truth as to the designs of the U. S.
government concerning them, except through Col. Pitchlyn who
was soon silenced & of the falsehoods told them as to the designs
of the Government, I do not wonder that they have joined the
rebels.

I saw strong men completely unmanned even to floods of tears
by the leaving of Dr. Hobbs and the thoughts of what was before
them.   I heard men say they did not want to fight but expected
to be forced to do it.

I trust the government will consider the circumstances of the
case & deal gently, considerately with the indians.   I do not like
to write such things of my brother missionaries but they are I
believe facts & though I love some of them very much I still must
say that, except Rev. Mr. Byington who was doubtful & Rev.
Mr. Balantine a missionary to the Chickasaws who was union,
all the ordained missionaries belonging to the Choctaw & Chickasaw Mission of the Presbyterian Board who remain there were
victims of the madness which swept over the South, were secessionists – One or two of the three Laymen who remained were
union men – Cyrus Kingsbury son of Rev. Dr. K. being
one.   .   .

The failure of the United States government to give
the Indians, in season, the necessary assurance that they
would be protected, no matter what might happen, can
not be too severely criticized.   It indicated a very short-
sighted policy and was due either to a tendency to ig-
nore the Indians as people of no importance or to a lack
of harmony and coöperation among the departments at
Washington.   Such an assurance of continued protec-

tion was not even framed until the second week in May
and then the Indian country was already threatened by
the secessionists.   Moreover, it was framed and intended to be given by one department, the Interior, and its
fulfilment left to another, the War.   It went out from
the Indian Office in the form of a circular letter,[114] addressed by Commissioner William P. Dole to the chief
executive[115] in each of the five great tribes.   It assured
the Indians that President Lincoln had no intention of
interfering with their domestic institutions or of allowing government agents or employees to interfere and
that the War Department had been appealed to to furnish all needed defense according to treaty guaranties.
The new southern superintendent, William G. Coffin
of Indiana, was made the bearer of the missive; but,
unfortunately, quite a little time elapsed[116] before the
military situation[117] in the West would allow him to as-

[114] The letter can be found in manuscript form in Indian Office, *Letter
Book*, no. 65, pp. 447-449, and in printed form in Commissioner of Indian
Affairs, *Report*, 1861, p. 34.

[115] *John Ross*, principal chief of the Cherokee Nation; *Cyrus Harris*, governor of the Chickasaw Nation; *M. Kennard*, principal chief of the Lower
Creeks; *Echo Hadjo* [Echo Harjo], principal chief of the Upper Creeks;
George Hudson, principal chief of the Choctaw Nation; and the unnamed
principal chief of the Seminoles west of Arkansas.

[116] It would seem that the letter was not given to Coffin immediately but
was held back on account of the insecurity of the mails [Dole to Creek and
Seminole chiefs, November 16, 1861, Indian Office, *Letter Book*, no. 67, pp.
78-79].

[117] The delay was not entirely due to the military situation. Coffin went
from Washington to his home in Indiana. He was there on the twentieth,
at Annapolis, Parke County, when Dole wrote urging him to hasten on his way,

I herewith enclose a slip taken from the National Intelligencer of
this date, being an extract from the Austin [Texas] State Gazette of the
4th Instant, by which you will perceive that efforts are being made to
tamper with the Indians within your Superintendency.

By this you will perceive the urgent necessity, that you should proceed at the earliest moment practicable to the vicinity of the duties in
your charge, that from your personal knowledge of the views of the
Government in relation to these Indians as well as by the instructions

sume his full duties or to reach his official headquarters,[118] and, in the interval, he was detailed for other

> and communications in your possession, you may be able to thwart the endeavors of any and all who have or shall attempt to tamper with these tribes and array them in hostility to the Government.
>
> I deem it of the utmost importance that no time be lost in this matter, as delay may be disastrous to the public service. – Indian Office, *Letter Book*, no. 65, p. 473.

By the nineteenth of June, Coffin had managed to reach Crawford Seminary, from which place he reported to Dole,

> We have at length reached the Indian Territory propper. . . I find Mr. Elder the Agent absent. I learned on my way down here that he had gone to Fort Scott with the view of locating the Agency there for the present which I supposed when I wrote you from the Catholic Mission might be propper from its close proximity to Missouri but as Mr. Phelps district is opposit here and he a good Union man and has been Stumping the district and I learn that the Union cause is growing fast in that part of the State I think there is now at least no Sort of excuse for removing, the buildings here are ample for a large family, watter good. . . – General Files, *Southern Superintendency, 1859-1862*, C1229.

The sequel showed that Agent Elder was right and Superintendent Coffin wrong about the security of the region. Coffin never reached Fort Smith at all and was soon compelled to vacate the Indian Territory. Indian Office, *Letter Book*, no. 66, which covers the period from June, 1861 to October, 1861, contains scarcely a letter to prove that the Indian Office was in communication with Indian Territory. Official connection with the country had been completely cut off. Military abandonment and dilatory officials had done their work.

[118] Official instructions were issued to Coffin, then in Washington, on the ninth, and gave him permission to change his headquarters at discretion. The following is an excerpt of the instructions:

> You having been appointed by the President to be Superintendent of Indian Affairs for the Southern Superintendency in place of *Elias Rector*, Esq. . . You will repair to Fort Smith, Arkansas, as early as practicable, for the purpose of relieving *Elias Rector*, Esq.
>
> In your progress from Indiana to Fort Smith, should you deem it expedient and advisable to pass down the Kansas line and among the Indians in that section, you will make it your business to inquire as to their sentiments and disposition with reference to the present disturbances in the neighboring countries, so far as time and opportunity will enable you to do so. On reaching Fort Smith you will also inform yourself as to the condition of Affairs there and surrounding country, and as to the prospect of the business of the Superintendency being carried on without molestation or other inconvenience, and should you find it necessary

work. The Indians, meanwhile, were left to their own devices and were obliged to look out for their own defense as best they could.

To all appearances neither the legislative action of the Chickasaws and of the Choctaws nor the work of the inter-tribal council was, at the time of occurrence, reported officially to the United States government or, if reported officially, then not pointedly so as to reveal its real bearings upon the case in hand. All the agents within Indian Territory were as usual southern men;[119] but may not have been directly responsible or even cognizant of this particular action of their charges. The records show that practically all of them, Cooper, Garrett, Cowart, Leeper, and Dorn, were absent[120] from their posts, with or without leave, the first part of the

---

from the circumstances that may surround you to remove the office of Superintendent from Fort Smith you are authorized to do so, selecting some eligible point in the proximate Indian Territory, or if required some point northwardly among the Indians in Kansas as your best discretion may dictate. I trust however that this discretionary authority may prove unnecessary and that in the legitimate discharge of your duties, you may suffer no interruption from any cause or source whatever. In a report from this Office of the 30th Ultimo, with reference to anticipated Indian troubles in your Superintendency consequent upon the removal of the troops from Fort Cobb, the attention of the *Hon. Secretary of the Interior* was called to the subject, and the enquiry as to the policy of the Government to keep in the country a sufficient force for the purpose of proper protection; and further calling his attention to the expression of friendship and loyalty made by the Choctaw and Chickasaw delegates lately in this City, recommended that a depot for arms be established within the Southern Superintendency, in order that the Indians there may be placed in possession of the means to defend themselves against any attack. As yet no response to this report has been received. . . – Indian Office, *Letter Book*, no. 65, pp. 442-443.

[119] Douglas H. Cooper, agent for the Choctaws and Chickasaws, was from Mississippi; William H. Garrett, agent for the Creeks, was from Alabama; Robert J. Cowart, agent for the Cherokees, was from Georgia; Matthew Leeper, agent for the Indians of the Leased District, was from Texas; and Andrew J. Dorn, agent at the Neosho River Agency, was from Arkansas.

[120] Telegram, Greenwood to Rector, January 19, 1861 [Indian Office, *Letter Book*, no. 65, p. 104].

new year and that every one of them became or was already an active secessionist.[121]

It has been authenticated and is well understood today that, as the Southern States, one by one, declared themselves out of the Union or were getting themselves into line for so doing, they prepared to further the cause of secession among their neighbors and, for the purpose, sent agents or commissioners to them, who organized the movement very much as the Committees of Correspondence did a similar movement prior to the American Revolution.   In short, in the spring of 1861, the seceding states entered upon active proselytism and at least two of them extended their labors to and among the Indians.   Those two were Texas and Arkansas. Missouri also worked with the same end in view, so did Colorado, but apparently not so much with the great tribes of Oklahoma as with the politically less important of Kansas.   Colorado, it is true, did operate to some extent upon the Cherokees of the Outlet and upon the Wichitas, but mostly upon the Indians of the western plains.   No one can deny that, in the interests of the Confederate cause, the project of sending emissaries even to the Indians was a wise measure or refuse to admit that the contrasting inactivity and positive indifference of the North was foolhardy in the extreme. It indicated a self-complacency for which there was no justification.   More than that can with truth be said; for, from the standpoint of political wisdom and foresight, the inactivity where the Indians were concerned was conduct most reprehensible.

[121] For information showing what Indian agents became adherents of the Confederate cause, see, among other things, an extract from a report of Albert Pike to be found in Indian Office, *Letter Book*, no. 130, pp. 237-238; and a letter from R. W. Johnson to L. P. Walker, published in *Official Records*, first ser., vol. iii, 598.

While Chickasaws and Choctaws, unsolicited,[122] were expressing themselves, the secessionist sentiment was de-

[122] The evidence on this point is not very convincing, either one way or the other. A number of documents might be cited bearing some brief, vague, or indefinite reference to the steps the Indians took from the beginning. The closing paragraph of the following report from E. H. Carruth, under date of July 11, 1861, is a typical case:

> Sir: I know not that any person has given information to any of the United States officers in regard to the position of the Indian Tribes connected with the Southern Superintendency.
>
> I am just arrived from the Seminole Country where for a year I have been employed as [illegible] to induce the Seminoles to establish schools. In Sept. last the chiefs applied to the Department to set aside $5000 for this purpose, but never heard from their application, and their Ag't soon became too deeply interested in the politics of the Country to pay much attention to the affairs of the tribe.
>
> From the time the secession movement began to ripen into treason, the Chief of the Seminoles has constantly sought information on the subject, and whenever I rec'd a mail he would bring an Interpreter & remain with me until all had been read and explained.
>
> After the Forts west were taken possession of by the Texans, the tribes living under the protection of Government around Fort Cobb came into the Seminole Country, seeking the counsel of the Seminoles as to what they should do, hostility to the Texans, being with them strengthened by the recollection of recent wrongs. The Seminoles gave them permission to reside on their lands, and advised them to interfere with neither party, should both be represented in the country.
>
> The Texan officers sent several letters among them & left Commissioners at Cobb to treat with them offering to them the same protection before enjoyed while the Government of the U. S. was represented among them. A letter was also sent to the Seminoles signed by Geo. W. Welch, "Capt – Commanding the Texan troops in the service of the Southern Confederacy" which asserted that the *Northern people were determined to take away their lands & negroes,* that the old Gov't would never be able to fulfill her treaty stipulations and wound up by asking them to place their interests under the protection of the Southern Confederacy.
>
> Very soon aferwards Capt- Albert G. Pike "Commissioner for the Confederate States of America" wrote to the Seminole Chief from the Creek Agency, asking that he should meet him at that place with six of his best men fully authorized to treat with him. He also asked for a body of Seminole warriors, & promised as "good perhaps better treaty" than their old one. His letter was backed up by one from Washburn (formerly Seminole Ag't) who gave a glowing description of treason, representing to the Indians that the U.S. could never pay one dollar of the moneys due them, that European Nations were committed to the

veloping rapidly in Texas. By the middle of February,
conditions were such that steps might be taken to order

cause of the Rebels, and entreated, prayed, almost commanded them to
take the step so essential to their political salvation. This Washburn
had once been engaged in a money transaction with two of the Chiefs
which swindled the nation out of many thousands of dollars, and while
they came near losing their heads in the operation, he escaped, & still
enjoys great personal popularity with the tribe. No man knows better
how to approach Indians. He was born among them of missionary
parents, & like all southern men, who regret their northern parentage,
he is the most rabid of violent traitors. The day after these letters were
rec'd the Chief (John Jumper) spent at my house. He felt true to the
treaties, & said that all his people were with the Government, but, the
Forts west were in possession of its enemies, their Agent would give
them no information on the subject, & he feared that his country would
be overrun, if he did not yield.

I told him plainly that Government was shamefully misrepresented,
that the treaties bound him to all the states alike, that the U.S. could not
fall with all the Army & Navy at her disposal, & that should the South
ever succeed in gaining her own independence the free States would
fight till not a man, woman or child was left, before yielding one inch
of Territory to the rebels. The war being entered into not so much
either for or against slavery in the states, as to protect the Constitutional
rights of Government in the Territories. The Chief told me that all the
full Indians everywhere were with the Gov't, that he did not wish to
fight, nor did his people, they had hoped to be left to themselves untill
the whites settled their quarrels, his people had enough of war in Florida, & were now anxious for peace. He would however go to the Creek
Agency & tell Capt. Pike & Ben McCulloch their determination. I believe the object of Pike in drawing the Seminoles to the Creek country
was that he could thus bring Creek influence to bear upon them. When
Pike's letter came, the Bearer sent word to the Chief to meet him ten
miles below, where they were read, but this caution did not keep them
out of sight, as the Chief immediately brought them to me, to whom as
clerk they should have come at first, but a "white man" was declared to
be the adviser of the Seminoles, for whom a black jack limb would soon
suffice. I knew it dangerous to await the arrival of my ranger friends,
& with my wife I left on horseback, traveling in a Kickapoo trail, coming in above the Creek country, as they had seceded – I was questioned
a good deal in the Cherokee Nation, but not interfered with as I was
personally acquainted with their leading half breeds, and my wife being
fortunate enough to have a Virginia birth and a brother in Missouri.

When within a half hour's travel of the Neosho River, my shot gun
was taken by a company of men, organized that day – the 2d after Sey-
mour was killed – they said "to clean out Kansas Jay hawkers."

The influence of Capt Pike the Rebel Commissioner is second to no

the evacuation of the state by Federal troops.   This was
finally done under authority of the Committee of Pub-

man's among the Southern Indians & I fear that he may succeed in his
intrigues with the other tribes, the Creeks, Chickasaws, & Choctaws
having already gone.   The Cherokees refuse to go as a Nation, & no one
is a firmer friend to the Union than John Ross, their Chief, but traitors
are scheming, and the half breeds in favor of the South, want an army
to come in, in which event they promise to be "forced in" to the Arms
of Jeff. Davis, & the select crowd of traitors at Montgomery.

There are many true & loyal men even among the half breeds, some
of the Judges of their courts I know to be so, while all the full blood
element is with the Gov't.

The half breeds belong to the K. G. C. a society whose sole object is
to increase & defend slavery and the full bloods have – not to be out-
done – got up a secret organization called the "pins" which meets among
mountains, connecting business with Ball-playing, and this is understood to be in favor of Gov't, at least when a half breed at Webers
falls raised a secession flag, the "pins" turned out to haul it down &
were only stopped by a superior force, they retired swearing that "it
should yet be done & its raiser killed" and now Sir, let me say a word
in behalf of the full Indians who make up in devotion to our Gov't
what they lack in knowledge.

I sometimes hear rejoicing on the part of Northern people, that these
tribes are seceding, because they say such violation of their treaties
will lose them their lands, whose beauty & fertility have long been admired by western farmers.   I have been twelve years among these
tribes & I know the full bloods to be loyal to the Gov't.   That Gov't
is bound by treaties to protect these nations, to keep up Forts for that
purpose.   The forts are deserted, the soldiers are gone.   The Agents
are either resigned or, working under "confederate" commissions.   The
Indians are told that the old Gov't is bankrupt, that it must die, that
England & France will help the South, That they are southern Indians
& own slaves, & have interests only with & in the south, That the war
is waged by the North for the sole purpose of killing slavery, & stealing the Indian lands etc. etc.   What have the Indians with which to
disprove this?   The "Confederate" Gov't is represented there by an
army & Commissioners, but the United States have not been heard from
for six months.   Every battle is believed to be against the old Gov't
& those who control the news know in what shape it should go to have
influence.   The Seminole Agent, Col. Rutherford, has never lifted his
finger to give information or advice to the Indians under his charge –
He said before Mr. Lincoln took his seat as President that he would not
receive a reappointment from him, but would serve until it should come,
which means that his love of money would enable him to make an occasional visit to the Agency buildings, but his fear for & sympathy with
Ark. rebels, would keep him from doing anything to endanger their

lic Safety [123] and the general in command, D. E. Twiggs
of Georgia, compliantly yielded. His small show of
resistance seemed, under the circumstances, a mere pretense, although he had his reasons, and good ones too,
perfectly satisfactory to himself, for doing what he did.
Two main conditions were attached to the agreement of
surrender; [124] one, exacted by General Twiggs, to the
effect that his men be allowed to retain their arms, commissary stores, camp and garrison equipage, and the
means of transportation; the other, exacted by the
Texan commissioners, that the troops depart by way of
the coast and not overland, as the United States War
Department had designed when, a short time before, it
had ordered a similar removal. [125] The precaution of

interests. A proper officer could have kept the Seminoles from sending
a delegation to Capt. Pike, as well as in the Creek country one could
have kept the Creeks loyal. That there has been the most culpable neglect on the part of its officers to the interests of the Genl Gov't needs
no demonstration – The cry has been: "More favorable treaties can now
be made with the South than after the war, as it will show that the
Indians are at heart with the South" – No doubt is allowed to be felt
as to the issue of the war. The agents who hold Commissions from
Mr. Lincoln & go to Montgomery to have Jeff. Davis endorse them,
show a faith in the issue, that is not lost upon the Indians.

A Capt. Brown of the Chickasaw tribe was commanding at Arbuckle, in the absence of Col. McKing who was at Tishimingo where
the legislature was in session. He informed me that the Texans would
not come over until the Choctaws & Chickasaws had given them to understand that "it would be all right" – At the time these nations did not
wish to invite them, it would have been too palpable a violation of
treaties, tho' they took command of the Fort, whether under their national authorities, or the "Confederate" I do not know which.

Letters now in possession of the Seminole Chief will prove much
herein stated. I told the chief to preserve those letters & all others
which he might receive of a like nature. . . – General Files, *Southern
Superintendency, 1859-1862*, C1348.

[123] *Official Records*, first ser., vol. i, 513.

[124] — *Ibid.*, 515-516.

[125] The order was one of the many, dictated by the policy of "no coercion,"
that issued in the last days of Buchanan's administration and the first of Lincoln's. A few of them, affecting or designed to affect the frontier, may as well

forcing a coastwise journey[126] was taken by the Texan commissioners to consume time and to prevent the troops being retained in states or territories through which transit lay for possible future use against Texas. The easy compliance of General Twiggs[127] undoubtedly merits some censure and yet was perfectly well justified to his own conscience by the exigencies of the situation and by the fact that he had repeatedly asked for orders as to what he should do in the event of an emergency and had received none. The circumstance of his surrender and the resulting triumph of the secessionist element could not fail to have its effect upon the watchful Indians to whom the exhibition of present power was everything.

That the Texan secessionists fully appreciated the strategic position of the Indian nations and the absolute necessity of making some sort of terms with them was brought out by the action of the convention at its first session. An ordinance was passed "to secure the friendship and co-operation of the Choctaw, Cherokee, Chickasaw, Creek, and Seminole Nations of Indians;" and three men, James E. Harrison, James Bourland, and Charles A. Hamilton, were appointed as commis-

---

be listed in chronological order. On the thirteenth of February, an abandonment of Fort Smith was ordered [*Official Records*, first ser., vol. i, 654]. The citizens protested and the order was countermanded [*ibid.*, 655]. On the fifteenth of the same month, General Scott ordered, in the event of secession, all United States troops from Texas, via Fort Belknap and the Indian country, to Fort Leavenworth [*ibid.*, 589]. On the eighteenth of March, a similar abandonment of Arkansas and the Indian country was arranged for [*ibid.*, 667].

126 *Official Records*, first ser., vol. liii, supplement, pp. 626, 628, 629.

127 General Twiggs was then waiting to be relieved of his command, having personally requested to be relieved, his sense of embarrassment being strong and his unwillingness to take responsibility, extreme. Robert E. Lee, brevet colonel, Second United States Cavalry, was relieved from duty in Texas and ordered to repair to Washington, by orders of February 4, 1861 [*Official Records*, first ser., vol. i, 586].

sioners[128] "to proceed to said nations and invite their

[128] Commissioners of some sort had been sent to the Indians even before this. They do not seem to have been, in any sense, agents of Texas, indeed, the ones particularly in mind were from Arkansas; but Texas may have taken her cue from their appointment. Their presence in the Indian country is sufficiently attested by the following correspondence:

I have been informed today that persons purporting to act in the capacity of Commissioners are now visiting the Indian nations on our frontier – preparatory to forming an alliance with them to furnish them with arms and munitions of war, in violation of subsisting treaties and the laws of the United States. Occupying the position I do as a Civil officer of the Government in discharge of my duty as well as instructions, It is my duty to make inquiry and report such a state of facts as may exist in relation to the same. And having no authentic information in relation to this matter other than public rumor, I have believed it my duty to address you knowing that if such projects are in embryo or consummation that they cannot escape your vigilance; and that from you I shall be informed of the same, that, they may be communicated from a reliable official source to the authorities at Washington for their action. – JOHN B. OGDEN, United States commissioner, to John Ross, dated Van Buren, February 15, 1861 [Indian Office, General Files, *Cherokee, 1859-1865*, O32].

I have received your communication of the 15th inst. – stating that you have been informed that persons purporting to act in the capacity of commissioners are now visiting the Indian Nations on the frontier preparatory to forming an alliance. . .

It is currently rumored in the Country that Mr. R. J. Cowart – the U. S. Agent – is officially advocating the secession policy of the Southern States and that he is endeavoring to influence the Cherokees to take sides and act in concert with the seceded States – At the same time uttering words of denunciation against all the distinguished Patriots who are exerting their efforts, to devise measures of reconciliation in Congress as well as those in the Peace Convention at Washington for the Preservation of the Union.

Mr. Cowart brought out with him from the State of Georgia a man named – Solomon – who is a notorious drunken brawling disunionist. He is strolling about Tahlequah under the permission of the socalled "U.S. Agent" – and is creating strife & getting into difficulties with citizens of the Nation – a perfect nuisance to the peace and good order of society.

The conduct and general deportment of this man, also of the Agent being in direct violation of the laws and Treaties of the United States – they should be removed out of the Cherokee Country.

For further information as to such facts relating to the subjects of your enquiry, I have to refer you at present to Mr. W. P. Ross for what he may be in possession of. . . – JOHN ROSS to John B. Ogden, February 28, 1861 [Indian Office, General Files, *Cherokee, 1859-1865*, O32].

prompt co-operation in the formation of a Southern Confederacy."[129]

Now before following these men in the execution of their mission, it may be advisable, for breadth of view, to illustrate how Texas still further made Indian relations an issue most prominent in all the earlier stages of her secession movement; but at the very outset it must be admitted that, in so doing, she differentiated carefully between the civilized and the uncivilized tribes. With the one group she was ready to seek an alliance, offensive and defensive, but with the other to wage a relentless, exterminating war. The failure of the United States central government to protect her against the aggressions and the atrocities so-called of the wild tribes was cited by her as one principal justification for withdrawal from the Union,[130] her obvious purpose being to gain thereby the adherence of the northern counties, non-slaveholding but frontier. Almost conversely, on the other hand, Governor Houston gave as one good and sufficient reason for not withdrawing from the Union, the fear that should the Union be dissolved the wild tribes, who were now, in a measure, restrained from committing depredations and enormities by the very nature of their treaty guaranties, would be literally let loose upon Texas.[131] As far as the civilized tribes were concerned, however, all were of one mind and that took the form of the conviction that so great was the necessity of gaining and holding the confidence of the Indians, that Texas must not procrastinate in joining

---

[129] *Official Records*, fourth ser., vol. i, 322.

[130] Tenney, W. J. *Military and Naval History of the Rebellion in the United States*, 134.

[131] Letter to the Alabama commissioner, J. M. Calhoun, January 7, 1861 [*Official Records*, fourth ser., vol. i, 74].

her fortunes with those of her sister states in the Confederacy.[132]

James E. Harrison and his colleagues started out upon the performance of the duties assigned them, February 27, 1861. Their report[133] of operations and of observations being somewhat difficult of access and its contents not easily summarized, is herewith appended. Its fullness of detail is especially to be commended.

We . . . crossed Red River and entered the Chickasaw Nation about thirty miles southwest of Fort Washita; visited and held a private conference with His Excellency Governor C. Harris and other distinguished men of that nation, who fully appreciated our views and the object of our mission. They informed us that a convention of the Chickasaws and Choctaws was in a few days to convene at Boggy Depot, in the Choctaw Nation, to attend to some municipal arrangements. We, in company with Governor Harris and others, made our way to Boggy Depot, conferring privately with the principal men on our route. We arrived at Boggy Depot on the 10th day of March. Their convention or council convened on the 11th. Elected a president of the convention (Ex-Governor Walker, of the Choctaw Nation); adopted rules of decorum. On the 12th we were waited on by a committee of the convention. Introduced as commissioners from Texas, we presented our credentials and were invited to seats. The convention then asked to hear us, when Mr. James E. Harrison addressed them and a crowded auditory upon the subject of our mission, setting forth the grounds of our complaint against the Government of the United States, the wrongs we had suffered until our patience had become exhausted, endurance had ceased to be a virtue, our duty to ourselves and children demanded of us a disruption of the Government that had ceased to protect us or to regard our rights; announced the severance of the old and the organization of a new Government of Confederate Sovereign States of the

---

[132] "Report of a Committee of the Convention, being an address to the people of Texas, March 30, 1861." – *Ibid.*, 199.

[133] *Official Records*, fourth ser., vol. i, 322-325.

South, with a common kindred, common hopes, common interest, and a common destiny; discussed the power of the new Government, its influence, and wealth; the interest the civilized red man had in this new organization; tendering them our warmest sympathy and regard, all of which met the cordial approbation of the convention.

The Choctaws and Chickasaws are entirely Southern and are determined to adhere to the fortunes of the South. They were embarrassed in their action by the absence of their agents and commissioners at Washington, the seat of Government of the Northern Confederacy, seeking a final settlement with that Government. They have passed resolutions authorizing the raising of a minute company in each county in the two nations, to be drilled for actual service when necessary. Their convention was highly respectable in numbers and intelligence, and the business of the convention was dispatched with such admirable decorum and promptness as is rarely met with in similar deliberative bodies within the States.

On the morning of the 13th, hearing that the Creeks (or Maskokys) and Cherokees were in council at the Creek agency, on the Arkansas River, 140 miles distant, we immediately set out for that point, hoping to reach them before their adjournment. In this we were disappointed. They had adjourned two days before our arrival. We reached that point on Saturday evening. On Sunday morning, hearing that there was a religious meeting five miles north of the Arkansas River, in the Creek Nation, Mr. James E. Harrison attended, which proved to be of the utmost importance to our mission. The Reverend Mr. H. S. Buckner was present, with Chilly McIntosh, D. N. McIntosh, Judge Marshall, and others, examining a translation of a portion of the Scriptures, hymn book, and Greek grammar by Mr. Buckner into the Creek language. Mr. Buckner showed us great kindness, and did us eminent service, as did also Elder Vandiven, at whose house we spent the night and portion of the next day with these gentlemen of the Creek Nation, and through them succeeded in having a convention of the five nations called by Governor Motey Kinnaird, of the Creeks, to meet at North Fork (Creek Nation) on the 8th of April.

In the intermediate time we visited the Cherokee Nation, calling on their principal men and citizens, conversing with them freely until we reached Tahlequah, the seat of government. Near this place Mr. John Ross resides, the Governor of the nation. We called on him officially. We were not unexpected, and were received with courtesy, but not with cordiality. A long conference was had with him, conducted by Mr. Harrison on the part of the commissioners, without, we fear, any good result. He was very diplomatic and cautious. His position is the same as that held by Mr. Lincoln in his inaugural; declares the Union not dissolved; ignores the Southern Government. The intelligence of the nation is not with him. Four-fifths, at least, are against his views, as we learned from observation and good authorities. He, as we learned, had been urged by his people to call a council of the nation (he having the only constitutional authority to do so), to take into consideration the embarrassed condition of political affairs in the States, and to give some expression of their sentiments and sympathies. This he has persistently refused to do. His position in this is that of Sam. Houston in Texas, and in all probability will share the same fate, if not a worse one. His people are already oppressed by a Northern population letting a portion of territory purchased by them from the United States, to the exclusion of natives, and we are creditably informed that the Governors of some two or more of the Western free-soil States have recommended their people emigrating to settle the Cherokee country. It is due Mr. John Ross, in this connection, to say that during our conference with him he frequently avowed his sympathy for the South, and that, if Virginia and the other Border States seceded from the Government of the United States, his people would declare for the Southern Government that might be formed. The fact is not to be denied or disguised that among the common Indians of the Cherokees there exists a considerable abolition influence, created and sustained by one Jones, a Northern missionary of education and ability, who has been among them for many years, and who is said to exert no small influence with John Ross himself.

From Tahlequah we returned to the Creek Nation, and had great satisfaction in visiting their principal men – the McIntoshes, Stidhams, Smiths, Vanns, Rosses, Marshalls, and others too numerous to mention. Heavy falls of rain occurred about the time the convention was to meet at North Fork, which prevented the Chickasaws and Choctaws from attending the council, the rivers and creeks being all full and impassable. The Creeks, Cherokees, Seminoles, Quapa, and Socks (the three latter dependencies of the Creeks) met on the 8th of April. After they had organized by calling Motey Kinnaird, the Governor of the Creeks, to the chair, a committee was appointed to wait on the commissioners present, James E. Harrison and Capt. C. A. Hamilton, and invite them to appear in the convention, when, by invitation, Mr. Harrison addressed the convention in a speech of two hours. Our views were cordially received by the convention. The Creeks are Southern and sound to a man, and when desired will show their devotion to our cause by acts. They meet in council on the 1st of May, when they will probably send delegates to Montgomery to arrange with the Southern Government.

These nations are in a rapid state of improvement. The chase is no longer resorted to as means of subsistence, only as an occasional recreation. They are pursuing with good success agriculture and stock raising. Their houses are well built and comfortable, some of them costly. Their farms are well planned and some of them extensive and all well cultivated. They are well supplied with schools of learning, extensively patronized. They have many churches and a large membership of moral, pious deportment. They feel themselves to be in an exposed, embarrassed condition. They are occupying a country well suited to them, well watered, and fertile, with extensive fields of the very best mineral coal, fine salt springs and wells, with plenty of good timber, water powers which they are using to an advantage. Pure slate, granite, sandstone, blue limestone, and marble are found in abundance. All this they regard as inviting Northern aggression, and they are without arms, to any extent, or munitions of war. They declare themselves Southerners by geographical position, by a common interest, by their social system, and by blood, for they are rapidly becoming a nation of whites. They have written constitutions, laws, etc., modeled after those of the Southern States. We recommend them to the fostering care of the South, and that treaty arrangements be entered into with them as soon as possible. They can raise 20,000 good fighting men, leaving enough at home to attend to domestic affairs, and under the direction of an officer from the Southern Government would deal destruction to an approaching army from that direction, and in the language of one of their principal men:

"Lincoln may haul his big guns about our prairies in the daytime, but we will swoop down upon him at night from our mountains and forests, dealing death and destruction to his army."

No delay should be permitted in this direction. They cannot declare themselves until they are placed in a defensible position. The Administration of the North is concentrating his forces at Fort Washita, about twenty-four miles from the Texas line, and within the limits of the Chickasaw Nation. This fort could easily be taken by a force of 200 or 300 good men, and it is submitted as to whether in the present state of affairs a foreign government should be permitted to accumulate a large force on the borders of our country, especially a portion containing a large number of disaffected citizens who repudiate the action of the State.

In this connection it may not be improper to state that from North Fork to Red River we met over 120 wagons, movers from Texas to Kansas and other free States. These people are from Grayton, Collin, Johnson, and Denton, a country beautiful in appearance, rich in soil, genial in climate, and inferior to none in its capacity for the production of the cereals and stock. In disguise, we conversed with them freely. They had proposed by the ballot box to abolitionize at least that portion of the State. Failing in this, we suppose at least 500 voters have returned whence they came.

All of which is respectfully submitted this April 23, 1861. . .

Presumably, the suggestions, contained in the closing paragraphs of the commissioners' report, in so far as they concerned Texas, were immediately acted upon by her. It was very true, as the commissioners had reported, that a change was taking place in the disposition of Federal troops within the Indian country.

About the middle of February, a complaint [134] had been
filed at the Indian Office by the Wichita agent, Matthew Leeper, to the effect that men, claiming to be
Choctaws and Chickasaws, were trespassing upon the
Leased District. The Reserve Indians asked for relief
and protection at the hands of their guardian, the
United States government. Shortly afterwards, perhaps in a measure in response to the appeal or more
likely, to a hint that everything was not quite as it
should be on the Texan border, Colonel William H.
Emory, First United States Cavalry, was ordered,
March 13, [135] to take post at Fort Cobb. He was then
in Washington and, immediately upon his departure
thence, was ordered, March 18, [136] to form his regiment
at Fort Washita instead, word having come from the
commander at that post, [137] in a report of the third instant, of a threatened attack by Texans. In explanation
of a policy so vacillating, Emory was given to understand that the change of destination was really made at
the solicitation of the agent and delegation of the Chickasaws. Those men were in Washington, out of reach
of and apparently out of sympathy with, the events
transpiring at home. Agent Cooper, secessionist
though he was, probably did not altogether approve of
the interference of the Texans. At any rate, he shared
the representations of the Chickasaw delegation that
Fort Washita stood in need of reënforcement, [138] and
the War Department acceded to their request on the
ground that, "The interests of the United States are

---

[134] Leeper to Greenwood, February 12, 1861 [General Files, *Wichita,
1860-1861*, L373].

[135] *Official Records*, first ser., vol. i, 656.

[136] — *Ibid.*

[137] — *Ibid.*, 660.

[138] — *Ibid.*, 648.

paramount to those of the friendly Indians on the reservation near Fort Cobb."[139]

Emory's orders further comprehended a concentration of all the troops at Fort Washita that were then at that place and at Forts Cobb and Arbuckle;[140] but the orders were discretionary in their nature and permitted his leaving a small force at the more northern posts should circumstances warrant or demand it. On the nineteenth, General Scott had had a conference with Senator Charles B. Mitchell of Arkansas and, in deference to Mitchell's opinion, still further modified his orders to Emory so that, while leaving him the bulk of his discretionary power, he recommended that, if advisable, Emory retain one company at Fort Cobb.[141] In any event, one company of infantry was to move in advance from Fort Arbuckle to Fort Washita.[142]

Up to the twenty-fourth of March, at which time he left Memphis, Colonel Emory made pretty good time in his attempt to reach his destination; but from Memphis on his movements were unavoidably and considerably hampered. Low water in the Arkansas detained him for several days so that he deemed it prudent to send his orders on ahead to the commanding officer at Fort Arbuckle "to commence the movement upon Fort Washita, and, in the event of the latter place being threatened, to march to its support with his whole force."[143] On reaching Fort Smith, Emory found that matters had come to a crisis in Arkansas and, touching

---

[139] *Official Records*, first ser., vol. i, 656.

[140] The Indian Office protested against a reduction of the forts because of treaty guaranties to the Indians [Dole to Smith, April 30, 1861, Indian Office, *Report Book*, no. 12, p. 152].

[141] Townsend to Emory, March 21, 1861 [*Official Records*, first ser., vol. i, 659].

[142] Same to same, *ibid.*, 660.

[143] Emory to Townsend, April 2, 1861 [*ibid.*, 660].

the disposition of his force and the objects of his mission, allowed himself to be unduly influenced in his judgment by men of local predilections.[144]   It was upon their advice and upon the urgent pleadings of Matthew Leeper,[145] Indian agent on the Leased District, that he exercised his discretionary power as to the disposal of troops, without listening to his military subordinates[146] or having viewed the locality for himself.   In the interests of these local petitioners,[147] he even enlarged upon Mitchell's recommendation and concluded to leave two companies at Fort Cobb as one was deemed altogether inadequate to the protection of so isolated

[144] At the time, when it was intended to remove all the troops from Fort Cobb for purposes of concentration farther south and nearer to the source of danger, instructions were issued that the Reserve Indians, whose peculiar protection Fort Cobb was, might remove within the limits of Fort Washita; but the Choctaws and the Chickasaws objected and, in deference to their wishes, Emory suspended the permission [*Official Records*, first ser., vol. i, 663], his excuse being that Fort Cobb was not to be abandoned anyway.   The contractors, Johnson and Grimes, whom Superintendent Rector had so much favored, had a good deal to do with the forming of this decision.   They told Emory that the Reserve Indians were not free to move; for they had no means and that they were "hutted and planting at Fort Cobb."   Quite naturally the food contractors did not wish the Indians to be taken out of their reach within the limits of a military reservation.

[145] Matthew Leeper was very insistent.   He not only wrote letters to Emory arguing his case but travelled from his agency to Fort Smith to interview him.

[146] Emory refused to grant the appeal of Major Sackett and Captain Prince not to abandon Fort Arbuckle [*Official Records*, first ser., vol. i, 666].

[147] This circumstance ought not, however, to be cited to the prejudice of Colonel Emory; for it was while he was yet at Fort Smith that he manifested some of the spirit that inspired Robert E. Lee, who, by the way, was in command of the 2nd regiment of United States cavalry and had been stationed, like Emory, in Texas, and who, whether he believed in the doctrine of secession or not, put, as many another high-minded Southerner did, the state before the nation in matters of pride, of allegiance, and of personal honor.   Such men as Lee belonged to quite another class from what the self-seeking politicians did who, in isolated cases at least, engineered the secession movement from hope of gain.   Many of the Indian agents and employees belonged to this latter class.   Emory was unlike Lee in the final result; for he did not ultimately conclude to go with his state.   It was he who later on commanded, as a Union brigadier-general, the defences of New Orleans.

a post. It never seems to have occurred to him that the attack would have to come from the south, from the direction of Fort Washita, and that a force large enough to be efficient at either Fort Washita or Fort Arbuckle would necessarily protect Fort Cobb and the Indians of the Leased District.

The position of the Indians in the Leased District was serious in the extreme. They lived in mortal terror of the Texans and their agent, the man placed over them by the United States government, was now an avowed secessionist. He was a Texan and declared, as so many another southerner did from General Lee down, that honor and loyalty compelled him to go with his state. In February, he had been in Washington City, settling his accounts with the government and estimating for the next two quarters in accordance with the rulings and established usage of the Indian Office. On his way west and back to his agency, he was waylaid by a man of the name of "Burrow," very probably Colonel N. B. Burrow, acting under authority from the state of Arkansas, who despoiled him of part of his travelling equipment and then suffered him to go on his way.[148] Leeper reached his agency to find the Indians greatly excited. He endeavored to allay their fears, assuring them that the Texans would do them no harm. Soon, however, came his own defection and he thenceforward made use of every means, either to make the way easy for the Texans or to induce the Indians to side with them against the United States.

While Emory was dilly-dallying at Fort Smith, the Texans made their preparations[149] for invading the In-

[148] See Appendix B, *Leeper Papers*.

[149] Very early, as has already been commented upon, the Texans bethought them of securing the Indian alliance. Additional evidence is to be found in such a request as Henry E. McCulloch made of Secretary Walker, on the occa-

dian country and a regiment of volunteers under William C. Young, once a planter of Braganza County and now state regimental colonel, moved towards the Red River. There is something to show that they came at the veiled invitation[150] of the Indians. At any rate they seem to have felt pretty sure of a welcome[151] and were close at hand when Colonel Emory reached Fort Washita. He reached Fort Washita to find that the concentration of troops, even of such as his ill-advised orders would permit, had not yet fully taken place, that his supplies had been seized by the Texans, and that a general attack by them upon the poorly fortified posts

sion of his brother Ben's having passed over to him the charge originally conferred upon himself of raising a regiment of mounted troops for the defence of the frontier. Henry E. McCulloch requested Secretary Walker to permit him

> To use some of the friendly Indians in the Indian Territory, if I can procure their services, in my scouting parties and expeditions against the hostile Indians. These people can be made of great service to us, and can be used without any great expense to the Government. – *Official Records*, first ser., vol. i, 618.

[150] Letter of Carruth, July 11, 1861.

[151] As proof that the Texans regarded the Choctaws and the Chickasaws as friends, the two following letters may be cited:

A letter from John Hemphill and W. S. Oldham, two of the representatives from Texas in the Provisional Congress, to Secretary Walker, March 30, 1861, outlining a scheme of defence for Texas in which the admission was made that, from the southwest corner of Arkansas to Preston on the Red River, Texas needed no defense as her neighbors on that side were, "the highly-civilized and agricultural tribes of Choctaws and Chickasaws, who are in friendship with Texas and the Confederate States." – *Official Records*, first ser., vol. i, 619.

A letter from E. Kirby Smith, major, Artillery, Confederate States of America, to Walker, April 20, 1861, to the effect that,

> In considering the defense of the line of the western frontier of Texas our relations with the civilized Indians north of Red River are of the utmost importance. Numbering some eight thousand rifles, they form a strong barrier on the north, forcing the line of operations of an invading army westward into a region impracticable to the passage of large bodies of troops. Regarding them as our allies, which their natural affinities make them, the line of the western frontier reduces itself to the country between the Rio Grande and Red River. – *Official Records*, first ser., vol. i, 628.

was to be hourly expected. Emory, thereupon, resolved to withdraw from Fort Washita towards Arbuckle and Cobb. The day after he did so, April 16, Young's troops entered in force. Emory hurried forward to strengthen Fort Cobb and, indeed, to relieve it, taking, in his progress, the open prairie road that his cavalry might be more available. On the way,[152] he was joined by United States troops from Fort Arbuckle, the Texans in close pursuit. Fort Arbuckle was occupied by them in turn and then Fort Cobb, Emory never so much as attempting to enter the place; for he found its garrison in flight to the northeast. Fugitives all together, the Federal troops, piloted by a Delaware Indian, Black Beaver,[153] hurried onwards towards Fort Leavenworth. They seem to have made no lengthy stop until they were safe across the Arkansas River[154]

---

[152] Between Fort Washita and Fort Arbuckle, Colonel Emory was overtaken by William W. Averell, second lieutenant, Regiment Mounted Rifles, with additional despatches from Townsend, ordering him, upon their receipt, immediately to repair to Fort Leavenworth, "with all the troops in the Indian country west of Arkansas" [*ibid.*, 667]. Lieutenant Averell's own account of his experiences on the journey between Washington City and Fort Washita, the hardships, difficulties, and delays, also the frenzied excitement of the Arkansas people over the prospect of secession, forms an interesting narrative [*ibid.*, vol. liii, supplement, 488, 493-496].

[153] Black Beaver had served creditably as United States interpreter for the Wichitas and recently Leeper had turned to him for help in allaying their fears [Leeper to Rector, dated Wichita Agency, March 28, 1861, *Leeper Papers*]. For services rendered on this expedition northward to Fort Leavenworth [Letter of W. S. Robertson, September 30, 1861, General Files, *Southern Superintendency, 1859-1862*, R1615], Black Beaver brought a claim against the United States [E. S. Parker to J. D. Cox, July 1, 1869, Indian Office, *Report Book*, no. 18, pp. 417-418; and same to same, April 25, 1870, *ibid.*, no. 19, p. 321]. Evidently Black Beaver served also in the Mexican War. He was then head of a company of mounted volunteers, Shawnees and Delawares [George W. Manypenny to Drew, August 8, 1854], which had been called and mustered into the service by Harney [P. Clayton, 2nd auditor, to A. K. Parris, 2nd comptroller, October 26, 1850].

[154] Emory to Townsend, May 19, 1861 [*Official Records*, first ser., vol. i, 648].

and their flight may well be said to have been a precipitous one. Behind them, at Fort Arbuckle, Colonel Young took possession of abandoned property and placed it in the care of the Chickasaw Indians,[155] who had materially aided him in his attack. His next move was to negotiate,[156] unauthoritatively, a treaty with the Reserve Indians, gaining the promise of their alliance upon the understanding that the Confederacy, in return, would feed and protect them. Fort Cobb was rifled and the Indians made rich, in their own estimation, with booty.[157] Colonel Young seems then to have drawn back towards the Red River; but for several months he continued to occupy with his forces,[158] under the authority of Texas and with the consent of the Chickasaw Indians, the three frontier posts that Emory had been instructed to guard; viz., Forts Washita, Arbuckle, and Cobb.

If Texas took time by the forelock in her anxiety to secure the Indian country and its inhabitants, Arkansas most certainly did the same; and, in the undertaking, various things told to her advantage, among which, not the least important was the close family relationship existing between her secessionist governor, Henry M.

---

[155] Captain S. T. Benning to Walker, May 14, 1861 [*Official Records*, first ser., vol. i, 653.]

[156] — *Ibid.*

[157] Leeper to Rector, January 13, 1862 [*Leeper Papers*].

[158] A note, communicated by X. B. Debray, aide-de-camp to the Governor of Texas, to Walker and dated, Richmond, August 28, 1861, says,

> The governor of Texas being convinced that the integrity of the soil of Texas greatly depends upon the success of the Southern cause in Missouri, and moved by an appeal to the people of Arkansas and Texas (published at the beginning of July by General Ben. McCulloch) ordered on the 25th ultimo the raising and concentration on Red River of 3,000 mounted men, besides the regiment commanded by Col. W. C. Young, which has been occupying for several months Forts Arbuckle, Cobb, and Washita, under authority of Texas, and at the request of the Chickasaw Indians. – *Official Records*, first ser., vol. iv, 98.

Rector, and the southern superintendent. They were cousins and, to all appearances, the best of friends. It is doubtful if in any state the executive authority thereof worked more energetically for secession or with greater consistency and promptitude than in Arkansas. Governor Rector had been elected, in the autumn of 1860, by the Democrats and old-line Whigs. He belonged to a numerous and most influential family, land-surveyors most of them, seemingly by inheritance, and, although from northern or border states originally, strongly committed to the doctrine of state sovereignty. The family connections were also powerful socially and politically. The gubernatorial inauguration came in November, 1860, and from that moment Henry M. Rector and his host of relations and friends worked for secession.

At the outset, Governor Rector identified the Indian interests with those of Arkansas. Even in his message[159] of December 11, 1860 he gave it as his opinion that the two communities must together take measures to prevent anti-slavery migration. It was rather late in the day, however, to intimate that men of abolitionist sentiments must not be allowed to cross the line, and a man of the political acumen of Henry M. Rector must have known it. Immediately after the general election there were evidences of great excitement in Arkansas and, when news[160] came that the disused arsenal at Little Rock was to be occupied by artillery under Captain James Totten from Fort Leavenworth, it broke out into expressions of public dissent. Little Rock was scarcely less radical and secessionist in its views than was Fort Smith and Fort Smith was regarded as a regular hot-bed of sectionalism. The legislature, too,

[159] House *Journal*, Arkansas, 1861, p. 304.
[160] *Confederate Military History*, vol. x, 4.

was filled with state-rights advocates and some of the actions taken there were almost revolutionary in their trend. With the new year came new alarms and false reports of what was to be. Harrell records[161] that the first message over the newly completed telegraph line between Memphis and Little Rock was a repetition of the rumor, quite without foundation, that Major Emory had been ordered from Fort Gibson to reinforce Totten at Little Rock, and that the effect upon Helena was electrical. It is no wonder that the newspapers and personal communications[162] of the time showed great

---

[161] *Confederate Military History*, vol. x, 7.

[162] Two letters found among the *Fort Smith Papers* may serve, in a measure, to illustrate the point:

LITTLE ROCK, ARKS, Jany 6, 1861.

DR THAD: I received your letter a few days ago . . . I am thankful that there are a few righteous men left and particularly gratified that you and Henry Lewis are true and faithful to the South.

I will endeavor to keep you posted so that you may hold your own with the Union savers — in sober truth the question is not whether the Union ought or can be saved but whether Arkansas shall go with the North or adhere to the South. Neither Fishback or anybody can preserve the Union – it now becomes us as wise men to put our house in order for the impending crisis. I wrote to Porter last night – the Senate have not passed the Convention bill and will not in anything like a right shape. . .   BEN T. DU VAL.

[Addressed to Capt. M. T. Tatum, Greenwood, Arks.].

LITTLE ROCK ARK, January 7th 1861.

DEAR THAD. I enclose you a copy of the printed bill now before our House to arm and equip the Militia of this State and to appropriate 100,000$ for that purpose. . . We have passed a bill through the House appropriating five hundred dollars to Porter to cover his losses to some extent in money which he has paid out in recovering fugitives, it ought to have been a good deal more, but I never worked harder for anything in my life to get what we did. I think it will pass the Senate. The news from South Carolina indicate a Tea party at Charleston before many days. From the general signs of the times I think a Compromise will be effect between the North and the South and the *Union saved*. The Convention bill has not passed the Senate yet but will in a few days I think. Give my respects to the boys generally   Your obt Servt   JOHN T. LONDON

[Addressed to Capt. M. T. Tatum, Greenwood, Sebastian County, Arkansas.]

intensity of feeling and a tendency to ring the changes on a single theme.

The public indignation following the receipt of the unsubstantiated rumor that Totten was to be reënforced seems to have compelled the action of Governor Rector in taking possession,[163] on February eighth, in the name of the state of Arkansas, of the United States arsenal at

---

[163] An interesting series of telegrams has a bearing upon that event.

February 1, 1861.

J. J. GREEN, WILLIAM WALKER, Van Buren, Ark.:

Not possible to leave here. Southern confederacy certain. Arkansas must save her children by joining it. Write by mail to-day.

JOHNSON and HINDMAN

Official Records, first ser., vol. liii, supplement, 617.

WASHINGTON, February 7, 1861.

JOHN POPE, ESQ., Little Rock, Ark.:

For God's sake do not complicate matters by an attack. It will be premature and do incalculable injury. We cannot justify it. The reasons that existed elsewhere for seizure do not exist with us.

ALBERT PIKE, R. W. JOHNSON.

— *Ibid.*, vol. i, 682.

U. S. SENATE, WASHINGTON, February 7, 1861.

HIS EXCELLENCY H. M. RECTOR, Little Rock, Ark.:

The motives which impelled capture of forts in other States do not exist in ours. It is all premature. We implore you prevent attack on arsenal if Totten resists.

R. W. JOHNSON, W. K. SEBASTIAN.

— *Ibid.*, 681.

WASHINGTON, February 7, 1861.

R. H. JOHNSON, JAMES B. JOHNSON, Little Rock:

Southern States which captured forts were in the act of seceding, were threatened with troops, and their ports and commerce endangered. Not so with us. If Totten resists, for God's sake deliberate and go stop the assault.

R. W. JOHNSON.

— *Ibid.*, 681-682.

WASHINGTON, February 7, 1861.

GOVERNOR RECTOR, Little Rock, Ark.:

For God's sake allow no attack to be made on Fort Totten.

A. RUST.

— *Ibid.*, vol. liii, supplement, 617.

February 7, 1861.

E. BURGEVIN, Little Rock:

For God's sake do not attack the arsenal. It can do no good and will be productive of great harm.

C. B. JOHNSON.

— *Ibid.*

Little Rock; but, as a matter of fact, Rector needed only
an excuse, and a very slight one at that, for doing more
than he had already done to prove his sectional bias.
Nor had he forgotten or neglected the Indians. Indeed, never at any time did he leave a single stone un-
turned in his search for inside and outside support; and,
notwithstanding the fact that the Arkansas Ordinance
of Secession was not passed until the sixth of May,
Governor Rector conducted himself, for months before
that, as though the state were a bona fide member of
the Confederacy. In all his audacious venturings, proposals, and acts, he had the full and unquestioning
support, not only of his cousin, Elias Rector,[164] in whose
honor Albert Pike had written the well-known par-

LITTLE ROCK, February 8, 1861.

C. B. JOHNSON, Washington:
    Spoke too late, like Irishman who swallowed egg. Arsenal in hands
of Governor.   EDMUND BURGEVIN.
Official Records, first ser., vol. liii, supplement, 617.

The senders and recipients of the telegraphic dispatches were, with one
or two exceptions, all relatives of each other, and all in public life. Robert
Ward Johnson and William K. Sebastian were, at the time, United States senators from Arkansas; Thomas C. Hindman and Albert Rust were Arkansas
representatives in Congress; Albert Pike was in Washington, prosecuting the
Choctaw Indian claim; Edmund Burgevin was the attorney-general of Arkansas and a brother-in-law of Governor Rector; Richard H. Johnson and
James Johnson were brothers of Robert W. Johnson, the former being proprie-
tor and editor of the Little Rock *Democrat* and the latter, in future years, a
colonel in the Confederate army. In 1868, R. W. Johnson moved to Washington City and became the law partner of Albert Pike. [Arkansas Historical Association, *Publications,* vol. ii, 268.] Hindman was the man who
sneered at the precautions taken to insure President-elect Lincoln's safety
[Stanwood, *History of Presidential Elections,* 235]. Sebastian was expelled
from the Senate because of his southern sympathies; but, as he really took no
active part in the Confederate movements, the resolution of expulsion was
rescinded in 1878.

    164 It would be interesting to know whether Elias Rector had as yet for-
mulated any such plan for personal aggrandizement such as must have been
in his mind when he wrote the letter to Douglas H. Cooper that called forth
from Cooper the following response:

ody[165] on "The Old Scottish Gentlemen;"[166] but of the leading citizens of Fort Smith and Little Rock, partic-

Private & Confidential

Copy   FORT SMITH May 1st 1861.
MAJOR ELIAS RECTOR

Dr. Sir: I have concluded to act upon the suggestion yours of the 28th Ultimo contains.

If we work this thing shrewdly we can make a fortune each, satisfy the Indians, stand fair before the North, and revel in the unwavering confidence of our Southern Confederacy.

My share of the eighty thousand in gold you can leave on deposite with Meyer Bro, subject to my order. Write me soon.   COOPER.

Indian Office, General Files, *Southern Superintendency, 1863-1864,* I435.

The foregoing letter of Cooper's was one of those referred to in the following telegraphic communication from Special Agent G. B. Stockton to Secretary Usher, dated Fort Smith, Arkansas, February 20, 1864:

I have just found & have now in this office a large desk containing indian papers treaties correspondence of Cooper Rector & others, correspondence of W. P. Dole as late as May fifteenth 1861 vouchers abstracts & correspondence convicting Rector & Cooper of enticing the various tribes to become enemies of the U. S. The papers extend back as far as 1834 will you please direct me what disposition to make of them.

Secretary Usher referred the matter to the Office of Indian Affairs and Mix instructed Stockton to send the papers on to Washington [Letter of February 20, 1864]. This Stockton did and notified the Commissioner of Indian Affairs in this wise, by telegraph:

I have boxed the Indian Papers which I found at this place, and this day send them by wagons to Leavenworth City, Kansas, to be thence forwarded by the American Express Company.

There seems to have been considerable delay in their transmittal after they had passed into the custodianship of the express company but they eventually reached the Indian Office and to-day form part of the Fort Smith collection.

[165] The melodious refrain of this,

> That fine Arkansas gentleman,
> Close to the Choctaw line.

unconsciously brings out one of the very ideas sought to be conveyed by the present chapter; namely, the extremely close connection between Arkansas and Indian Territory.

[166] This old, old song, "written on the model and to the air of 'The Old Country Gentleman'," runs thus:

> The song I'll sing, though lately made, it tells of olden days,
> Of a good old Scottish gentleman, of good old Scottish ways;

ularly of those whose previous occupations, residence, inclinations, or interests had made them conversant with Indian affairs and, therefore, unusually appreciative of the strategic value of the Indian country. Under such circumstances, it is not at all surprising that Governor Rector seized, as he did, the earliest[167] opportunity to approach the Cherokees. Fort Smith at the junction of the Arksansas and Poteau Rivers was only eighty miles from Fort Gibson.

Before taking up for special comment Governor Rector's negotiations with the Cherokees through their principal chief, John Ross, it might be well to retrace our steps a little in order to show how, in yet other ways, Arkansas interested herself more than was natural in the concerns of the Indians and made some of her citizens, in the long run, more than ordinarily responsible for the development of secessionist sentiment among the southern tribes.

When David Hubbard, journeying westward as special secessionist commissioner[168] from Alabama to Arkansas, reached Little Rock – and that was in the early winter of 1861 – he soon discovered that many Arkansans were not willing for their state to go out of the Union unless she could take Indian Territory with her. Hubbard's letter,[169] descriptive of the situation, is very elucidating. It is addressed to Andrew B.

When our barons bold kept house and hold, and sung their olden lays
And drove with speed across the Tweed, auld Scotland's bluidy faes,
Like brave old Scottish gentlemen, all of the olden time.

Scottish Songs, printed by W. G. Blackie and Company (Glasgow).

[167] The commissioners to whom Ogden referred in his letter of February 15, 1861, may have been the tangible evidence of Governor Rector's first attempt to influence the Indians.

[168] Fleming, *Civil War and Reconstruction in Alabama*, 46, footnote 1.

[169] Smith, *Debates of the Alabama Convention*, 443-444; *Official Records*, fourth ser., vol. i, 3.

Moore,[170] governor of Alabama, and bears date Kinloch, Alabama, January third.

MY DEAR SIR: On receipt of your letter and appointment as commissioner from Alabama to Arkansas, I repaired to Little Rock and presented my credentials to the two houses, and also your letter to Governor Rector, by all of whom I was politely received. The Governor of Arkansas was every way disposed to further our views, and so were many leading and influential members of each house of the Legislature, but neither are yet ready for action, because they fear the people have not yet made up their minds to go out. The counties bordering on the Indian nations – Creeks, Cherokees, Choctaws, and Chickasaws – would hesitate greatly to vote for secession, and leave those tribes still under the influence of the Government at Washington, from which they receive such large stipends and annuities. These Indians are at a spot very important, in my opinion, in this great sectional controversy, and must be assured that the South will do as well as the North before they could be induced to change their alliances and dependence. I have much on this subject to say when I get to Montgomery, which cannot well be written. The two houses passed resolutions inviting me to meet them in representative hall and consult together as to what had best be done in this matter. When I appeared men were anxious to know what the seceding States intended to do in certain contingencies. My appointment gave me no authority to speak as to what any State would do, but I spoke freely of what, in my opinion, we ought to do. I took the ground that no State which had seceded would ever go back without full power being given to protect themselves by vote against anti-slavery projects and schemes of every kind. I took the position that the Northern people were honest and did fear the divine displeasure, both in this world and the world to come, by reason of what they considered the national sin of slavery, and that all who agreed with me in a belief of their sincerity must see that we could not remain quietly in the same Government with them. Secondly, if they were dishonest hypocrites, and only lied to im-

[170] Governor Moore had appointed the commissioners, including Hubbard, on his own initiative before the convention met. See his address, Smith's *Debates*, 35.

pose on others and make them hate us, and used anti-slavery arguments as mere pretexts for the purpose of uniting Northern sentiment against us, with a view to obtain political power and sectional dominion, in that event we ought not to live with them. I desired any Unionist present to controvert either of these positions, which seemed to cover the whole ground. No one attempted either, and I said but little more. I am satisfied, from free conversations with members of all parties and with Governor Rector, that Arkansas, when compelled to choose, will side with the Southern States, but at present a majority would vote the Union ticket. Public sentiment is but being formed, but must take that direction. . .

What, in addition to that just cited, Hubbard had to say about the Indians or about the profit accruing from close contact with them, we have no way of knowing; but we have a right to be suspicious of the things that have to be communicated by word of mouth only, especially in this instance, when we remember that white men have always made the Indians subjects of exploitation and that Hubbard was the man whom the southern Confederacy chose for its first commissioner of Indian affairs, also that Hubbard's first outline of work, as commissioner, in truth, his only outline, comprehended an extended visit to the Indians before whom he proposed to expatiate on the financial advantages of an adherence to the Confederacy and the inevitable financial ruin that must come from continued loyalty to the Union. All things considered, it would surely seem that in Hubbard's mind the money question was always uppermost.

But there were others to whom the Indian income was a thing of interest. At the earlier meeting of the Arkansas convention, a resolution [171] had been passed, March 9, 1861, authorizing an inquiry to be made into the annual cost to the United States government of the

---

[171] House *Journal*, Arkansas, 38.

Indian service west of Arkansas. The state administration had already seized[172] the Indian funds on hand,
an opportunity to do so having offered itself upon the
occasion of the death[173] of the United States disbursing
officer, Major P. T. Crutchfield. But, later, for fear
that this might work prejudice with the Indians a resolution[174] was passed providing that the money should
not be diverted from its proper uses. Because of such
actions and others of like direction, it is certainly safe
to assume that pecuniary considerations made the fron-
tiersmen of 1861 vitally interested in Indian affairs.
The same influences that moved Hubbard to write his
letter to Governor Moore with special mention of the
Indians unquestionably moved the citizens of Boonsboro to try,[175] without much further ado, the temper of
the Cherokees.

[172] House *Journal*, Arkansas, 314, 445.

[173] January 12, 1861.

[174] The resolution is found in House *Journal*, Arkansas, 167 and in *Official
Records*, fourth ser., vol. i, 307. Its text is as follows:

Resolved, That no money or property of any kind whatever, now in
the hands of the Superintendent of Indian Affairs, or of any Indian
agent, being placed there, or designed for the Indians on the western
frontier of Arkansas, shall be seized, but that the same shall so remain
to be applied to and for the use of the several Indian Nations, faithfully,
as was designed when so placed in their hands for disbursement.

And the people of the State of Arkansas, here in sovereign convention assembled, do hereby pledge the sovereignty of the State of Arkansas, that everything in their power shall be done to compel a faithful
application of all money and property now in the hands of persons or
agents designed and intended for the several Indian tribes west of
Arkansas.

Adopted in and by the convention May 9, 1861.

DAVID WALKER, President of the Arkansas State Convention.
Attest.   ELIAS C. BOUDINOT, Secretary of the Convention.

[175]

BOONSBOROUGH, ARK., May 9, 1861.
HON. JOHN ROSS:

Dear Sir: The momentous issues that now engross the attention of
the American people cannot but have elicited your interest and attention
as well as ours. The unfortunate resort of an arbitrament of arms seems
now to be the only alternative. Our State has of necessity to co-operate

Returning now to Govenor Rector and to a recital of his endeavors with the same Indian people, it is seen that his approach to the Cherokees was made, as has been already intimated, through their principal chief, John Ross, and by means of the following most excellently worded letter:

THE STATE OF ARKANSAS, EXECUTIVE DEPARTMENT,
Little Rock, January 29, 1861.

To HIS EXCELLENCY JOHN ROSS,
    Principal Chief Cherokee Nation:

SIR: It may now be regarded as almost certain that the States having slave property within their borders will, in consequence of repeated Northern aggressions, separate themselves and withdraw from the Federal Government.

South Carolina, Alabama, Florida, Mississippi, Georgia, and Louisiana have already, by action of the people, assumed this attitude. Arkansas, Missouri, Tennessee, Kentucky, Virginia, North Carolina, and Maryland will probably pursue the same course by the 4th of March next. Your people, in their institu-

---

with her natural allies, the Southern States. It is now only a question of North and South, and the "hardest must fend off." We expect manfully to bear our part of the privations and sacrifices which the times require of Southern people.

This being our attitude in this great contest, it is natural for us to desire, and we think we may say we have a right, to know what position will be taken by those who may greatly conduce to our interests as friends or to our injury as enemies. Not knowing your political status in this present contest as the head of the Cherokee Nation, we request you to inform us by letter, at your earliest convenience, whether you will co-operate with the Northern or Southern section, now so unhappily and hopelessly divided. We earnestly hope to find in you and your people true allies and active friends; but if, unfortunately, you prefer to retain your connection with the Northern Government and give them aid and comfort, we want to know that, as we prefer an open enemy to a doubtful friend.

With considerations of high regard, we are, your obedient servants,

MARK BEAN,	J. A. MCCOLLOCH,
W. B. WELCH,	J. M. LACY,
E. W. MACCLURE,	J. P. CARNAHAN,
JOHN SPENCER,	*And many others.*

Official Records, first ser., vol. xiii, 493-494; Indian Office, General Files, *Cherokee, 1859-1865*, C515.

JOHN ROSS, PRINCIPAL CHIEF OF THE CHEROKEES
[*From Smithsonian Institution, Bureau of American Ethnology*]

tions, productions, latitude, and natural sympathies, are allied to the common brotherhood of the slaveholding States. Our people and yours are natural allies in war and friends in peace. Your country is salubrious and fertile, and possesses the highest capacity for future progress and development by the application of slave labor. Besides this, the contiguity of our territory with yours induces relations of so intimate a character as to preclude the idea of discordant or separate action.

It is well established that the Indian country west of Arkansas is looked to by the incoming administration of Mr. Lincoln as fruitful fields, ripe for the harvest of abolitionism, freesoilers, and Northern mountebanks.

We hope to find in your people friends willing to co-operate with the South in defense of her institutions, her honor, and her firesides, and with whom the slaveholding States are willing to share a common future, and to afford protection commensurate with your exposed condition and your subsisting monetary interests with the General Government.

As a direct means of expressing to you these sentiments, I have dispatched my aide-de-camp, Lieut. Col. J. J. Gaines, to confer with you confidentially upon these subjects, and to report to me any expressions of kindness and confidence that you may see proper to communicate to the governor of Arkansas, who is your friend and the friend of your people. Respectfully, your obedient servant,

HENRY M. RECTOR, Governor of Arkansas.[176]

Lieutenant Gaines duly started out upon his mission and upon reaching Fort Smith interviewed Superintendent Rector and received from him a letter of introduction[177] to John Ross, which was, in effect, a hearty endorsement of the governor's project. An inkling of what Gaines was about soon came to the ears of A. B. Greenwood, an Arkansan, a state-rights man, and United States commissioner of Indian affairs. At the

[176] Indian Office, *General Files, Cherokee, 1859-1865,* C515; *Official Records,* first ser., vol. i, 683-684; vol. xiii, 490-491.

[177] Indian Office, *General Files, Cherokee, 1859-1865,* C515; *Official Records,* first ser., vol. i, 683.

moment he was the official, intent upon doing his duty, nothing more.   It was then in his official capacity that he straightway demanded of Agent Cowart an explanation of Gaines's movements; but Cowart was privy to Governor Rector's plans undoubtedly, a Georgian, a secessionist, and one of those illiterate, disreputable, untrustworthy characters that frontier or garrison towns seem always to produce or to attract, the kind, unfortunately for its own reputation and for the Indian welfare, that the United States government has so often seen fit to select for its Indian agents.   More than that, Cowart was a man of such base principles that he could commercialize with impunity a great cause and calmly continue to hold office under and to draw pay from one government while secretly plotting against it in the interests of another.   On this occasion he attempted a denial [178] of the presence of Rector's commissioner at

---

[178] In a letter to A. B. Greenwood, dated Fort Smith, February 13, 1861, he says:

On the 11th Inst. I sent a dispatch to you asking for Troops and yesterday rec'd an answer making enquiries as to the Object for which they are wanted, and asking if the Governor's Commissioner was here & what was his Object.

I have just replyed in a Dispatch, that the Gov. has no Com. here and has had none. I suppose you have been Tehlegraphed that there was a Com. and that for mischief. Now the following are the facts in the case as far as I have been able to learn them. On Saturday or Sunday last there came a young man by the name of Gains called Dr. Gains from Little Rock. He stated his object was to visit the Indian Tribes west of this to cultivate with them friendly Relations and stated moreover that he was authorized to do so by the Gov. of Arkansas. When I returned your Dispatch I went to Dr. Gains and asked him in the presents of witnesses if he was acting as Com. for the Gov. of Arkansas he replyed that he was not, and now Sir I am sorry to learn to day that a rumor is afloat that I am here to aid in taking this post & that by having Troops sent from here to weaken the forces. Nothing can be more false. In the first place, the Citizens have no Disposition to interfere with this post in any way and the truth is I see no persons but the Officers and I will not judge of their motives.

Them and myself are all friendly as far as I know except it may be

Fort Smith; but the Indian Office had soon good proof [179] that a commissioner had been there and that he

they object to a Speach I made here on Monday night last. I can say and prove by all the best citizens of the Place that my remarks were mild and conciliatory and could not be objectionable to any true Southern man this the citizens of the City will bare me out, the truth is the only objection they could make to my speach was that it was unanswerable I told you the same when in Washington. I appeal to the Citizens for the truth of what I say. I desire troops to protect the Cherokees from Abolition forays from Kansas & the Neutral land. I am told that there are three times the No. of Intruders now that there was there last fall and that violent threats have been made by Kansas.

In the next place I can do nothing without Troops there and a No. of lawless murderers in the Nation that cannot without Troops, and I told you those things when with you last and in addition to the above facts the Troops can live and support quite as comfortable and for less money out there than they can here. – Indian Office, General Files, *Cherokee, 1859-1865.*

[179] The proof appeared in the correspondence of John B. Ogden, commissioner of the district court of the United States for the western district of Arkansas. On March 4, 1861, Ogden wrote from Van Buren to the Secretary of the Interior the following letter:

Having learned on the 15th of Feby last from rumor the person appointed as Comr had been sent by Gov. Rector of the State of Arkansas to the Indian tribes upon our frontier for co-operation in secession movements, and the same being in violation of treaty stipulations and the laws enacted by Congress regulating trade and Intercourse, I addressed a letter of inquiry to John Ross principal chief of the Cherokee Nation in relation to the same, which letter accompanies this with his reply – The letter to me I think was intended to be confidential from its language and from my conversation with the messenger who was the bearer of it to me, of this however I cannot positively judge and have thought best to forward the same. John Ross was unable to give me an imediate answer as he was not personally advised of the subject matter. But upon the return of Mr W. P. Ross who was a delegate from the Cherokees to a General Council being held of the tribes West of Arkansas in relation to their own international policy, he became advised of the matter of inquiry and for the purpose of furnishing the required information sent Mr W. P. Ross the bearer of this letter to Van Buren that he might fully communicate with me in the matter. I learn from him that one Dr J. J. Gains late editor of a secession sheet at Little Rock, did attend the said Council held by the Indian tribes west of Arks in the Choctaw Nation, and that said Gains announced to the Council his mission to be that of a Comr from Arkansas accredited by the Govr to consult with them in relation to co-operation with the seceding States – That he submitted a written Statement to them in reference

had proceeded thence to the Cherokee country. It was no other than Gaines, of course, who, when once he had delivered the Rector letters to Ross, saw fit, in the further interests of his mission, to attend the inter-tribal council at the Creek Agency.

to their interests and future relations in the event of a dissolution of the Union – but that he was guarded in his propositions – You will learn from Mr John Ross' letter that he informs me officially that the present (agent) of the Cherokees "is officiously advocating the secession policy of the southern States and that his endeavoring to influence the Cherokees to take sides and act in Concert with the Seceding Sates." – I can state from my own information that when said Agent is in Arks he is invariably to be found upon the stump "open-mouthed and – " for disunion, to the great anoyance of the good people of the Country. These people should be heard and their grievances redressed and the causes removed, and some man of correct constitutional morals appointed in his stead. We have hosts of such men in this State, and as the Incoming Administration are not advised of persons in this country, allow me to suggest that on application to the Hon. A. B. Greenwood now of Washington the selection of a suitable person could be named. I have no doubt, that would be satisfactory – pardon this apparent officiousness – At this time my great anxiety for the preservation of the Union must be my apology for what I have said.

I also enclose you a copy of a permit furnished me by Mr Ross issued by said agent. – Indian Office, General Files, *Cherokee, 1859-1865*, O32.

Inclosures

1. John Ogden to John Ross, February 15, 1861.
2. John Ross to John B. Ogden, February 28, 1861.
3.   CHEROKEE AGENCY, near Tahlequah, C.N.

Isaac G. Freeman, a citizen of what was formerly the United States and a farmer by occupation has permission to remain with J. C. Cunningham near Park Hill in said Nation and labor for the said Cunningham for twelve months from this date subject to be removed by the Agent at any time for cause.   R. J. COWART, U.S. Cherokee Agent. [Endorsement]   A true copy from the original as taken by me March 1st 1861   WILL P. ROSS

4. Newspaper clippings, one containing the Choctaw resolutions of February 7, 1861, and the other this:

Dr. J. J. Gains, (an old editor) dropped in upon us, last week, on his way to Little Rock, from the Indian country. His mission was one of peace, and not to *"incite rebellion"* as was telegraphed to Washington City, by some officious person. We were glad to learn from him, that our border friends are all right.

John Ross did not reply to Governor Rector's communication until the anniversary of George Washington's birthday and he then expressed the same ideas of concern, of sympathy, but also those of positive neutrality that had characterized his advice to the Indian conferees. He scouted, though, the very idea of the incoming administration's planning to abolitionize the Indian country while at the same time he manifested his utter disapproval of it. This is what he said:

TAHLEQUAH, CHEROKEE NATION, February 22, 1861.
HIS EXCELLENCY HENRY M. RECTOR, Governor of Arkansas:

Sir: I have the honor to acknowledge the receipt of Your Excellency's communication of the 29th ultimo, per your aide-de-camp, Lieut. Col. J. J. Gaines.

The Cherokees cannot but feel a deep regret and solicitude for the unhappy differences which at present disturb the peace and quietude of the several States, especially when it is understood that some of the slave States have already separated themselves and withdrawn from the Federal Government and that it is probable others will also pursue the same course.

But may we not yet hope and trust in the dispensation of Divine power to overrule the discordant elements for good, and that, by the counsel of the wisdom, virtue, and patriotism of the land, measures may happily be adopted for the restoration of peace and harmony among the brotherhood of States within the Federal Union.

The relations which the Cherokee people sustain toward their white brethren have been established by subsisting treaties with the United States Government, and by them they have placed themselves under the "protection of the United States and of no other sovereign whatever." They are bound to hold no treaty with any foreign power, or with any individual State, nor with the citizens of any State. On the other hand, the faith of the United States is solemnly pledged to the Cherokee Nation for the protection of the right and title in the lands, conveyed to them by patent, within their territorial boundaries, as also for the protection of all other of their national and individual rights and interests of persons and property. Thus the Cherokee people are inviolably allied with their white brethren of the United States in war and friends in peace. Their institutions, locality, and natural sympathies are unequivocally with the slave-holding States. And the contiguity of our territory to your State, in connection with the daily, social, and commercial intercourse between our respective citizens, forbids the idea that they should ever be otherwise than steadfast friends.

I am surprised to be informed by Your Excellency that "it is well established that the Indian country west of Arkansas is looked to by the incoming administration of Mr. Lincoln as fruitful fields ripe for the harvest of abolitionism, free-soilers, and Northern mountebanks." As I am sure that the laborers will be greatly disappointed if they shall expect in the Cherokee country "fruitful fields ripe for the harvest of abolitionism," &c., you may rest assured that the Cherokee people will never tolerate the propagation of any obnoxious fruit upon their soil.

And in conclusion I have the honor to reciprocate the salutation of friendship.

I am, sir, very respectfully, Your Excellency's obedient servant,   JNO. ROSS, Principal Chief Cherokee Nation.[180]

The Arkansas state convention, sanctioned by popular vote, met, by authority of the governor's proclamation, March fourth. Its members were inclined to temporize, however; for, as Harrell says, they were coöperationists [181] rather than secessionists and their policy of temporizing they carried out even in the provision made for reassembling after adjournment. David Walker, the president of the convention, was out of sympathy with this; and, at the first news of the attack upon Fort Sumter and while passion and excitement were still at fever heat, called [182] an extra session for the sixth of May. The regular session was not to come until the nineteenth of August. Coincidently Governor

[180] General Files, *Cherokee, 1859-1865*, C515; *Official Records*, first ser., vol. xiii, 491-492.

[181] Stephens says they were almost equally divided on the question of secession [*Constitutional View of the Late War between the States*, vol. ii, 363].

[182] On April 20, 1861.

Rector again showed where his sympathies lay by refusing[183] President Lincoln's call for troops.

The Arkansas Ordinance of Secession was passed on the sixth of May. S. R. Cockrell had proved himself a good prophet; for, writing jubilantly to L. P. Walker, on the twenty-first of April, on the progress of secession, he had said,[184] "Arkansas will go out 6th of May before breakfast. The Indians come next." His closing remark had some foundation for its utterance. Intelligent and prominent Indians were to be found in the very ranks of the Arkansas secessionists. E. C. Boudinot, a Cherokee, an enemy and rival of John Ross, and later Cherokee delegate in the Confederate Congress, was secretary[185] of the convention. M. Kennard, a leading and a principal Creek chief, seems also to have been influential. The alliance of the Indians was yet being sought.[186]

The secession ordinance once safely launched, the Arkansas convention turned its attention without equivocation to Indian concerns. On the tenth of May, for instance, it followed the example set by Texas and passed a resolution,[187] authorizing the president of the convention to appoint three delegates to visit Indian Territory. The men appointed were, S. L. Griffith of Sebastian County (the same man, interestingly enough to whom the United States government had recently offered[188] the Southern Superintendency), J. Murphy of

---

[183] Stephens, *op. cit.*, vol. ii, 375; *Official Records*, first ser., vol. i, 674, 687.

[184] *Official Records*, first ser., vol. i, 686.

[185] *Journal*, Arkansas Convention, 369.

[186] The importance of such an alliance seems never to have been lost sight of. In his message of May 6, 1861, Governor Rector called attention to the fact that Arkansas was the most exposed state in the Union, because of the Indians on the west [*Journal*, 153]. In various ways, he emphasized the strategical value of Indian Territory [*ibid.*, 156].

[187] *Journal*, Arkansas Convention, 183.

[188] See page 183.

Madison County, and G. W. Laughinghouse of St. Francis County. Two of these counties were on or near the border. Sebastian was on the border and Madison not far inland, so Griffith and Murphy very probably realized the full significance of their mission. On the eleventh of May, the convention tried to pass another resolution,[189] indicative of a community of interests between Arkansas and the Indian country. This resolution failed, but, had it passed, it would have prayed the president of the Confederate States to erect a military department or division out of Arkansas and Indian Territory. As it was, the convention contented itself, on this occasion, with empowering[190] Brigadier-general Pearce[191] to coöperate with Brigadier-general McCulloch.[192]   It took this action on the twenty-first of May and on the twenty-eighth it received a communication[193] from Elias Rector concerning the Choctaws and Chickasaws.

Almost simultaneously with this legislative activity, solicitation of the Indians came from yet other directions. On the eighth of May, Brigadier-general B. Burroughs of the Arkansas militia took it upon himself to make an appeal to the Chickasaws, which he did in this wise:

HEADQUARTERS EIGHTH BRIGADE, FIRST DIVISION, ARKANSAS MILITIA, Fort Smith, Ark., May 8, 1861.

GOV. C. HARRIS: To-day we have information that Arkansas, in Convention, has seceded, by a vote 69 to 1. Tennessee

---

[189] *Journal*, Arkansas Convention, 189.

[190] — *Ibid.*, 295.

[191] N. Bart Pearce had just been created by the convention "brigadier-general of Arkansas, to command the Western frontier."

[192] On the thirteenth of May, the Confederate War Department had assigned Ben McCulloch to the command of the district embracing Indian Territory.

[193] *Journal*, Arkansas Convention, 369.

has also seceded, and made large appropriations and ordered an army of 50,000 men.

Arkansas has for several days past been in arms on this frontier for the protection (of) citizens, and the neighboring Indian nations whose interests are identical with her own.

I have news through my scouts that the U. S. troops have abandoned the forts in the Chickasaw country.

Under my orders from the commander-in-chief and governor of Arkansas, I feel authorized to extend to you such military aid as will be required in the present juncture of affairs to occupy and hold the forts.

I have appointed Col. A. H. Word, one of the State senators, and Captain Sparks, attached to this command, commissioners to treat and confer with you on this subject. These gentlemen are fully apprised of the nature of the powers intrusted to myself by the governor of this State, and are authorized to express to you my views of the subject under consideration. I ask, therefore, that you express to them your own wishes in the premises, and believe, my dear sir, that Arkansas cherishes the kindest regards for your people.

I have the honor to subscribe myself, with sentiments of regard, your excellency's friend and servant,

B. BURROUGHS, Brigadier-General, Commanding.[194]

The impudence and calm effrontery of this has its humorous side and would seem even ridiculous were it not for the fact that we are bound to remember that the Indians took it all so very seriously. It was true enough, as Burroughs said, that the Federal troops had abandoned the Indian country; but against whom were the forts to be held? Surely not against the Federals. Furthermore, what need was there for Arkansas to interest herself in the Chickasaw forts, since the Texan troops were already in possession? Is it possible to suppose that Burroughs's scouts, who had found out so much about the withdrawal of the Federal forces, had not discovered the work of the Texans in contributing

[194] *Official Records*, first ser., vol. i, 691.

thereto? The Chickasaws were particularly friendly
to the secessionists and, in this same month of May,
passed, by means of their legislature, those eight resolutions [195] in which they gave such strong expression to

[195] These resolutions are found in the *Official Record*, first ser., vol. iii,
585-587 and are as follows:

*Resolutions of the Senate and House of Representatives of the Chick-
asaw Legislature assembled*, May 25, 1861: Whereas the Government
of the United States has been broken up by the secession of a large
number of States composing the Federal Union – that the dissolution has
been followed by war between the parties; and whereas the destruction
of the Union as it existed by the Federal Constitution is irreparable, and
consequently the Government of the United States as it was when the
Chickasaw and other Indian nations formed alliances and treaties with
it no longer exists; and whereas the Lincoln Government, pretending
to represent said Union, has shown by its course towards us, in withdrawing from our country the protection of the Federal troops, and
withholding, unjustly and unlawfully, our money placed in the hands of
the Government of the United States as trustee, to be applied for our
benefit, a total disregard of treaty obligations toward us; and whereas
our geographical position, our social and domestic institutions, our feelings and sympathies, all attach us to our Southern friends, against
whom is about to be waged a war of subjugation or extermination, of
conquest and confiscation – a war which, if we can judge from the declarations of the political partisans of the Lincoln Government, will sur-
pass the French Revolution in scenes of blood and that of San Domingo
in atrocious horrors; and whereas it is impossible that the Chickasaws,
deprived of their money and destitute of all means of separate self-pro-
tection, can maintain neutrality or escape the storm which is about to
burst upon the South, but, on the contrary, would be suspected, oppressed,
and plundered alternately by armed bands from the North, South, East,
and West; and whereas we have an abiding confidence that all our
rights – tribal and individual – secured to us under treaties with the
United States, will be fully recognized, guaranteed, and protected by
our friends of the Confederate States; and whereas as a Southern people
we consider their cause our own: Therefore,

Be it resolved by the Chickasaw Legislature assembled, 1st. That the
dissolution of the Federal Union, under which the Government of the
United States existed, has absolved the Chickasaws from allegiance to
any foreign government whatever; that the current of the events of the
last few months has left the Chickasaw Nation *independent*, the people
thereof free to form such alliances, and take such steps to secure their
own safety, happiness, and future welfare as may to them seem best.

2d. *Resolved*, That our neighboring Indian nations – Choctaws, Cherokees, Creeks, Seminoles, Osages, Senecas, Quapaws, Comanches, Kio-

their views, at the same time, however, giving the
Southern States clearly to understand that they knew

was, together with the fragmentary bands of Delawares, Kickapoos,
Caddoes, Wichitas, and others within the Choctaw and Chickasaw country who are similarly situated with ourselves, be invited to co-operate,
in order to secure the independence of the Indian nations and the defense
of the territory they inhabit from Northern invasion by the Lincoln
hordes and Kansas robbers, who have plundered and oppressed our red
brethren among them, and who doubtless would extend towards us the
protection which the wolf gives to the lamb should they succeed in over-
running our country; that the Chickasaws pledge themselves to resist by
all means and to the death any such invasion of the lands occupied by
themselves or by any of the Indian nations; and that their country shall
not be occupied or passed through by the Lincoln forces for the purpose
of invading our neighbors, the States of Arkansas and Texas, but, on
the contrary, any attempt to do so will be regarded as an act of war
against ourselves, and should be resisted by all the Indian nations as in-
sulting to themselves and tending to endanger their Territorial rights.

3d. *Resolved*, That it is expedient, at the very earliest day possible,
that commissioners from other Indian nations for the purpose of forming
a league or confederation among them for mutual safety and protection,
and also to the Confederate States in order to enter into such alliance
and to conclude such treaties as may be necessary to secure the rights,
interests, and welfare of the Indian tribes, and that the co-operation of
all the Indian nations west of the State of Arkansas and south of Kansas
be invited for the attainment of these objects.

4th. *Resolved*, That the Chickasaws look with confidence especially
to the Choctaws (whose interests are so closely interwoven with their
own, and who were the first through their national council to declare
their sympathy for, and their determination, in case of a permanent dissolution of the Federal Union, to adhere to the Southern States), and
hope they will speedily unite with us in such measures as may be necessary for the defense of our common country and a union with our natural allies, the Confederate States of America.

5th. *Resolved*, That while the Chickasaw people entertain the most
sincere friendship for the people of the neighboring States of Texas and
Arkansas, and are deeply grateful for the prompt offer from them of
assistance in all measures of defense necessary for the protection of our
country against hostile invasion, we are desirous to hold undisputed
possession of our lands and all forts and other places lately occupied by
the Federal troops and other officers and persons acting under the authority of the United States, and that the governor of the Chickasaw Nation be, and he is hereby, instructed to take immediate steps to obtain
possession of all such forts and places within the Choctaw and Chickasaw country, and have the same garrisoned, if possible, by Chickasaw
troops, or else by troops acting expressly under and by virtue of the au-

the extent of their own rights and were determined to hold fast to them.   They also declared that they wished to hold their forts themselves.

On the ninth of May, the Indians were still further addressed and this time by the citizens of Boonsboro, Arkansas, whose appeal has already been referred to and quoted.[196]   The appeal was made through the medium of a letter to John Ross and of him the citizens of Boonsboro inquired where he intended to stand; inasmuch as they much preferred "an open enemy to a

thority of the Chickasaw or Choctaw nations, until such time as said forts, Indian agencies, etc., may be transferred by treaty to the Confederate States.

6th. *Resolved*, That the governor of the Chickasaw Nation be, and he is hereby, instructed to issue his proclamation to the Chickasaw Nation, declaring their *independence*, and calling upon the Chickasaw warriors to form themselves into volunteer companies of such strength and with such officers (to be chosen by themselves) as the governor may prescribe, to report themselves by filing their company rolls at the Chickasaw Agency, and to hold themselves, with the best arms and ammunition, together with a reasonable supply of provisions, in readiness at a minute's warning to turn out, under the orders of the commanding general of the Chickasaws, for the defense of their country or to aid the civil authorities in the enforcement of the laws.

7th. *Resolved*, That we have full faith and confidence in the justice of the cause in which we are embarked, and that we appeal to the Chickasaw people to be prepared to meet the conflict which will surely, and perhaps speedily, take place, and hereby call upon every man capable of bearing arms to be ready to defend his home and family, his country and his property, and to render prompt obedience to all orders from the officers set over them.

9th [8th]. *Resolved*, That the governor cause these resolutions to be published in the National Register, at the Boggy Depot, and copies thereof sent to the several Indian nations, to the governors of the adjacent States, to the President of the Confederate States, and to Abraham Lincoln, President of the Black Republican Party.

Passed the House of Representatives May 25, 1865.

A. ALEXANAN, Speaker House Representatives.

Attest: C. CARTER, Clerk House Representatives

Passed the Senate.   JOHN E. ANDERSON, President of Senate.

Attest: JAMES N. McLISH, Clerk of Senate.

Approved, Tishomingo, May 25, 1861.   C. HARRIS, Governor.

196 See *footnote 175.*

doubtful friend." They earnestly hoped, they said, to find in him and his people "true allies and active friends." On the fifteenth of May, J. R. Kannady, lieutenant-colonel, commanding at Fort Smith, also communicated [197] with Ross and on the same subject, his immediate provocation being the report that Senator James H. Lane was busy raising troops in Kansas to be used against Missouri and Arkansas. Of the Kannady letter, John B. Luce was the bearer and, to it, Ross replied [198] on the seventeenth, the very day that he published his great proclamation [199] of neutrality; for the otherwise most sensible John Ross labored under the delusion that the Indians would be allowed to figure as silent witnesses of events. In this respect, he was, however, on slightly firmer ground than were the citizens of such a state as Kentucky; but, none the less, he labored under a delusion as he soon found out to his sorrow. His proclamation of neutrality was intended as a final and conclusive answer [200] to all interrogatories like that from Boonsboro.

---

[197] General Files, *Cherokee, 1859-1865*, C515; *Official Records*, first ser., vol. xiii, 492.

[198] General Files, *ibid.*; *Official Records*, first ser., vol. xiii, 492-493.

[199] The text of this is to be found in various places. The most convenient of such places are, *Official Records*, first ser., vol. xiii, 489-490 and Moore's *Rebellion Record*, vol. ii, 145-146. A manuscript copy of the proclamation may be found in General Files, *Cherokee, 1859-1865*, C515; and a synopsis of its contents in Moore's *Rebellion Record*, vol. ii, 1-2.

[200] Ross gave the citizens of Boonsboro their direct answer, May 18, 1861 [General Files, *Cherokee, 1859-1865*, C515; *Official Records*, first ser., vol. xiii, 494-495].

III. THE CONFEDERACY IN NEGOTIATION WITH THE INDIAN TRIBES

The provisional government of the Confederate States showed itself no less anxious and no less prompt than the individual states in its endeavor to secure the Indian country and the Indian alliance. On the twenty-first of February, 1861, the very same day that the law was passed for the establishment of a War Department of which Leroy P. Walker of Alabama took immediate charge, William P. Chilton, member [201] of the Provisional Congress from Alabama, offered in that body a resolution to the effect, that the Committee on Indian Affairs be instructed to inquire into the expediency of opening up negotiations with the Indian tribes of the West in relation to all matters concerning the mutual welfare of said tribes and the people of the Confederate States. [202] The resolution was adopted. Four days later, Edward Sparrow of Louisiana asked that the same committee be instructed to consider the advisability of appointing agents to those same Indian tribes. [203] The Indian committee, at the time, was composed of Jackson Morton of Florida, Lawrence M. Keitt of South Carolina, and Thomas N. Waul of Texas. Robert W. Johnson became a member after Arkansas had seceded and had been admitted to the Confederacy.

---

[201] The official list of members of the Confederate congresses can be found in *Official Records*, fourth ser., vol. iii, 1185-1191.

[202] Provisional Congress of the Confederate States, *Journal*, vol. i, 70.

[203] — *Ibid.*, 81.

Preliminary steps such as these led naturally to a comprehension of the need for a Bureau of Indian Affairs[204] and, on the twelfth of March, President Davis recommended[205] that one be organized and a commissioner of Indian affairs appointed. His recommendations were acted upon without delay and a law[206] in conformity with them passed. This happened on the fifteenth of March and on the day following, the last of the session, Davis nominated David Hubbard,[207] ex-commissioner[208] from Alabama to Arkansas, for the Indian portfolio. For some time, however, Hubbard had little to do.[209]   It is wise therefore to leave him for

[204] Under the second section of the law of February 21, 1861, Indian affairs had been left for general supervision to the War Department [*Provisional and Permanent Constitutions of the Confederate States and Acts and Resolutions of the First Session of the Provisional Congress*, 48]. The Bureau of Indian Affairs, created by the law of March 15, 1861, was made a bureau of the War Department.

[205] Provisional Congress *Journal*, vol. i, 142; Richardson, *Messages and Papers of the Confederacy*.

[206] *Provisional and Permanent Constitutions*, 133-134.

[207] Provisional Congress *Journal*, vol. i, 154.

[208] Hubbard had occupied other and earlier positions of importance; but it must certainly have been upon the basis of the experience gained in filling this one that his nomination for commissioner of Indian affairs was made. Hubbard had been a state senator, a representative in the twenty-sixth and in the thirty-first United States congresses, and presidential elector on the Democratic ticket in 1844 and on the Breckinridge and Lane ticket in 1860 [*Biographical Congressional Directory, 1774-1903*, 608].

[209] The Bureau of Indian Affairs . . . has been organized. . . So far this Bureau has found but little to do. The necessity for the extension of the military arm of the Government toward the frontier, and the attitude of Arkansas, without the Confederacy, have contributed to circumscribe its action. But this branch of the public service doubtless will now grow in importance in consequence of the early probable accession of Arkansas to the Confederacy; of the friendly sentiments of the Creeks, Cherokees, Choctaws, and Chickasaws, and other tribes west of Arkansas toward this Government; of our difficulties with the tribes on the Texas frontier; of our hostilities with the United States, and of our probable future relations with the Territories of Arizona and New Mexico. — Extract from the Report of Secretary Walker to President Davis, April 27, 1861 [*Official Records*, fourth ser., vol. i, 248].

a while and resume the examination of congressional work.

The journal entries through February and March show that the Provisional Congress had, not infrequently, Indian matters placed before it and, at times presumably, communications direct from the tribes. On the fourth of March, Robert Toombs, himself on the Finance Committee and at the same time Secretary of State,[210] offered the following resolution:[211]

> *Resolved*, That the President be, and he is hereby authorized to send a suitable person as special agent of this Government to the Indian tribes west of the State of Arkansas.

Whether this was called forth by the investigations of the Committee on Indian Affairs under the Chilton resolution of the twenty-first of February or whether it grew out of a correspondence between Toombs and Albert Pike does not appear. Toombs and Pike were friends, brother Masons[212] in fact, and then or soon afterwards in intimate correspondence on the subject of Indian relations. The resolution passed, but there the matter seems to have rested for a time. On the tenth of May, William B. Ochiltree proposed[213] that the Committee on Indian Affairs consider the condition of Reserve Indians in Texas; and, on the fifteenth, a most important measure was introduced[214] in the shape of a bill, reported by Keitt from the Committee on Indian Affairs, "for the protection of certain Indian tribes." This opened up the whole subject of prospective rela-

[210] Davis would have preferred to have had Toombs for secretary of the treasury [Rhodes, *History of the United States*, vol. iii, 295, *note* 7].

[211] *Journal*, vol. i, 105.

[212] Both Pike and Toombs reached in time the thirty-second degree, or Scottish Rite. Note Pike's glowing tribute to Toombs, quoted in Richardson, *Messages and Papers of the Confederacy*, vol. ii, 142.

[213] *Journal*, vol. i, 205.

[214] — *Ibid.*, 225.

tions with the great tribes of Indian Territory and, taken in connection with the provision for a special commissioner, was fruitful of great results.

On the seventh of May, Thomas A. Harris of Missouri had made the Provisional Congress acquainted with some Choctaw and Chickasaw resolutions,[215] which, in themselves, seemed indicative of a friendly disposition towards the South. This fact lent to the bill for the assumption of a protectorate a large significance. Congress considered it, for the most part, in secret session. The text of the act as finally passed does not appear in any of the published[216] statutes of the Confederate States; but, under the act, Albert Pike, special commissioner for the purpose appointed by President Davis, negotiated all his remarkable treaties with the western tribes. Three sections of the law, those added to the original bill by way of amendment, appear in the Provisional Congress *Journal.*[217] They are strictly financial in their nature and are as follows:

Sec. 6. And be it further enacted, That the Confederate States do hereby assume the duty and obligation of collecting and paying over as trustees to the several Indian tribes now located in the Indian Territory south of Kansas, all sums of money accruing, whether from interest or capital of the bonds of the several States of this Confederacy now held by the Government of the United States as trustees for said Indians or any

---

[215] Just what particular sets of resolutions those were I have no means of knowing. The most important set of Chickasaw resolutions, those issued under date of May 25, 1861 [*Official Records*, first ser., vol. iii, 585-587] had not yet been passed. The Choctaw resolutions presented may have been and very probably were those of February 7, 1861 [*ibid.*].

[216] On the twenty-first of May, President Davis approved "An Act for the protection of the Indian Tribes" [*Journal*, 263], it having gone through its various stages of amendment and having passed Congress, May seventeenth [*ibid.*, 244]. Adjutant-general G. W. Andrews reports, November 4, 1912, that nothing additional concerning the text of this law is to be found in the Confederate archives.

[217] *Journal*, vol. i, 244.

of them; and the said interest and capital as collected shall be paid over to said Indians or invested for their account, as the case may be, in accordance with the several treaties and contracts now existing between said Indians and the Government of the United States.

Sec. 7. That the several States of this Confederacy be requested to provide by legislation or otherwise that the capital and interest of the bonds issued by them respectively, and held by the Government of the United States in trust for said Indians, or any of them, shall not be paid to said Government of the United States, but shall be paid to this Government in trust for said Indians.

Sec. 8. That it shall be the duty of the Commissioner of Indian Affairs to obtain and publish, at as early a period as practicable, a list of all the bonds of the several States of this Confederacy now held in trust by the Government of the United States as aforesaid, and to give notice in said publication that the capital and interest of said bonds are to be paid to this Government and to no other holder thereof whatever.

Before this bill for the protection of the Indians had come up for discussion or had even emerged from the rooms of the Committee on Indian Affairs, Albert Pike, in letters to Toombs and R. W. Johnson, had pointed out most emphatically the military necessity of securing [218] the Indian country. His conviction was strong that the United States had no idea of permanently abandoning the same but would soon replace the regular troops, it had withdrawn from thence, by volunteers. Pike discussed the matter with N. Bart Pearce and the two agreed [219] that there was no time to lose and that something must be done forthwith to prevent the

---

[218] Governor Clark of Texas, also, at this time displayed great interest in the matter. On the fifteenth of May, he wrote to President Davis that he was constituting James E. Harrison, a man thoroughly conversant with the whole subject, "the duly accredited agent of Texas to convey" the Report of April 23, 1861 to Richmond [*Official Records*, fourth ser., vol. i, 322].

[219] See letter from Pearce to President Davis, May 13, 1861 [*ibid.*, first ser., vol. iii, 576].

possibility of Federal emissaries gaining a foothold among the great tribes; for, if they did gain such a foothold, their influence was likely to be very great, especially among the Cherokees who might be regarded as predisposed to favor them, they having many abolitionists on their tribal rolls. Whether, at so early a date, Pike thought formal negotiation, as had been customary, the preferable method of procedure, we are not prepared to say, positively. Formal negotiation was scarcely consistent with the southern argument of Jackson's time or consonant with present state-rights doctrine. When writing [220] to Johnson on the eleventh of May, Pike seems to have been thinking simply of Indian enlistment and of the use of white and red troops in the defense of the Indian country. At that date his own appointment [221] as diplomatic agent for the negotiation of treaties of amity and alliance was certainly not prominently before him. He expressed himself to Johnson in such a way, indeed, as would lead us to suppose that the position he half expected to get, and did not altogether want, was that of commander of an Indian Department which he hoped would be created.

For such a position Pike was not entirely unfitted. He had served in the Mexican War and had attained the rank of captain; but his tastes were certainly not what one would call military. He was a poet [222] of acknowledged reputation and a lawyer of eminence. Arkansas had recognized him as one of her foremost citizens by sending him as her one and only dele-

---

[220] *Official Records*, fourth ser., vol. i, 572-574.

[221] Pike was appointed under authority of a resolution passed by Congress, March 5, 1861. See Message of President Davis, December 12, 1861 [*ibid.*, fourth ser., vol. i, 785].

[222] To-day he is, perhaps, best known by his parody on "Dixie" and by his singularly beautiful and pathetic "Every Year" [*Poems*, Roome's edition, 31-34].

gate to the Commercial Convention[223] of Southern and Western States, held at Charleston, South Carolina, April, 1854. Just recently, at the time when the question of secession was before the people of Arkansas, he had issued a pamphlet, entitled, *State or Province, Bond or Free*, described by a contemporary as, "a most specious argument for secession, but a re-production of the political heresies, that thirty years ago called down on John C. Calhoun, the anathema maranatha of Andrew Jackson."[224] To the men of his time, it seemed all the more astonishing that Albert Pike should take such a pronounced stand on the subject of state rights, not because he was a New Englander by birth, for there were many such in Arkansas and in the ranks of the secessionists, but because he was the author of that stirring poem against the idea of national disintegration, published some time before under the title of, "Disunion."[225]

---

[223] See *Journal of Proceedings*, no. 273 of Johns Hopkins University Civil War Pamphlets.

[224] Bishop, *Loyalty on the Frontier*, 148-151.

[225] The poem is printed entire in Bishop's *Loyalty on the Frontier*, 149-150. The first two stanzas are here given:

DISUNION

Ay, shout! 'Tis the day of your pride,
    Ye despots and tyrants of earth;
Tell your serfs the American name to deride,
    And to rattle their fetters in mirth.
Ay, shout! for the league of the free
    Is about to be shivered to dust,
And the rent limbs to fall from the vigorous tree,
Shout! shout! for more firmly established, will be
Your thrones and dominions beyond the blue sea.

Laugh on! for such folly supreme,
    The world has yet never beheld;
And ages to come will the history deem,
    A tale by antiquity swelled;
For nothing that time has upbuilt
    And set in the annals of crime,

On the twentieth of May, Pike wrote[226] again to
Toombs and by that time he certainly knew[227] of his
commission to treat with the Indian tribes, but had
apparently not received any very definite instructions
as to the scope of his authority. One little passage in
the letter brings out very clearly the essential fair-
mindedness of the man, a marked characteristic in all[228]

> So stupid and senseless, so wretched in guilt,
>   Darkens sober tradition or rhyme.
> *It will be like the fable of Eblis' fall,*
> *A by-word of mockery and horror to all.*

[226] *Official Records*, first ser., vol. iii, 580-581.

[227] In a letter to Commissioner D. N. Cooley, under date of February 17,
1866, Pike said that Toombs requested him in May of 1861 to visit the Indian
country as commissioner. I have not been able to find out whether Toombs
made his request in writing or verbally. The correspondence of Toombs recently edited by U. B. Phillips does not furnish any additional information on
this point.

[228] On one very important occasion, Albert Pike was not strictly fair to the
Indians. That occasion was after the war when the United States Indian
Office was endeavoring to make a settlement with the Cherokees on the basis of
their adherence to the Confederate cause. Pike was appealed to and threw
the weight of his influence against John Ross, but most unjustly as it would
seem. The letter embodying his views is a narrative of the events of 1861 as
they happened in the Indian country under his scrutiny, and may as well be
inserted here in full. It is to be found in the Indian Office in a bundle la-
beled, "Loyalty of John Ross, Principal Chief of the Cherokees: Letter of
Albert Pike (original), Feb. 17, 1866 – and *Copies* of several of Ross' letters –
relative to his *loyalty* in 1861 & 1862, etc."

> 5.   *Albert Pike to the Commissioner of Indian Affairs*
>
> MEMPHIS, TENNESSEE, 17th February 1866.
>
> SIR: I have received, to-day, a copy of the "Memorial" of the
> "Southern Cherokees," to the President, Senate and House of Representa-
> tives, in reply to the Memorial of other Cherokees claiming to be "loyal."
>
> It is not for me to take any part in the controversy between the two
> portions of the Cherokee People, nor have I any interest that could lead
> me to side with one in preference to the other. Nor am I much in-
> clined, having none of the rights of a Citizen, to offer to testify in any
> matter, when my testimoney may not be deemed worthy of credit, as
> that of one not yet restored to respectability and creditability by a pardon.
>
> But, as I know it to be contemptible as well as false, for Mr. John
> Ross and the "loyal" Memorialists to pretend that they did not volun-
> tarily engage themselves by Treaty Stipulations to the Confederate

his dealings with the Indians, but at once his strength

States, and as you have desired my testimony, I have this to say, and I think no man will be bold enough to deny any part of it.

In May, 1861, I was requested by Mr. Toombs, Secretary of State of the Confederate States, to visit the Indian Country as Commissioner, and assure the Indians of the friendship of those States. The Convention of the State of Arkansas, anxious to avoid hostilities with the Cherokees, also applied to me to act as such Commissioner. I accordingly proceeded to Fort Smith, where some five or six Cherokees called upon General McCulloch and myself, representing those of the Cherokees who sympathized with the South, in order to ascertain whether the Confederate States would protect them against Mr. Ross and the Pin Indians, if they should organize and take up arms for the South. We learned that some attempts to raise a Secession flag in the Cherokee Country on the Arkansas had been frustrated by the menace of violence; and those who came to meet us represented the Pin Organization to be a Secret Society, established by Evan Jones, a Missionary, and at the service of Mr. John Ross, for the purpose of abolitionizing the Cherokees and putting out of the way all who sympathized with the Southern States.

The truth was, as I afterwards learned with certainty, the Secret Organization in question, whose members for a time used as a mark of their membership a *pin* in the front of the hunting shirt, was really established for the purpose of depriving the half-breeds of all political power, though Mr. Ross, himself a Scotchman and a McDonald by the father and the mother, was shrewd enough to use it for his own ends. At any rate, it was organized and in *full* operation, long before Secession was thought of.

General McCulloch and myself assured those who met us at Fort Smith, that they should be protected; and agreed to meet, at an early day then fixed, at Park Hill, where Mr. Ross resided. Upon that I sent a messenger with letters to five or six prominent members of the Anti-Ross party, inviting them to meet me at the Creek Agency, two days after the day on which General McCulloch and I were to meet at Park Hill.

I did not expect to effect any arrangement with Mr. Ross, and my intention was to treat with the heads of the Southern party, Stand Watie and others.

When we met Mr. Ross at Park Hill, he refused to enter into any arrangement with the Confederate States. He said that his intention was to maintain the neutrality of his people; that they were a small and weak people, and would be ruined and destroyed if they engaged in the war; and that it would be a cruel thing if we were to engage them in our quarrel. But, he said, all his interests and all his feelings were with us, and he knew that his people must share the fate and fortunes of Arkansas. We told him that the Cherokees *could* not be neutral.

and his weakness.   He succeeded with the red man for

We used every argument in our power to change his determination, but in vain; and finally General McCulloch informed him that he would respect the neutrality of the Cherokees, and would not enter their Country with troops, or place troops in it, unless it should become necessary in order to expel a Federal force, or to protect the Southern Cherokees.

So we separated.   General McCulloch kept his word, and no Confederate troops ever were stationed in or marched into the Cherokee Country, until after the Federal troops invaded it.

Before leaving the Nation I addressed Mr. Ross a letter, which I afterwards printed, and circulated among the Cherokee people.   In it I informed him that the Confederate States would remain content with his pledge of neutrality, although he would find it impossible to maintain that neutrality; that I should not again offer to treat with the Cherokees, and that the Confederate States would not consider themselves bound by my proposition to pay the Cherokees for the neutral land, if they should lose it in consequence of the war.   I had no further communication with Mr. Ross until September.

Meanwhile, he had persuaded Opoth le Yahola, the Creek leader, not to join the Southern States, and had sent delegates to meet the Northern and other Indians in Council near the Antelope Hills, where they all agreed to be neutral.   The purpose was, to take advantage of the war between the States, and form a great independent Indian Confederation – I defeated all that, by treating with the Creeks at the very time that their delegates were at the Antelope Hills in Council.

When I had treated with them and with the Choctaws and Chickasaws, at the North Fork of the Canadian, I went to the Seminole Agency and treated with the Seminoles.   Then I went to the Wichita Agency, having previously invited the Reserve Indians to return there, and invited the prairie Comanches to meet me.   After treating with these, I returned by Fort Arbuckle, and before reaching there, met a nephew of Mr. Ross, and a Captain [Keld? *sic*] in the prairie, bearing a letter to me from Mr. Ross and his Council, with a copy of the resolutions of Council, and an invitation in pressing terms to repair to the Cherokee Country and enter into a Treaty.

I consented, fixed a day for meeting the Cherokees, and wrote Mr. Ross to that effect, requesting him also to send messengers to the Osages, Quapaws, Shawnees, Senecas, &c. and invite them to meet me at the same time.   He did so, and at the time fixed I went to Park Hill, and there effected Treaties.

When I first entered the Indian Country, in May, I had as an escort one company of mounted men.   I went in advance of them to Park Hill; General McCulloch went there without an escort.   At the Creek Agency I sent the Company back: I then remained without escort or guard, until I had made the Seminole Treaty, camping with my little party and displaying the Confederate flag.   When I went to the Wichita Country,

the very same reason that he failed with the white, be-

I took an escort of Creeks and Seminoles. These I discharged at Fort Arbuckle on my return, and went, accompanied only by four young men, through the Creek Country to Fort Gibson, refusing an escort of Creeks offered me on the way.

From Fort Gibson eight or nine companies of Colonel Drew's Regiment of Cherokees, chiefly full-bloods and Pins, escorted me to Park Hill. This regiment was raised by order of the National Council, and its officers appointed by Mr Ross, his nephew William P. Ross, Secretary of the Nation, being Lieut. Colonel, and Thomas Pegg, President of the National Committee, being its Major.

I encamped, with my little party near the residence of the Chief, unprotected even by a guard, and with the Confederate flag flying. The terms of the Treaty were fully discussed and the Cherokee authorities dealt with me on equal terms. Mr. John Ross had met me as I was on my way to Park Hill, escorted by the National Regiment, and had welcomed me to the Cherokee Nation, in an earnest and enthusiastic speech; and seemed to me throughout to be acting in perfect good faith. I acted in the same way with him.

After the treaties were signed, I presented Colonel Drew's Regiment a flag, and the chief in a speech exhorted them to be true to it: and afterwards, *at his request, I wrote the Cherokee Declaration of Independence* which is printed with the Memorial of the Southern Cherokees. I no more doubted, then, that Mr. Ross' whole heart was with the South, than that mine was. *Even in May he said to General McCulloch and myself, that if Northern troops invaded the Cherokee Country, he would head the Cherokees and drive them back.* "*I have borne arms*" he said, "*and though I am old I can do it again.*"

At the time of the treaty there were about nine hundred Cherokees of Colonel Drew's Regiment encamped near, and fed by me, and Colonel Watie, who had almost abandoned the idea of raising a regiment, had a small body of men, not more, I think, than eighty or ninety, at Tahlequah. When the flag was presented, Col. Watie was present, and after the ceremony the chief shook hands with him and expressed his warm desire for union and harmony in the Nation.

The gentlemen whom I had invited to meet me in June at the Creek Agency did not do so. They were afraid of being murdered, they said, if they openly sided with the South. In October they censured me for treating with Mr. Ross, and were in an ill humour, saying that the regiment was raised in order to be used to oppress *them*.

The same day that the Cherokee Treaty was signed, the Osages, Quapaws, Shawnees and Senecas signed treaties, and the next day they had a talk with Mr. Ross at his residence, smoked the great pipe and renewed their alliance, being urged by him to be true to the Confederate States.

I protest that I believed Mr. John Ross, at this time and for long after, to be as sincerely devoted to the Confederacy as I myself was.

cause he gave to the Indians the consideration and the

He was frank, cheerful, earnest, and evidently believed that the independence of the Confederate States was an accomplished fact. I should dishonour him if I believed that he then dreamed of abandoning the Confederacy or turning the arms of the Cherokees against us in case of a reverse.

Before I left the Cherokee Country, part of the Creeks, under Opoth-le-Yaholo left their homes, under arms and threatened hostilities. Mr. Ross, at my request, invited the old Chief to meet him, and urged him to unite with the Confederate States. Colonel Drew's regiment was ordered into the Creek Country, and afterwards, on the eve of the action at Bird Creek, abandoned Colonel Cooper, rather than fight against their neighbours. But after the action, the regiment was again reorganized. The men were eager to fight, they said, against the Yankees; but did not wish to fight their own brethren, the Creeks.

When General Curtis entered North Western Arkansas, in February 1862, I sent orders from Fort Smith to Colonel Drew to move towards Evansville and receive orders from General McCulloch. Colonel Watie's Regiment was already under General McCulloch's command. Colonel Drew's men moved in advance of Colonel Watie, with great alacrity, and showed no want of zeal at Pea Ridge.

I do not *know* that any one was scalped at that place or in that action, except from information. None of my officers knew it at the time. I heard of it afterwards. I cannot say to which regiment those belonged who did it. But it has been publicly charged on some of the same men who afterwards abandoned the Confederate cause and enlisting in the Federal Service were sent into Arkansas to ravage it.

After the actions at Pea Ridge and Elk Horn, the Regiment of Colonel Drew was moved to the mouth of the Illinois, where I was able, after a time, to pay them $25 cash, the commutation for six months' clothing, in Confederate money. Nothing more, owing to the wretched management of the Confederate government, was ever paid them; and the clothing procured for them was plundered by the commands of Generals Price and Van Dorn. The consequence was that when Colonel Weer entered the Cherokee Country, the Pin Indians joined him *en masse.*

I had procured at Richmond, and paid Mr. Lewis Ross, Treasurer of the Cherokee Nation, about the first of March 1862, in the Chief's house and in the Chief's presence, the moneys agreed to be paid them by Treaty, being about $70,000 (I think) in coin, and among other sums $150,000 in Confederate Treasury notes, loaned the Nation by way of advance on the price expected to be paid for the Neutral land. This sum had been promised in the Treaty at the earnest solicitation of Mr. John Ross; and it was generally understood that it was desired for the special purpose of redeeming scrip of the Nation issued long before, and much of which was held by Mr. Ross and his relatives. That such *was*

justice which were their due. This is the significant

the case, I do not know. I only know that the moneys were paid, and that I have the receipts for them, which, with others, I shall file in the Indian Office.

In May, 1862, Lieut. Colonel William P. Ross visited my camp at Fort McCulloch, near Red River, and said to me that "the Chief" would be gratified if he were to receive the appointment of Brigadier General in the Confederate Service. I did not ask him if he was authorized by the Chief to say so; but I did ask him if he were *sure* that the appointment would gratify him; and being so assured, I promised to urge the appointment. I did so, more than once, but never received a reply. It was not customary with the Confederate War Department to exhibit any great wisdom; and in respect to the Indian Country its conduct was disgraceful. Unpaid, unclothed, uncared for, unthanked even, and their services unrecognized, it was natural the Cherokees should abandon the Confederate flag.

When Colonel Weer invaded the Cherokee Country, Mr. Ross refused to have an interview with him, declaring that the Cherokees would remain faithful to their engagements with the Confederate States. There was not then a Confederate soldier in the Cherokee Nation, to overawe Mr. Ross or Major Pegg or any other "loyal" Cherokee. Mr. Ross sent me a copy of his letter to Colonel Weer, and I had it printed and sent over Texas, to show the people there that the Cherokee Chief was "loyal" to the Confederate States.

Afterwards, when Stand Watie's Regiment and the Choctaws were sent over the Arkansas into the Cherokee Country, and Mr. Ross considered his life in danger from his own people, in consequence of their ancient feud, he allowed himself to be taken prisoner by the Federal troops. At the time, I believed that if white troops had been sent to Park Hill, who would have protected him against Watie's men, he would have remained at home and adhered to the Confederacy: for either he was true to his obligations to the Confederate States, voluntarily entered into, – true at heart and in his inmost soul, – or else he is falser and more treacherous than I can believe him to be.

The simple truth is, Mr. Commissioner, that the "loyal" Cherokees hated Stand Watie and the half-breeds and were hated by them. They were perfectly willing to kill and scalp Yankees, and when they were hired to change sides, and twenty two hundred of them were organized into regiments in the *Federal* Service, they were just as ready to kill and scalp when employed against us in Arkansas. *We* did *not* pay and clothe them, and the United States *did*. They scalped for those who paid, for and clothed them. As to "loyalty" they had none at all.

I entered the Indian Country in May, and left it in October. For five months I travelled and encamped in it, unprotected by white troops, alone with the four young men, treating with the different tribes. If there had been any "loyalty" among the Indians, I could not have gone

passage from his letter to Toombs:[229]

> a mile in safety. Opoth-le-Yaholo was not "loyal." He feared the
> McIntoshes, who had raised troops, and who, he thought, meant to kill
> him for killing their father long years before. He told me that he did
> not wish to fight against the Southern States, but only that the Indians
> should all act together. If Mr. Ross had treated with us at first, *all* the
> Creeks would have done the same. If Stand Watie and his party took
> *one* side, John Ross and his party were sure, in the end, to take the
> other, *especially when that other proved itself the stronger.*
>
> So far from the Watie party overawing the party which upheld Mr.
> Ross, I *know* it to be true that they were *afraid* to actively cooperate
> with the Confederate States, to organize, to raise Secession flags, or even
> to meet me and consult with me. They feared that Colonel Drew's
> Regiment would be used to harrass them, and they never dreamed of
> *forcing* the authorities into a Treaty.
>
> After the action at Elkhorn, murders were continually complained of
> by Colonels Watie and Drew, and the Chief solicited me to place part
> of Colonel Drew's Regiment at or near Park Hill, to protect the govern-
> ment and its records. I did so. There never was a time when the
> "loyal" Cherokees had not the power to destroy the Southern ones.
>
> As to myself, I dealt fairly and openly with all the Indians. I used
> no threats of force or compulsion, with any of them. The "loyal"
> Cherokees joined us because they believed we should succeed, and left
> us when they thought we should not. At their request I wrote their
> declaration of Independence and acceptance of the issues of war; and if
> any men voluntarily, and with their eyes open, and of their own motion
> acceded to the Secession movement, it was John Ross and the people
> whom he controlled. I am, Sir, Very res[py], Your obt Svt
>
> ALBERT PIKE
>
> D. N. Cooley Esq, Commissioner of Ind. Aff.

[229] In writing this letter, Pike most certainly addressed himself to Toombs
officially and with the idea in mind that he was holding his commission under
the Confederate State Department. That he was serving under that department and that he did not get his appointment until May seem scarcely to admit
of a doubt, notwithstanding the fact that Judah P. Benjamin, Secretary of War
later in the year, December [14?], 1861, in reporting to President Davis, could
make the following statement:

> At the first session of the Congress an act was passed providing for
> the sending of a commissioner to the Indian tribes north of Texas and
> west of Arkansas, with the view of making such arrangements for an
> alliance with and the protection of the Indians as were rendered neces-
> sary by the disruption of the Union and our natural succession to the
> rights and duties of the United States, so far as these Indians were
> concerned. The supervision of this important branch of administrative
> duty was confided to the State Department, by which Brig.-Gen. Albert
> Pike was selected as commissioner. At a later period of the same ses-

I very much regret that I have not received distinct authority to give the Indians guarantees of all their legal and just rights under treaties. It cannot be expected they will join us without them, and it would be very ungenerous, as well as unwise and useless, in me to ask them to do it. Why should they, if we will not bind ourselves to give them what they hazard in giving us their rights under treaties?

As you have told me to act at my discretion, and as I am not directed not to give the guarantees, I shall give them, formal, full, and ample, by treaty, if the Indians will accept them and make treaties. General McCulloch will join me in this, and so, I hope and suppose, will Mr. Hubbard, and when we shall have done so we shall, I am sure, not look in vain to you, at least, to affirm these guarantees and insist they shall be carried out in good faith.

There was an implied doubt of Hubbard in Pike's reference to him and a single future declaration almost justified the doubt, notwithstanding the fact that Hubbard was supposed to have been chosen as commissioner of Indian affairs because of his "well known sympathy for the Indian tribes and the deep concern" he had ever "manifested in their welfare." Hubbard's

sion a Bureau of Indian Affairs was created by law and attached to this Department, charged with the management of our relations with the Indian tribes. . . - *Official Records*, fourth ser., vol. i, 792.

Now, if Benjamin was correct in his chronology, the appointment of Pike must have antedated that of Hubbard, a very unlikely state of affairs unless, indeed, the Confederate government from the start, taking cognizance of the very advanced condition of the Indians under discussion and of the very extreme delicacy of the situation, concluded it would be wisest to act upon the assumption that the great tribes were independent enough to be dealt with almost as foreign powers and so left everything to the discretion of the State Department.

In November, 1861, the Provisional Congress considered the advisability of transferring the whole Indian Bureau to the Department of State [*Journal*, November 28, 1861, vol. i, 489]. The transfer was probably suggested by the fact that the relations to date of the Confederate States with the Indians had been conducted altogether upon a basis of diplomacy. An added reason might have been, that the ordinary business of the War Department was sufficiently onerous without the details of Indian complications being made a part of it. Yet the transfer was never made.

official position was that of Commissioner of Indian Affairs; but the unorganized character of the Confederate administration in early 1861 is well attested by the way Secretary Walker confounded the name and functions of that office with those of an ordinary superintendent. On the fourteenth of May, he addressed Hubbard as "Superintendent of Indian Affairs" and instructed him

> To proceed to the Creek Nation, and to make known to them, as well as to the rest of the tribes west of Arkansas and south of Kansas . . . the earnest desire of the Confederate States to defend and protect them against the rapacious and avaricious designs of their and our enemies at the North. . . You will, in an especial manner, impress upon the Creek Nation and surrounding Indian tribes the imperious fact that they will doubtless recognize, that the real design of the North and the Government at Washington in regard to them has been and still is the same entertained and sought to be enforced against ourselves, and if suffered to be consummated, will terminate in the emancipation of their slaves and the robbery of their lands. To these nefarious ends all the schemes of the North have tended for many years past, as the Indian nations and tribes well know from the character and conduct of those emissaries who have been in their midst, preaching up abolition sentiments under the disguise of the holy religion of Christ, and denouncing slaveholders as abandoned by God and unfit associates for humanity on earth.
>
> You will be diligent to explain to them, under these circumstances, how their cause has become our cause, and themselves and ourselves stand inseparably associated in respect to national existence and property interests; and in view of this identification of cause and interests between them and ourselves, entailing a common destiny, give to them profound assurances that the Government of the Confederate States of America, now powerfully constituted through an immense league of sovereign political societies, great forces in the field, and abundant resources, will assume all the expense and responsibility of protecting them against all adversaries. . .
>
> Give them to understand, in this connection, that a brigadier-

general of character and experience has been assigned to the military district embracing the Indian Territories south of Kansas, with three regiments under his command, while in Texas another military district has been formed. . .

In addition to these things, regarded of primary importance, you will, without committing the Government to any especial conduct, express our serious anxiety to establish and enforce the debts and annuities due to them from the Government at Washington, which otherwise they will never obtain, as that Government would, undoubtedly, sooner rob them of their lands, emancipate their slaves, and utterly exterminate them, than render to them justice. Finally, communicate to them the abiding solicitude of the Confederate States of America to advance their condition in the direction of a proud political society, with a distinctive civilization, and holding lands in severalty under well-defined laws, by forming them into a Territorial government; but you will give no assurance of State organization and independence, as they still require the strong arm of protecting power, and may probably always need our fostering care; and, so far as the agents of the late Government of the United States may be concerned, you will converse with them, and such of them as are willing to act with you in the policy herein set forth you are authorized to substantiate in the employment of this Government at their present compensation. . .[230]

Hubbard's mission to the west was quite independent[231] of Pike's, although both missions were undoubtedly part of the one general plan of securing as quickly, as surely, and as easily as possible the friendly coöperation of the Indians. At about the same moment that they were devised, the Confederacy took yet another means of accomplishing the same object and one referred to in the letter of Secretary Walker just quoted. On the thirteenth of this same month of May, 1861, it assigned Brigadier-general Ben McCulloch

[230] *Official Records*, first ser., vol. iii, 576-578.

[231] Hubbard's ill-health, however, seems to have made it incumbent upon Pike to assume much the larger share of official responsibility and practically to do Hubbard's work as well as his own; that is, so much of it as was not transacted in Richmond.

"to the command of the district embracing the Indian Territory lying west of Arkansas and south of Kansas." McCulloch's orders [232] were "to guard that Territory against invasion from Kansas or elsewhere," and, for the purpose, in addition to three regiments of white troops, "to engage, if possible, the service of any of the Indian tribes occupying the Territory referred to in numbers equal to two regiments."

Hubbard's part in the prosecution of this great endeavor may as well be disposed of first. It was of short duration and seemingly barren of direct results. Hubbard was long in reaching the western boundary of Arkansas. On the way out he was seized with pneumonia and otherwise delayed by wind and weather. On the second of June he was still in Little Rock, apparently much more interested [233] in the local situation in Arkansas than in the real object of his mission. His intention was to "go up the river to Fort Smith," June third. From that point, on the twelfth, he addressed the Cherokee chief, John Ross, and the Confederate general, Ben McCulloch. The letter was more particularly meant for the former.

> As Commissioner of Indian Affairs of the Confederate States it was my intention to have called upon you and consulted as to the mutual interests of our people. Sickness has put it out of my power to travel, and those interests require immediate consideration, and therefore I have determined to write, and make what I think a plain statement of the case for your consideration, which I think stands thus: If we succeed in the South – succeed in this controversy, and I have no doubt of the fact, for we are daily gaining friends among the powers of Europe, and our people are arming with unanimity scarcely ever seen in the world before – then your lands, your slaves, and your sep-

---

[232] Adjutant and Inspector-General S. Cooper to McCulloch, May 13, 1861 [*Official Records*, first ser., vol. iii, 575-576].

[233] Hubbard to Walker, June 2, 1861 [*ibid.*, 589-590].

arate nationality are secured and made perpetual, and in addition nearly all your debts are in Southern bonds, and these we will also secure. If the North succeeds you will most certainly lose all. First your slaves they will take from you; that is one object of the war, to enable them to abolish slavery in such manner and at such time as they choose. Another, and perhaps the chief cause, is to get upon your rich lands and settle their squatters, who do not like to settle in slave States. They will settle upon your lands as fast as they choose, and the Northern people will force their Government to allow it. It is true they will allow your people small reserves – they give chiefs pretty large ones – but they will settle among you, overshadow you, and totally destroy the power of your chiefs and your nationality, and then trade your people out of the residue of their lands. Go North among the once powerful tribes of that country and see if you can find Indians living and enjoying power and property and liberty as do your people and the neighboring tribes from the South. If you can, then say I am a liar, and the Northern States have been better to the Indian than the Southern States. If you are obliged to admit the truth of what I say, then join us and preserve your people, their slaves, their vast possessions in land, and their nationality.

Another consideration is your debts, annuities, &c., school funds due you. Nearly all are in bonds of Southern States and held by the Government at Washington, and these debts are nearly all forfeited already by the act of war made upon the States by that Government. These we will secure you beyond question if you join us. If you join the North they are forever forfeited, and you will have no right to believe that the Northern people would vote to pay you this forfeited debt. Admit that there may be some danger take which side you may, I think the danger tenfold greater to the Cherokee people if they take sides against us than for us. Neutrality will scarcely be possible. As long as your people retain their national character your country cannot be abolitionized, and it is our interest therefore that you should hold your possessions in perpetuity.[234]

The effect that such a communication as the forego-

[234] *Official Records*, first ser., vol. xiii, 497-498; General Files, *Cherokee, 1859-1865*, C515.

ing might well have had upon the Indians can scarcely be overestimated. Time out of number they had been over-reached in dealings financial. Only the year before, bonds in which Indian trust funds were invested had been abstracted [235] from the vaults of the Interior Department; and, for this cause and other causes, Indian money had not been readily forthcoming for the much needed relief of Indian sufferers from the fearful drought that devastated Indian Territory, Kansas, and other parts of the great American desert in 1860.

Comment upon Hubbard's letter from the standpoint of historical inaccuracy seems hardly necessary here. Suffice it to say that the distortion of facts and the shifting of responsibility for previous Indian wrongs from the shoulders of Southern States to those of a federal government made up entirely of northern states must have seemed preposterous in the extreme to the Indians. One can not help wondering how Hubbard dared to say such things to the Indian exiles from Southern States and particularly to John Ross who like all of his tribe and of associated tribes was the victim of southern aggression and not in any sense whatsoever of northern.

To Hubbard's gross amplification and even defiance of his instructions, also to his extravagant utterances touching the repudiation of debts and southern versus northern justice and generosity, Chief Ross replied, [236]

---

[235] Rhodes, *op. cit.*, vol. iii, 237-238; also *Report* of the Select Committee to Investigate the Abstraction of Bonds Held by the United States Government in Trust for Indian Tribes, being House *Report*, 36th congress, second session, no. 78. Dole, in his *Annual Report* for 1861, p. 27, urged that the government make the loss good to the Indians and also appropriate money "to meet the unpaid interest on those trust bonds of the revolted States yet in custody of the Secretary of the Interior." There ought never, either from the standpoint of national faith or of that of political expediency, to have been any hesitation in the matter.

[236] The entire letter is to be found in *Official Records*, first ser., vol. xiii, 498-499; also in General Files, *Cherokee, 1859-1865*, C515.

by way of strong contrast, in terms dignified and convincing:

> It is not the province of the Cherokees to determine the character of the conflict going on in the States.   It is their duty to keep themselves, if possible, disentangled, and afford no grounds to either party to interfere with their rights.   The obligations of every character, pecuniary and otherwise, which existed prior to the present state of affairs between the Cherokee Nation and the Government are equally valid now as then.   If the Government owe us, I do not believe it will repudiate its debts.   If States embraced in the Confederacy owe us, I do not believe they will repudiate their debts.   I consider our annuity safe in any contingency.
>
> A comparison of Northern and Southern philanthropy, as illustrated in their dealings toward the Indians within their respective limits, would not affect the merits of the question now under consideration, which is simply one of duty under existing circumstances.   I therefore pass it over, merely remarking that the "settled policy" of former years was a favorite policy with both sections when extended to the acquisition of Indian lands, and that but few Indians now press their feet upon the banks of either the Ohio or the Tennessee. . .

Judging from all the instructions that Secretary Walker sent out on Indian matters in May of 1861, it would seem that he had very much at heart the enlistment of the Indians and their actual participation in the war. Mention has already been made of how General McCulloch was told by Adjutant-general Cooper to add, if possible, two Indian regiments to his brigade and of how Walker had written Hubbard urging him to persuade the Indians to join forces and raising the number of Indian regiments desired from two to three.   In a similar strain Walker wrote[237] to Douglas H. Cooper

---

[237]   WAR DEPARTMENT, C.S. ARMY, MONTGOMERY, May 13, 1861. MAJOR DOUGLAS H. COOPER, Choctaw Nation:

Sir: The desire of this Government is to cultivate the most friendly relations and the closest alliance with the Choctaw Nation and all the

on the occasion of definitely asking him to give his services to the South.   In all these letters no special stress was laid upon an intention to use the Indians as home guards exclusively.   On the contrary, one might easily draw, from the letters, a quite opposite inference and

Indian tribes west of Arkansas and south of Kansas. Appreciating your sympathies with these tribes, and their reciprocal regard for you, we have thought it advisable to enlist your services in the line of this desire.   From information in possession of the Government it is deemed expedient to take measures to secure the protection of these tribes in their present country from the agrarian rapacity of the North, that, unless opposed, must soon drive them from their homes and supplant them in their possessions, as, indeed, would have been the case with the entire South but for our present efforts at resistance.   It is well known that with these unjust designs against the Indian country the Northern movement for several years has had its emissaries scheming among the tribes for their ultimate destruction.   Their destiny has thus become our own, and common with that of all the Southern States entering this Confederation.

Entertaining these views and feelings, and with these objects before us, we have commissioned General Ben. McCulloch, with three regiments under his command, from the States of Arkansas, Texas, and Louisiana, to take charge of the military district embracing the Indian country, and I now empower you to raise among the Choctaws and Chickasaws a mounted regiment, to be commanded by yourself, in co-operation with General McCulloch.   It is designed also to raise two other similar regiments among the Creeks, Cherokees, Seminoles, and other friendly tribes for the same purpose.   This combined force of six regiments will be ample to secure the frontiers upon Kansas and the interests of the Indians, while to the south of the Red River three regiments from Texas, under a different command, have been already assigned to the Rio Grande and western border.

It will thus appear, I trust, that the resources of this Government are adequate to its ends, and assured to the friendly Indians.   We have our agents actively engaged in the manufacture of ammunition and in the purchase of arms, and when your regiment has been reported organized in ten companies, ranging from 64 to 100 men each, and enrolled for twelve months, if possible, it will be received into the Confederate service, and supplied with arms and ammunition.   Such will be the course pursued also in relation to the two other regiments I have indicated.

The arms we are purchasing for the Indians are rifles, and they will be forwarded to Fort Smith.   Respectfully,

L. P. WALKER, Secretary of War.

Official Records, first ser., vol. iii, 574-575.

conclude that the Indian troops, if raised, were to be used very generally and exactly as any other volunteers might be used. This is important in view of the stand, and a very positive one it was, that Albert Pike took some time afterwards. In his own letter[238] to Johnson of May 11, 1861, he does not specifically say that the Indian soldiers, whose mustering he has in contemplation, are not to be used outside of the Indian country; but he does insist that that country be occupied by them and by a certain number of white regiments – another important point as subsequent events will divulge.

General McCulloch took up his part of the task of securing the Indians in his own characteristic way. He had great energy and great enthusiasm and both qualities were displayed to the fullest extent on the present occasion. He first laid his plans for taking possession forthwith of the Indian country, it having come to his knowledge that Colonel Emory with the Federal forces had abandoned it.[239] Apparently, it had never occurred to McCulloch that the Indians themselves might be averse to such a proceeding on his part but he was soon made aware of it; for when he consulted[240] with John Ross, he found, to his discomfiture and deep chagrin, that the desire and the determination of this greatest of all the Indians was to remain strictly neutral. On the twelfth of June, McCulloch still further communicated[241] with Ross and informed him that he would respect his wishes in so far as expediency justified but that he would have to insist upon the inherent right of the individual Cherokees to organize themselves into a force

[238] *Official Records*, first ser., vol. iii, 572-574.

[239] — *Ibid.*, 583.

[240] See McCulloch to Walker, May 28, 1861, *ibid.*, 587; also same to same, June 12, 1861, *ibid.*, 590-591.

[241] — *Ibid.*, 591-592; also vol. xiii, 495.

of Home Guards should they feel so inclined.   Then
he closed his letter by this note of warning:

> Should a body of men march into your Territory from the
> North, or if I have an intimation that a body is in line of march
> for the Territory from that quarter, I must assure you that I
> will at once advance into your country, if I deem it advisable.

Once again the forbearance of Chief Ross had been
put to a severe test, but he none the less replied to Mc-
Culloch with his customary dignity.   Ross was then at
Park Hill, McCulloch at Fort Smith, where he had
halted hoping that the permission would be forthcoming for him to cross the line.   Ross's reply [242] came by
return mail, so to speak, and was dated the seventeenth.
It was largely a reiteration of the reasons he had already given for preserving neutrality, but it was also
a positive refusal to allow the individual Cherokees to
organize a Home Guard.   The concluding paragraph
gives the lie direct to those intriguing and self-interested politicians who, in later years, endeavored to im-
pugn Ross's sincerity:

> Your demand that those people of the nation who are in
> favor of joining the Confederacy be allowed to organize into
> military companies as Home Guards, for the purpose of defend-
> ing themselves in case of invasion from the North, is most re-
> spectfully declined.   I cannot give my consent to any such or-
> ganization for very obvious reasons: First, it would be a pal-
> pable violation of my position as a neutral; second, it would
> place in our midst organized companies not authorized by our
> laws but in violation of treaty, and who would soon become
> efficient instruments in stirring up domestic strife and creating
> internal difficulties among the Cherokee people.   As in this
> connection you have misapprehended a remark made in conver-
> sation at our interview some eight or ten days ago, I hope you
> will allow me to repeat what I did say.   I informed you that I

---

[242] General Files, *Cherokee, 1859-1865*, C515; *Official Records*, first ser., vol.
iii, 596-597 and vol. xiii, 495-497.

had taken a neutral position, and would maintain it honestly, but that in case of a foreign invasion, old as I am, I would assist in repelling it. . .

It will develop later how Ross's wishes with respect to the enrollment of Home Guards were successfully and adroitly circumvented, with the connivance of General McCulloch, by men of the Ridge faction in Cherokee politics. From the beginning, McCulloch seemed determined not to take Ross seriously, yet he duly informed Secretary Walker of the turn events were taking. On the twelfth of June, for instance, he wrote[243] to him and gave an account of his recent interview with the Cherokee chief. It was rather a misleading account, however; for it conveyed to Walker the idea that Ross was only waiting for provocation from the North to throw in his lot with the Confederacy. On the twenty-second of June, McCulloch wrote[244] to Walker again

---

[243] *Official Records*, first ser., vol. iii, 590-591.

[244]
HEADQUARTERS McCULLOCH'S BRIGADE,
Fort Smith, Ark., June 22, 1861.

HON. L. P. WALKER, Secretary of War:

Sir: I have the honor to transmit the inclosed copy of a communication from John Ross, the principal chief of the Cherokee Nation.

Under all the circumstances of the case I do not think it advisable to march into the Cherokee country at this time unless there is some urgent necessity for it. If the views expressed in my communication to you of the 14th instant are carried out, it will, I am satisfied, force the conviction on the Cherokees that they have but one course to pursue – that is, to join the Confederacy. The Choctaw and Chickasaw regiment will be kept on the south of them; Arkansas will be to the east; and with my force on the western border of Missouri no force will be able to march into the Cherokee Nation, and surrounded as they will be by Southern troops, they will have but one alternative at all events. From my position to the north of them, in any event, I will have a controlling power over them. I am satisfied from my interview with John Ross and from his communication that he is only waiting for some favorable opportunity to put himself with the North. His neutrality is only a pretext to await the issue of events.

I have the honor to be, sir, your obedient servant,
BEN. McCULLOCH, Brigadier-General Commanding.
Official Records, first ser., vol. iii, 595-596.

and to the same effect as far as his belief that Ross was not sincere in his professions of neutrality was concerned, even though, in the interval between the two letters, he had been carefully corrected by Ross himself and even though he was, at the very time, sending on to Richmond, the correspondence that denied the truth of his own statement. He did, however, add that his belief now was that Ross was awaiting a favorable moment to join forces with the North.

Albert Pike, special commissioner from the State Department of the Confederate States to the Indian tribes west of Arkansas, had accompanied General McCulloch on his visit to Ross, the latter part of May, and had been present at the resulting interview. He had told[245] Toombs that he would leave Little Rock for Fort Smith the twenty-second and go at once[246] to the Cherokee country. At Fort Smith, Pike met McCulloch and the two, seeking the same object, agreed to go forward together,[247] having already been approached by an anti-Ross element of the Cherokee Nation.[248] Ross, as has been shown, insisted upon maintaining an attitude of strict neutrality, which probably did not surprise his interviewers, since, according to Pike's own testimony, he and McCulloch had not gone to Park Hill expecting to be able to effect any arrangement with Chief Ross.[249] Ross, however, did go so far

---

[245] See Pike to Toombs, May 20, 1861 [*Official Records*, first ser., vol. iii, 580-581].

[246] On the twenty-ninth of May, Pike wrote to Toombs again and informed him that he was leaving for Tahlequah that very morning [*ibid.*, fourth ser., vol. i, 359].

[247] See McCulloch to Walker, May 28, 1861 [*Ibid.*, first ser., vol. iii, 587-588].

[248] See Pike to Cooley, February 17, 1866 [Indian Office, *Miscellaneous Files*].

[249] — *Ibid.*

as to promise[250] that within a short while he would call a meeting of the Cherokee Executive Council and confer with it further on the policy to be pursued. Ross doubtless felt that it was a part of political wisdom to do this. His was an exceedingly difficult position; for, within the nation, there was a large element in favor of secession. It was a minority party, it is true; but, none the less, it represented for the most part, the intelligence and the property and the influence of the tribe. Opposed to it and in favor of neutrality, was the large majority, not nearly so influential because made up of the full-bloods and of those otherwise poverty-stricken and obscure. In the light of previous tribal discords, the minority party was the old Ridge, or Treaty, Party, now headed by Stand Watie and E. C. Boudinot, while the majority party was the Ross, or Non-treaty Party. Ross himself, his nephew, William P. Ross, and a few others were the great exceptions to the foregoing characterization of their following. Of sturdy Scotch extraction and honest to the core, they personally stood out in strong contrast to the rank and file of the non-secessionists and it was they who so guided public sentiment that John Ross had the nation back of him when, on May 17, 1861, he issued his memorable Proclamation of Neutrality:[251]

Proclamation to the Cherokee people

Owing to the momentous state of affairs pending among the people of the several States, I, John Ross, Principal Chief, hereby issue this my proclamation to the people of the Cherokee Nation, reminding them of the obligations arising under their treaties with the United States, and urging them to the faithful

---

[250] McCulloch to Walker, June 12, 1861 [*Official Records*, first ser., vol. iii, 591].

[251] *Official Records*, first ser., vol. xiii, 489-490.

observance of said treaties by the maintenance of peace and friendship toward the people of all the States.

The better to obtain these important ends, I earnestly impress upon all my fellow-citizens the propriety of attending to their ordinary avocations and abstaining from unprofitable discussions of events transpiring in the States and from partisan demonstrations in regard to the same.

They should not be alarmed by false reports thrown into circulation by designing men, but cultivate harmony among themselves and observe in good faith strict neutrality between the States threatening civil war. By these means alone can the Cherokee people hope to maintain their rights unimpaired and to have their own soil and firesides spared from the baleful effects of a devastating war. There has been no declaration of war between the opposing parties, and the conflict may yet be averted by compromise or a peaceful separation.

The peculiar circumstances of their condition admonish the Cherokees to the exercise of prudence in regard to a state of affairs to the existence of which they have in no way contributed; and they should avoid the performance of any act or the adoption of any policy calculated to destroy or endanger their territorial and civil rights. By honest adherence to this course they can give no just cause for aggression or invasion nor any pretext for making their country the scene of military operations, and will be in a situation to claim and retain all their rights in the final adjustment that will take place between the several States. For these reasons I earnestly impress upon the Cherokee people the importance of non-interference in the affairs of the people of the States and the observance of unswerving neutrality between them.

Trusting that God will not only keep from our own borders the desolations of war, but that He will in infinite mercy and power stay its ravages among the brotherhood of States.

Given under my hand at the executive office at Park Hill this 17th day of May, 1861.

JNO. ROSS, Principal Chief Cherokee Nation.

The discretion of the Cherokees, their wily diplomacy if, under the circumstances, you should please to call it such, was more than counterbalanced by the indiscretion and the impetuosity of some of their neighbors. It has already been noted how the Chickasaws expressed their southern sympathies in the legislative resolves[252] of the twenty-fifth of May, but not as yet how the Choctaws took an equally strong stand. Both tribes were so very pronounced in their show of affection for the Confederacy that they gave a secessionist color to the whole of the Indian Territory, so much so, in fact, that Lieutenant-colonel Hyams could report[253] to Governor Moore of Louisiana, on the twenty-eighth of May, and upon information given him by some Indian agent.

. . . That the nations on the borders of this State (Arkansas) are anxious and desirous to be armed; that they can and will muster into the service 25,000 men; that they have immense supplies of beeves, sufficient to supply the meat for the whole Confederate service. All they ask is arms and enrollment. If within your power to forward their views with the President, it would be a great step in the right direction, and erect a more effectual barrier against the Kansas marauders than any force that could be sent against them, and thereby protect the northern boundary of both Arkansas and Louisiana. The reasons why every effort should be made to arm these people (now heart and soul with us) to defend themselves and us are so palpable, that I do not attempt to urge them upon you, but do solicit your attention, so far as is compatible with your high position, to this matter, to impress its importance on the President, and use your well-known influence to effect this much desirable result. . .

General McCulloch, in a letter[254] also of the twenty-eighth of May, more particularly specified the tribes that were friendly to the South, but he too mentioned some of them, the Choctaw and the Chickasaw, as "anxious to join the Southern Confederacy." It should not be a matter of surprise then to find that on the four-

[252] *Official Records*, first ser., vol. iii, 585-587.
[253] — *Ibid.*, 589.
[254] — *Ibid.*, 587.

teenth of June, George Hudson, principal chief of the Choctaw Nation, acting in accordance with the will of the General Council, which had met four days before, publicly declared[255] the Choctaw Nation, "free and *independent.*" The chief's proclamation was, in effect, a conscription act and provided for the enrollment, for military service in the interests of the Confederacy, of all competent males between the ages of eighteen and forty-five years. The General Council had authorized this and had further arranged for the appointment of commissioners "to negotiate a treaty of alliance and amity" with the Confederate States.

Under such conditions, the work of Albert Pike must have seemed all plain sailing when once he was safely beyond the Cherokee limits; but his efforts,[256] vain though they were, to persuade that tribe into an alliance did not end[257] with the first recorded interview with Ross. He kept up his intercourse with the Ridge faction; but finally decided that as far as Ross and the nation as a whole were concerned it would be best to await the issue of events. It was only too apparent to all the southern agents and commissioners that Ross would never yield his opinion unless compelled thereto by one of three things or a combination of any or all of them. The three things were, pressure from within the tribe; some extraordinary display of Confederate strength that would presage ultimate success for southern arms; and encroachment by the Federals. It was the com-

---

[255] — *Ibid.*, 593-594.

[256] See Albert Pike to John Ross, June 6, 1861 and John Ross to Albert Pike, July 1, 1861 in General Files, *Cherokee, 1859-1865,* C515.

[257] It would appear that, failing with John Ross, Pike tried to negotiate with the disaffected Cherokees under the control of Stand Watie, Boudinot, and others. See *Office Letter* to President Johnson, February 25, 1866. Pike himself says that he invited some of these men to meet him at the Creek Agency. See Pike to Cooley, February 17, 1866.

bination that eventually won the day. Pike, meanwhile, had passed on to the Creek country.

At the North Fork Village, in the Creek country, the work of negotiating Indian treaties in the interests of the Confederacy really began and it did not end until a rather long series of them had been concluded. The series consisted of nine main treaties [258] and the nine group themselves into three distinct classes. The basis of classification is the relative strength or power of the tribe, or better, the degree of concession which the Confederacy, on account of that strength or that power or under stress of its own dire needs, felt itself obliged to make. This is the list as classified:

FIRST CLASS

1. Creek, negotiated at North Fork, Creek Nation, July [259] 10, 1861
2. Choctaw and Chickasaw, negotiated at North Fork, July 12, 1861
3. Seminole, negotiated at the Seminole Council House, August 1, 1861
4. Cherokee, negotiated at Tahlequah, Chreokee Nation, October 7, 1861

SECOND CLASS

1. Osage, negotiated at Park Hill, Cherokee Nation, October 2, 1861
2. Seneca and Shawnee, negotiated at Park Hill, October 4, 1861
3. Quapaw, negotiated at Park Hill, October 4, 1861

---

[258] The text of the treaties is to be found in the *Confederate Statutes* and also in *Official Records*, fourth ser., vol. i, as follows:

Creek Treaty, 426-443
Choctaw and Chickasaw Treaty, 445-466
Seminole Treaty, 513-527
Wichita Treaty, 542-548
Comanche Treaty, 548-554
Osage Treaty, 636-646
Seneca and Shawnee Treaty, 647-658
Quapaw Treaty, 659-666
Cherokee Treaty, 669-687

[259] Although the Creek Treaty was negotiated July tenth and was the first to be negotiated, Dole was ignorant of its existence as late as October second

THIRD CLASS

1. Wichita, etc., negotiated at the Wichita Agency near the False Washita River, August 12, 1861
2. Comanche, negotiated at the Wichita Agency, August 12, 1861

Although all the treaties, made in 1861 by Albert Pike, were negotiated under authority[260] of the Act of the Provisional Congress of the Confederate States, approved May 21, 1861, by which the Confederacy offered and agreed to accept the protectorate of the Indian tribes west of Arkansas and Missouri, only those made with the great tribes contained a statement,[261] definitely showing that the protectorate had been formally offered, formally accepted and formally assumed. Thus, in a very unequivocal way, Creeks, Choctaws, Chickasaws, Seminoles, and Cherokees, all signified[262] their willingness to transfer their allegiance from the United to the Confederate States. The smaller tribes seem not to have been asked to make the same concession and their nationality was, in no sense, recognized. They acted more or less under duress or compulsion, and the very negotiation of treaties with them was taken as a full compliance with the confederate scheme.

The nationality of the great tribes, or more properly speaking, their political importance, was still further

---

[*Report*, 1861, 39], which only goes to prove how very slight was the Federal communication with Indian Territory through all that critical time.

[260] President Davis, in his message of December 12, 1861, said,

Considering this act as a declaration by Congress of our future policy in relation to those Indians, a copy of that act was transmitted to the commissioner and he was directed to consider it as his instructions in the contemplated negotiation. [Richardson, *Messages and Papers of the Confederacy*, vol. i, 149; *Official Records*, fourth ser., vol. i, 785.]

[261] All the treaties of the First Class contain a *Preamble*, lacking in the others, which specifically outlines the assumption of the protectorate. In addition, those same treaties have a special clause accepting the full force of the Act of May twenty-first.

All references to these treaties, unless otherwise noted, will be page refer-

recognized by clauses guaranteeing territorial and political integrity,[263] representation by delegates[264] in the

ences to the treaties as found in the *Statutes at Large* of the Provisional Government of the Confederate States of America.

[262] See Creek Treaty, Articles II and IV, pp. 289, 290; Choctaw and Chickasaw Treaty, Articles II and VII, pp. 312, 313; Seminole Treaty, Articles II and IV, pp. 332, 333; Cherokee Treaty, Articles II and V, pp. 395, 396.

[263] ARTICLE VIII (Creek Treaty). The Confederate States of America do hereby solemnly agree and bind themselves that no State or Territory shall ever pass laws for the government of the Creek Nation; and that no portion of the country hereby guaranteed to it shall ever be embraced or included within or annexed to any Territory or Province; nor shall any attempt ever be made, except upon the free, voluntary and unsolicited application of the said nation, to erect the said country, by itself or with any other, into a State or any other territorial or political organization, or to incorporate it into any State previously created [p. 291].

Compare with similar articles in the other treaties; viz., Article X of the Choctaw and Chickasaw, p. 314; Article VIII of the Seminole, p. 334; Article VIII of the Cherokee, p. 397; Articles VIII and XXVI of the Osage, pp. 364, 367; Articles VIII and XIX of the Seneca and Shawnee, pp. 376, 377; Article VII of the Quapaw, p. 387.

[264] ARTICLE XL (Creek Treaty). In order to enable the Creek and Seminole Nations to claim their rights and secure their interests without the intervention of counsel or agents, and as they were originally one and the same people and are now entitled to reside in the country of each other, they shall be jointly entitled to a delegate to the House of Representatives of the Confederate States of America, who shall serve for the term of two years, and be a member of one of the said nations, over twenty-one years of age, and labouring under no legal disability by the law of either nation; and each delegate shall be entitled to the same rights and privileges as may be enjoyed by delegates from any territories of the Confederate States to the said House of Representatives. Each shall receive such pay and mileage as shall be fixed by the Congress of the Confederate States. The first election for delegate shall be held at such time and places, and be conducted in such manner as shall be prescribed by the agent of the Confederate States, to whom returns of such election shall be made, and he shall declare the person having the greatest number of votes to be duly elected, and give him a certificate of election accordingly, which shall entitle him to his seat. For all subsequent elections, the times, places, and manner of holding them and ascertaining and certifying the result shall be prescribed by law of the Confederate States [p. 297].

Compare with Article XXVII of Choctaw and Chickasaw Treaty [p. 318], the chief point of difference between the two being that, in the latter treaty the delegate to which the two tribes, parties to the treaty, were entitled jointly,

Confederate Congress, and the prospect[265] of ultimate statehood.   The guarantee of territorial integrity was,

was to be elected from them alternately.   The Choctaw and Chickasaw Treaty also stipulated that the delegate was to be a member by birth or blood on either the father's or the mother's side.   The corresponding provision in the Cherokee Treaty, Article XLIV [pp. 403-404], said that the delegate should be a native born citizen.   The Seminole arrangement, Article XXXVII [p. 339], was, as might be expected, exactly the same as the Creek.

[265] The Choctaw and Chickasaw Treaty was the only one that developed this idea.   We might presume that the Creeks were even opposed to it.   This is how it appears in Articles XXVIII, XXIX, and XXX, of the Choctaw and Chickasaw Treaty [pp. 318-319]:

ARTICLE XXVIII.   In consideration of the uniform loyalty and good faith, and the tried friendship for the people of the Confederate States, of the Choctaw and Chickasaw people, and of their fitness and capacity for self-government, proven by the establishment and successful main- tenance, by each, of a regularly organized republican government, with all the forms and safe-guards to which the people of the Confederate States are accustomed, it is hereby agreed by the Confederate States, that whenever and so soon as the people of each nation shall, by ordi- nance of a convention of delegates, duly elected by majorities of the legal voters, at an election regularly held after due and ample notice, in pursuance of an act of the Legislature of each, respectively, declare its desire to become a State of the Confederacy, the whole Choctaw and Chickasaw country, as above defined, shall be received and admitted into the Confederacy as one of the Confederate States, on equal terms, in all respects, with the original States, without regard to population; and all the members of the Choctaw and Chickasaw Nations shall thereby become citizens of the Confederate States, not including, how- ever, among such members, the individuals of the bands settled in the leased district aforesaid.

Provided, That, as a condition precedent to such admission, the said nations shall provide for the survey of their lands, the holding in sev- eralty of parts thereof by their people, the dedication of at least one section in every thirty-six to purposes of education, and the sale of such portions as are not reserved for these, or other special purposes, to citi- zens of the Confederate States alone, on such terms as the said nation shall see fit to fix, not intended or calculated to prevent the sale thereof.

ARTICLE XXIX.   The proceeds of such sales shall belong entirely to members of the Choctaw and Chickasaw Nations, and be distributed among them or invested for them in proportion to the whole population of each, in such manner as the Legislatures of said nations shall pro- vide; nor shall any other persons ever have any interest in the annuities or funds of either the Choctaw or Chickasaw people, nor any power to legislate in regard thereto.

ARTICLE XXX.   Whenever the desire of the Creek and Seminole people and the Cherokees to become a part of the said State shall be

of a certainty, not new. It had been inserted into various removal treaties as a safeguard against a repetition of the injustice that had been meted out to the Indians by the Southern States in Jackson's day. It comprised, in effect, a solemn promise that no state or territorial lines should ever again circumscribe the particular domain of the Indian nation securing the guarantee; and that state or territorial laws, as the case might be, should have no operation within the Indian country. The idea of congressional representation [266] was also not new, but where it had previously been but a promise or a mere contingency, it was now an assured fact, a thing definitely provided for. Ultimate statehood had, however, attached to it the old time elements of uncertainty, which is not at all surprising, considering that Walker, in his instructions [267] to Hubbard, had positively spoken against it.

All the treaties, without distinction of class, recognized the land rights of the Indians and their existing territorial limits, but with the usual restriction upon alienation to foreign powers. A sale or cession to a foreign state, without the consent of the Confederate States, was to result in forfeiture and reversion to the Confederate States. By the Choctaw and Chickasaw Treaty, the arrangement,[268] already satisfactorily reached, for a Chickasaw country distinct from a Choc-

---

expressed, in the same manner and with the same formalities, as is above provided for in the case of the Choctaw and Chickasaw people, the country of the Creeks and Seminoles, and that of the Cherokees, respectively, or either by itself, may be annexed to and become an integral part of said State, upon the same conditions and terms, and with the same rights to the people of each, in regard to citizenship and the proceeds of their lands.

[266] Abel, "Proposals for an Indian State in the Union, 1778-1878," in the American Historical Association, *Report*, 1907, pp. 89-102.

[267] *Official Records*, first ser., vol. iii, 577.

[268] Articles V and VI.

taw was continued, the Indians of both tribes being given the privilege of having their particular land surveyed and sectionized whenever they might so please, provided it be done by regular legislative process.[269] The same treaty transferred[270] the lease of the Wichita Reserve from the United to the Confederate States and limited it to ninety-nine years. Practically the same bands of Indians were to be accommodated in this Leased District as before; namely, those whose permanent ranges were south of the Canadian or between it and the Arkansas. The New Mexican Indians were still to be absolutely excluded. The Choctaw and Chickasaw Indians reserved the right to pass upon the accommodation of any other Indians than those specifically mentioned in the treaty. The individual bands, so accommodated in the Leased District, were to be settled upon reserves and to hold the same in fee. Finally, the treaty placed,[271] for the time being, the Wichitas and their fellow reservees exclusively under the control of the Confederate States with a limited jurisdiction resting in the Choctaw Nation and a full right of settlement in Choctaws and Chickasaws.

In regard to special features of the land rights of tribes other than those already mentioned, it is well to observe, perhaps, that the title to the reservation then occupied by the Seminoles was admitted to be dependent upon Creek sufferance;[272] that the United States patent of December 31, 1838, was recognized[273] as protecting the Cherokee; and that the Osage lands in Kansas were inferentially covered by the Confederate guar-

---

[269] Article VIII.

[270] Article XI.

[271] Article XII.

[272] Article VII of the Seminole Treaty [p. 334], and Article VII likewise of the Creek Treaty [p. 291].

[273] Article IV of the Cherokee Treaty [pp. 395-396].

antee, given that tribe, of title in perpetuity.²⁷⁴ The Confederate States, moreover, agreed to indemnify²⁷⁵ the Cherokees should their Neutral Lands be lost to them through the misfortune of the war. It is rather interesting to see that this new government, in promising the insignificant tribes a permanent occupancy of their present holdings, made use of the same high-flown, meaningless language that the United States had so long used; but Albert Pike knew better than to assure the truly powerful tribes that they should hold their lands themselves and in common "as long as the grass should grow and the waters run." That language could yet be made appealing and effective, though, in official dealings with weak Wichitas,²⁷⁶ Senecas, and Shawnees,²⁷⁷ and, strange as it may seem, even with Creeks.²⁷⁸ In reciprocal fashion, the wild Comanches could most naïvely promise²⁷⁹ to hold the Confederate States "by the hand, and have but one heart with them always."

Speaking of indemnification, we are reminded of other very important financial obligations assumed by the Confederacy when it made its famous treaties with the Indians west of Arkansas. Those financial obligations comprised the payment of annuities due the tribes from the United States in return for land cessions of enormous extent. They also comprised the interest on various funds, such as the Orphan Creek fund, education funds, and the like. Albert Pike had been given no specific authority to do this but he knew well that no

---

²⁷⁴ In the matter of the guarantee of territorial integrity, the treaties of the Second Class were strictly on a par with those of the First Class. See Article VIII of the Osage Treaty [p. 364], Article XIX of the Seneca and Shawnee Treaty [p. 378], Article VII of the Quapaw [p. 387].

²⁷⁵ Article XLVII [pp. 407-408].

²⁷⁶ Article V [p. 348].

²⁷⁷ Article III [pp. 374-375].

²⁷⁸ Article V [p. 291].

²⁷⁹ Article I [p. 354].

treaties could possibly be made without it.   It was not very likely that the slaveholding tribes would surrender so much wealth for nothing, and so Pike argued, when justifying himself and his actions later on.   In his capacity as commissioner with plenary powers, he also promised the Indians that the Confederacy would see to it that their trust funds, secured by southern bonds, should be rendered safe and negotiable.   Over and above all this, the government of the Confederate States made itself responsible for claims for damages of various sorts that the different tribes had brought or were to bring against the United States.   Three good instances of the same are the following: the claim of the Cherokees for losses, personal and national, incident to the removal from Georgia; the claim[280] of the Sem-

---

[280] For an illustration of how the Seminoles had been preferring the claim, see the following affidavit:

Be it known that on this 22d day of January, A.D. 1856, personally appeared before me, J. W. Washbourne, United States' Agent for Seminoles, in open Council, the following named Chiefs and Head men of the Seminole tribe of Indians, and deposed to the subsequent statement.

That sometime during the war between the United States and the Seminoles, Gen. Thomas S. Jessup, then commanding the U.S. troops in Florida, issued a proclamation to the effect that all negroes belonging to the hostile Seminoles who should come in and take service under the Government against their masters, or in any way render service to the United States against the Seminoles, or induce them to sue for peace and emigrate west, they, the negroes, should be declared free: That many negroes took advantage of said illegal proclamation and did take service in Florida under Government, but that, by far the larger number of negro slaves who took refuge under said proclamation and thereby claimed their freedom, did so after the immigration west was determined or consummated: That said negro slaves, in great numbers and to the great injury of their owners, and against their orders, took refuge within the United States' post, Fort Gibson, Cherokee Nation, where they were for upwards of three years protected by the United States officers at that Post, although the Seminoles claimed them, the negroes, as their lawful slaves, and protested against this procedure of the U.S. officers: That while these negro slaves were thus protected by military officers, it was impossible to keep their slaves at home who were continually flying to Fort Gibson, where they were beyond the reach of their masters: That this occurred during the years 1845-'6-'7: That

inoles for losses sustained by reason of General Thomas

through the instrumentality of their former Sub Agent and attornies employed by them, they after long delay and at great expense and loss of slaves, presented the matter to the attention of the Secretary of War, Hon. Wm. L. Marcy, and that finally from him, as such Secretary of War, there issued an order bearing date the 5th of August 1848, directed to the commanding officer at Fort Gibson, enjoining him to protect no longer said negro slaves at that Post and commanding him to deliver all of said slaves to the Seminoles their rightful owners: That even after this order the nuisance did not abate, for another order dated July 31st 1850 required the commanding officer of Fort Gibson to give no further protection to these "Seminole negroes": That by this order of the Secretary of War, as was just and right, the United States recognised the ownership of these said slaves as being in the Seminoles, and that they were entitled by law and right to said slaves and their service: That in consequence of the withdrawal of the protection afforded them at Fort Gibson and from their having so long considered themselves free, said slaves in great numbers escaped, some of whom reached Mexico, some were killed by the wild Indians, and the remainder were only captured at great and ruinous expense: That the owners of these said negro slaves are justly and equitably entitled to the service of said slaves, while unlawfully and against the power and protests of the Seminoles, detained at Fort Gibson for the space of more than three years, by U.S. officers: That the number of said negro slaves so unlawfully detained and kept from the service due their masters, as near as now can be estimated was Two Hundred and Thirty-four or thereabouts: That the services of these said slaves for these three years and upwards were amply worth at the time Seventy five dollars each per annum, making the sum of Fifty two Thousand Six hundred and fifty dollars ($52.650.00,) to which the Seminole owners of said slaves are fully and fairly, in law and equity, entitled, and which ought to be paid to them by the Government of the United States.

JOHN JUMPER, P. Chief Seminoles X his mark

PAH SUC AH YO HO LAH, Speaker Council X his mark

CHITTO-TUSTO-MUGGEE X his mark

ARHAH-LOCK-TUSTO-MUGGEE X his mark

NOKE-SU-KEE X his mark

PARS-CO-FER X his mark

TESI-KI-AH X his mark

ALLIGATOR X his mark

TALLA-HASSA X his mark

GEORGE CLOUD X his mark

HO-TUL-GEE-HARJO X his mark

TAR-HAH FIXICO X his mark

Sworn to and subscribed before me, in open Council Jany 22d 1856.

J. W. WASHBOURNE U.S. Agent for Seminoles.

Witnesses: GEORGE M. AUD

S. Jesup's emancipation[281] order during the progress of the Second Seminole War; and the claim of the Wichitas against the United States government for having granted to the Choctaws the land that belonged by hereditary preëmption to them and had so belonged from time out of mind. It is exceedingly interesting to know that these Wichitas had been colonized on the very land they claimed as indisputably their own.

In all the treaties, negotiated by Pike, except the two of the Third Class,[282] the Wichita and the Comanche, the institution of slavery was positively and particularly recognized, recognized as legal and as having existed from time immemorial. Property rights in slaves were guaranteed. Fugitive Slave Laws were declared operative within the Indian country, and the mutual rendition of fugitives was promised throughout the length and breadth of the Confederacy. The First Class of treaties differs from the Second in this matter but only in a very slight degree. The latter condenses in one clause[283] all that bears upon slavery in its various aspects, the former separates the discussion of the legality of the institution from that of the rendition of slaves. Of the First Class, the Creek Treaty[284] constituted the

---

[281] President Polk seems to have been of the opinion that negro slaves could not be freed by military proclamation [*Diary* (Quaife's edition), vol. iii, 504].

[282] Slavery was not completely ignored even in the treaties of the Third Class. In Article IX of their treaty [p. 348], the Wichitas promised to do all in their power to take and return any negroes, horses, or other property stolen from white men or from Indians of the great tribes. The corresponding article in the Comanche Treaty [p. 355], was to like purpose.

[283] Article XXXVII of the Osage Treaty, Article XXVIII of the Seneca and Shawnee Treaty, and Article XXVIII of the Quapaw Treaty.

[284] The following are the Creek clauses and the Choctaw and Chickasaw, Articles XLV and XLVII, the Seminole, Articles XXIX and XXXIII, and the Cherokee, Articles XXXIV and XXXVII, are similar:

ARTICLE XXIX. The provisions of all such acts of Congress of the Confederate States as may now be in force, or may hereafter be enacted, for the purpose of carrying into effect the provision of the constitution

model; of the Second, the Osage.[285]

Aside from the things to which reference has already been made, the Confederate Indian treaties were, in a variety of ways and to the same extent that the Confederate constitution itself was, a reflection upon past history. To avoid the friction that had always been present between the red men and their neighbors, an attempt was now made to redefine and to readjust the relations of Indians with each other both within and without the tribe; their relations with white men considered apart from any political organization; their relations, either as individuals or as tribes, with the several states of the Confederacy; and their relations with the central government. In general, their rights, civil, political, and judicial, as men and as semi-independent communities were now specified under such conditions as made for what in times past would have been regarded as full recognition, and even for enlargement. Indian rights were at a premium because Indian alliances were in demand.

---

in regard to the re-delivery or return of fugitive slaves, or fugitives from labour and service, shall extend to, and be in full force within the said Creek Nation; and shall also apply to all cases of escape of fugitive slaves from the said Creek Nation into any other Indian nation or into one of the Confederate States, the obligation upon each such nation or State to re-deliver such slaves being in every case as complete as if they had escaped from another State, and the mode of procedure the same [p. 296].

ARTICLE XXXII. It is hereby declared and agreed that the institution of slavery in the said nation is legal and has existed from time immemorial; that slaves are taken and deemed to be personal property; that the title to slaves and other property having its origin in the said nation, shall be determined by the laws and customs thereof; and that the slaves and other personal property of every person domiciled in said nation shall pass and be distributed at his or her death, in accordance with the laws, usages and customs of the said nation, which may be proved like foreign laws, usages & customs, and shall everywhere he held valid and binding within the scope of their operation [p. 296].

[285] P. 369.

The relations of Indians with Indians need not be considered at length. Suffice it to say that many clauses were devoted to the regulation of the affairs of those tribes that were, either politically or ethnologically, closely connected with each other; as, for example, the Choctaws and Chickasaws on the one hand and the Creeks and Seminoles on the other. Still other clauses assured the tribes of protection against hostile invasion from red men and from white, and assured all the great tribes, except the Cherokees,[286] of similar protection against domestic violence.[287] The Cherokees, very possibly, were made an exception because of the known intensity of their factional strife and hatred, which, purely for its own selfish ends, the Confederacy had done so much to augment. There may also have been some lingering doubt of John Ross's sincerity in the matter of devotion to the Confederacy. The time had been and might come again when the Confederacy would find it very expedient to play off one faction against another. Injuries coming to the Indians from a failure to protect were to be indemnified out of the Confederate treasury. Could the United States, throughout the more than a hundred years of its history have had just such a law, its national treasury would have been saved millions and

---

[286] Article XVII of the Cherokee Treaty [p. 399].

[287] ARTICLE XV (Creek Treaty). The Confederate States shall protect the Creeks from domestic strife, from hostile invasion, and from aggression by other Indians and white persons not subject to the jurisdiction and laws of the Creek Nation, and for all injuries resulting from such invasion or aggression, full indemnity is hereby guaranteed to the party or parties injured, out of the Treasury of the Confederate States, upon the same principle and according to the same rules upon which white persons are entitled to indemnity for injuries or aggressions upon them committed by Indians [p. 293].

See also Article XXI of the Choctaw and Chickasaw Treaty and Article XV of the Seminole Treaty.

millions of dollars paid out in claims, just and unjust, of white men against the Indians.

As affecting their relations with white men, the Indians were conceded the right to determine absolutely, by their own legislation, the conditions of their own tribal citizenship. This would mean, of course, the free continuance of the custom of adoption, a custom more pernicious in Indian history than even the principle of equal apportionment in Frankish; because it was the entering wedge to territorial encroachment. The white man, once adopted into the tribe as a citizen, was to be protected against unjust discrimination or against the forfeiture of his acquired status. The provisions against intruders were legitimately severe, those of the United States had never been severe enough. The executive power had always been very weak and very lax but now it was to reside in the tribal Council and would bid fair to be firm because interested, or, perhaps, we should say disinterested. The Confederacy, on its part, promised that the aid of the military should be forthcoming for the expulsion of intruders on application by the agent, should the tribal authority prove inadequate. The Indians might compel the removal of obnoxious men from agency and military reserves. Unauthorized settlement within the Indian country by citizens of the Confederate States was absolutely forbidden under pain of punishment by the tribe encroached upon.

With respect to Indian trade, there was considerable innovation and considerable modification of existing laws. For years past, the Indians of the great tribes had chafed under the restrictions which the United States government had placed upon their trade and, unquestionably, no other single thing had irritated them more than the very evident monopoly right which the United States had given to a few white men over it. Indian trade, under federal regulations, was nothing more nor less than an extension of the protective policy, a policy that was destructive of all competition and that put the Indian, often to the contempt of his intelligence, at the mercy of the white sharper. Indian commissioner after Indian commissioner had protested against it, but all in vain. George W. Manypenny, particularly, had tried [288] to effect a change; for he was himself convinced that, if the Indians were capable of self-government, they were certainly capable of conducting their own trade. Needless to say, Manypenny's efforts were entirely unavailing. The Indian trade in the hands of the licensed white trader, although a pernicious thing for the Indian, was an exceedingly lucrative business for enterprising American citizens, white men who were, unfortunately, in possession of the elective franchise but of little else that was honorable and the government, controlled by constituents with local interests, dared not surrender it to the unenfranchised Indians no matter how highly competent they might be. Thus the Indian country, throughout its entire extent, was exploited for the sake of the frontiersman. Moreover, the annuity money, a just tax upon a government that had received so much real estate from the aborigines, instead of being spent judiciously to meet the ends of civilization and in such a way as to reflect credit upon the donor, who after all was a self-constituted guardian, went right back into the pockets of United States citizens but, of necessity, into those of only a very limited number of them.

[288] Manypenny to Dean, November 30, 1855 [Indian Office, *Letter Book*, no. 53, pp. 94-95]. Dean to Manypenny, December 25, 1855 [*Letter Press Book*].

Because it was a matter of expediency and not because it was a principle that it believed in, otherwise it would have given it to the weak tribes as well as to the strong, the Confederacy gave to the Indians of the great tribes, but not to all in exactly the same measure,[289] the control of their own trade. It did not do away with the post trader, as it ought to have done in order to make its reform complete, but it did deprive him of his monopoly privileges. It hedged his license about with restrictions,[290] made it subject, on complaint of the Indian and in the event of arrearages, to revocation; and, to all of the great tribes except the Seminoles, it gave the power of taxing his goods, his stock in trade, usually a rather paltry outfit. No better precaution could have possibly been devised against exorbitant charging. An ad valorem tax would most certainly have quite eliminated the fifty, the one hundred, and the two hundred per cents of profit. As a matter of fact, the extravagantly high prices of the ordinary Indian trader would be, for most persons, positively prohibitive. The Confederacy further bound itself to pay to the Indians an annual compensation for the land and timber used by the trader.

The questions settled as between the several states and the Indian tribes were chiefly[291] of property rights and

---

[289] Compare Article xx of the Cherokee Treaty and Article xxiv of the Choctaw and Chickasaw Treaty with Article xvi of the Creek Treaty and all of these with Article xvi of the Seminole Treaty.

[290] See, for example, Article xviii of the Seminole Treaty [p. 336].

[291] One other important right was conceded and that was the right of free transit. The concession is well stated in the Creek Treaty and occurs in connection with a prohibition against the pasturing of stock by outsiders within the Creek country.

ARTICLE XXII. No citizen or inhabitant of the Confederate States shall pasture stock on the lands of the Creek Nation, under the penalty of one dollar per head for all so pastured, to be collected by the authorities of the nation; but their citizens shall be at liberty at all times, and

of civil and criminal rights and procedure. In addition to their property right in slaves, the Indians were at last admitted to have a possible right in other things, in land, for instance, that might lie within the limits of a state. This they were henceforth to hold, dispose of as they pleased, and bequeath by will.[292] Restrictions, likewise, upon their power freely to dispose of their chattels,[293] were removed, a coördinate concession, but one that did not so much affect their relations with a given individual state as their relations with the central government. To such[294] of the Indians as were not to be brought within the jurisdiction of the Confederate States District Courts[295] that were to be created within the Indian country, the right was given to sue and to implead in any of the courts of the several states. To Indians generally of the great tribes was given the right to be held competent as witnesses[296] in state courts, and, if indicted there themselves, to subpoena witnesses and to employ counsel.[297] The Cherokees, the Choc-

whether for business or pleasure, peaceably to travel the Creek country; and to drive their stock to market or otherwise through the same, and to halt such reasonable time on the way as may be necessary to recruit their stock, such delay being in good faith for that purpose.

ARTICLE XXIII. It is also further agreed that the members of the Creek Nation shall have the same right of travelling, driving stock and halting to recruit the same in any of the Confederate States as is given citizens of the Confederate States by the preceding aricle [p. 295].

[292] Article LXV of the Creek Treaty, Article XXVI of the Choctaw and Chickasaw Treaty, Article XXXI of the Seminole Treaty, and Article XXII of the Cherokee Treaty.

[293] Article XVIII of the Creek Treaty, Article XXV of the Choctaw and Chickasaw Treaty, Article XIX of the Seminole Treaty, and Article XXI of the Cherokee Treaty.

[294] Article LXV of the Creek Treaty and Article XXXI of the Seminole Treaty.

[295] Tush-ca-hom-ma at Boggy Depot and Cha-lah-ki at Tahlequah.

[296] Article XXX of the Creek Treaty, Article XLIII of the Choctaw and Chickasaw Treaty, Article XXX of the Seminole Treaty, and Article XXXV of the Cherokee Treaty.

[297] Article XXVIII of the Creek Treaty, Article XLIV of the Choctaw and

taws, and the Chickasaws were also granted the right of recovery [298] as against citizens of the Confederate States. Should recovery not be possible, the Confederacy was to stand the loss. But more than anything else reciprocal right of extradition was henceforth to be accorded. This was to exist as between tribe and tribe [299] and, with some slight exceptions, as between tribe and state. An examination of the various treaties reveals a steady development in the matter of this concession. The Creek Treaty,[300] which was the first to be negotiated, made extradition a rather one-sided [301] affair. The tribe was to yield the criminal to the state, but, not reciprocally, the state to the tribe. This verbal inequality would not have so much mattered had there been a possibility that in the sequel it would have been interpreted, as in the

Chickasaw Treaty, Article xxviii of the Seminole Treaty, Article xxxiii of the Cherokee Treaty, Article xxxvi of the Osage Treaty, Article xxvii of the Seneca and Shawnee Treaty, and Article xxvii of the Quapaw Treaty.

[298] Article xxix of the Cherokee Treaty and Article xxiii of the Choctaw and Chickasaw Treaty.

[299] ARTICLE XXXI (Cherokee Treaty). Any person duly charged with a criminal offence against the laws of either the Creek, Seminole, Choctaw or Chickasaw Nations, and escaping into the jurisdiction of the Cherokee Nation, shall be promptly surrendered upon the demand of the proper authority of the nation within whose jurisdiction the offence shall be alleged to have been committed; and in like manner, any person duly charged with a criminal offence against the laws of the Cherokee Nation, and escaping into the jurisdiction of either of the said nations, shall be promptly surrendered upon the demand of the proper authority of the Cherokee Nation [pp. 401-402].

Note the development from the corresponding extradition clause in the earlier treaties of the series. In the Creek and Seminole treaties, extradition was as between Creeks and Seminoles exclusively. In the Choctaw and Chickasaw Treaty, it was as between Choctaws and Chickasaws exclusively. In this treaty of the Cherokees, all the tribes were to be sharers in the extradition privilege; but it is difficult to understand how a clause in the Cherokee Treaty could be made legally binding upon other Indians than Cherokee.

[300] Article xxvi.

[301] It was also a one-sided affair in the treaties of the Second Class. See Article xxxiv of the Osage Treaty, Article xxv of the Seneca and Shawnee Treaty, and Article xxv of the Quapaw Treaty.

states, in terms of executive courtesy and discretion; but the chances were that a state would have made it a matter of absolute obligation with the tribe. Reciprocity[302] found its way into the second treaty, however, and also into all the later ones of the First Class. Finally, be it remarked, that as a climax to this series of judicial concessions, full faith and credit[303] were to be given by the one Indian nation or Confederate state, as the case might be, to all legal processes, decisions, and acts of the other.

There yet remain two provisions[304] of importance that were intended to put the Indian nations on a basis of equality with the states. They are provisions rather particular in their nature, however, and, in their full operation, would have affected Texas and Arkansas much more nearly than any other members of the Southern Confederacy. The first of these provisions is to be found, as a grant of mutual rights, only in treaties of the First Class and in two only of those, the Choctaw and Chickasaw and the Cherokee. The omission from the Creek and Seminole treaties was due, most likely, to geographical conditions; but the lack of reciprocity in the Osage, the one treaty of the Second Class in which a suggestion of the provision occurs, was just as surely due to the weakness of the tribe from which the privilege was exacted. The provision comprehended the use of navigable streams within the limits of the Confederacy and the Indians specified

302 Article xxxvii of the Choctaw and Chickasaw Treaty [p. 320], and Article xxxii of the Cherokee Treaty [p. 402].

303 Article xxxi of the Creek Treaty, Article xlvi of the Choctaw and Chickasaw Treaty, Article xxxii of the Seminole Treaty, and Article xxxvi of the Cherokee Treaty. Note that the enjoyment of the privilege by the Seminole Nation was to be conditioned upon its own establishment of regular courts.

304 There were also secret articles to some of the treaties. The indications are that such secret articles entailed the customary bribery of chiefs and influential men upon whose support depended successful negotiation.

were to have the same rights in the premises as the citizens of the Confederate States. Osage[305] streams and water courses were, however, to be open to white people but not conversely Confederate waters to the Osages. The clauses in treaties of the First Class, embodying this provision, comprehended all navigable streams whatsoever but had particular application to the Red and Arkansas Rivers, the Choctaw[306] and Chickasaw to the former and the Cherokee[307] to the latter. The rights of ferrying on these streams were to be open alike to white and red men living upon their banks.

The second provision was couched in terms of general amnesty. The Indians were to forgive wholesale the citizens of the individual Confederate states for their past offences and, reciprocally, the states were to forgive and pardon the Indians for theirs, or, rather, the government of the Confederate States was to use its good offices to persuade and induce them to do so.[308] The Choctaw and Chickasaw Treaty contained, in addition to this general clause, a particular one bringing out again the close connection with Texas and Arkansas. It reads thus:

> . . . And the Confederate States will especially request the States of Arkansas and Texas to grant the like amnesty as to all offences committed by Choctaw or Chickasaw against the laws of those States respectively, and the Governor of each to reprieve or pardon the same, if necessary.[309]

Some evidence of the special interest Texas might have in the matter came out rather prominently in the

---

[305] Article VII of the Osage Treaty [p. 364].

[306] Article XIII of the Choctaw and Chickasaw Treaty [p. 315].

[307] Article IX of the Cherokee Treaty [p. 397].

[308] Article LXVI of the Creek Treaty, Article XLIV of the Seminole, Article LIII of the Cherokee.

[309] Article LXIV [p. 330].

treaties of the Third Class, the amnesty in them was particular while the amnesty in the treaties of the other two classes was general. This is what the Wichita and Comanche say:

> It is distinctly understood by the said several tribes and bands, that the State of Texas is one of the Confederate States, and joins this Convention, and signs it when the Commissioner signs it, and is bound by it; and all hostilities and enmities between it and them are now ended and are to be forgotten and forgiven on both sides.[310]

It soon developed that Texas was not pleased to find her consent so thoroughly taken for granted and that the Reserve Indians were no better satisfied.   The enmity between the two continued as before.

As regarded the relations between the Indian tribes and the Confederate States proper, the Pike treaties were old law in so far as they duplicated the earlier United States treaty arrangements and new law only in so far as they met conditions incident to the war. United States laws and treaties were specifically continued in force wherever possible, and, in most cases, the name of the one government was simply substituted for that of the other.   Considerable emphasis was laid upon the right of eminent domain.   The Indians conceded to the Confederacy the power to establish agency reserves,[311] military posts[312] and fortifications, to main-

---

[310] Article XL of the Wichita Treaty and Article X of the Comanche.

[311] Article XI of the Creek Treaty, Article XVI of the Choctaw and Chickasaw Treaty, Article XI of the Seminole Treaty, Article XIII of the Cherokee Treaty, Article IV of the Osage Treaty, Article V of the Seneca and Shawnee Treaty, and Article IV of the Quapaw Treaty.

[312] Article XII of the Creek Treaty, Article XVII of the Choctaw and Chickasaw Treaty, Article XII of the Seminole Treaty, Article XIV of the Cherokee Treaty, Article V of the Osage Treaty, Article VI of the Seneca and Shawnee Treaty, and Article V of the Quapaw Treaty.   After the war the posts in certain specified cases were to be garrisoned by native troops.

tain post and military roads,[313] and to grant the right of way,[314] upon payment of an indemnity,[315] to certain corporations for purposes of internal improvement, mainly railway and telegraph lines. Most of this would have contributed very materially to the good of the southern cause in guarding one of the approaches to Texas and in increasing the convenience of communication. The Confederate States assumed the wardship of the tribes, exacted a pledge of loyalty from the weaker and one of alliance,[316] offensive and defensive, but without the entail of pecuniary responsibility, from the stronger. In its turn, the Confederacy promised to the Indians many things, deserving of serious mention and far too important for mere enumeration. As a matter of fact, the South paid pretty dearly, from the view-point of historical consistency, for its Indian alliance. In the light of Indian political history, it yielded far more than at first glance appears and, as a consequence, the great tribes gained nearly everything that they had been contending for for half a century.

As has just been intimated, the concessions made by the Confederacy to the Indians were somewhat significant. In addition to the things noted a few paragraphs back, congressional delegates, control of trade, and others of like import, Pike, the lawyer commissioner and the man of justice, promised the establishment of Confederate States courts within the Indian country. There were to be two of them, one in the

---

[313] The reference is the same as the foregoing with two exceptions; viz., Article xxviii of the Osage Treaty and Article xx of the Quapaw Treaty.

[314] Article xiii of the Creek Treaty, Article xviii of the Choctaw and Chickasaw Treaty, and Article xiii of the Seminole Treaty.

[315] The provision in the Osage Treaty was one exception to this. It was definitely said there that there should be no compensation.

[316] The details of this will come out in the chapter following.

Choctaw country[317] and one in the Cherokee.[318]   They
were to be District Courts with a limited Circuit Court
jurisdiction.   The importance of the concession cannot
well be over-estimated; for it struck at the root of one
of the chief Indian grievances.   The territorial extent
of the districts was left a little vague and the jurisdiction
was not fairly distributed.   Here again we have an illustration of might conditioning right.   The Osages,[319] the
Senecas and Shawnees,[320] and the Quapaws[321] were all
brought within the limits of the Cha-lah-ki, or Cherokee district, but it is not clear that, as far as they
were concerned, any other offences than those against
the Fugitive Slave[322] laws, were to come within the

---

[317] ARTICLE XXXVIII (Choctaw and Chickasaw Treaty).   In order to
secure the due enforcement of so much of the laws of the Confederate
States in regard to criminal offences and misdemeanors as is or may be
in force in the said Choctaw and Chickasaw country, and to prevent
the Choctaws and Chickasaws from being further harassed by judicial
proceedings had in foreign courts and before juries not of the vicinage,
the said country is hereby erected into and constituted a judicial district
of the Confederate States to be called the Tush-ca-hom-ma District,
for the special purposes and jurisdiction hereinafter provided; and there
shall be created and semi-annually held, within such district, at Boggy
Depot, a district court of the Confederate States, with the powers of a
circuit court, so far as the same shall be necessary to carry out the provisions of this treaty, and with jurisdiction co-extensive with the limits
of such district, in such matters, civil and criminal, to such extent and
between such parties as may be prescribed by law, and in conformity to
the terms of this treaty [p. 320].

Articles XXXIX, XL, XLI, and XLII more specifically define the jurisdiction.

[318] See Article XXIII of the Cherokee Treaty, and, for the jurisdiction of the
court, see Articles XXIV, XXV, and XXVI.

[319] Article XXXV.

[320] Article XXVI.

[321] Article XXVI.

[322] In other ways than this, the treaties with the minor tribes stressed the
"peculiar institution."   Consider, for instance, in the matter of extradition, how
it was not the criminal generally, but only the fugitive slave that was to be
reciprocally extradited.   Moreover, as a rule, the weak tribes all pledged themselves to try to return negroes and other property and were assured that negroes should come under the jurisdiction of tribal laws.

purview of the court. The Wichitas and Comanches were left entirely unassigned, although naturally, they would have come within the Tush-ca-hom-ma, or Choctaw district.

The Confederacy reinstituted the agency system and continued it with modifications. These modifications were in line with reiterated complaints of the Indians. They restricted the government patronage to some extent and, in certain instances, allowed a good deal of tribal control. As a general thing, to each tribe was allowed one agent and to each language, one interpreter. An exception to the first provision was to be found wherever it had been found under the earlier régime. Thus there was a single agent for the Choctaws and Chickasaws, another for the fragmentary tribes of the Leased District, and another for those of the Neosho River country. In the minor treaties, it was stipulated, for very evident and very sound reasons, most of them based upon experiences of past neglect, that the agent should be faithful in the performance of his duties, that he should reside at his agency continually, and never be absent for long at a time or without good and sufficient cause.

There were also certain things the Indians were forbidden to do, many of them familiar to us in any ordinary Bill of Rights and having reference to ex-post facto laws, laws impairing the obligation of contracts, due process of law, and the like. The Confederacy, in turn, bound itself not to allow farming on government reserves or settlement there except under certain conditions and not to treat[323] with Cherokee factions. It inserted into the treaties with the minor tribes the usual number of civilization clauses, promising agri-

[323] Article II [p. 395].

cultural and industrial support; and into the Cherokee some things that were entirely new, notably a provision that the congressional delegation from each of the great tribes should have the right to nominate a youth to membership in any military academy that might be established.[324]   It also promised to maintain a postal system throughout the Indian country, one that should be, in every particular, a part of the postal system of the Confederate States with the same rates, stamps, and so on.   To the Cherokees, it promised the additional privilege[325] of having the postmasters selected and appointed from among their own people.   From the foregoing analysis of the treaties, it is clearly seen that the characteristic feature of them all was conciliation and conciliation written very, very large.   Of the great tribes, the Confederacy asked an alliance full and complete; of the middle tribes, such as the Osage, it asked a limited alliance and peace; and of the most insignificant tribes it asked simply peace but that it was prepared, not only to ask, but, if need be, to demand. Between the Cherokees and the Wichitas, there was a wide, wide gulf and one that could be measured only in terms of political and military importance.

So much for the contents of the treaties but what about the detailed history of their negotiation?   When Albert Pike first came within reach of the Indian country, he communicated[326] officially or semi-officially

---

[324] Article LII [p. 410].

[325] Article XXXIX [p. 403].

[326] Without doubt some preliminary sounding of Leeper must have preceded the accompanying document. Pike would hardly have written with such assurance or given such instructions unless he had been very sure of his ground.

FORT SMITH, ARKANSAS, 26th May 1861.

SIR: I have been appointed by the President of the Confederate States of America Commissioner to the Indian Tribes West of Arkansas, with discretionary powers, for the purpose of making treaties of alli-

with the men belonging or recently belonging to the Indian field service, agents and agency employees, or, at least, with those of them that were known as Confederate sympathizers.   A few very necessary changes

ance with them, and of enlisting troops to act with the forces of the Confederate States.

In the exercise of the powers entrusted to me, I hereby authorize and request you to exercise the powers of Agent for the Wichitas and other Indians in the Country leased from the Choctaws and Chickasaws, until you shall receive a regular commission therefor. Your compensation will be the same as that received from the United States, to commence from the day when you resigned as agent of the United States.

And you are hereby instructed forthwith to repair to your agency, and to inform the Indians under your charge that the Confederate States of America will take you themselves and fully comply with all the obligations entered into by the United States in their behalf; securing and paying all that may be due them from injury; and especially that they will continue to supply them with rations, as it has heretofore been done, until they shall no longer need to be supplied.

You will also please inform them that I shall in a short time be among them, to enter into a treaty with them, on the part of the Confederate States.

You will impress upon them that the people of Texas are now a part of the Confederate States, and must no longer be looked upon as enemies: and if any troops from Texas should come within your jurisdiction, you will particularly warn them against doing any harm to the Indians under your charge.

You will make known to the Delawares, and if practicable to the Kickapoos, that it is my desire, and I have authority, to enlist a battalion of 350 men, of the Delawares, Kickapoos, and Shawnees, and will especially assure the Kickapoos, that if they have any cause of complaint against any of the people of Texas, it will be inquired into, and reparation made, and that they must in no case commit any act of hostility against Texas.

I shall be greatly obliged to you for all assistance you can render in securing the services in arms of the Kickapoos and Delawares. They will be paid like other mounted men, receiving 40 cents a day for use and risk of their horse, in addition to their pay, rations, and clothing.

I need not say that I place much reliance on your zeal and intelligence and assure you that your services will not fail to be appreciated by the Government of the Confederate States.   Most respectfully yours

ALBERT PIKE, Comm^r C.S.A. to the
Indian Tribes, West of Arkansas.

Matthew Leeper Esq.
Leeper Papers.

had been made in the service with the inauguration of President Lincoln but the changes were not always such as could, in any wise, have strengthened the Federal position. First, as regards the southern superintendency, an attempt had been made to find a successor to Elias Rector [327] at about the same time that Harrison

[327] It is not clear as to just when Elias Rector left the United States service or when he entered the Confederate. The Indian Office in Washington was communicating with him officially for some little time after Griffith had been notified of his appointment. There seems no reason to doubt that Rector was working in the interests of the Southern Confederacy all through the spring of 1861; and, when he went over openly to the South, he did not close his accounts with the United States Indian Office. He was accordingly regarded as a defaulter and there was talk of confiscating his property at Fort Smith [W. G. Coffin to Dole, January 29, 1864, General Files, *Southern Superintendency, 1863-1864*, I640; Dole to Usher, February 2, 1864, Indian Office, *Report Book*, no. 13, p. 297].

In the course of his official connection with the United States government Elias Rector had frequently been accused of irregularities and even of crookedness [General Files, *Southern Superintendency, 1859-1862*, C1222]. As touching the Seminole removal from Florida, he had much that was peculiar to explain away. Apparently he quite frequently made queer contracts, was given to making over-charges for mileage and to favoring his friends at the expense of the Indians and of the government. In 1861, he rendered a voucher showing he had paid a certain Henry Pape $6000.00 for building the Wichita Agency house. On various matters connected with his official record, see Rector's *Letter Press Book* and Indian Office, *Letter Books*, no. 64, p. 342; no. 65, p. 49; no. 66, p. 26. In 1865, Rector made application to be allowed to straighten out his accounts [J. B. Luce to Cooley, November 2, 1865].

Returning, however, to the subject of Rector's incumbency: on the twelfth of June, 1861, he wrote quite frankly to John Schoenmaker, principal of the Osage Mission,

. . . I have no connection at this time with the Indian Department under the old U. S. Government. I am now acting as Superintendent under the Government of the Confederate States, and as no treaties have as yet been concluded between the Southern confederacy and the tribes of Indians with whom you are engaged I of course can say nothing to you on the subject matter of your letter. . . – General Files, *Southern Superintendency, 1859-1862*.

The Confederate southern superintendency had not at the time been filled, but Rector seems to have been considered the most competent candidate. Johnson, in recommending various men to Walker for various positions, recommended Rector in strong terms of implied commendation,

Dr. Griffith wants to be appointed superintendent in place of E.

B. Branch[328] of Missouri had been appointed central superintendent in the stead of A. M. Robinson. The man chosen was Samuel L. Griffith[329] of Fort Smith to whom the new Secretary of the Interior, Caleb B. Smith, telegraphed on the fifth of April, tendering the position. Similarly by wire, on the ninth, Griffith accepted; and, on the tenth, explained[330] the delay in the following letter:

> Being a member of our State Convention on the Union side, I hesitated a day or two, as to the propriety of accepting, fearing it might affect the union cause, but on mature deliberation and counsel with union friends, and on the receipt of a memorial signed by a large number of names of men of all parties, I concluded to accept. . .
>
> Col. W. H. Garret Agt. for the Creeks, passed through this place on the 8th. . .
>
> Col. S. Rutherford left here this morning for his agency (the Seminole). I desired him to ascertain on his way through the Creek and Choctaw Nations, the facts, as to the rumor that two men from Texas were in the Creek Nation for the purpose of meeting the several nations in Council &c. and to report to me immediately. . .

Dr. Griffith's solicitude for the Union interests appar-

Rector. Do not allow this to be done. Hold everything as it is until peace and unity are attained, and then make all the changes you think proper; but not now – not now, by all manner of means.

I do earnestly beg you to keep your agencies as they were. They are good and true men, and popular and qualified with the tribes and their business. Restore and commission Elias Rector, superintendent; John Crawford, Cherokee agent; William Quesenbury, Creek agent; Samuel M. Rutherford, Seminole agent; and Matthew Leeper, Wichita agent; and if Cooper has resigned (which I fear is the case), appoint Richard P. Pulliam (who is the next best living man on earth for the place, I believe) as agent of the Choctaws. With this programme you will have peace and success; without it, no one can tell your troubles or our misfortunes on this frontier. . . – *Official Records*, first ser., vol. iii, 598.

[328] Dole to Robinson, April 9, 1861 [Indian Office, *Letter Book*, no. 65, 323].
[329] Dole to Rector, April 6, 1861 [— *ibid.*, p. 317].
[330] General Files, *Southern Superintendency, 1859-1862*, G463.

ently soon vanished. On the twentieth of April, he wrote[331] that, "under the circumstances," he could not hold office. Coffin of Indiana was then selected[332] for the place of southern superintendent and, in a very little while, Griffith was among the applicants[333] for the corresponding position in the Confederate States. Between the dates of the two activities, morever, he had been appointed by the Arkansas Convention one of the three special agents to interview the Indian tribes in the interests of secession. That was on the tenth of May.

The changes in the agency incumbents proved equally temporary and unfortunate. Particularly was this the case with two determined[334] upon on the sixth of April. Four days later, William Quesenbury[335] of Fayetteville, Arkansas was notified that he had been appointed to succeed William H. Garrett as agent for the Creeks, and John Crawford[336] of the same place that he had been appointed to succeed Robert J. Cowart as agent for the Cherokees. Both went over to the Confederacy. Nothing else could well have been expected of Crawford, or of Quesenbury either for that matter, and it is rather surprising that their past records were not more thoroughly examined. Quesenbury, like Richard P. Pulliam, was a sort of protégé of Elias Rector. Pulliam had been Rector's clerk in the office and

[331] General Files, *Southern Superintendency, 1859-1862,* G463.

[332] Smith to Dole, May 4, 1861; Dole to Rector, May 9, 1861 [Indian Office, *Letter Book,* no. 65, p. 440].

[333] Johnson to Walker, June 25, 1861 [*Official Records,* first ser., vol. iii, 598].

[334] Caleb B. Smith to Dole, April 6, 1861 [General Files, *Southern Superintendency, 1859-1862*].

[335] Dole to Quesenbury [Indian Office, *Letter Book,* no. 65, p. 330]. In the middle of the summer, George A. Cutler became United States agent for the Creeks [*ibid.,* no. 66, p. 200].

[336] Dole to Crawford [*ibid.,* no. 65, p. 331].

Quesenbury his clerk in the field.[337] Crawford had been very prominent[338] in the Arkansas legislature the preceding winter in the expression of ideas and sentiments hostile to Abraham Lincoln. He accepted the office of Cherokee agent under Lincoln, notwithstanding, and he subsequently said[339] that he did so because the Indians would not have liked a northern man to come among them. Before Crawford's commission arrived, Cowart had departed[340] and Cherokee affairs were in dire confusion.[341] John J. Humphreys[342] of Tennessee had

---

[337] Rector to Greenwood, August 31, 1860 [*Letter Press Book*].

[338] November 27, 1860, he voted in the affirmative on a resolution against Lincoln's election and against the advisability of Arkansas members of Congress taking their seats during his administration [Arkansas House *Journal*, thirteenth session, 1860-1861, p. 234].

[339] On the thirteenth of June, when Crawford wrote, resigning his commission, he said in extenuation of his conduct,

> I only accepted through the influence of friends knowing then the Cherokee Indians was Southern in their feelings and did not wish a Northern man sent among them to act as Agent & as the Government of the Southern Confederacy has in their wisdom thought best to take charge of all the Indian Tribes south of Kansas and the Indians all being anxious to join in with the South and oppose to the bitter end the course now pursued by the Northern Government – I most respectfully decline acting as agent for the Cherokee Indians under the Administration of A. Lincoln. – CRAWFORD to Dole, June 13, 1861 [General Files, *Cherokee, 1859-1865*, C1376].

[340] Crawford to Dole, May 20, 1861 [*ibid.*].

[341] The excitement here is at an alarming pitch for the last few days I trust to God that those in power will do something to settle this interruption in the government and something must be done soon or War will ensue troops were drilling here last night at ten oclock, State troops, strong talk of attacking Fort Smith the President of the Convention has called the Convention to meet on the 6th day of May and the State will secede if there is not something done immediately perhaps war will be commenced before you receive my letter though I trust not. I should very much to know that the North and South were engaged in a war, if you can do anything to have those troubles settled use your influence with the President in calling a national convention or something else to have peace. . . – CRAWFORD to Dole, dated Van Buren, April 21, 1861 [General Files, *Cherokee, 1859-1865*, C1044].

[342] Smith to Dole, April 20, 1861 [General Files, *Wichita, 1860-1861*, I320].

meanwhile been offered the Wichita Agency[343] and Peter P. Elder[344] of Kansas, the Neosho River. The Choctaw and Chickasaw Agency seems to have been left vacant. Truth to tell, there was no longer any such agency under United States control. Cooper had thrown in his lot with the secessionists and was already working actively in their cause.

The defection of Douglas H. Cooper, United States agent for the Choctaws and the Chickasaws, can not be passed by so very lightly; for it had such far reaching effects. The time came during and after the war, when the United States Indian Office came to have in its possession various documents[345] that proved conclusively that Douglas H. Cooper had been most instrumental in organizing the secession movement among the Indians of at least his own agency. It was even reported[346] that material was forthcoming to show how he "was engaged in raising troops for the Rebel Army, during the months of April, May, and June, 1861, while holding the office of U.S. Indian Agent." His successor had been appointed considerably before the end of that time, however, and, when the war was over, the Indians themselves exonerated him from all responsibility in the matter of their own defection.[347] Notwithstanding, he most certainly did manifest unusual activity in behalf of the slaveholding power. Even his

[343] Some slight account of the Wichita Agency and of Agent Leeper's defection has already been narrated. A number of documents elucidating the subject are to be found in the "Appendix."

[344] Dole to Elder, April 29, 1861 [Indian Office, *Letter Book*, no. 65, pp. 390-391]; Mix to Elder, August 22, 1861 [*ibid.*, no. 66, pp. 283-284].

[345] See, for instance, Stockton to Usher, February 20, 1864 [General Files, *Southern Superintendency, 1863-1864*].

[346] See Isaac Coleman, United States Indian agent, to Superintendent Elijah Sells, a copy of which letter is retained in the Office of Indian Affairs, the original having been sent to the office of the United States attorney-general, October 10, 1865.

[347] Commissioner of Indian Affairs, *Report*, 1865, pp. 310, 345.

motives for manifesting activity are, in a sense, impugned as instanced by the following most extraordinary letter, which, written by Cooper to Rector privately and in confidence and later transmitted to Washington out of the ordinary course of official business, has already been quoted once for the purpose of forming a correct estimate of the recipient's character. It is gratifying to know that such letters are very rare in connection with the history of the American Civil War.

Private & Confidential

[*Copy*]   FORT SMITH May 1st 1861.
MAJOR ELIAS RECTOR
  Dr. Sir: I have concluded to act upon the suggestion yours of the 28th Ultimo contains.
  If we work this thing shrewdly we can make a fortune each, satisfy the Indians, stand fair before the North, and revel in the unwavering confidence of our Southern Confederacy.
  My share of the eighty thousand in gold [348] you can leave on deposite with Meyer Bro. subject to my order. Write me soon.

COOPER.

---

[348] The reference is, presumably, to a portion of the money that the United States government had allowed the Choctaws in satisfaction of claims arising under the treaties of 1830 and 1855 [Act of March 2, 1861, U. S. *Statutes at Large*, vol. xii, 238]. The episode of the Corn Contract was directly connected with the expenditure of the money. For documents bearing upon it, see Land Files, *Choctaw, 1874-1876*, Box 39, C1078, particularly documents labelled "N," "O," and "P." Document "N" is a communication from Albert Pike to the General Council of the Choctaw Nation, received at the June session, 1861, and is most interesting as showing how Pike mixed up private and public business and, indeed, gave to private the preference.

  FRIENDS AND BROTHERS: You are aware that since the year 1854 Mr John T. Cochrane and myself, aided by Col. Cooper your agent and by your delegates, have been engaged at Washington in prosecuting the just claims of your people under the treaty of 1830 before the Government of the United States.

  We have succeeded in procuring a final award of the Senate, giving you the net proceeds of all the lands which you ceded by that treaty, and a Report from the Committee of Indian Affairs, estimating the sum due you at over two millions three hundred thousand dollars.

  At the last session of Congress, we succeeded in procuring an ap-

When Captain Pike [349] reached the North Fork Vil-

propriation on account of this debt of \$250,000 in money and \$250,000 in bonds of the United States.

Owing to the unfortunate difficulties between the Northern and Southern States, one hundred and thirty-eight thousand dollars, only, of the sums, has been paid, \$135,000 of which was placed in your Agent's hands, ostensibly to purchase corn; and most of it remains unexpended.

Towards my expenses while prosecuting your claims and towards my fee, I have received the sum of sixteen hundred dollars. My expenses alone, in four years have been five thousand dollars.

I have had to abandon my other business, to attend to yours: and unless some part of my compensation is paid, or my expenses repaid me, my property will have to be sold to pay my debts. I am entirely without money, and have you only to look to.

I have labored for you very faithfully; and am sure your Delegates will tell you that, but for me your claims would never have been allowed; and but for me, after they were allowed, the appropriation would not have been obtained.

The whole of the claims will be paid whenever peace is restored, either by the United States, or by the Confederate Southern States. I shall take it in charge and never desert you until all is paid.

I respectfully and earnestly request you to cause to be paid to me, out of the moneys now in the Agent's hands, for my expenses, and on account of my fee, such sum of money as you may think just and right; and which I hope will not be less than seven thousand five hundred dollars.

I also desire to inform you that I have been appointed by the President of the Confederate States, a Commissioner to your Nation, and all the other Nations and Tribes west of Arkansas; that I shall at the proper time come among you to counsel with you, and that I shall take your interests in charge, and see that your title to your lands, and all annuities, and other moneys due you by the United States are assumed and guaranteed by the Confederate States. On this you may implicitly rely; as it is the promise of one who never breaks his word.

Let your people therefore, and the Chickasaws remain perfectly quiet until the proper time arrives, and look to me for advice. If any emissaries from Arkansas come among you, hear them and say nothing. So it is that wise men do. The State of Arkansas has nothing whatever to do with you, and cannot protect you. The Confederate States are both able and willing to do so; and when they have guaranteed your rights, it will be time enough for you to act. Your friend

(signed) ALBERT PIKE.

Office of the National Secretary of the Choctaw Nation.

[Endorsement]   I hereby certify that the foregoing is a true copy from the original letter from Albert Pike on file in the National Secretary's Office.

lage, very probably still attended by the escort that the

Given under my hand and official seal. Done at Chahta Tamaha, November 1st A.D. 1873.
(signed) JNO. P. TURNBULL, National Secretary Choctaw Nation.

349 Pike's programme of operations is outlined in his letter to Toombs of May 29, 1861:

SIR: I leave this morning for Tahlequah, the seat of government of the Cherokee Nation, and Park Hill, the residence of Governor Ross, the principal chief. Since 1835 there have always been two parties in the Cherokee Nation, bitterly hostile to each other. The treaty of that year was made by unauthorized persons, against the will of the large majority of the nation and against that of the chief, Mr. Ross. Several years ago Ridge, Boudinot, and others, principal men of the treaty party, were killed, with, it was alleged, the sanction of Mr. Ross, and the feud is today as bitter as it was twenty years ago. The full-blooded Indians are mostly adherents of Ross, and many of them – 1,000 to 1,500 it is alleged – are on the side of the North. I think that number is exaggerated. The half-breeds or white Indians (as they call themselves) are to a man with us. It has all along been supposed, or at least suspected, that Mr. Ross would side with the North. His declarations are in favor of neutrality. But I am inclined to believe that he is acting upon the policy (surely a wise one) of not permitting his people to commit themselves until he has formal guarantees from an authorized agent of the Confederate States. These I shall give him if he will accept them. General McCulloch will be with me, and I strongly hope that we shall satisfy him, and effect a formal and firm treaty. If so, we shall have nearly the whole nation with us, and those who are not will be unimportant. If he refuses he will learn that his country will be occupied; and I shall then negotiate with the leaders of the half-breeds who are now raising troops, and who will meet me at the Creek Agency on Friday of next week. Several of those living near here I have already seen.

On Wednesday of next week I will meet the chiefs of the Creeks at the North Fork of the Canadian. I will then fix a day for a council of the Creeks, and go on to meet the Choctaws at Fort Washita. When I shall have concluded an arrangement with them I will go to the Chickasaw Country, and thence to the Seminoles.

I hope to meet the heads of the Wichitas, Caddos, Iowas, Toncawes, Delawares, Kickapoos, and Reserve Comanches at Fort Washita. I have requested their agent to induce them to meet me there. The Creek chiefs have a council with the wild Indians, Comanches and others, high up on the North Fork of the Canadian, on the 10th proximo. I shall endeavor, through the Creek chiefs, to have an interview with the heads of the wild tribes at Fort Washita and induce them to come in and settle on the reserve upon the False Washita River near Fort Cobb.

As I shall be absent from this post some six weeks or more, it is not

Military Board of Arkansas had graciously – or perhaps officially since Pike, according to his own con-

likely that I shall be able to give you frequent advice of my movements. There are no mails in the Indian country and I shall have to
employ expresses when I desire to send on letters.

We shall have no difficulty with the Creeks, Seminoles, Choctaws,
and Chickasaws, either in effecting treaties or raising troops. The
greatest trouble will be in regard to arms. Not one in ten of either of
the tribes has a gun at all, and most of the guns are indifferent double-
barreled. I do not know whether the Bureau of Indian Affairs is a part
of the Department of State, and of course whether this is properly addressed to you. I do not address the Commissioner because I understand he is on his way hither. The suggestions I wish to make are important and I venture to hope that you will give them their proper
direction. I have already spoken of arms for the Indians. Those arms,
if possible, should be the plain muzzle-loading rifle, large bore, with
molds for conical bullets hollowed at the truncated end, which I suppose
to be the minie-ball. Revolvers, I am aware, cannot be had, and an
Indian would not pick up a musket if it lay in the road.

Our river is falling and will soon be low, when steam-boats will not
be able to get above Little Rock, if even there. To embody the Indians
and, collecting them together, keep them long without arms would dis-
gust them, and they would scatter over the country like partridges and
never be got together again. The arms should, therefore, be sent here
with all speed.

No funds have been remitted to me, nor have I any power to procure or draw for any, for my expenses or for those of the councils I
must hold. It has always been customary for the Indians to be fed at
such councils, and they will expect it. I have borrowed $300 of Mr.
Charles B. Johnson, giving him a draft on the Commissioner of Indian
Affairs, for incidental expenses, and if I have a council at Fort Washita
shall contract with him to feed the Indians. I have seen Elias Rector,
late superintendent of Indian affairs at Fort Smith, and William Quesenbury, appointed agent for the Creeks by the Government at Washington, but who did not accept, and Samuel M. Rutherford, agent for the
Seminoles, who forwards his resignation immediately; and have written to Matthew Leeper, agent for the Wichitas and other Reserve Indians; and have formally requested each to continue to exercise the
powers of his office under the Confederate States. They are all citizens
of Arkansas and Texas and have readily consented to do so.

If we have declared a protectorate over these tribes and extended
our laws over them we have, I suppose, continued in force there the
whole system. Even if we have not we cannot dispense with the superintendent and agents. I shall also see Mr. Crawford, agent for the
Cherokees, and request him to continue to act, as I have requested
Colonel Cooper to do as agent for the Choctaws and Chickasaws. Unless all this were done there would be both discontent and confusion,

fession, was acting as commissioner from Arkansas[350] as well as from the Confederacy – furnished[351] him,[352] he found the Creeks awaiting his approach with some anxiety. Among them were Motey Kennard,[353] prin-

and I therefore earnestly request that my action may be immediately confirmed and these officers assured that they shall be continued, and that their compensation shall be the same as under the United States and date from the day of the resignation of each or of his acceptance of office under the Confederate States. And I also strenuously urge that no changes be made in these offices. The incumbents are all good men and true, competent, and honest, and are, or will be, very acceptable to the Indians. To make changes will be to make mischief.

Mr. Charles B. Johnson is feeding the Wichitas and other Reserve Indians under a contract which ends on the 30th of June. I have instructed him to continue feeding them during the present season under the same contract, *i.e.*, on the same terms, which I know to be reasonable.

It is very important that some funds should be at my disposition. The State of Arkansas has furnished me an escort of a company and General McCulloch has procured me transportation. To meet contingent expenses it is necessary that at least $1000 should be placed here subject to my draft; and, as I have several times urged, money should be placed in the proper hands to pay a bounty to each Indian that enlists.

I wish I had more definite instructions and power more distinctly expressed, especially power in so many words to make treaties and give all necessary guarantees. For without giving them nothing can be done, and I am [not] sure that John Ross will be satisfied with my statement or assurance that I have the power, or with anything less than a formal authority from the Congress. He is very shrewd. If I fail with him it will not be my fault.

I have the honor to be, sir, very truly and respectfully, yours,

ALBERT PIKE, Commissioner, &c.

Official Records, fourth ser., vol. i, 359-361.

[350] Pike to Cooley, February 17, 1866.

[351] *Official Records*, first ser., vol. liii, supplement, 688.

[352] A military escort had also been furnished by the Arkansas Military Board to General McCulloch [*ibid.*, 687].

[353] Motey, or Moty, Kennard is occasionally spoken of, in the records, as the principal chief of the entire Creek Nation. The tribe was, however, very sharply divided into the Lower and the Upper Creeks. Their differences had been accentuated by the unpleasant and even dishonorable and tragic circumstances of their removal from Georgia and Alabama. The Lower Creeks represented the faction that had stood back of William McIntosh and that had consented to the fraudulent treaty of Indian Springs, the Upper Creeks were the dissenters [Abel, *History of Indian Consolidation*, chapters vi and vii; Phillips, *Georgia and State Rights*, 56-57].

cipal chief of the Lower Creeks, and Echo Harjo, principal chief of the Upper Creeks, both of whom had been absent[354] in Washington at the time the intertribal council of the spring had been planned. They had gone to Washington, in company with John G. Smith, as a delegation, greatly concerned about the prospect of Creek finances and the continuance of Creek integrity should the quarrel between the North and the South continue. Greenwood had tried to reassure them; but, when shortly afterwards, all Indian allowances were suspended[355] by the United States Indian Office for fear that remittances might fall, en route, into the hands of the disaffected, the distrust and the dissatisfaction of the Indians revived and increased, thus rendering them peculiarly susceptible to the plausible secessionist arguments of men like Agent Garrett. Sometime in May, therefore, a delegation was sent to Montgomery[356] to confer with authorities of the Confederate States, who by the time of the arrival of the Creeks had moved on to Richmond.

At the North Fork Village, everything seemed to be working in Pike's favor. There was scarcely a white man[357] around who was willing to say a word for the North; and leading Indians, who were known to be anti-secessionists, were away[358] treating with the Indians

---

[354] Letter from Greenwood to the Delegation, February 4, 1861 [Indian Office, *Letter Book*, no. 65, pp. 140-141].

[355] Commissioner of Indian Affairs, *Report*, 1861. Note that as early as March 18, 1861, Secretary Smith had ordered the suspension of the issuance of all requisitions to ordinary disbursing officers in the seceding states. This order probably affected indirectly even the Indian Territory [Smith to commissioner of Indian affairs, March 18, 1861, *Miscellaneous Files, 1858-1863*].

[356] Governor Thomas O. Moore of Louisiana to President Davis, May 31, 1861 [*Official Records*, first ser., vol. iii, 588].

[357] See letter of W. S. Robertson to the Secretary of the Interior [General Files, *Southern Superintendency, 1859-1862*, R1664].

[358] See statement of the "Loyal" Creek Delegation at the Fort Smith Coun-

of the Plains. Opoeth-le-yo-ho-la, who was to become the stanch leader of the opposition, was not with the absentees, it would seem; but then that, at the time, did not so much signify because he was not a ranking chief and so had little influence.[359] On the tenth of July, the treaty that Pike and the Creek commissioners had been working on for days was finally submitted for signature and the names of Motey Kennard, Echo Harjo, Chilly McIntosh, Samuel Checote and many

---

cil, September, 1865 [Land Files, *Indian Talks, Councils, etc., 1865-1866*, Box 4; Commissioner of Indian Affairs, *Report*, 1865, pp. 328-329].

[359] Opoeth-le-yo-ho-la was nevertheless a very prominent man among the Upper Creeks and had been prominent even before the exodus from Georgia and Alabama. At all events he was sufficiently prominent to protest with others against the transportation contracts that had been made by the War Department [Lewis Cass to Opoeth-le-yo-ho-la and other Creek chiefs, dated Tuckabatchytown, Alabama, January 27, 1836]. Again in 1838, Opoeth-le-yo-ho-la headed a party of protest, that time against the selling of certain Creek lands left unsold at the time of emigration [*Creek Reservation Papers*, 25].

Opoeth-le-yo-ho-la seems to have been one of the assassins of William McIntosh; that is, if the subjoined statement of Acting-superintendent William Armstrong is to be trusted:

CHOCTAW AGENCY August 31, 1836

C. A. HARRIS Esqr, Comr of Ind Affairs,

Sir: The first party of emigrating Creeks are now on the opposite side of the river Arkansas, on their way up. I shall leave tomorrow so as to meet them at Gibson; while there, I will see the McIntosh party and endeavor to learn the state of feelings amongst the several parties. Many threats have been made; and much dissatisfaction manifested by both Chilly & Rolly McIntosh, the latter has sworn to kill A-po-the-ho-lo who was concerned in taking the life of his Father. Rolly McIntosh and the other Chiefs now over, are opposed to Ne-a-math-la the Chief who is with the party emigrating, upon the ground mainly that they may probably be superseded, or their authority abridged. I will however report to you, fully, after I shall have informed myself, of the state of feeling &c, and will endeavor with Genl Arbuckle, to bring about a reconciliation. Respectfully Your Obt Servt

WM ARMSTRONG Act Supt Westn Tery

War Department Files, A37.

Early in the forties, Opoeth-le-yo-ho-la posed as a trader in the Creek country. He was the partner of J. W. Taylor, a white man. The company so composed failed, in 1843, "to give bond and license" and so Agent J. L. Dawson closed its store [Communication of J. L. Dawson, September 5, 1843, *War Department Files*, I1537].

other less prominent Creeks were attached to it. On the twentieth, the general council approved it and more names were attached, that of Jacob Derrysaw being among them. On one or the other occasion, several white men signed. William Quesenbury, who was acting as Pike's secretary, Agent Garrett, Interpreter G. W. Stidham,[360] and W. L. Pike. Soon came the return of the travellers and much subsequent commotion. They expressed themselves as opposed to the whole proceeding, yet three of them found that, in their absence, their names had been forged[361] to the document that was passing as a treaty between the Creeks and the Confederate States. The three whose names were forged were, Ok-ta-ha-hassee Harjo (better known subsequently as "Sands" and who became in reconstruction days the great rival of Samuel Checote for the office of principal chief), Tallise Fixico, and Mikko Hutke. It is a matter of dispute what course Opoeth-le-yo-ho-la had taken[362] in the treaty conference but not what he did afterwards; for he became the intrepid

---

[360] G. W. Stidham was probably a half-breed. Naturally, being the official interpreter, he signed as the interpreter and not as a member of the tribe.

[361] We the loyal Creek Indians represented by the Delegation now present, solemnly declare that the Treaty of July 10, 1861 was alone made by the rebel portion of the Creek Indians, and never was executed or assented to by the Union portion of the Nation, and is, not now, and never has been, obligatory upon them and the names to said treaty, of the loyal party, was a forgery – Land Files, *Indian Talks, Councils, etc.*, Box 4, 1865-1866; Commissioner of Indian Affairs, *Report*, 1865, p. 330.

[362] The document herewith given presents one view of the case:

The undersigned Delegates from the Creek Nation would respectfully ask to make the following statement concerning the alliance between the said Creek Nation and the so-called Confederate States of America. To the end that the Creek Nation may be put upon a proper footing in the estimation of your honorable body and that there may be no misapprehension on the part of the Government you here represent we beg leave to state:

1st. The Alliance entered into by the Creek Nation with the Con-

leader of the so-called "Loyal Creeks" and the foremost of the "Refugees."

If the Creeks were disturbed about their national

---

federate Government was entered into voluntarily, and without the interference of any person or persons other than members of our tribe. In taking that step the assembled wisdom of the Nation in council, thought they were acting for the best interests of the Nation and of their posterity.

2d. Hopoethle Yoholo the far-famed leader of those members of our tribe who battled against us, was not at the time of the making of the treaty with Albert Pike Commissioner on the part of the Confederate States, a Chief, counsellor or head man in said tribe and had no voice in the council, he was however present at the making of said Treaty and give said Pike to understand that he fully concurred in the result of our deliberations. After the making of the Treaty Hopoethle Yoholo collected together his adherents, and for reasons entirely of a domestic character and in no wise connected with the National question at issue, withdrew from the country and assumed a hostile attitude. With this exception the Creeks were united as one man in action and were ever united as one man in principle on the National question then agitated.

3d. Although the Nation we represent would not attempt at this time to urge anything in palliation of the course of conduct they adopted in this matter, other than to ask your honorable body to esteem the error as one of the "head and not of the heart" – but we beg leave to state that at the time of the forming of the Alliance above refered to circumstances over which we could not possibly exercise control seemed to *demand* an adoption of the course taken. The protection always borne with the idea of allegiance, was taken from our Nation by the withdrawal of the United States forces from the Indian Territory. This movement left the Nations entirely without the support of the United States government, and had they desired to remain neutral or to take active measures on the side of the United States they could not possibly have done so without having their Country desolated, or by abandoning their homes. Surrounded by States, in a tumult of angry excitement attendant upon a dissolution of their connection with the United States, they were completely in the power of those States, without having United States forces to call to their aid or assistance. An alliance under such circumstances were [was] indispensible to the safety of the country. Viewing the matter in this light the Treaty was made, and once having linked our destiny with those of the Confederacy, we could not in honor betray our trust. In conclusion we beg leave to say that as long as events cannot be controlled by human wisdom and foresight and until an honorable adherence to promises made voluntarily, is dishonorable so long must we deem ourselves in one sense at least – guiltless of any criminality in this matter. – Land Files, *Indian Talks, Councils, etc., Box 4, 1865-1866.*

finances, the Choctaws[363] were even more so. There were many suspicious circumstances connected with a certain corn contract and with the expenditure generally of the huge sum of money that the United States Congress had appropriated in satisfaction of claims arising under the treaty of removal, payment on which it had recently suspended to the displeasure of the Indians and the discomfiture of the speculators. Wherever suspicion rested, Pike attempted elaborate explanations and, wherever affairs could be turned to the account of the Confederacy, he labored with redoubled zeal. His task was an easy one comparatively-speaking, though, for the Choctaws were already committed[364] to the southern cause. The two Folsoms, Peter and Sampson, who were among the special commissioners sent to Washington to inquire about the money and who had lingered at Montgomery, were his eager coadjutors. Just how far George Hudson, principal chief, was readily compliant, it is difficult to say. It is supposed that he issued his proclamation[365] of June 14, announcing independence and calling for troops, under compulsion and, in July, he may still have been secretly in favor of neutrality. The joint treaty for the Choctaws

---

[363] They were also worried over rumors of sequestration:

Statements having found their way into some of the public prints, to the effect that supplies purchased for the use of the Choctaws, have been detained by citizens of the Northern States, which statements if uncontradicted may engender hostile feelings between those Indians and the Government, I have thought proper to forward to you the enclosed copies of official correspondence in relation to this subject, that you may be able authoritatively to contradict such statements and satisfy the Choctaws that the Government intends faithfully to preserve and perpetuate the amicable relations subsisting between itself and those people. – DOLE to Rector and same to Coffin, May 16, 1861 [Indian Office, *Letter Book*, no. 65, p. 458].

[364] Particularly by means of the resolutions of the National Council, June 10, 1861.

[365] *Official Records*, first ser., vol. iii, 593.

and Chickasaws was completed on the twelfth of July and again prominent men, the most prominent in the tribes, no doubt, endorsed the action by affixing their signatures. R. M. Jones, the chief[366] of the secessionists, W. B. Pitchlynn, Winchester Colbert, and James Gamble,[367] who was soon afterwards selected as the first delegate[368] to the Confederate Congress, were among the signers; but Agent Cooper was not. Perchance, he and Pike had already begun to dispute over the propriety of an Indian agent's holding a colonelcy in the Confederate army. Cooper[369] wanted to be both agent and colonel.

Having disposed satisfactorily of the Creeks, Choctaws, and Chickasaws, Pike passed on, with his group of white and red friends, to the Seminoles and met them in council[370] at their own agency. Rector was now[371] one

---

[366] For evidence of this and for the fullest extant account of the progress of secession among the Choctaws, see letter of S. Orlando Lee to Dole, March 15, 1862.

[367] The following is found in the *Fort Smith Papers*:

Tishomingo, C.N. Nov. 26, 1861.

GEN. A. G. MAYERS

Sir: Having been appointed as a Delegate from this Nation (the Chickasaw) to the Southern Congress, am at a loss (to know) when the Congress does meet. I have all along understood from newspaper accounts that it was to be on the 22d of February, but some seems to think it is sooner. Will you please inform me at your earliest convenience at what time the S. Congress does meet. Your attention to the above is respectfully requested. I am yours very Respectfully   JAMES GAMBLE.

P.S. Please continue to send me the Parallel. I will make it all right with you when on my way to Va.   J. G.

[368] In the list of members of the Confederate congresses, given in *Official Records*, fourth ser., vol. iii, 1184-1191, no Indian delegate is specified until 1863.

[369] Cooper to President Davis, July 25, 1861 [*ibid.*, first ser., vol. iii, 614].

[370] E. H. Carruth, in a letter to General Hunter of November 26, 1861 [Commissioner of Indian Affairs, *Report*, 1861, p. 47], would have us understand that the Seminoles as a tribe did not negotiate with Pike, but that the whole affair was as between Pike and Jumper, Jumper being assisted by four chosen friends. The five were probably bribed. That Pike was not averse to the use of money for such ends, his letter to Walker of June twelfth would

of his assistants. The poor Seminoles, according to their own story of what happened, were taken completely unawares;[372] and, after some skilful maneuvering, Pike succeeded in inducing about half[373] of them, headed by one of their principal chiefs, John Jumper,[374] and a town chief, Pas-co-fa, to agree to "perpetual peace and friendship" with the Confederate States. There was nothing specifically said about an alliance, offensive and defensive, but it was understood and was immediately provided for.[375] The head chief, Billy Bowlegs,[376] and other chiefs of present and future impor-

---

lead us to suspect [*Official Records*, first ser., vol. iii, 590]. We have, however, no definite proof of the same. John Jumper was early rewarded by the Confederate government. By act of the Provisional Congress, January 16, 1861 [*Statutes at Large*, p. 284], he was made an honorary lieutenant-colonel of the army of the Confederate States. Carruth further says that the family influence of Jumper "enabled him to raise forty-six men, not all Seminoles, and Ben McCulloch authorized him to call to his aid six hundred rangers from Fort Cobb, that he might crush out the Union feeling in his tribe."

[371] It is just possible that Rector had been with him all the time. At all events Rector subsequently entered an expense account against the C.S.A. for services from July tenth to August twenty-fourth inclusive. See Appendix A, *Fort Smith Papers*.

[372] See letter of Agent Snow, dated March 10, 1864, and its enclosures, one of which is a speech of Long John, who became principal chief when the aged Billy Bowlegs died, and another, a speech of Pas-co-fa, who, provided his signature to the treaty be genuine, eventually must have repented of his Confederate alliance. He was soon, with Bowlegs and Chup-co, in the ranks of Opoeth-le-yo-ho-la [General Files, *Seminole, 1858-1867*, S291].

[373] The report of the United States commissioner of Indian affairs for 1863 estimates the loyal Seminoles at about two-thirds of the tribe [House *Executive Documents*, 38th congress, first session, vol. iii, 143], that of the Confederate States commissioner of Indian affairs as fully one-half [S. S. Scott to Secretary Seddon, January 12, 1863, *Official Records*, fourth ser., vol. ii, 353].

[374] While at the Creek Agency, Pike had communicated, so it seems, with John Jumper and had asked him to meet him there with six others competent and authorized to make a treaty. Up to the time of hearing from Pike, John Jumper seems to have been inclined to adhere faithfully to the United States government. The excellent report of E. H. Carruth, July 11, 1861 gives full particulars of this whole affair.

[375] See supplementary Article [*Official Records*, fourth ser., vol. i, 525].

[376] See communications from Bowlegs [So-nuk-mek-ko] to Commissioner of Indian Affairs, March 2, 1863 and May 13, 1863 [General Files, *Seminole,*

tance, like John Chup-co,[377] refused [378] to sign the treaty and, before many days had elapsed, joined the party of the "Loyal Creeks." Various ones of the "Southern" Creeks, notably Motey Kennard, were present at the treaty-making and used their influence to strengthen that of Pike, Rector, Agent Rutherford,[379] Contractor Charles B. Johnson, and a host of minor enthusiasts, like J. J. Sturm and H. P. Jones, all of whom had formerly been in the United States employ and were now, or soon to be, in the Confederate.[380]

Pike's military escort had surely left him by this time and had returned to Arkansas and yet never had it been more needed; for the Confederate commissioner and his party were about to go into the western country to confer with the tribes of the Leased District whose friendship as yet could scarcely be counted upon, notwithstanding the fact that their agent had openly thrown in his fortunes with the South [381] and was using

---

1858-1869, B131, B317]. See also Dole to Coffin, March 24, 1863 [Indian Office, *Letter Book*, no. 70, pp. 208-209].

[377] Commissioner of Indian Affairs, Report, 1869 [House *Executive Documents*, 41st congress, second session, vol. iii, part 3, p. 521].

[378] See letter of E. H. Carruth.

[379] William P. Davis of Indiana had been given the United States Seminole Agency but he never reached his post [Dole to John D. Davis, April 5, 1862, Indian Office *Letter Book*, no. 68, p. 39]. Consequently, the Confederate States agent, Rutherford, had sole influence there. Not until George C. Snow of Indiana became United States Seminole agent, did the non-secessionist Indians get the encouragement and support they ought to have had all along.

[380] See Appendix B – *Leeper Papers*.

[381] The *Leeper Papers*, printed in the Appendix, furnish convincing proof of this. Note also that July 4, 1861, Rector wrote to Leeper from Fort Smith as follows:

> In the 3rd section of the law of the Confederate Congress, regulating the Indian service connected with said government, and making provision for the continuance in office of the Superintendent and Agents heretofore connected with the original U. S. government, you will be continued upon the same terms and at the same salary, as heretofore received from the federal government, and before entering upon your duties as such it will be your duty to take an oath before a proper

every form of persuasive art to induce them to do the same. Fearing, perhaps, some show of hostility from the Wichitas, Comanches, and Tonkawas, and hoping that a show of force on his part would intimidate them, Pike gathered together, before proceeding to the Leased District, a company of fifty-six [382] mounted men, friendly Creeks and Seminoles, and with them left the Seminole Council House. The Leased District once reached, some of the hardest work of the whole negotiation began and two treaties [383] were ultimately concluded, one

officer of a State of the Confederate States, to support the Constitution of and accept a Commission from the Confederate States of America. . . — *Leeper Papers.*

[382] Pike to Walker, dated Seminole Agency, July 31, 1861 [*Official Records*, first ser., vol. iii, 624]. Writing to Benjamin, December 25, 1861 [*ibid.*, vol. viii, 720], Pike said he had "64 men."

[383] These two treaties are interesting in various particulars. They contained fewer concessions, fewer departures from established practice than any others of the nine. They were made primarily for the maintenance of peace on the Texan frontier. That fact is only too evident from their contents and from the circumstances of their negotiation. One of the chief reasons, cited by Texas, for her withdrawal from the Union was the failure of the United States to protect her from Indian ravages. It seems never to have occurred to her to mention the fact that her citizens, by their aggressions, had constantly provoked the ravages, if such we can call them. The northern counties of Texas were not "Southern" in climate or industries, so it was especially necessary to enlist their sympathy in the Confederate cause by keeping the Indians of the plains quiet and peaceful.

The Comanche treaties were also interesting in the matter of their signatures and of their schedules. The signatures included that of Rector, of the Creek chiefs, Motey Kennard and Chilly McIntosh, and of the Seminole chief, John Jumper. The schedules promised such things as the following to the Indians but in amounts that were beautifully indefinite:

Blue drilling, warm coats, calico, plaid check, regatta cotton shirts, socks, hats, woolen shirts, red, white and blue blankets, red and blue list cloth, shawls and handkerchiefs, brown domestic, thread, yarn and twine, shoes, for men and women, white drilling, ribbons, assorted colors, beads, combs, camp kettles, tin cups and buckets, pans, coffee pots and dippers, needles, scissors and shears, butcher knives, large iron spoons, knives and forks, nails, hatchets and hammers, augers, drawing knives, gimlets, chopping axes, fish-hooks, ammunition, including powder, lead, flints and percussion caps, tobacco.

Two of a kind would have satisfied most of the requirements of these

with some of the legitimate residents of the locality and one with wandering bands who came in for the purpose. It is well to note at the outset, however, that the Wichitas proper refused to be either cajoled or intimidated and that, in consequence, they who had always, under United States control, been the most important of the reservees, the ones to give the name to the entire group, were now reduced to a subordinate position and some of the Comanches [384] elevated to the first rank. The first treaty then, the one made with reservees, was thus designated, "Treaty with Comanches and Other Tribes and Bands." The second treaty, made with Indians be-

schedules. The list of things is interesting from the standpoint of domesticity and general utility and also from the standpoint of the things that the same Indians had previously seemed to need in such immense quantities. For illustration it would be well to note that when Agent Leeper handed in his last accounts to the United States government, he claimed to have issued during the second quarter of 1861 to the Indians at the Wichita Agency, 550 pounds of coffee, 550 pounds of sugar, 650 pounds of soap, 600 pounds of tobacco, etc.

In conclusion, with respect to these Comanche treaties, we may say that, since the Choctaw and Chickasaw Treaty had put the Leased District under the jurisdiction of the C.S.A., there was very little for the reservees themselves to do, except take the protection and other things offered by the Confederacy (the Comanches of the Prairie and Staked Plain had promised to become reservees on the Leased District) and be content. Pike did not bother about promising to make them citizens eventually or about making them admit the legality of the institution of slavery. Their political status had never been high and it was no higher under the Confederacy than it had been under the Union.

[384] The Tonkawas seem to have been the ones who were the most completely persuaded of all to adhere to the South and they continued unwaveringly loyal thereafter to its failing fortunes [S. S. Scott to Governor Winchester Colbert, dated Fort Arbuckle, November 10, 1862; Colbert to Scott, same date; Moore's *Rebellion Record*, vol. vi, 6; Commissioner of Indian Affairs, *Report*, 1863, House *Executive Documents*, 38th congress, first session, vol. iii, 143; Indian Office, *Report Book*, no. 19, pp. 186-188]. Apparently the Confederacy was rather careful in carrying out its obligations to the Tonkawas. Among the *Leeper Papers* are various documents proving this, such as an unsigned receipt for money received from Pike, July 19, 1862, to carry out the terms of Articles XVI and XVII of the treaty of August 12, 1861; and a copy of a letter, from Leeper probably, to J. J. Sturm, commissary, dated November 30, 1861, complaining that Sturm had not followed "instructions in making issues to Tonkahua Indians."

longing outside the Leased District was designated, "Treaty with the Comanches of the Prairies and Staked Plain."

The negotiation of the remaining treaties of the Pike series came as an immediate effect of Confederate military successes and belongs, in its description, to the next chapter. It is proper now to return to a consideration of the work of the Confederate Congress, in so far, at least, as that work had a bearing upon the alliance with the tribes. On the twenty-eighth of August, Hugh F. Thomason of Arkansas, offered the following resolution:

> *Resolved*, That the Committee on Indian Affairs be instructed to inquire whether any, and if so what, treaties have been made with any of the Indian tribes, and if so, with which of them; and whether any, and if so, what legislation is necessary in consequence thereof; and that they have leave to report at such time and in such manner as to them shall seem proper.[385]

There the matter rested until after the whole series of treaties had been completed which was in ample time for President Davis to submit[386] Pike's report[387] and the tangible evidence of his successful work to the Provisional Congress at its winter session.

President Davis's message of December 12, 1861, transmitting the Pike treaties to the Provisional Congress, summarized their merits and their defects and gave direction to the consideration and discussion that ended in their ratification. It called particular attention to the pecuniary obligations[388] assumed and to the

---

[385] *Journal*, vol. i, 565.

[386] Message of Dec. 12, 1861 [Richardson, *op. cit.*, vol. i, 149-151; *Official Register*, fourth ser., vol. i, 785-786].

[387] This report I have been unable to find.

[388] The pecuniary obligations of these treaties are of great importance. Apart from the annuities secured to them by former treaties, and which we are to assume by those now submitted, these tribes have large permanent funds in the hands of the Government of the United States as

contemplated change of status.   Regarding the latter,
Davis said,

> Important modifications are proposed in favor of the respective
> local governments of these Indians, to which your special atten-
> tion is invited.   That their advancement in civilization justified
> an enlargement of their power in that regard will scarcely ad-
> mit of a doubt; but whether the proposed concessions in favor
> of their local governments are within the bounds of a wise policy
> may well claim your serious consideration.   In this connection
> your attention is specially invited to the clauses giving to certain
> tribes the unqualified right of admission as a State into the com-
> pact of the Confederacy, and in the meantime allowing each of
> these tribes to have a delegate in Congress.   These provisions

their trustee.   These funds may be divided into three classes: First.
Money which the Government of the United States stipulated to invest
in its own stocks or stocks of the States, and which has been partly invested in its own stocks and partly uninvested, remains in its Treasury,
but upon which it is bound to pay interest.   Second. Funds invested in
the stocks of States not members of this Confederacy.   Third. Money invested in stocks of States now members of this Confederacy. . .   By
the treaties now submitted to you the first and second class are absolutely
assumed by this Government; but this Government only undertakes as
trustee to collect the third class from the States which owe the money
and pay over the amounts to the Indians when collected.   It is fortunate
for the Indians and ourselves that the amounts embraced in classes one
and two are relatively small, and the obligations incurred by their assumption cannot be onerous, as the amount due by States of the Confederacy on account of investments in the funds of Northern Indians considerably exceeds the amount to be assumed under this provision of the
treaties.   We thereby have the means to compel the Government of the
United States to do justice to the Indians within the jurisdiction of the
Confederate States, or to indemnify ourselves for its breach of faith.
  . . . I also submit to you the report of Albert Pike, the commissioner, which contains a history of his negotiations and submits his reasons for a departure from his instructions in relation to the pecuniary
obligations to be incurred.   [The reference here is to a letter from Pike
to Toombs, May 20, 1861, *Official Records*, first ser., vol. iii, 581.]   In
view of the circumstances by which we are surrounded, the great importance of preserving peace with the Indians on the frontier of Texas,
Arkansas, and Missouri, and not least, because of the spirit these tribes
have manifested in making common cause with us in the war now existing, I recommend the assumption of the stipulated pecuniary obligations, and, with the modifications herein suggested, that the treaties
submitted be ratified. – *Official Records*, fourth ser., vol. i, 786.

are regarded not only as impolitic but unconstitutional, it not being within the limits of the treaty-making power to admit a State or to control the House of Representatives in the matter of admission to its privileges. I recommend that the former provision be rejected, and that the latter be so modified as to leave the question to the future action of Congress; and also do recommend the rejection of those articles in the treaties which confer upon Indians the right to testify in the State courts, believing that the States have the power to decide that question, each for itself, independently of any action of the Confederate Government.[389]

Again Arkansas was in the lead in the exhibition of interest and, on the motion[390] of one of her delegation, Robert W. Johnson, the president's message and the documents accompanying it were referred to the Committee on Indian Affairs. This was on the thirteenth of December and Johnson was the chairman of the committee. On the nineteenth, the treaties began to be considered[391] in executive session. The first to be so considered was the Choctaw and Chickasaw, and interest concentrated on its twenty-seventh article,[392] the one giving to the two tribes jointly a delegate in the Confederate Congress. This provision was finally amended[393] so as to leave the delegate's status, his rights and his privileges, just as Davis had recommended, to the House of Representatives. Then came the consideration of the twenty-eighth article,[394] which promised ultimate statehood, and that also was amended in such a way as to leave the final determination to Congress,

By whose act alone, under the Constitution, new States can be

[389] *Official Record*, fourth ser., vol. i, 785-786.
[390] *Journal*, vol. i, 564, 565.
[391] — *Ibid.*, 590-596.
[392] — *Ibid.*, 590-591.
[393] *Statutes at Large*, 330.
[394] *Journal*, vol. i, 591-592.

admitted and whose consent it is not in the power of the President or the present Congress to guarantee in advance. . .[395]

In the afternoon of December twenty-first, the Provisional Congress resumed[396] its consideration of the Indian treaties. The day previous, it had decided upon this order of procedure and had agreed[397] that the Comanche treaties, being of the least importance, should be left to the last. The work of the twenty-first was on the judicial clauses and, on the question of the qualification of the Indians to be competent witnesses in civil and criminal suits. Article XXXVI[398] of the Osage Treaty, dealing with the right to subpoena witnesses and to have counsel, seemed likely to create prejudice.[399] At length Waul of Texas suggested[400] that Commissioner Pike be invited to be present at future sessions in order that some very necessary explanations of scope, of motives, and of reasons might be forthcoming. In the end, the only changes made in the grant of judicial privileges were along the line of safe-guarding the existing rights of the individual states. In illustration of this, take the Choctaw and Chickasaw Treaty as typical of all of the treaties of the First Class. Articles XLIII and XLIV were amended. To the former was added,

> And the Confederate States will request the several States of the Confederacy to adopt and enact the provisions of this article, in respect to suits and proceedings in their several courts.[401]

From the latter, the phrase, "or of a State," was stricken

---

[395] *Statutes at Large*, 331.
[396] *Journal*, vol. i, 597.
[397] — *Ibid.*, 593.
[398] *Statutes at Large*, 367.
[399] *Journal*, 601.
[400] — *Ibid.*, 598.
[401] *Statutes at Large*, 331.

out and this substitution made; "or of a State, subject to the laws of the State." [402]

On the whole, the Indian treaties took up a very large share of the attention of the Confederate Congress throughout the month of December; and, after debate, President Davis's advice in every particular was followed, even to the assumption of the pecuniary obligations. On the twenty-third of December, Johnson reported [403] back the treaty with the Cherokees and some of its clauses were then considered. On the same day, Johnson offered [404] a resolution of ratification for the Seminole Treaty and it was unanimously adopted, the same changes identically having been made in the treaty as had been made in the Choctaw and Chickasaw in so far as the two treaties corresponded originally with each other. Congress also ratified a supplementary article to the Seminole Treaty. The last of the month, the Comanche treaties were reached [405] and soon pushed through with only very slight modifications. Then came the final consideration of the treaty with the Creek Indians. It was ratified [406] with the customary amendments the same day. The Quapaw Treaty came [407] next and with its congressional ratification, the work of diplomatically securing the Indians was practically done. The later Indian ratification was more or less perfunctory.

---

[402] *Statutes at Large*, 331.
[403] *Journal*, vol. i, 610.
[404] — *Ibid.*
[405] — *Ibid.*, 632-633.
[406] — *Ibid.*, 634.
[407] — *Ibid.*, 635.

IV. THE INDIAN NATIONS IN ALLIANCE WITH THE CONFEDERACY

The work of soliciting the military support of the Indians and, to a large extent, that of securing it, antedated very considerably the formal negotiation of treaties with their constituted authorities. Whether it be true or not, that Douglas H. Cooper, United States agent for the Choctaws and the Chickasaws, did, as early as April, 1861, begin to enroll his Indians for the service of the Confederate States, it is indisputable that, immediately upon receiving Secretary Walker's communication [408] of May thirteenth, he began to do it in real earnest and, from that time forward, gained his recruits with astonishing ease. There were many [409] to recommend the employment of the Indians and some to oppose it. A certain F. J. Marshall, writing [410] to Jefferson Davis from Marysville, Kansas, on the twentieth of May, mapped out a tremendous programme of activities in which Indians were to play their part and to help secure everything of value between the Missouri line and the Pacific coast. Henry McCulloch thought [411] they might be used advantageously in Texas and on her borders. Pike believed [412] not more than thirty-five hundred could be counted upon, maybe five

---

[408] *Official Records*, first ser., vol. iii, 574.

[409] Chief Justice M. H. McWillie of La Mesilla, Arizona, was among the number. See his letter to President Davis, June 30, 1861, quoted in *Official Records*, vol. iv, 96.

[410] *Official Records*, first ser., vol. iii, 578-579.

[411] — *Ibid.*, vol. i, 618.

[412] Letter to Johnson, May 11, 1861, *ibid.*, vol. iii, 572.

thousand, but whatever the number, he would engage them quickly and provide them with the necessary equipment. He wanted also to employ[413] a battalion of those Indians that more strictly belonged to Kansas. Presumably, then, he would not have confined Confederate interest to the slaveholding tribes. Others besides Pike were doubtless of the same mind. Marshall was, for instance, and southern emissaries were frequently heard of, north of the Neosho River. Henry C. Whitney, one of two United States special agents (Thomas C. Slaughter was the other), sent[414] out to Kansas to investigate and with a view to relieve under congressional appropriation[415] the distress among the Indians, caused by the fearful and widespread drouth of 1860, met[416] with many traces of secessionist influence.[417]

---

[413] Letter to Toombs, May 20, 1861, *ibid.*, 581.

[414] Commissioner of Indian Affairs, *Report*, 1861, p. 14.

[415] Act of March 2, 1861, U.S. *Statutes at Large*, vol. xii, 239.

[416] On the twenty-second of May, Whitney reported, generally, on the condition of several tribes:

> Owing to the extremely dangerous state of political affairs in Missouri especially along the line of the H. & St. Jo. R.R., I have refrained from writing to you. . . Although the *Delawares* were not especially refered to in my instructions yet I visited the Mission & Agent as it was quite convenient . . . and ascertained to my complete satisfaction . . . that they were a wealthy tribe and that although many of their individual members were *necessitous* yet they were not of the *destitute* kind contemplated by your department: 2d. that the new agent who had heard of this movement towards relief was very anxious to make it appear that his tribe was very needy & to have large amounts of relief furnished at his residence on the Missouri River away from the agency & also from a central point. . .
>
> I next visited the Osage River Agency and ascertained that all of the tribes belonging to that Agency were in rather a destitute condition, they having used and still (are) using their school fund in buying provisions: the Miamis of that agency I found to be the most needy & it might be said that they were *suffering* to some extent. . .
>
> . . . In reference to the Neosho Agency, as that was such a long distance I engaged three trains of wagons before leaving Leavenworth. . .

Whitney speaks harshly of the Osages as lazy vagabonds and continues,

The efforts of Cooper, coupled with those of Pike and McCulloch, in this matter of the enlistment of In-

> . . . The general famine throughout Kansas had but little to do with their sufferings as they cultivate nothing of consequence . . . and therefore . . . they are not morally & strictly proper objects of government charity. . .
>
> . . . Systematic and well planned solicitations had been and are being made by Missourians to them to take up arms against the borderers to which the people throughout this entire section feared they might be induced on account of the neglect of Government [and because the whites steal their ponies] – Land Files, *Central Superintendency, 1852-1869,* W223.

Note that Whitney thought the reports of border ruffian inducements, though true in a measure, had been exaggerated. On the eighth of June, he reported again,

> When I got within reach of the H. & St. J. R. R. it became apparent that my produce would be at best somewhat exposed to seizure by the secessionists and that such hazard would be very greatly enhanced if it was known to be government property and especially if it should be known to be going to the Indians whom the Missourians were even then as was reported upon authority endeavoring to excite against the borderers. . . – Land Files, *Central Superintendency, 1852-1869,* W223.

Slaughter had less to report; but even he, on the twenty-first of June, said, while insisting that the reports had been exaggerated,

> I have no doubt overtures have been held out to them [the more northern tribes], but whether from authorized parties from [the] South no one can tell. It is all matter of conjecture. A general council of the tribes it is understood has been solicited by some of the Southern Indians, but I doubt whether it will be held. – General Files, *Central Superintendency, 1860-1862,* S404.

Slaughter further surmised, from personal observations, that the northern tribes would remain loyal to the United States. See his letter to Dole, June 15, 1861. Other people were of the same opinion, although, in early 1861, the various tribes had much to complain of, much to make them discontented and therefore very susceptible to bad influences. Some of the Miamis were preferring charges against Agent Clover for misapplication of funds and other things [Louis Lefontaine, etc. to Greenwood, January 13, 1861, Land Files, *Osage River, 1860-1866*]; the Kaws were suffering and R. S. Stevens slowly working out the details of his preposterous graft in the construction of houses for them [M. C. Dickey to Greenwood, February 26, 1861, General Files, *Kansas, 1855-1862,* D250, and same to same, March 1, 1861, *ibid.,* D251]; the Shawnees were having the usual troubles over their tribal elections, Joseph White having recently been elected second chief in place of Eli Blackhoof [Robinson to Greenwood, February 19, 1861, Land Files, *Shawnee, 1860-1865*]; and then, even farther north, from among the Otoes, came additional complaints;

dian troops, were soon rewarded. Chief Hudson's proclamation of June fourteenth, besides being a declaration of independence, was a call for troops and a call that was responded to by the Choctaws with alacrity. A little more than a month later, the enlistment of Indians had so far advanced that McCulloch was able to speak[418] positively as to his intended disposition of them. It was to keep them, both the Choctaw-Chickasaw regiment, which was then well under way towards

for Agent Dennison, who by the way, became a secessionist and a defaulter [Dole to Thaddeus Stevens, May 26, 1862, Indian Office, *Report Book*, no. 12, pp. 388-389], was withholding annuities and an uprising was threatening in consequence [General Files, *Otoe, 1856-1862*].

[417] The alien influence extended itself even to the wild Indians of the Plains. On the sixth of August, 1861 [General Files, *Pottawatomie, 1855-1861*, B704], Branch reported bad news that he had received from Agent Ross regarding the hostile approach of these Indians and remarked,

> I think there can be little doubt but what emissaries of the Rebels have been and are actively engaged in creating dissatisfaction against the government with every tribe of Indians that they dare approach on that subject.
>
> As soon as I can get the business of this office in a shape so I can conveniently leave my office duties I propose visiting the most of the tribes under this superintendency with a view to reconciling them and enjoining peace. . .

Similarly Captain Elmer Otis from Fort Wise, August 17, 1861, and A. G. Boone from the Upper Arkansas Agency, September 7, 1861, reported the Texans' tampering with the Kiowas [Land Files, *Upper Arkansas, 1855-1865*, O40, B772], who seem successfully to have resisted their threats and their blandishments. The Comanches of Texas were also approached but they fled rather than yield [Boone to Mix, October 19, 1861, *ibid.*, B861]. They, however, importunately demanded a treaty from the United States government in return for their loyalty. They were poor, they said, and had lost their hunting-grounds. Boone made good use of them as scouts and spies against the Texans [Letter of December 14, 1861, *ibid.*, B1006]. They were of the Comanches who had treated with Pike and who had solemnly pledged themselves, under duress and temporary excitement, to amity and allegiance. Secret agents from the South went also among the Blackfeet and Agent Thomas G. McCulloch sent an ex-employee of the American Fur Company, named Alexander Culbertson and married to the daughter of the Blackfeet chief, as a secret agent to counteract their influence [General Files, *Central Superintendency, 1860-1862*].

[418] Letter to Walker, July 18, 1861 [*Official Records*, first ser., vol. iii, 611].

organization, and the Creek, which was then forming, at Scullyville, situated fifteen miles, or thereabouts, from Fort Smith, as a check upon the Cherokees. Evidently the peace-loving element among the Cherokees was yet the dominant one. On the twenty-fifth of July, Cooper furnished further information,

> The organization of the Choctaw and Chickasaw Regiment of Mounted Rifles will be completed this week, but as yet no arms [419] have been furnished at Fort Smith for them. I hope speedy and effectual measures will be taken to arm the people of this (Indian) Territory – the Creeks, Seminoles, Cherokees. . . . The Choctaws and Chickasaws can furnish 10,000 warriors [420] if needed. The Choctaws and Chickasaws are extremely anxious to form another regiment.

[419] The scarcity of arms proved to be a serious matter. On the thirtieth of July, the assistant-quartermaster general, George W. Clark, telegraphed to Walker that arms had not yet arrived and that the Indians, encamped at the Old Choctaw Agency, were, in consequence, showing signs of discontent [*Official Records,* first ser., vol. iii, 620].

[420] Cooper probably spoke the truth, for the Choctaws and Chickasaws together had a population of twenty-three thousand.

In 1861, the Indian population of the Southern Superintendency was, as reported by Dole upon inquiry from Hon. J. S. Phelps of Missouri [John C. G. Kennedy, of the Census Office, to Dole, August 9, 1861]:

Chickasaws	5,000
Choctaws	18,000
Cherokees	21,000
Creeks	13,550
Seminoles (of which 1,247 were males) . . .	2,267

[Dole's answer, August 10, 1861].

In April, the report from the Indian Office had been:

Choctaws	18,000
Chickasaws	5,000
Total .	23,000
Creeks	13,550
Cherokees	17,530
Seminoles	2,267
Neosho Agency	4,863
Leased District	2,500
Total .	63,710

[Indian Office, *Report Book,* no. 12].

There seems to be a disposition to keep the Indians at home.
This seems to me bad policy. They are unfit for garrison duty,
and would be a terror to the Yankees.[421]

All this time, of course, Pike had been making progress with his treaties and undoubtedly simplifying
Cooper's task by embodying in those treaties the principles of an active alliance. These clauses from the
Creek Treaty will illustrate the point:

ARTICLE I. There shall be perpetual peace and friendship,
and an alliance offensive and defensive, between the Confederate
States of America, and all of their States and people, and the
Creek Nation of Indians, and all its towns and individuals.[422]

ARTICLE XXXVI. In consideration of the common interests of
the Creek Nation and the Confederate States, and of the protection and rights guaranteed to the said nation by this treaty,
the Creek Nation, hereby agrees that it will, either by itself or
in conjunction with the Seminole Nation, raise and furnish a
regiment of ten companies of mounted men to serve in the armies
of the Confederate States for twelve months, the company officers whereof shall be elected by the members of the company,
and the field officers by a majority of the votes of the members
of the regiment. The men shall be armed by the Confederate
States, receive the same pay and allowances as other mounted
troops in the service, and not be moved beyond the limits of the
Indian country west of Arkansas without their consent.[423]

ARTICLE XXXVII. The Creek Nation hereby agrees and
binds itself at any future time to raise and furnish, upon the re-

---

[421] Letter to President Davis [*Official Records*, first ser., vol. iii, 614].

[422] Identical with Article 1 of both the Cherokee and the Choctaw and
Chickasaw, but different from the Seminole in that the Seminole provided
simply for "perpetual peace and friendship."

[423] The corresponding Choctaw and Chickasaw Article [XLIX] stipulated
that the colonel of the regiment should be appointed by the president. Of
course, Douglas H. Cooper, was at this time, the one and only candidate for
the place and there is no doubt that the exception was made for his especial
benefit. However, Pike objected to his holding, in addition to the colonelcy,
the office of Indian agent [*Official Records*, first ser., vol. iii, 614].

Agent Garrett wanted the position of colonel in the Creek regiment and
Pike recommended him, but McCulloch objected saying,

I hope the appointment will not be made, for Colonel Garrett is in no
way qualified for the position, and from what I know of his habits, I

quisition of the President, such number of troops for the defence
of the Indian country, and of the frontier of the Confederate

am satisfied that a worse appointment could not be made. – *Official Records*, first ser., vol. iii, 597.

This was before the treaty had been negotiated and, after it had been negotiated, Pike wrote to Walker as follows:

When I recommended the appointment of William H. Garrett, the
present agent for the Creeks, to be colonel of the Creek regiment, I had
not sufficiently estimated the ambition and desire for distinction of the
leading men of that nation, and I also supposed that Mr. Garrett, popular with them as an agent, would be acceptable as colonel of their
regiment; but when I concluded with them the very important treaty
of July 10, instant, they strenuously insisted that the colonel of the
regiment to be raised should be elected by the men. As the public interest did not require I should insist upon a contrary provision, by
which I might have jeoparded the treaty, I yielded, and the consequence is that by the treaty, as signed and ratified by the Creek council, the field officers are all to be elected by the men of the regiment.

This being the case, I have this day written Colonel Garrett, requesting him to inform the Creeks immediately, as I have already done,
that notwithstanding his appointment they will elect their colonel. If
he should not do so he will cause much mischief, and would deserve severe censure; but I do not doubt he will promptly do it. . . – *Official
Records*, first ser., vol. iii, 623-624.

On the twenty-fourth of August, the matter was settled at Richmond by
Walker's writing to Pike,

In order that there shall be no misunderstanding with the friendly
Indians west of Arkansas, this Department is anxious that the article in
the treaty made by you, guaranteeing to them the right of selecting
their own field officers, shall be carried out in good faith. The name of
Mr. Garrett will therefore be dropped as colonel of the Creek regiment,
and that regiment will proceed to elect its own officers. The regiment
being formed among the Seminoles will exercise the same right. Reassure the tribes of the perfect sincerity of this Government toward
them. – *Ibid.*, 671.

The corresponding Cherokee Article [XL] differed slightly from the Creek.
It seems to have taken certain things, like the choice of officers, both company
and field, for granted. It reads thus:

In consideration of the common interest of the Cherokee Nation and
the Confederate States, and of the protection and rights guaranteed to
the said nation by this treaty, the Cherokee Nation hereby agrees that
it will raise and furnish a regiment of ten companies of mounted men,
with two reserve companies, if allowed, to serve in the armies of the
Confederate States for twelve months; the men shall be armed by the
Confederate States, receive the same pay and allowances as other mounted troops in the service, and not be moved beyond the limits of the
Indian country west of Arkansas without their consent.

States as he may fix, not out of fair proportion to the number of its population, to be employed for such terms of service as the President may fix; and such troops shall always receive the same pay and allowances as other troops of the same class in the service of the Confederate States.[424]

ARTICLE XXXVIII.   It is further agreed by the said Confederate States that the said Creek Nation shall never be required or called upon to pay, in land or otherwise, any part of the expenses of the present war, or of any war waged by or against the Confederate States.[425]

ARTICLE XXXIX.   It is further agreed that, after the restoration of peace, the Government of the Confederate States will defend the frontiers of the Indian country, of which the Creek country is a part, and hold the forts and posts therein, with native troops, recruited among the several Indian Nations included therein, under the command of officers of the army of the Confederate States, in preference to other troops.[426]

Although John Ross had positively forbidden the recruiting of any force within the limits of the Cherokee country, that while nominally for home defense, should be in reality a reserve force for the Confederacy, he was unable to prevent individuals from going over, on their own responsibility entirely, to McCulloch; and many did go and are believed to have fought[427] with his

[424] Identical with Article LI of the Choctaw and Chickasaw Treaty and with Article LXI of the Cherokee.

[425] Identical with Article L of the Choctaw and Chickasaw Treaty, with Article XLII of the Cherokee, and with Article XXXVI of the Seminole.

[426] Identical with Article LII of the Choctaw and Chickasaw Treaty and with Article XLIII of the Cherokee.

[427] Frémont reported to Townsend, August 13, 1861, that Cherokee half-breeds, judging from the muster roll and from the corroborating testimony of prisoners, were with McCulloch in this battle, fought about ten miles south of Springfield, August 10, 1861 [*Official Records*, first ser., vol. iii, 54]. Connelley says, in 1861, Quantrill, returning from Texas, lingered in the Cherokee Nation with a half-breed Cherokee, Joel Mayes,

> Who, many years after the war, was elected Head Chief of the Nation. Mayes espoused the cause of the Confederacy and was captain of a company or band of Cherokees who followed General Ben McCulloch to Missouri. – *Quantrill and the Border Wars*, 198].

A letter, written by McCulloch to Colonel John Drew, September 1, 1861,

brigade at the Battle of Oak Hills, or Wilson's Creek. That battle proved the determining point in this period of Cherokee history. It was a Confederate victory, and a victory gained under such circumstances [428] that the watchful Indians had every reason to think that the southern cause would be triumphant in the end.

The dissensions [429] among the Cherokee and the constant endeavors of the Ridge Party to develop public sentiment in favor of the Confederacy, to undermine the popularity of John Ross, and to destroy his influence over the full-bloods were, and there is no gainsaying it, the real causes of the ultimate Cherokee defection. The Battle of Wilson's Creek was only the occasion, only the immediate cause, the excuse, if you please, and of itself could never have brought about a decision. Yet its effect [430] upon Cherokee opinion was unquestionably great and immediate, and that effect was noticeably strengthened and intensified by the memory of

seems to indicate that individual Cherokees had joined him [*Official Records*, first ser., vol. iii, 691].

[428] The Federal defeat was believed by contemporaries to have been due to mismanagement, to army friction, to the incompetency and sloth of Sigel, and to Frémont's failure to reinforce the redoubtable Lyon, who fell in the engagement. An investigation into Sigel's conduct was subsequently made by Halleck, Sigel's bitter enemy. Halleck hated Sigel, because Sigel so greatly admired Frémont, whom Halleck supplanted; and because Sigel was the hero of the Germans, and one of them. For the Germans, Halleck had a great antipathy. Many of them were "pfälzisch-badischen Revolutionäre" and Halleck regarded them as adventurers or as refugees from justice. They in turn referred to Halleck as one of the West Point "bunglers" who were so numerous in the northern army, the really efficient and capable West Pointers, so they said, having all gone with the South [Kaufmann's "Sigel und Halleck" in *Deutsch-Amerikanische Geschichtsblätter*, Band, 210-216, October 1910].

[429] Even in the latter part of May, these were so serious as to threaten a Cherokee civil war [Letter of John Crawford, May 21, 1861, General Files, *Cherokee, 1859-1865*; Mix to Crawford, June 4, 1861, Indian Office, *Letter Book*, no. 66, pp. 15-16].

[430] Ben McCulloch to Walker, September 2, 1861 [*Official Records*, first ser., vol. iii, 692]; Pike to Benjamin, December 25, 1861 [*ibid.*, vol. viii, 720].

other Federal reverses along the Atlantic seaboard, especially the more recent and more serious one of Manassas Junction, on the twenty-first of July.

Up to about that time, the neutral policy of John Ross seems to have received the endorsement of a majority of the Cherokee people. In the last days of June, the Executive Council had been called together and had, after a session of several days, publicly and officially approved [431] of the stand the principal chief had taken to date. But events were already under way that were to make this executive action in no sense a true index to popular feeling. The secessionists were secretly organizing themselves, ready to seize the first opportunity that might appear. The full-bloods, or non-secessionists, were also organized and, under the name of "Pins," were holding meetings of mutual encouragement among the hills. Encounters between the two factions were not infrequent and the half-breeds resorted to all sorts of expedients for persuading, or that failing, of frightening the full-bloods into a compliance with their wishes. They told them that the Kansas people had designs upon their lands (which was not altogether untrue), and that the Federal government would free their slaves and otherwise dispossess, degrade, and humiliate them. Such arguments had their effect and there was little at hand to counteract it, none in the memory of the past, none in the neglect and embarrassment of the present, none in the prospect of the future. There were no Federal troops, no new Federal assurances of protection. Agent Crawford, who was the only agent within reach, added his threats and his Confederate promises to those of the half-breeds. Then came the Battle of Wilson's Creek with its disastrous

---

[431] "Meetings and Proceedings of the Executive Council of the Cherokee Nation, July 2, 1861" [General Files, *Cherokee, 1859-1865*, C515].

Federal showing, and the exhausted resisting power of the Pins went down before the renewed secessionist ardor.

A meeting of the Cherokee Executive Council had been called for August first, and John Ross, Joseph Vann, James Brown, John Drew, and William P. Ross, all prominent non-secessionists, had attended it. On this occasion, a general, or mass, meeting of the Cherokee people was arranged for, in response to a public appeal, and the date for it was fixed for the twentieth of August.[432] In the interval came the news from Springfield and another communication from Albert Pike.[433]

The convention which met at Tahlequah in August of 1861 ended in the secession of the Cherokee Nation. While it was in progress, the events of the last few months were gone over in thorough review and emphasis placed upon those of recent occurrence. The attendance at the convention was large.[434] Both political factions were well represented and there seems to have been only a slight show of force, if any, from the secessionists. The Reverend Evan Jones is our authority for thinking that some "seventy or eighty of them appeared there in arms with the intention to break up the meeting;" but that only two of them succeeded in making

[432] See "Meetings and Proceedings of the Cherokee Executive Council, August 1, 1861" [General Files, *Cherokee, 1859-1865*, C515].

[433] Pike to Ross, August 1, 1861 [*ibid.*].

[434] A general meeting of the Cherokee people was held at Tahlequah on Wednesday, the 21st day of August, 1861. It was called by the executive of the Cherokee Nation for the purpose of giving the Cherokee people an opportunity to express their opinions in relation to subjects of deep interest to themselves as individuals and as a nation. The number of persons in attendance, almost exclusively adult males, was about 4,000, whose deportment was characterized by good order and propriety, and the expression of whose opinions and feelings was frank, cordial, and of marked unanimity. – *Report of the Proceedings at Tahlequah, August 21, 1861*, transmitted to General McCulloch by the Executive Council, August 24, 1861 [*Official Records*, first ser., vol. iii, 673].

any disturbance.[435] In the course of the meeting, Agent Crawford put in an appearance and again asserted himself in behalf of the Confederacy. He "appeared on the platform," says an eyewitness,

> And stated that although for some time past he had been among the Cherokees acting as U. S. Agent, it had been by the advice and consent of the Confederate authorities, and with the understanding that when the proper time arrived he should declare himself the Agent of the C.S.A. That time had now come making this the proudest day of his life.[436]

---

[435] Evan Jones of the Baptist Mission, Cherokee Nation, to Dole, dated Lawrence, Kansas, November 2, 1861 [General Files, *Cherokee, 1859-1865,* J503].

[436] W. S. Robertson, who for twelve years had been "teaching in the Tullahassee Manual Labor School in the Creek Nation under the care of the Presbyterian Board of Foreign Missions" [Robertson's Letter of September 30, 1861, General Files, *Southern Superintendency, 1859-1862,* R1615].

Robertson says, that

> Having witnessed the whole struggle between the Loyal & War parties, when the latter prevailed, I was on the 25th of August ordered by a party of the "Creek Light Horse" acting under the written orders of Moty Kenard and Jacob Derrysaw, Chief of the Creeks, to leave within twenty-four hours from the Creek country. I retired to my friends at Park Hill in the Cherokee where the same struggle was going on.
>
> At Park Hill I enjoyed every facility for knowing the feelings of the people, the designs of the Executive.
>
> When at last the Rebel flag flaunted over the council ground at Tahlequah, I left the Cherokee country with my family, and after encountering many dangers, succeeded in reaching Rolla, on the 23rd Sept. without giving any pledge to the enemy.
>
> Having written to the Sec. of the Interior (from St. Louis, Oct. 1st) stating my long residence among the Creeks and Cherokees, my means of information, and my desire to give any information that would benefit our Gov't or my loyal friends among the Indians – and having forwarded all the printed correspondence between the Rebels and Chief Ross (except the last letter of the Rebel commissioner, Albert Pike) together with Chief Ross' speech at the Cherokee Convention at Tahlequah, on the 21st of Aug. and the resolutions passed at said Convention, without receiving any answer, I concluded that Col. Humphrey's (of Tenn.) mysterious movements were all right, that he was loyal, and kept our Gov't well informed as to the Rebel doings among the Indians. That I had redeemed my pledge to loyal Creeks & Cherokees.
>
> Recent letters from St. Louis, & New York stating that "Gov't agents are seeking information everywhere," and urging me to write to "Gen.

Such a confession of baseness seems hardly credible. The secessionist was entitled to his opinions touching the doctrine of state rights, for which a difference of view found its justification both in fact and in theory. He might even conscientiously believe in the righteousness of negro enslavement, inasmuch as it really did offer an easy solution of a labor problem; and more-

Hunter" & Washington, induce me to send you my address, to urge you in the name of humanity and justice not to take decisive measures against the betrayed and oppressed people, until you have heard all that can be said in their behalf. – Letter to Department of the Interior and referred to Commissioner of Indian Affairs, dated January 7, 1862 [General Files, *Southern Superintendency, 1859-1862,* R1664].

Mix answered it February 14, 1862 [Indian Office, *Letter Book,* no. 67, p. 357].

In a somewhat earlier letter, the one from which the extract, in the body of the text was taken, Robertson had said,

I am . . . deeply interested in their welfare, acquainted with the feelings of the people, well informed as to the men and measures which have detached these nations from their allegiance to the U.S.

Chief among the traitors were not only the Superintendent of that District, and the Agents under him appointed by the late Administration but others claiming to have received commissions as Indian Agents "since the 4th of March last" from the U.S. Gov't.

On the 21st of Aug. last I was in Tahlequah, the capital of the Cherokee Nation, at a convention of the Cherokee people called by their Chief Jno. Ross. . .– ROBERTSON to President Lincoln, dated Winneconne, Wisconsin, December 12, 1861 [General Files, *Southern Superintendency, 1859-1862,* R1658].

Concerning the responsibility attaching to government agents for Indian defection, E. C. Boudinot and W. P. Adair wrote, January 19, 1866, to Cooley,

The Southern Indians have repeatedly repudiated the idea that they were induced by the machinations of any persons to ally themselves with the rebellion, but accept the full responsibility of their acts without such excuse.

The passage above quoted [meaning one from Coffin's report of September 24, 1863 – "They resisted the insidious influences which were brought to bear upon them by Rector, Pike, Cooper, Crawford and other rebel emissaries for a long time."] however does great injustice to all the parties named, particularly to Genl Cooper, who had no earthly connection with the Cherokees until several months after. Mr. John Ross made the treaty with the so-called Confederate States. – General Files, *Cherokee, 1859-1865,* B60.

over, would work under a benign paternalism, for the thorough, because so gradual, development of an inferior race; but by no standard of personal honor, or of moral rectitude could conduct such as Crawford's be condoned.

John Ross had opened the meeting with an address in which he had defined its purposes and his own good intentions, both past and present. Personally, he seemed still inclined to maintain a neutral attitude but designing persons had made his position most difficult.[437]

. . . Our soil has not been invaded, our peace has not been molested, nor our rights interfered with by either Government. On the contrary, the people have remained at home, cultivated their farms in security, and are reaping fruitful returns for their labors. But for false fabrications, we should have pursued our ordinary vocations without any excitement at home, or misrepresentations and consequent misapprehensions abroad, as to the real sentiments and purposes of the Cherokee people. Alarming reports, however, have been pertinaciously circulated at home and unjust imputations among the people of the States. The object seems to have been to create strife and conflict, instead of harmony and good-will, among the people themselves, and to engender prejudice and distrust, instead of kindness and confidence, towards them by the officers and citizens of the Confederate States. . .

. . . The great object with me has been to have the Cherokee people harmonious and united in the full and free exercise and enjoyment of all their rights of person and property. Union is strength; dissension is weakness, misery, ruin. In time of peace, enjoy peace together; in time of war, if war must come, fight together. As brothers live, as brothers die. While ready and willing to defend our firesides from the robber and murder-

---

[437] "Ross was overborne. It is said that his wife was more staunch than her husband and held out till the last. When an attempt was made to raise a Confederate flag over the Indian council house, her opposition was so spirited that it prevented the completion of the design." – Howard, *My life and experiences among our hostile Indians*, 100.

COLONEL ADAIR, CHEROKEE
[From Smithsonian Institution, Bureau of American Ethnology]

er, let us not make war wantonly against the authority of the United or Confederate States, but avoid conflict with either, and remain strictly on our own soil. We have homes endeared to us by every consideration, laws adapted to our condition of our own choice, and rights and privileges of the highest character. Here they must be enjoyed or nowhere else. When your nationality ceases here, it will live nowhere else. When these homes are lost, you will find no others like them. Then, my countrymen, as you regard your own rights, as you regard the welfare of your posterity, be prudent how you act. The permanent disruption of the United States is now probable. The State on our border and the Indian nations about us have severed their connection from the United States and joined the Confederate States. Our general interests are inseparable from theirs, and it is not desirable that we should stand alone. The preservation of our rights and of our existence are above every other consideration. And in view of all the circumstances of our situation I do say to you frankly that in my opinion the time has now come when you should signify your consent for the authorities of the nation to adopt preliminary steps for an alliance with the Confederate States upon terms honorable and advantageous to the Cherokee Nation.[438]

After having received this most solemn of warnings, "and a few pertinent and forcible remarks from Colonel Crawford," the meeting organized with Joseph Vann as president and William P. Ross as secretary. To effect a reconciliation between the contending factions and to decide upon some national policy that should be acceptable to the majority of the people, were, undoubtedly, the objects sought and so, after much discussion, a series of resolutions was adopted in which these ideas were given prominence as well as some of kindred importance. The resolutions asserted the legal and constitutional right of property in slaves and, in no doubtful terms, a friendship for the Confed-

[438] For the entire address of John Ross, see *Official Record*, first ser., vol. iii, 673-675.

eracy. Yet the convention itself took no definite action towards consummating an alliance but left everything to the discretion of the constituted authorities of the nation, in whom it announced an unwavering confidence.

Whereas we, the Cherokee people, have been invited by the executive of the Cherokee Nation, in compliance with the request of many citizens, to meet in general meeting, for the purpose of drawing more closely the bonds of friendship and sympathy which should characterize our conduct and mark our feelings towards each other in view of the difficulties and dangers which have arisen from the fearful condition of affairs among the people of the several States, and for the purpose of giving a free and frank expression of the real sentiments we cherish towards each other, and of our true position in regard to questions which affect the general welfare, and particularly on that of the subject of slavery: Therefore be it hereby

Resolved, That we fully approve the neutrality recommended by the principal chief in the war pending between the United and the Confederate States, and tender to General McCulloch our thanks for the respect he has shown to our position.

Resolved, That we renew the pledges given by the executive of this nation of the friendship of the Cherokees towards the people of all the States, and particularly towards those on our immediate border, with whom our relations have been harmonious and cordial, and from whom they should not be separated.

Resolved, that we also take occasion to renew to the Creeks, Choctaws, Seminoles, Chickasaws, and Osages, and others, assurances of continued friendship and brotherly feeling.

Resolved, That we hereby disavow any wish or purpose to create or perpetuate any distinctions between the citizens of our country as to the full and mixed blood, but regard each and all as our brothers, and entitled to equal rights and privileges according to the constitution and laws of the nation.

Resolved, That we proclaim unwavering attachment to the constitution and laws of the Cherokee Nation, and solemnly pledge ourselves to defend and support the same, and as far as in us lies to secure to the citizens of the nation all the rights and privileges which they guarantee to them.

Resolved, That among the rights guaranteed by the constitution and laws we distinctly recognize that of property in negro slaves, and hereby publicly denounce as calumniators those who represent us to be abolitionists, and as a consequence hostile to the South, which is both the land of our birth and the land of our homes.

Resolved, That the great consideration with the Cherokee people should be a united and harmonious support and defense of their common rights, and we hereby pledge ourselves to mutually sustain our nationality, and to defend our lives and the integrity of our homes and soil whenever the same shall be wantonly assailed by lawless marauders.

Resolved, That, reposing full confidence in the constituted authorities of the Cherokee Nation, we submit to their wisdom the management of all questions which affect our interests growing out of the exigencies of the relations between the United and Confederate States of America, and which may render an alliance on our part with the latter States expedient and desirable.

And which resolutions, upon the question of their passage being put, were carried by acclamation. JOSEPH VANN, President. Wm. P. Ross, Secretary.

Tahlequah, C.N., August 21, 1861.[439]

In making his plans, prior to the Battle of Wilson's Creek, for effecting a junction with Price and coöperating with him and others in southwest Missouri, McCulloch acted, not under direct orders from Richmond, but from his own desire to take such a position opposite the Cherokee Neutral Lands, once so outrageously intruded upon by Kansas settlers and now being made the highway of marauders entering Missouri, as would make it appear to the Cherokees that he was there as their friend and as the protector of their interests. After the battle, he refused, and rightly in view of his

---

[439] *Official Record*, first ser., vol. iii, 675-676. A slightly incorrect copy of these same resolutions is to be found in vol. xiii, 499-500.

own special commission, to accompany Price in his forward march towards the Missouri River. Instead he drew back into the neighborhood of the Cherokee boundary and there developed his plans for attacking Kansas, should such a course be deemed necessary in order to protect Indian Territory.

It was at this juncture that the Cherokees as a nation expressed their preference for the South and for the southern cause, moved thereto, however, by the peculiarities and the difficulties of their situation. The Executive Council lost no time in communicating [440] to McCulloch the decision of the Tahlequah mass-meeting and their own determination to carry out its wishes by effecting an alliance with the Confederacy "as early as practicable." They realized very clearly that this might "give rise to movements against the Cherokee people upon their northern border" and were resolved to be prepared for such an emergency. They, therefore, authorized the raising of a regiment of mounted men, home guards they were to be and to be so designated, officered by appointment of the principal chief, Colonel John Drew being made the colonel. It would appear that the nucleus of this regiment, and with a strong southern bias, had made [441] its appearance prior to the Tahlequah meeting and the circumstance gave rise to the suspicion that the Cherokees had not been acting in good faith. After the war, the suspicion concentrated, very unjustly, upon John Ross and was made the most of by Commissioner Cooley at the Fort Smith

---

[440] John Ross and others to McCulloch, August 24, 1861 [*Official Records,* first ser., vol. iii, 673].

[441] Commissioner of Indian Affairs, *Report,* 1865. The Report of the Commissioner of Indian Affairs to President Johnson, February 25, 1866, in answer to the Cherokee protest against Chief Ross's deposition contains this statement:

As early as June or July, the exact date is not known, John Ross authorized the raising of Drew's Regiment, for the Southern army. . .

conference; in order to accomplish, for reasons dishonorable to the United States government, the aged chief's deposition.

Drew's regiment of home guards was tendered to McCulloch and he agreed to accept it[442] but not until after a treaty of alliance should have been actually consummated between the Cherokees and the Confederate States. Pending the accomplishment of that highly desirable object, McCulloch promised to protect the Cherokee borders with his own troops and confessed[443] that he had already authorized the enlistment of another force of Cherokees under the command of Stand Watie, which had been designed to protect that same northern border but "not to interfere with the neutrality of the Nation by occupying a position within its limits."

It is not easy to decide just when or by whom the use of Indians by the Federals in the border warfare[444] was

[442] McCulloch to Ross, September 1, 1861 [*Official Records*, first ser., vol. iii, 690].

[443] —*Ibid.*; McCulloch to John Drew, September 1, 1861 [*ibid.*, 691].

[444] In the course of the war, both inside and outside of Kansas, many instances occurred of Indians' expressing a wish to fight or of their services being earnestly solicited. In late April of 1861, a deputation, headed by White Cloud, came east and tendered to the United States government the services of some three hundred warriors, Sioux and Chippewas [Moore's *Rebellion Record*, vol. i, 43].

Agent Burleigh, in charge of the Yancton Sioux, asked permission to garrison Fort Randall with Indians [Commissioner of Indian Affairs, *Report*, 1861, p. 118]. The Omahas manifested great interest in the war, so their agent, O. H. Irish, reported [*ibid.*, p. 65]. Towards the end of the struggle a young recruiting officer, who went among them, persuaded about thirty youths, mostly students at the Mission School, to enlist. Their terms had not expired when the war closed, so they were sent out as scouts to protect the Union Pacific Railroad, in course of construction from Denver to Salt Lake City, against the Sioux who were attacking workmen and emigrants. Even Senecas from the far away Cattaraugus Reservation, New York, offered to enlist [Dole to Strong, December 7, 1861, Indian Office *Letter Book*, no. 67, p. 129]; and so did the Pawnees from the great plains. The United States government, however, refused to accept the Pawnees for anything but scouts and,

first suggested. As late as May twenty-second, Governor Charles Robinson of Kansas, in a letter [445] to Superintendent Branch, protested against even so much as arming them, which would certainly indicate that a

in that capacity, they proved exceedingly useful [Commissioner of Indian Affairs, *Report*, 1869, p. 472]. Winnebagoes were in the United States employ [Indian Office, *Report Book*, no. 13, pp. 276-277], as were also many individuals from other tribes. Some Indians became commissioned officers and a number were at the head of companies. Captain Dorion of Company B, Regiment Fourteenth Kansas Volunteers was an Iowa [*ibid.*, 261] and Eli S. Parker on General Grant's staff was a Seneca.

After the Enrollment Act of March 3, 1863 [United States *Statutes at Large*, vol. xii, 731-737] was passed, several attempts were made to force the Indians to serve in the army but Mix, the Acting Commissioner of Indian Affairs, declared they were exempt from the draft [Letter to Agent D. C. Leach, September 4, 1863, Indian Office, *Letter Book*, no. 71, p. 354]. On the sixteenth of July, 1863, the United States War Department inquired very particularly as to the Indian eligibility for enrollment and Secretary Usher took occasion to instruct Mix that the respective agents should be

Directed to offer no resistance to the enrolling officers, after notifying said officers of the fact, that the tribe or tribes under their charge are composed of Indians who have not acquired the rights of Citizenship, but immediately upon being informed of the drafting of any member of his tribe, he will report the case to the Com^r of Indian Affairs, for such action as may be necessary to procure the exemption of the Indians from military service. – Letter of Secretary Usher, September 12, 1863, *Miscellaneous Files, 1858-1863*.

[445] The bearer has a train of goods at this point en route for the Indians on the western border of the State, containing quite a quantity of arms & ammunition.

There is great excitement in the community with reference to arming the Indians at the present time, as for several days past reports have come to us that our frontier settlements are in danger of attack from hostile Indians who are collecting in the neighborhood. I am daily importuned to send them aid. Also, report says, and it seems very reliable, that the Indians on our southern border are arming themselves against our citizens. In addition to these Indian rumors it is believed by many that these arms are in danger of falling into the hands of secessionists, before reaching their destination. Quite a number of that class of men have recently passed up this way (Topeka) and through Riley County. In this condition of affairs I do not think these arms & ammunition can be taken west without an escort, as the rabble will be almost certain to waylay them as soon as they get on the Pottawatomie Reserve. I can protect them while in this county & will do so, but cannot follow them. Would it not be well, if you have the

general use of their services had not yet been thought
of or resorted to; but, in August, when Senator James
H. Lane was busy organizing his brigade of volunteers
for the defense of Kansas, he resolved,[446] rather offi-

authority, to direct the bearer to leave that part of his freight in charge
of the U.S. Marshal, or in my charge, until there shall be a change
of circumstances, or until further orders from Washington?

Although I would not undertake to oppose the action of Government
in the matter and would not interfere unless it should be to prevent
the property from falling into the hands of a mob, yet I do think under
the circumstances it is very bad policy to arm the Indians on the border. I feel very sure from what I learn, they will be used against our
citizens within three months time. I am ready to co-operate at all
times with the U.S. authorities. . . – General Files, *Central Superintendency, 1860-1862*, B479. See also Branch's reply, May 23, *ibid.*

[446] H. B. Branch to Mix, September 16, 1861, transmitting a letter from
Agent Farnsworth of September 13, 1861, enclosing communications from Senator Lane, Captain Price, and others, "relative to organizing the Indians for
the defense of the Government" [General Files, *Kansas, 1855-1862*, B774].

> Headquarters K.B. Ft. Lincoln, Aug. 22d 1861.
> To Indian Agents Sac and Foxes – Shawnees – Delawares – Kicka-
> poos – Potawatomies – and Kaws – Tribes of Indians
> GENTS: For the defence of Kansas I have determined to use the
> loyal Indians of the Tribes above named. To this end I have appoint-
> ed Augustus Wattles, Esq to confer with you and adopt such measures
> as will secure the early assembling of the Indians at this point.
>
> If you have the means within your control I would like to have you
> supply them when they march with a sufficient quantity of powder,
> lead & subsistence for their march to this place, where they will be fed
> by the Government.
>
> You can assure them for the Govt that they will not be marched
> out of Kansas without their consent – that they will be used only for the
> defence of Kansas.
>
> I enjoin each of you to be prompt and energetic that an early as-
> sembling of said Indians at this point may thereby be secured.
>
> > J. H. LANE, Commanding Kansas Brigade.
> > By ABRAM CUTLER, Acting assistant Adgt-Gen.
>
> The danger is imminent. Hordes of whites & half breeds in the
> Indian country are in arms driving out & killing Union men. They
> threaten to overrun Kansas and exterminate both whites & Indians. It
> it rumored that John Ross, the Cherokee Chief is likely to be overcome
> unless he is assisted.
>
> The Osages also need assistance. Gen. Lane intends to establish a
> strong Indian camp near the neutral lands as a guard to prevent forage
> into Kansas. He is very solicitous that you should come if possible

ciously, one might think, upon using some of the Kansas River tribes in establishing "a strong Indian camp near the neutral lands to prevent forage into Kansas" and arranged for a conference with the Indians at Fort

> with the Chiefs & see him at Ft. Lincoln on the Little Osage 10 miles south of Mound City.
>
> If you do come, please bring all the fighting men you can, of all Kinds. Men are needed.
>
> If you do not come, please authorise some responsible man to lead the Indians as far as Ft. Lincoln where Gen. Lane will receive them and give them a big war talk. Bring an interpreter. Expenses will be paid.
>
> Congress will undoubtedly make suitable acknowledgements to the Kaws, as an independent nation, for any valuable services which they may render. . .
>
> P.S. A Captain's wages will be given to any competent man whom you may appoint to take the lead of the band, provided there are fifty or more. – AUGUSTUS WATTLES to Major Farnsworth, dated Sac and Fox Agency, Kansas, August 25, 1861.

Wattles had evidently not yet heard of the Tahlequah mass-meeting. Postal connections with Indian Territory were, of necessity, very poor. Dole had recommended, May 29, 1861, to Secretary Smith a new postal route through southwest Missouri or southern Kansas instead of the old route through Arkansas [Indian Office, *Report Book*, no. 12, p. 170].

The Confederates were similarly embarrassed. On the twenty-seventh of May, the postmaster at Fort Smith had complained to the postmaster-general J. H. Reagan,

> Enclosed please find letter of G. B. Hester (a Choctaw who was made quarter-master and commissary in the First Choctaw Regiment and, in 1865, "cotton agent for the Creek Indians who were at that time squatting in the Chickasaw Nation." See O'Beirne's *Leaders and Leading Men of the Indian Territory*) at Boggy Depot, C.N. You will see they are without mails in that country. For three weeks the mails for the Indian country have been accumulating in this office. I sent forward all the mail that could be packed on a single horse. . . I cannot get men to carry the mail. They say they are afraid of being robbed or murdered. . . Our neighbours, the Indians must suffer great inconvenience on account of the stoppage of mail facilities. All tribes are in favor of the South except the Cherokees. A little good talk would do them good, perhaps a little powder and lead might help the cause. Ross and his party are not to be relied on. – *Fort Smith Papers*.

Mayers wrote Reagan in a similar vein a month later, on June 26, 1861,

> Our mails throughout the Cherokee, Choctaw, Chickasaw & Creek nations have all been stopped by the old mail carriers. . . – *Ibid.*

Lincoln, his headquarters. Soon, however, a stay of execution was ordered [447] until the matter could be discussed, in its larger aspects, with Commissioner Dole, to whom courtesy, [448] at least, would have demanded that the whole affair should have been first submitted.

Dole was then in Kansas [449] and before long became aware [450] that General Frémont was also favoring the

---

[447] On August 26, 1861, Wattles wrote Farnsworth from Lawrence,

I wrote you a few days ago concerning the employment of the Indians in the defence of our frontier.

The necessity seemed imperative. But on hearing that the Commissioner of Indian Affairs was in Kansas and will probably see you – I think it best to say nothing to the Indians till he is consulted in the matter.

Gen. Lane has 60 miles of the Missouri border to guard, and an army of at least double his to hold in check, which employs all his force night & day.

Besides this, he has the Indian frontier on the south of about 100 miles. This he intends to intrust to the loyal Indians – I will add, if the Commissioner agrees to it.

The stay of execution was not of long duration, however; for, September 10, 1861, J. E. Prince sent Farnsworth from Fort Leavenworth a circular requesting immediate enrollment and an estimate of the strength of the loyal Indians.

[448] The conduct of Lane was presumptuous, arrogant, dictatorial; but he had interfered in yet other ways in Indian concerns. He must have had quite a hold, political or otherwise, over several of the agents and they appealed to him in matters that ought, in the first instance, to have been referred to the Indian Office and left there. Thus, in July, Agent F. Johnson had approached Lane on the subject of having Charles Journeycake appointed Delaware chief in place of Rock-a-to-wa deceased. Both Pomeroy and Lane endorsed the appointment but it was unquestionably entirely out of their province to do so. Tribal politics were assuredly no concern of the Kansas delegation in Congress.

[449] Dole had gone to Kansas in the latter part of August "to submit in person the amendments, made by the Senate at its last session, to the Delaware treaty of May 30, 1860" [Commissioner of Indian Affairs, *Report*, 1861, p. 11].

[450] I find here your letter to the Agent of the Delaware, requesting *Fall Leaf* to organize a party of 50 men for the service of your Department. *Mr. Johnson* the Agent called the tribe together before I arrived here, and found the Chiefs unwilling that their young men should enter the service as you desired. Since my arrival I have seen the Chiefs and stated to them that the Government was not asking them to enter the war as a tribe but that we wished to employ some of the tribe

enlistment of Indians, or, at all events, their employment by the army in some capacity. He had approached Agent Johnson on the subject, his immediate purpose being to request Fall Leaf, a Delaware, "to organize a party of 50 men for the service of" his department. Agent Johnson called the tribe together and discovered that the chiefs were much averse to having their young men enlist. Dole inquired into the matter and assured [451] the chiefs that a few braves only were needed and those simply for special service and that there was no intention of asking the tribe, as a tribe, to give its services. The chiefs refused consent, notwithstanding; but Fall Leaf and a few others like him did enlist. [452] They were probably among the fifty-three Delawares, subsequently reported [453] as having been employed by Frémont to act as scouts and guides. Fall Leaf attained the rank of captain. [454] Superintendent

---

for Special Service and wished the Chiefs to make no objection. I could not however get their consent even to acquiesce in their men Volunteering for the service as you desired, & *Fall Leaf* and several of the tribe are here and determined to tender you their Services, with my consent. I have advised them that they are at Liberty to join you if they choose. *Fall Leaf* says he will be able to report at Fort Leavenworth in a very few days with twenty to twenty five men. Should you require more men, you will have probably to call on some other tribe. Those men who volunteer against the advice of their Chiefs should be particularly remembered by the Gov't. – DOLE to Frémont, dated Leavenworth City, September 13, 1861 [Indian Office, *Letter Book*, no. 66, p. 485].

451 — *Ibid.*

452 I am instructed to acknowledge the receipt of your letter of the 13th inst., and to state that the Commanding General will accept with pleasure the services of Fall Leaf and his men.

Other tribes will be applied to immediately. I have written to the same effect to Mr. Johnson, at the Deleware Agency. – JOHN R. HOWARD, captain and secretary, to William P. Dole, dated Headquarters, Western Department, at St. Louis, September 20, 1861 [General Files, *Central Superintendency, 1860-1862*].

453 F. Johnson to Dole, June 6, 1862 [General Files, *Delaware, 1862-1866*].

454 Dole to Captain Fall Leaf, November 12, 1863 [Indian Office, *Letter Book*, no. 72, p. 109].

Branch,[455] be it said, and also Commissioner Dole,[456] at this stage of the war, were strongly opposed to a general use of the Indians for purposes of active warfare. They knew only too well what it was likely to lead to. Indeed, the most that Dole had, up to date, agreed[457] to, was the supplying the Indians with the means of their own defense when United States troops had shown themselves quite unavailable.

Dole's opinion being such, it is scarcely to be supposed that he could have considered favorably Senator Lane's idea of an Indian camp in the Cherokee Neutral Lands or the one, developed later, of an Indian patrol along the southern boundary of Kansas. Lane's troubles, quite apart from his Indian projects, were daily increasing; and, considering the method of warfare indulged in by him and encouraged in his white troops, the same one that pro-slavery and free-state men had equally experimented with in squatter-sovereignty days, it would have been simply deplorable to have permitted him the free use of Indian warriors. Complaints[458] of Lane and of his brigade, of their jayhawking and of their marauding were being made on every

---

[455] Report to Dole, October 22, 1861 [Commissioner of Indian Affairs, *Report*, 1861, p. 50]; Report to Dole, September 17, 1862 [Commissioner of Indian Affairs *Report*, 1862, p. 98].

[456] I send you a letter to *General Fremont open* that you may read and understand its object. *Fall Leaf* will call upon you probably this afternoon and receive from you such information as you see proper to give him. I am disinclined to encourage the Indians to engage in this war except in extreme cases, as guides. I have in this case used my influence in favor of the formation of this Company, without any knowledge of the views of Gov't, supposing Gen¹ Fremont was a special need of them or he would not have made the request. . . – DOLE to Captain Price, dated Leavenworth, September 13, 1861 [Indian Office, *Letter Book*, no. 66, pp. 485-486].

[457] Letter of August 15, 1861 [Commissioner of Indian Affairs, *Report*, 1861, p. 39].

[458] General Orders, no. 23 [*Official Records*, first ser., vol. iii, 539].

hand. Governor Robinson[459] reported these complaints and endorsed them. Secretary Cameron, while making his western tour of investigation, heard[460] them and reported them also. Lane attributed[461] them to personal dislike of him, to envy, to everything, in fact, except their true cause; but we know now that they were all well-grounded. Yet, remarkable to relate, Lane's influence with Lincoln and with the War Department suffered no appreciable decline. His suggestions[462] were acted upon; and, as we shall presently see, he was even permitted to organize a huge jayhawking expedition at the beginning of the next year.

The mention of Lane's jayhawking expedition calls to mind the conditions that made it seem, at the time, an acceptable thing and takes us back in retrospect to Indian Territory and to the events occurring there after the Tahlequah mass-meeting of the twenty-first of August. As soon as the meeting had broken up, John Ross despatched[463] a messenger to Albert Pike to inform him of all that had happened and of the Cherokee willingness, at last, to negotiate with the Confederacy. It was arranged that Pike should come to the Cherokee country, taking up his quarters temporarily at Park Hill,

---

[459] Villard says, as early as 1856, rivalry had developed between Robinson and Lane [*John Brown*, 108].

[460] Thomas to Frémont, October 14, 1861 [*Official Records*, first ser., vol. iii, 533].

[461] Lane to Lincoln, October 9, 1861 [*ibid.*, 529].

[462] It would seem as if Lane were remotely responsible for the division of the Western Department into the Department of Kansas and the Department of Missouri. In his letter to President Lincoln of October 9, 1861, he described the good work that his Kansas Brigade had done and asked that, in order that it might be enabled to continue to do effective work, a new military department be created, one that should group together Kansas, Indian Territory, and so much of Arkansas and the territories as should be advisable [*ibid.*].

[463] Ross's Address to Drew's Regiment, December 19, 1861 [Commissioner of Indian Affairs, *Report*, 1865, p. 355]; Letter of Albert Pike to D. N. Cooley, February 17, 1866.

the home of Ross near Tahlequah, and that a general
Indian council should be called. A special effort was
made to have the fragmentary bands of the northeast
represented and Pike sent out various agents[464] to urge
an attendance. John Ross was also active in the same
interest. He, personally, communicated with the
Osages[465] and with the Creeks[466] by letter; but the

[464] "Chisholm" the well known interpreter has been sent to the Comanches, Creeks to the Osages – Matthews to the Senecas Quapaws
&c. . . – ROBERTSON in a letter, dated St. Louis, September 30, 1861
[General Files, *Southern Superintendency, 1859-1862*, R1615].

. . . In the fall of the same year Albert Pike called a General
Council of the same tribes to meet at Talloqua and in order to secure
their attendance stated that John Ross was to make a speech . . . he
sent Dorn late U.S. Indian Agent to notify the Osages, Quapaws Senecas & Shawnees that there was to be a Council at Talloqua and that
Ross was going to talk at the same time to tell them that the U.S.
Government was breaking up – that they would get no more money and
that they were about to send an Army to take their Negroes and drive
them from the country and pointed to Missouri in proof of it, when
the Council met at Talloqua instead of Ross the council was opened by
Pike who told them "We are here to protect our property and to save
our Country. . . – BAPTISTE PEORIA.

Baptiste Peoria, in the spring and summer of 1862, went around as a
secret agent of the United States government among the southern Indians
finding out their real sentiments respecting the war. The report from which
the above extract is taken is dated May 1, 1862, and is in General Files, *Osage
River, 1855-1862*, B1430.

[465]   FORT SMITH, ARKANSAS, September 19th 1865.

In a talk held at the rooms of the Commission, with Commissioners
Sells and Parker, the following statement was this day voluntarily made
by Shon-tah-sob-ba ("Black Dog") the Chief of the Black Dog band of
the Osage Indians, relating to a treaty with the so-called Confederate
States. In answer to a question by Commissioner Sells, "How did you
happen to be in this Southern Country?" Shon-tah-sob-ba (Black Dog)
replied "I am glad you have asked that question, for I wish to make
some statements in explanation. We came down here upon the invitation
of John Ross, Principal Chief of the Cherokee Nation, who sent us a
letter asking us to attend a Council for the purpose of making a treaty
with Albert Pike" –

COMMR SELLS – Have you that letter now in your possession?

ANSWER: We don't know where the letter is. It was sent to Clermont, whose son had it in his possession when he died & we suppose it
was buried with him. But I have it here in my head & will never

Creeks,[467] like Evan Jones,[468] seem to have been incredulous as to Cherokee defection. They seem to have doubted the genuineness of the letter sent to them and

forget it. John Ross, the Cherokee Chief, said in that letter, "My Bros. the Osages, there is a distinguished gentleman sent by the Confederate States who is here to make treaties with us. He will soon be ready to treat, and I want you to come here in order that we may all treat together with him. My Brothers, there is a great black cloud coming from the North, about to cover us all, and I want you to come here so that we can counsel each other & drive away the black cloud." This is all that he said & signed his name. All the Osages went. We were all there together, Pike, John Ross and I, sitting as you are. Pike told us he was glad that we had come to make peace & a treaty. All your other brothers have made treaties & shook hands, & if *you* want to, you can do so too. I will tell you what John Ross said at the time. John Ross told us, "My Red Bros. you have come here as I asked you & I am glad to see you & hope you will do what the Commissioner wants you to do. The talk the Commissioner has made is a good talk & I want you to listen to it & make friends with the Confederate States. You can make a treaty or not, but I advise you, as your older brother, to make a treaty with them. It is for your interest & your good." After he finished talking, John Ross told us we could consult among ourselves over there (pointing to our camp near his residence) & decide among ourselves. We consulted on the matter, & on the request of John Ross we signed the treaty. He asked us to do it. He was the man that made us make that treaty, and that's how we came to be away from our country.

The above statement was endorsed by Wah-tah-in-gah, Chief Counselor of the Black Dog & Clermont bands of the Osage Indians.

The above is a correct statement as interpreted.

E. S. PARKER Com^r   GEO. L. COOK Ass't Sec^y.

ELIJAH SELLS Com^r

Papers relating to the Council at Fort Smith, September, 1865, *Indian Office Files.*

[466] Commissioner of Indian Affairs, *Report,* 1865, pp. 353-354.

[467] These Creeks, of course, were the Upper Creeks, the anti-McIntosh Creeks, the following of Opoeth-le-yo-ho-la. Some of the confidence that Opoeth-le-yo-ho-la seems to have had in John Ross, in his discretion and in his integrity, may have dated from the days when John Ross had refused, as he must have refused, to share in the plan for a betrayal of his country, at the instance of William McIntosh. The following document will explain that circumstance:

NEWTOWN 21th October 1823

MY FRIEND: I am going to inform you a few lines as a friend. I want you to give me your opinion about the treaty wether the chiefs will be willing or not. If the chiefs feel disposed to let the United

made inquiries about it, only to be assured [469] again and again by Ross that all was well and that he wished the Indians en masse to join the Southern States.

The council at Tahlequah, viewed in the light of its immediate object, was unusually successful. Four treaties were negotiated, one [470] at Tahlequah itself, October seventh, with the Cherokees and three at Park Hill. Of these three, one [471] was with four bands of the Great Osages, Clermont's, White Hair's, Black Dog's, and the Big Hill, October second; another [472] with the Quapaws, October fourth; and the third, [473] on the same day, with the Senecas [474] (once of Sandusky) and the Shawnees (once of Lewistown and now of the mixed

States have the land part of it, I want you to let me know. I will make the United States commissioner give you two thousand dollars, A. McCoy the same and Charles Hicks $3000 for present, and no body shall know it, and if you think the land wouldent sold, I will be satisfied. If the land should be sold, I will get you the amount before the treaty sign, and if you got any friend you want him to Receive it, they shall recd the same. nothing moore to inform you at present. I remain your affectionate Friend   Wm McIntosh
John Ross – an answer return
NB. the whole amount is $12000. you can divide among your friends. exclusive $7000.

This letter is on file in the United States Indian Office and bears the following endorsement:

rec^d on the 23rd Oct. 1823.
              MR John Ross President *N. Committee*
Letter from Wm McIntosh to Mr John Ross read & exposed in open
        Council in the presence of Wm McIntosh Oct 24th 1823   J Ross

[468] Letters to Dole, October 31, 1861 [Commissioner of Indian Affairs, *Report*, 1861, p. 42] and November 2, 1861 [General Files, *Cherokee, 1859-1865*, J503].

[469] Commissioner of Indian Affairs, *Report*, 1865, pp. 353, 354.

[470] *Official Records*, fourth ser., vol. i, 669-687.

[471] — *Ibid.*, 636-646.

[472] — *Ibid.*, 659-666.

[473] — *Ibid.*, 647-658.

[474] The Senecas of the mixed band of Senecas and Shawnees were not originally parties to the treaty, but provision was duly made for their becoming so.

band of Senecas and Shawnees). Hereditary[475] chiefs
alone signed for the Great Osages, the merit chief, Big
Chief, being, apparently, not present. The notorious
ex-United States agent, J. W. Washbourne,[476] was very
much in evidence as would most likely also have been
the equally notorious and disreputable Indian trader,

[475] Ka-hi-ke-tung-ka for Clermont's Band, Pa-hiu-ska for White Hair's,
Shon-tas-sap-pe for Black Dog's, and Chi-sho-hung-ka for the Big Hill.

[476] For information concerning Washbourne [Washburne or Washburn]
and charges against him, see Dean to Manypenny, December 28, 1855, December 31, 1855 [Dean's *Letter Book*, Indian Office]; and Elias Rector to Secretary
Thompson, October 1, 1859 [Rector's *Letter Book*, Indian Office]. Rector's
letter was as follows:

> An important sense of my duty as Superintendent of Indian Affairs
> for the Southern Superintendency compells me to recommend, most earn-
> estly, the immediate removal of the present incumbent of the Seminole
> Agency,
> The performance of this unpleasant duty is forced upon me by the
> following consideration, –
> 1st The neglect of duty and disregard of the orders and Regulations
> of the Department in absenting himself repeatedly and for protracted
> periods, from his Agency without authority for so doing; to the preju-
> dice of the public interests entrusted to him, –
> On this point I presume it is not necessary for me to enlarge, or to
> urge upon the Department my views of the paramount necessity of In-
> dian Agents residing at their Agencies and being at all times present
> at their Stations as well to cultivate the respect and confidence, and a
> just knowledge of the character and wants of the people entrusted to
> their care, as to be in position to execute promptly the orders, and to
> promote the views of the Department, –
> 2nd I consider him unworthy of the trust reposed in him from certain
> facts connected with the late payment of money to the Indians under his
> charge, which have come to my knowledge –
> Of the $90.000 recently paid to those Indians, appropriated by Con-
> gress expressly to pay such of them as should remove under the late
> Treaty; for their improvements and to assist in defraying their removal
> expences I have ascertained, and it is notorious, that thirteen thousand
> Dollars or more passed into the hands of Mr Washbourne, through Col-
> lusion with the principal Chiefs, $5000 of which he received under a
> private Contract with Senator Yulee of Florida for services in obtain-
> ing the consent of the Chiefs to the payment of thirty thousand dollars
> of this money to Senator Yulee on an old claim presented by him of long
> standing in behalf of one Gov Humphreys of Florida. The balance of
> the $13000 received by Mr Washbourne was probably awarded him in
> consideration of his permitting the Chiefs to appropriate certain por-

John Mathews,[477] had he not recently received his deserts at the hands of Senator Lane's brigade.

tions of the money they paid over to them in trust for the legetimate claimants, to their own use and benefit,

I have informed you in a late letter of the pains I took to make the Chiefs acquainted with the true object of the appropriations. Having been instructed to pay over the whole amount to the authorities of the Nation, this was all I could do in furtherance of the intentions of Congress; my efforts to accomplish which were thus frustrated by Mr Washbourne and his advances. –

3d The breach of good faith in the Chiefs towards the Indians, prompted by Mr Washbourne in the distribution of this $90.000 as explained in my late letter, has incensed the Indians to such degree that bloodshed has been threatened and is seriously to be apprehended, –

4th The influence of Mr Washbourne over the Chiefs acquired through his Collusion with them in this swindling the intended legal recipients of this money is such that, the Chiefs have intimated that they will not send a delegation to Florida unless Mr Washbourne shall accompany them, and I have reason to believe that in case he is not permited to accompany them, he is prepared to throw every obstacle in the way of the accomplishment of this, so much desired measure of the Government,

The conduct of the Chiefs and their Agent in the distribution of the $90000 and the enclosed letter from Mr Jacoway U S Marshal of this District, whose acquaintance you have made, taken in connection with the declarations of the Chiefs, that they will not go without him (or that they desire that he should go with and have charge of them) justifies the apprehension that there is another scheme in embryo between them to perpetrate another swindle. Should circumstances favour its accomplishment; and if it is the intention of the Department to charge me with conducting the negotiations of a Delegation to Florida, I must decline the performance of this duty if one in whom I have so little confidence is permited to accompany the Delegation in the capacity of Agent; for I hesitate not to say, that if disappointed in his hopes of making a profitable employment of his influence he would exert himself to defeat any negotiations that might be set on foot, and there is good reason to fear that he might be successful, –

For these reasons I beg leave respectfully to urge upon the Department the immediate removal of Mr Washbourne and the appointment in his stead of some gentleman who will perform the duties of the office with a high appreciation of the trust confided to him and with a view, rather to the honest discharge of this trust, than to his own profit,

I make this communication direct to the Sec't of Interior instead of sending it through the Indian office for the reason that I learn that the Comr Ind Affrs is absent on official acct.

[477] Agent Elder to Coffin, September 30, 1861 [Commissioner of Indian

An accurate and connected account of the occurrences at the Tahlequah council, it is well nigh impossible to obtain. Some intimidation[478] seems to have been used, and there was a report of a collision[479] between the Ross and Ridge factions some days previous to the meeting. Drew's regiment, which, when organized, had been placed as a guard[480] on the northern border, escorted[481] Commissioner Pike to Park Hill and later took up its station on the treaty ground. Some of Stand Watie's Confederate forces were also in the

Affairs, *Report*, 1861, p. 37]; Coffin to Dole, October 2, 1861 [*ibid.*, p. 38]; Moore's *Rebellion Record*, vol. iii, 33.

478 We the loyal Cherokee Delegation acknowledge the execution of the treaty of Oct. 7, 1861. But we solemnly declare that the execution of the Treaty was procured by the coercion of the rebel army [Land Files, *Indian Talks, Councils, etc.*, Box 4, 1865-1866].

479 Hon. J. S. Phelps to C. B. Smith, dated Rolla, Mo., October 3, 1861 [General Files, *Cherokee, 1859-1865*, P44].

480 A difference of opinion seems to exist as to the original object of the organization of Drew's regiment. When Ross wrote his despatches to McCulloch concerning the proceedings at Tahlequah, he sent them for transmission to the C.S.A. quartermaster at Fort Smith, Major George W. Clark, to whom he imparted the information that the Cherokees were going to raise a regiment of mounted men immediately and place it under the command of Colonel John Drew, "to meet any emergency that may arise." "Having espoused," said he, "the cause of the Confederate States, we hope to render efficient service in the protracted war which now threatens the country, and to be treated with a liberality and confidence becoming the Confederate States." – Moore's *Rebellion Record*, vol. iii, 155, Document 63½.

Those, who afterwards wanted to put the Cherokee position in the best possible light, declared repeatedly that Drew's regiment had no sectional bias in the work mapped out for it, that it was nothing more than a home guard. Writing to Dole, January 21, 1862, the Reverend Evan Jones said,

A regiment of Cherokees was raised for home protection, composed of one company for each of eight Districts, and either two or three companies for the District of Tahlequah. But these were altogether separate and distinct from the rebel force. . . The great majority of officers and men, in this case, being decidedly loyal Union men Four of the Captains and four hundred men, gave evidence of their loyalty, in the part they acted, at the battle in which Opothleyoholo was attacked by the Texan rangers & rebel Creeks & Choctaws, under Cooper. . . – General Files, *Cherokee, 1859-1865*, J556.

481 Commissioner of Indian Affairs, *Report*, 1865, p. 355.

neighborhood.[482] In 1865, at the Fort Smith Council, held for the readjustment of political relations with the United States government, the Indians of the Neosho Agency gave[483] a rather picturesque description of the way they had been prevailed upon to sign the treaty with the Confederate States. The real object of the Tahlequah meeting was evidently not revealed to them until they had actually reached the treaty ground. Agent Dorn had told them that they had to go to the meeting. They went and were there taken in hand by Pike who said,

> If you don't do what we lay before you, we can't say you shall live happy.

The Indians

> feeling badly, just looked on, and the white man went to work, got up a paper and said I want you to sign that. The Indian did not want to, but he compelled him. You know yourself that, under such circumstances, he would do anything to save his life. . .

Now that the history of the diplomatic relations between the Indian tribes and the Confederacy has been brought thus far, nothing seems more fitting than to return to the consideration of the Federal government and its representatives, its purposes, and its plans, beginning the account with the Indian Office and Commissioner Dole. Dole's early attempt to prevail upon the War Department to resume its occupation of Indian Territory was followed up by the convincing letter of the thirtieth of May in which he likened the Indians to the Union element in some of the border states and ended by throwing the full responsibility for any disloyalty that might appear among them upon the Fed-

---

[482] Cooley's Report to President Johnson, February 25, 1866. This letter was found in the loose files of the Indian Office and is not to be found in Indian Office, *Report Book*, no. 15, where it would properly belong.

[483] Commissioner of Indian Affairs, *Report*, 1865, p. 321.

eral autho̱rities; inasmuch as they had neglected and were still ne̱glecting to give the support and protection that any ordinary guardian is bound in honor to give to his wards.   Dole said in writing to Secretary Smith,

> .   .   .   Experience has shown that the presence of even a small force of federal troops located in the disaffected States has had the effect to preserve the peace, encourage the friends of the Union, and induce the people to return to their allegiance.
>
> That this same result would be produced in the Indian country I cannot doubt, as they can have no inducement to unite with the enemies of the United States unless we fail as a nation to give them that protection guaranteed by our treaty stipulations, and which is necessary to prevent designing and evil-disposed persons from having free intercourse with them, to work out their evil purposes.   .   .[484]

Nothing came of Dole's application and thus was exemplified, as often before and often since, a very serious defect in the American administrative system by which the duty of doing a certain thing rests upon one department and the means for doing it with quite another.   It is surely no exaggeration to say that hundreds and hundreds of times the Indians have been the innocent victims of friction between the War and Interior Departments.

But if the authorities at Washington were indifferent to the Indian's welfare, Senator Lane was neither indifferent to nor ignorant of the strategical importance of Indian Territory.   With him the defence of Kansas and the means of procuring that defence were everything.   Indian Territory and the Indian tribes came within the scope of the means.   And so it happened that, while he was organizing his Kansas brigade, he commissioned[485] a man, E. H. Carruth, who had for-

---

[484] Commissioner of Indian Affairs, *Report*, 1861, p. 35; Indian Office, *Report Book*, no. 12, p. 176.

[485] Enclosed pleaz find a coppy of a Commission given by General

merly posed as an educator[486] among the Seminoles, to communicate with the various tribes for the purpose of determining their real feelings towards the United States government and of obtaining, if possible, an interview between Lane and some of their accredited representatives. The interview was to take place "at Fort Lincoln on the Osage or some point convenient thereto."[487]

Now a considerable portion of the Creek tribe was in just the right mood and in just the right situation to receive such overtures in the right spirit. That portion consisted of those who, after the treaty of July tenth had been negotiated in the manner already described, had rallied around Opoeth-le-yo-ho-la; and who, in a Creek convention that had been called for August fifth had declared that the chiefs, who had signed a treaty outside the National Council, had violated a fundamental law of the tribe and had thereby forfeited their administrative rank. The criticism applied to Motey Kennard and to Echo Harjo, the principal and the sec-

Lane to E. H. Carruth together with coppies of Letters sent by him to the various Tribes in the Indian Territory. I had an interview with Mr. Carruth yesterday. I find him a very Inteligent man and thougherly posted as to all matters relating to the Southern Indians he is very confident that most if not all the Southern Indians written to will Send deligations to Fort Scott as requested there ware three Creek Indians came up to se General Lane who came to Iola for Caruthe to go with them to General Lane which he did and they ware the barers of letters of which the enclosed are coppies. I am going to Fort Scott today and will make arrangements with Agent Elder to give the notice imediately on their arrival or Bring them to Humboldt. I shall try to secure the assistance of Mr. Caruthe tho he is now a voluntear in the Home Guards for protection. I very much feer the service required of me at the Sacks & Fox and Kaw agencies will take me to far off but will try to attend to all if possible – General Files, *Southern Superintendency, 1859-1862*, C1348.

[486] Manypenny to Dean, April 9, 1855 [Indian Office, *Letter Book*, no. 51, pp. 232-233].

[487] Extract from commission, dated Fort Scott, August 30, 1861, issued to Carruth by authority of J. H. Lane, Commanding the Kansas Brigade [*ibid.*].

ond chief respectively. Kennard, as we have seen, was the leader of the Lower Creeks and Harjo of the Upper. A further division in Creek ranks was now inevitable and it came forthwith, the Non-treaty Party, made up mostly of Upper Creeks, proceeding to recognize [488] Ok-ta-ha-hassee Harjo (better known as "Sands") as the acting principal chief of the tribe. It also betook itself westward so as to be as much as possible out of the reach of the secessionists. When once in a position of at least temporary security, it despatched Mik-ko Hut-kee (White Chief), Bob Deer, Jo Ellis, and perhaps others to Washington to confer with the "Great Father." [489]

[488] Commissioner of Indian Affairs, *Report*, 1865, p. 328.

[489] The loyal Creeks testified, in 1865, that they sent their "chief" and others to Washington and leave the reader to infer that the chief meant was "Sands;" but the accredited delegates were most certainly Mik-ko Hut-kee, Bob Deer, and Jo Ellis. These three men signed their names, or rather attached their mark, to an address to the president of which the following is a certified copy:

SHAWNEE AGENCY, LEXINGTON, September 18, 1861.

SIR, we the Chiefs, Head Men, and Warriors, of the Creek Nation of Indians, in the Indian Territory, through our delegates, the undersigned desire to state to your excellency the condition of our people. Owing to the want of correct information as to condition of the Country and Government our people are in great distress. Men have come among us, who claim to represent a New Government, who tell us that the Government represented by Our Great Father at Washington, has turned against us and intends to drive us from our homes and take away our property, they tell us that we have nothing to hope from our old Father and that all the Friends of the Indian have joined the New Government. And that the New Government is ready to make treaties with the Indians and do all and more for them than they can claim under their old treaties. they ask us to join their armies and help sustain the Government that is willing to do so much for us. But we doubted their statements and promises and went to talk with the Agent and Superintendent which Our father has always kept among us but they were both gone and then some of our people began to think that Our Great Father had forsaken us and a very few joined the Army of the New Government and our people were in great trouble and we called a Grand Council of the Chiefs of Creeks, Cherokees, Chickasaws, Shawnees, Senecas, Quapaws, Kickapoos, Delawares, Weas, Peankeshaws,

The Creek delegates, Mik-ko Hut-kee and his companions, went, on their way to Washington, northward through Kansas, saw Superintendent Coffin[490] and, later, Lane's agent, E. H. Carruth. This was about the second week of September and Carruth was at Barnesville, Lane's headquarters. Carruth received the Creeks kindly, read sympathetically the letter[491]

Witchetaws Tribes and bands of Comanches, Seminoles, and Cadoes. And after a long discussion of the source of their troubles, decided to remain loyal to our Government and if possible neutral. The Chiefs went among their people (and as a general thing) counteracted the influence of the emissaries of the New Government. But these emissaries are still among us giving us great trouble, while our Government has no one who can officially represent itself. And we most earnestly ask that some person shall be sent here who shall meet the Chiefs of the above mentioned tribes in Council at some suitable place, and then make known to them the condition, policy and wishes of the Government so far as the interests of the Indians are concerned. If your Excellency should deem it best to comply with our request, we would suggest that Humboldt Allen County Kansas be the place for holding the Council. A notice sent to the Agent of the Shawnees, will immediately be forwarded by a messinger to the Chiefs. Very Respectfully, your Obedient Servants   WHITE CHIEF X his mark

BOBB DEER X his mark

JOSEPH ELLIS X his mark Interpreter

P.S. The Choctaws were not present at the Council and we have reason to feer that they have gone with the Southern Confederacy. It will take near forty days to notify the Chiefs and get them together after the notice gets at this place.   WHITE CHIEF X his mark

[490] They also saw Agent Abbot [Commissioner of Indian Affairs, *Report*, 1865, p. 330] and received new assurances from him.

[491] Perchance the same letter, either the original or a copy of which, Superintendent Branch transmitted to Dole along with an explanatory letter from Agent Abbott. The "talk" of the Creek chiefs was accompanied by a sort of Seminole and Chickasaw endorsement. Dole replied to the Creek and Seminole delegate appeals, November 16, 1861 [Indian Office, *Letter Book*, no. 67, pp. 78-79]. This is what the Creek chiefs said:

CREEK NAT. Aug 15, 1861.

Now I write to the President our Great Father who removed us to our present homes, & made a treaty, and you said that in our new homes we should be defended from all interference from any people and that no white people in the whole world should ever molest us unless they come from the sky but the land should be ours as long as grass grew or waters run, and should we be injured by anybody you would come with

that they brought from their distressed chiefs, Sands and Opoeth-le-yo-ho-la, assured the equally distressed delegates of the continued fatherly interest of the United States government, and sent them on their way, greatly comforted. It was while these Creek delegates were lingering at Barnesville that Carruth made a special effort to induce the southern Indians generally to send representatives for an interview with Lane. He wrote personally to Ross,[492] to the two Creek chiefs,[493]

your soldiers & punish them, but now the wolf has come, men who are strangers tread our soil, our children are frightened & the mothers cannot sleep for fear. This is our situation now. When we made our Treaty at Washington you assured us that our children should laugh around our houses without fear, & we believed you. Then our Great Father was strong. And now we raise our hands to him we want his help to keep off the intruder & make our homes again happy as they used to be. . .

I was at Washington when you treated with us, and now White People are trying take our people away to fight against us and you. I am alive. I well remember the treaty. My ears are open & my memory is good. This is the letter of Your Children by

OPOTHLEHOYOLA
OUKTAHNASERHARJO

The Seminoles also send the same word & the full Indians of the Chickasaws too send to the P –

The reply to this letter was made by Dole, November 16, 1861. See Indian Office, *Letter Book,* no. 67, pp. 79-80.

Pascofar the chief of Seminoles was present   he was not able to come with us now but sent word. And if our Great Father want us we will come to see him.   MICEO HULKA   JO ELLIS
ROB DEER

General Files, *Creek, 1860-1869,* B787.

492 There is a delegation of the Creeks now at Gen'l Lanes Head Quarters.

We wish to see delegations from the tribes loyal to the U.S. Government. You will send us a delegation who will report to the Head Quarters of the Kansas Brigade where commissioners of the Government will meet and confer with them.

You are probably aware of the falsehoods resorted to by the enemies of the U.S. to induce the Indians to withdraw their allegiance from the Government. Could you come in person it would be grattifying to the Commissioners. – Letter of September 11, 1861 [General Files, *Southern Superintendency, 1859-1862,* C1348].

493 Your letter by Micco Hutka is received. You will send a delega-

and to the Wichita chief, Tusaquach,[494] and, in addition, wrote to the Seminole chiefs and headmen [495] and to the "loyal" Choctaws and Chickasaws.[496]

Presumably, Superintendent Coffin did not altogether approve of Senator Lane's taking it upon himself to confer with the Indians who, after all, were officially Coffin's charges; for, in October, we find him, likewise, planning for an intertribal conference to be held at Humboldt.[497] It is rather interesting to look back upon all this and to realize, as perforce we must, that every plan for conferring with the southern tribes

tion of your best men to meet the Commissioners of the United States Government in Kansas.

I am authorized to inform you that the President will not forget you. Our armies will soon go south and those of your people who are true and loyal to the Government will be treated as friends – Your rights & property will be respected. The Commissioners from the Confederate States have deceived you they have two tongues.

They wanted to get the Indians to fight and they will rob and plunder you if they can get you into trouble. But the President is stil alive his soldiers will soon drive these men who have treacherously violated your homes from the land they have entered. When your Delegates Return to you they will be able to inform you when and where your monies will be paid those who stole your orphan funds will be punished and you will learn that the people who are tru to the Government which has so long protected you are your Friends. – Letter to Opoth-le-ho-yo-ho, Ho-so-tau-hah-sas Hayo, dated Barnesville, September 11, 1861. – General Files, *Southern Superintendency, 1859-1862*, C1348.

The author's opinion is that the mistakes in spelling were made by the illiterate Coffin, who probably made a copy of Carruth's letters for transmission to the Indian Office. He may also have made a slight alteration in the date of the letter to the Creeks; for the original of the letter, bearing the date of September 10, 1861, was found in Opoeth-le-yo-ho-la's camp after the Battle of Chustenahlah, December 26, 1861 [*Official Records*, first ser., vol. viii, 25].

494 *Official Records*, first ser., vol. viii, 26.

495 In his letter to the Seminole chiefs and headmen, Carruth reminds them that he was with them when letters came from Pike and that Pike "is the man who has tried so hard to get your lands sectionalized" and asks, "who brought up a bill in Congress to bring your tribes under Territorial laws, Johnson of Arkansas. . ."

496 — *Ibid.*, 26.

497 Coffin to Dole, October 2, 1861 [Commissioner of Indian Affairs, *Report*, 1861, pp. 38-39].

in the interests of the United States government, at this critical time, contemplated a meeting at some place outside of Indian Territory.   Here were agents of the Indian's "Great Father" offering protection to the red men and yet giving incontestable proof in the very details of the offer that they did not themselves dare to venture [498] beyond the Kansas boundary.   As a matter of fact, all such plans for a general conference came to nothing, although, as late as November, Lane had still the idea of one in mind.   He was, at the time, hoping to meet the Indians at Leroy [499] in Coffey County, Kansas, on the twenty-fourth.   Lane also continued to advocate the use of the friendly Indians as soldiers.   A little earlier, Agent Johnson had endorsed [500] Lane's plan in a letter to Commissioner Dole; but the coming of General Hunter upon the scene considerably affected the sphere of influence.

Dissatisfaction with Frémont on account of his extravagance, his haphazard way of issuing commissions,

---

[498] Evan Jones wrote, October 31, 1861 [Commissioner of Indian Affairs, *Report*, 1861, pp. 41-43] that he had found it impossible to get anyone who would undertake to carry a message to John Ross. The risk was too great.

[499] Dole to Hunter, November 16, 1861 [*ibid.*, p. 44].

[500] On consultation with Gen'l Jas. H. Lane he thinks an auxiliary Regiment of Indians are necessary to the service and could be used to great advantage in this department. If it meets with your approbation I would like and ask the privilege of Raising such Regt which I think I could do in thirty days. I have made my estimate of the number of men which I think would be furnished by each tribe as follows

Iowas & Kickapoos	225
Delawares	125
Potawatomies	250
Shawnees, Miamies, & Weas	100
Sacks & Foxes	250
Senecas & Wyandotts	125
	1075

This will be laid before you by Gen'l Lane in person I hope it will meet with your approval and that you will grant the permission to raise

his tardiness, and, above all, his general military incompetence had crystallized in September; and, by orders[501] of General Scott on the twenty-fourth of October, Hunter was directed to relieve him. Hunter reached his post in early November and almost immediately thereafter, either upon his own initiative or after consultation with someone like Coffin (it could hardly have been with Lane; for Lane had gone[502] to Washington, or with Branch; for Branch was strongly op-

the Regt and if necessary I have no doubt but a Brigade of Indians could be organized by embracing the Osages and Loyal Creeks and Cherokees. – Letter of October 10, 1861 [General Files, *Delaware, 1855-1861*].

[501] *Official Records*, first ser., vol. iii, 553.

[502] I am not certain of the exact date of Lane's departure for Washington. Spring says [*Kansas*, 279] that he went there in November. When an Indian delegation reached Fort Scott, seeking him, some time about the middle of the month, he had already handed over his command to Colonel James Montgomery and "had gone to Washington" [Cutler to Coffin, September 30, 1862, Commissioner of Indian Affairs, *Report*, 1862, p. 138]. Yet Dole's letter to General Hunter would convey the impression that Lane was still in Kansas the middle of the month and expected to be there on the twenty-fourth. I am also in doubt as to when Hunter reached his post. He communicated with Agent Cutler from St. Louis, November 20, 1861 [*ibid.*, 1861, p. 44]. Hunter and Lane may very well have met even outside of Kansas and have exchanged views and opinions that would have given a basis for the representations that Lane must have made to Lincoln and Cameron regarding Hunter's approval of the "Jayhawking Brigade." McClellan seems to have advised the forward movement in the direction of the Indian Territory; for he says, when writing to Hunter, December 11, 1861 [*Official Records*, first ser., vol. viii, 428]:

Immediately after you were assigned to your present department I requested the Adjutant-General to inform you that it was deemed expedient to organize an expedition under your command to secure the Indian territory west of Arkansas, as well as to make a descent upon Northern Texas, in connection with one to strike at Western Texas from the Gulf. The general was to invite your prompt attention to this subject, and to ask you to indicate the necessary force and means for the undertaking.

It is only fair to say that Lane had always advocated a more southern concentration of forces. He more than any other northern man seems to have appreciated fully the importance of Indian Territory. He continually recommended using Fort Scott as a base for such military operations as had the protection of Kansas as their main object.

posed to the project intended), he telegraphed[503] to the War Department "for permission to muster a Brigade of Kansas Indians into the service of the United States, to assist the friendly Creek Indians in maintaining their loyalty." Evidently, the request was not granted,[504] but duties akin to it were, by arrangement of President Lincoln, conferred upon Hunter which involved his assuming the responsibility of holding, if such a plan were feasible, an intertribal council so as to renew the confidence of the southern Indians in the United States government. A letter[505] from Dole, outlining the plan, reveals an astonishing ignorance of just how far those selfsame Indians had gone in their defection, because of the loss of the confidence.

In the giving of these new duties to General Hunter, there was not the slightest intention of ignoring Senator Lane. In fact, Dole expressly mentioned that Lane had called for just such an Indian conference[506] and suggested that, if Hunter's military duties prevented his

---

[503] Hunter to Thomas, dated Leavenworth, January 15, 1862 [General Files, *Southern Superintendency, 1859-1862*].

[504] In January, 1862, Hunter deplored the fact that his request had not been acceded to and said,

> Had this permission been promptly granted, I have every reason to believe that the present disastrous state of affairs, in the Indian country west of Arkansas, could have been avoided. I now again respectfully repeat my request – *Ibid.*

[505] Dole to Hunter, November 16, 1861 [Indian Office, *Letter Book*, no. 67, pp. 80-82; Commissioner of Indian Affairs, *Report*, 1861, pp. 43-44].

[506] Lane's proposed conference called for the assembling of representatives of Kansas tribes as well as of Indian Territory tribes. Judging from Hunter's letter to Agent Cutler of November 20, 1861 [Commissioner of Indian Affairs, *Report*, 1861, pp. 44-45], I infer that Hunter's conference was to be confined to the southern Indians. The purpose of Lane's must have been represented to the Kansas Indians as Creek needs [Shawnee "talk" to the Creeks, November 15, 1861, *ibid.*, p. 45]. Hunter intended to hold his conference at his headquarters, Fort Leavenworth, which was making the southern Indians come a pretty long way [Hunter to Cutler, November 20, 1861, *ibid.*, p. 44; Dole to Cutler, December 3, 1861, Indian Office, *Letter Book*, no. 67, p. 107].

meeting the Indians in person, Lane might take his place, "provided he can be spared from his post." The whole affair was incident to the reorganization that had recently, under general orders[507] of the ninth of November, taken place in the Western Department, from which had resulted a Department of Kansas, separate and distinct from the Department of Missouri. The Department of Kansas included "the State of Kansas, the Indian Territory west of Arkansas, and the Territories of Nebraska, Colorado, and Dakota" and was to be under the command of Major-general David Hunter[508] with headquarters at Fort Leavenworth. The idea governing this division of the old western department was, ostensibly, as Nicolay and Hay express[509] it, that Kansas might be protected, Indian Territory repossessed, and Texas reached. As we shall presently see, a similar reorganization took place, about the same time, in the Confederate western service and for very much the same reason, the condition of the Indian country being a very large proportion of that reason. It is barely possible that, as far as the United States was concerned, Senator Lane's recommendation[510] of the ninth of October was almost wholly accountable for the change.

It was, undoubtedly, high time that something vigorous was being done to stay Confederate progress in Indian Territory. Indeed, events were happening there

---

[507] *Official Records,* first ser., vol. iii, 567.

[508] Major-general H. W. Halleck was to command the sister department of Missouri.

[509] *Abraham Lincoln,* vol. v, 81-82.

[510] I earnestly request and recommend the establishment of a new military department, to be composed of Kansas, the Indian country, and so much of Arkansas and the Territories as may be thought advisable to include therein. – LANE to Lincoln, dated Leavenworth City, Kansas, October 9, 1861 [*Official Records,* first ser., vol. iii, 529].

at this very moment that made all plans for an inter-
tribal conference exceedingly out of date. The Confederate government had now a large Indian force[511] in
the field and expectations of an increase, provided the

[511] By the end of July, the First Regiment of Choctaw and Chickasaw
Mounted Rifles had been completely organized [*Official Records*, first ser., vol.
iii, 620, 624] and eight companies of a prospective Creek regiment [*ibid.*, 624].
By October twenty-second, when McCulloch ordered him [*ibid.*, 721] to take
up a position in the Cherokee Neutral Lands, Stand Watie's battalion had apparently reached the proportions of a regiment, the First Cherokee Mounted
Rifles. On the twenty-seventh of November, Pike who was then in Richmond
informed Benjamin,

> We have now in the service four regiments, numbering in all some
> 3,500 men, besides the Seminole troops and other detached companies, in-
> creasing the number to over 4,000. An additional regiment has been of-
> fered by the Choctaws and another can be raised among the Creeks. If
> I have the authority I can enlist even the malcontents among that people.
> I can place in the field (arms being supplied) 7,500 Indian troops, not
> counting the Comanches and Osages, whom I would only employ in case
> of an invasion of the Indian country. . . – *Official Records*, first ser.,
> vol. viii, 697.

A supposed report of Agent Garrett, sent to the United States Indian Office
under the following endorsement, is not without interest as bearing upon the
strength of the Confederacy within the Indian country:

> The copy of a letter herewith, is without signature, but is said to be
> in the handwriting of the late Col. Garret, who at that date, was U.S.
> Indian Agent of the Creeks. It is not of much importance, but yet, as
> historical and statistical, is not without some interest. I obtained it a
> few weeks ago, found among other papers at the Agency, and I presume
> is a retained copy of the original.   CREEK AGENCY C.N. Dec. 16th 1861.

> SIR: I have the honor to acknowledge the receipt of your letter of
> the 2d ultimo, requiring certain information from me in regard to the
> number of Creek Indians; and their relations or feelings towards the
> Confederate States. Owing to the great irregularity of the mails, I did
> not receive your communication as soon as I ought. The difficulty at
> the time I received your letter in regard to answering it properly, caused
> me to delay a few days, so that I might answer it definitely. Incidental
> to the confusion here, I could not state to you who were reliable, and
> who were not, for I did not know myself, and believing that a battle
> would be fought in a few days where every one would have to show
> his hand, I thought I could give you more reliable information: and
> from the valor and fidelity of the Creeks engaged then I can give you
> reliable information.

> The Creeks number in all 14630, a portion of whom reside in Ala-

necessary arms[512] were obtainable. On the twenty-second[513] of November, by special orders[514] from Rich-

bama, Texas and Missouri, leaving about 13000 within the limits of the Creek Nation: – From the best information I can get, there are among the lower Creeks 1650 warriors, 375 of them are unfriendly – Among the Upper Creeks there are 1600 warriors – only 400 of them are friendly – to sum up the whole matter there are 1675 Creek warriors friendly to the Confederate States and 1575 unfriendly – Of those friendly there are in the service of the Confederate States 1375 – One Regiment is commanded by Col. Chilly McIntosh, numbering 400 – and an independent company commanded by Capt. J. M. C. Smith numbering 75 men, all in the service, and armed with a very few exceptions, and I think from recent indications are willing to do service wherever ordered, and circumstances justify it.

The Regiment, Battalion and Company were all mustered into service for twelve months. This comprises nearly all the friendly warriors in the Nation. I cannot answer you in regard to the number that are willing to serve during the war. My opinion is, though, that the number now in the service, and perhaps more, are willing to remain in the service as long as they may be wanted. The Hostiles are headed by Ho path ye ho lo who has engaged in his cause portions of several tribes viz a portion of the Seminoles, Kickapoos, Shawnees, Delawares, Wichitas, Comanches, and Cherokees – 400 of whom deserted a few days before the recent battle from Col. John Drews Regiment Cherokee Volunteers and joined Hopathyeholo who is in communication with the federal forces in Kansas, and has received goods and ammunition from them: His force is estimated from 2500 to 3000 – I would give you a more detailed account of the battle, but I do not think it proper in this communication and I presume the commanding officer Col. Cooper has made his report of the Battle to the Secretary of War – I may be mistaken to some extent, in regard to the friendly and hostile Creeks, but I think I am not, and it is correct from the best information I can get, and my own knowledge of the facts. It will afford me much pleasure, to communicate to you at any time anything of importance to the Confederate States. Very Respectfully Your Obt Servt.
Hon. David Hubbard, Com. Indian Affairs
   Richmond Va.

[512] Therein lay the whole difficulty. It was simply impossible for the Confederate government to honor all requisitions for arms.

[513] The matter must have been even earlier under advisement; for, on the twenty-sixth of October, J. P. Benjamin, Acting Secretary of War, sent this notice to "General Albert Pike, Little Rock, Ark.:"

I cannot assign to your command any Arkansas troops at this moment. Governor Rector is applying for return of the regiments in Tennessee. – *Official Records*, first ser., vol. iii, 727.

[514] — *Ibid.*, vol. viii, 690.

mond, Indian Territory had been erected into a separate military department and Albert Pike, now a brigadier-general, assigned to the command of it. For the present, however, things seem to have remained much as they were with McCulloch nominally in command and Cooper in actual charge. Moreover, long before Pike reappeared upon the scene, matters had come to an issue between the secessionist and unionist Creeks.

Determined not to allow themselves to be over-persuaded or intimidated by the secessionist element in their nation, the unionist Creeks, under Opoeth-le-yo-ho-la, had withdrawn from active intercourse with the rival faction and, resisting all attempts of Cooper and others to inveigle them into an interview that might result in compromise, they had encamped at or near the junction of the Deep and North Forks of the Canadian River. Cooper resolved to attack them there and, for the purpose, gathered [515] together an effective fighting force of about fourteen hundred men, all Indians except for a detachment of Texas cavalry. On the fifth of November, Opoeth-le-yo-ho-la broke camp and took up the line of march for Kansas, hoping that, in Kansas, he and his followers would receive either succor or refuge. It has been estimated that Opoeth-le-yo-ho-la's force, at this time, was less than two thousand men and that it comprised, besides Creeks and Seminoles, some two or three hundred negroes. His traveling cortège was, however, very much larger; for it included women and children, the sick and the aged. Approximately half of the Creeks were on the move for pastures new. For many of them it was a second exodus.

Colonel D. H. Cooper reached the deserted camp of Opoeth-le-yo-ho-la on the fifteenth of November and,

---

[515] *Daily State Journal* (Little Rock), Nov. 8, 1861.

finding his enemy gone and locating his trail, moved himself in a slightly northeasterly direction towards the Red Fork of the Arkansas. He came up with the unionist Creeks at Round Mountain on the night of the nineteenth and an indecisive engagement[516] followed, both sides claiming the victory. Under cover of darkness, Opoeth-le-yo-ho-la managed to slip away and crossed into the Cherokee country where there were plenty of disaffected full-bloods to give him sympathy. It is more than likely that they had invited him there and had prepared for his coming. Cooper did not attempt to pursue the Creek refugees, having been called back to the Arkansas line, there to wait in readiness to reënforce McCulloch should the Federals make a forward march southward from Springfield, as then seemed probable. But that danger soon passed, passed even before Cooper had had time to take the post indicated or to leave his own camp at Concharta, after a brief recuperation. He was now free to follow up the meagre advantage of the nineteenth.

The next opportunity to crush Opoeth-le-yo-ho-la came in the Battle of Bird Creek [Chusto-Talasah, Little High Shoals, or the Caving Banks],[517] fought December 9, 1861. On the twenty-ninth of the preceding month, a part of Cooper's force had set out for Tulsey Town and an advance guard had been sent up the Verdigris in the direction of a place, called "Coody's Settlement," where Colonel John Drew with a detachment of his regiment of Cherokee full-bloods was posted. The orders were that Drew should effect a junction with Cooper's main force and, on December eighth they were all encamped on Bird Creek in the south-

[516] Colonel D. H. Cooper's "Report" [*Official Records*, first ser., vol. viii, 5].

[517] Colonel D. H. Cooper's "Report" [*Official Records*, first ser., vol. viii, 7, 709].

western corner of the Cherokee Nation. At this juncture, word came that Opoeth-le-yo-ho-la wished to treat
for peace and Major Pegg, a Cherokee, with three companions was sent forward to confer with him. They
found the Creek chief, surrounded by his warriors and
ready for battle. It was evening and Colonel Cooper
had scarcely heard the news of the Creek determination
to fight when a message came that four companies of
Drew's regiment, horrified at the thought of fighting
with their neighbors, had dispersed and gone over to
Opoeth-le-yo-ho-la. The incident did not promise well
for success on the morrow and the Battle of Bird
Creek was another indecisive engagement, although
the Creeks, eager and resplendent with their yellow
corn-shuck badges, seem to have had all the advantage
of position. Again they made their escape and again
Colonel Cooper was prevented from following them,
this time because he was exceedingly fearful lest the
Cherokee desertion might have a lasting and disastrous
effect upon the remaining Indian forces, particularly
upon the small group that was all that was left of the
original First Cherokee Mounted Rifles. Cooper's personal opinion was, that the defection was widespread
among the Cherokees and that it would be sheer folly to
start out after Opoeth-le-yo-ho-la until more white
troops had been added to the pursuing force, by way
both of reënforcement and of encouragement.

Instead, therefore, of continuing northward, Colonel
Cooper drew off in the direction of Fort Gibson and,
from that point, sent for aid to Colonel James McIntosh at Van Buren. He then occupied himself with his
own troops and prevailed upon John Ross to rally[518] the
Cherokees. It was now the nineteenth of December and

---

[518] Commissioner of Indian Affairs, *Report*, 1865, pp. 355-357.

the aged chief did his best to keep his people true to the faith that the nation had pledged in the treaty of the seventh of October. He recalled to their minds the fact that it was, by all odds, the best treaty that the Cherokees had ever secured, the one that gave them the fullest recognition of their rights as a semi-independent people, and he might have added with sad, sad truth that it was the best that they could ever hope to get. He made no such pessimistic reflection, however, but concluded,

> It is, therefore, our duty and interest to respect it, and we must, as the interest of our common country demands it. According to the stipulations of the treaty we must meet enemies of our allies whenever the south requires it, as they are our enemies as well as the enemies of the south; and I feel sure that no such occurrence as the one we deplore would have taken place if all things were understood as I have endeavored to explain them. Indeed the true meaning of our treaty is, that we must know no line in the presence of our invader, be he who he may. . .[519]

Colonel Cooper then addressed [520] the Indians and, after him, Major Pegg; [521] but they were not convinced and many of them went home, positively refusing to march farther with the army.

Meanwhile Cooper's call for reënforcements had reached McIntosh [522] and, as the need seemed so urgent,

---

[519] Extract from John Ross's address to Drew's regiment [Commissioner of Indian Affairs, *Report*, 1865, p. 356].

[520] Commissioner of Indian Affairs, *Report*, 1865, p. 357.

[521] — *Ibid.*

[522] McIntosh, at the time, was in charge of McCulloch's brigade, McCulloch having gone to Richmond to explain to the authorities there why he had persistently laid himself open to the charge of refusing to coöperate with Sterling Price in his many Missouri ventures, planned subsequent to the Battle of Wilson's Creek. McCulloch's orders from the Confederate War Department were that he should guard the Indian Territory. Price's great idea was to occupy the Missouri River country. Had McCulloch gone northward with Price, he would, so he ably argued, have removed himself altogether from his base.

McIntosh resolved to supply it and notified Cooper to that effect. Subsequently, he decided[523] to take the field in person and to head a column, separate from Cooper's. What induced him to do this, nobody can well say. Cooper always felt that the incompleteness of the victory over Opoeth-le-yo-ho-la, which was soon to come, was mainly attributable to the divided effort of the attacking force. In the two former engagements, Opoeth-le-yo-ho-la's force, such as it was, untrained and miscellaneous, had greatly outnumbered the Confederate; but now the two were more equally matched in point of numbers and the chances of success were all on the southern side because of superior training and equipment, so Cooper was probably correct in his conjecture. McIntosh's excuse[524] for advancing precipitately and alone was, notwithstanding, very reasonable. The scarcity of forage made it expedient to march compactly; and the two generals had agreed, so McIntosh declared, when in conference at Fort Gibson, "that either force should attack the enemy on sight."

The privilege of attacking Opoeth-le-yo-ho-la fell, under this arrangement, supposing it was made, to McIntosh, who had been able to push on in advance of Cooper. The Battle of Chustenahlah was fought in the early afternoon of Decmber 26, 1861, and ended in what seemed the complete defeat of the Creeks. McIntosh reported that, although their position was strong, they were forced to retreat

> To the rocky gorges amid the deep recesses of the mountains, where they were pursued by our victorious troops and routed in every instance with great loss. They endeavored to make a stand at their encampment, but their efforts were ineffectual, and

---

[523] *Official Records*, first ser., vol. viii, 11.
[524] — *Ibid*, 22.

we were soon in the midst of it. The battle lasted until 4 o'clock, when the firing gradually ceased.[525]. .

And then the Creeks fled, leaving practically everything in the shape of property behind them. Cooper came up and detachments of his troops pursued them almost to the Kansas line. The weather was bitterly cold, provisions scarce, the country rough and bleak. The pursuit took the form of a seven day scout; but the Creeks, no matter how great their dispersion, were headed straight for Walnut Creek, Kansas.

Their coming was anticipated. Hearing of their approach, Superintendent Coffin had directed[526] all the agents[527] under his charge to report to him for duty at a place on the Verdigris River called Fort Roe[528] "about thirty-five or forty miles from Leroy and Burlington." It was Coffin's intention to meet the refugees upon their first arrival; but, as Commissioner Dole was expected soon to be at Fort Leavenworth, he thought it best to wait[529] and consult with him. It does not seem to have been recorded on just what date the first of the Indian refugees crossed the Kansas line, but they were very soon crossing in great numbers and, by the time Coffin finally reached them, their condition was truly pitiable. They took up their station on the bare prairies between the Verdigris and the Arkansas Rivers and stretched

[525] *Official Records*, first ser., vol. viii, 23-24.

[526] Commissioner of Indian Affairs, *Report*, 1862, p. 136.

[527] The agents were, George A. Cutler, Creek, Charles W. Chatterton, Cherokee, Isaac Coleman, Choctaw and Chickasaw, G. C. Snow, Seminole, and Peter P. Elder, Neosho River. Agent Elder did not report for duty.

[528] The Indian agents usually referred to it as "Fort Roe" but the military men, with a few possible exceptions, when meaning identically the same locality, spoke of "Roe's Fork." There is no such place as Fort Roe given in the *Lists of Military Posts, etc., established in the United States from its earliest settlement to the present time*, published by the United States War Department, 1902. That list, however, is far from being complete.

[529] Commissioner of Indian Affairs, *Report*, 1862, p. 138.

themselves in almost hopeless confusion over about two hundred miles of country. Fortunately the land upon which they camped was Indian land, New York Indian land, and the few white men thereon were legally intruders and could not consistently object to the presence of the refugees. The numbers of the refugees were variously estimated. Starting with about forty-five hundred,[530] they increased daily and at an astonishing rate; for the exodus of the Creeks was but the signal for the flight of other tribesmen from Indian Territory, of all those, in fact, who were either tired of their alliance with the Confederacy or had never been in sympathy with it and were only too eager to take the first chance to escape from it.

The suffering of the refugees, due to destitution and exposure, was something horrible to think upon. Superintendent Coffin had little to give them. He appealed to General Hunter for an allowance from the army supplies and Hunter sent down his chief commissary of subsistence, Captain J. W. Turner, to do what he could to relieve the distress. Hunter also sent Brigade-surgeon A. B. Campbell; for it was not simply food and clothing, that were needed and roof shelter, but medical at-

---

[530] In compliance with instructions from Major-General Hunter, contained in your order of the 22d. ultimo, I left this place on the 22d. and proceeded to Burlington, where I learned that the principal part of the friendly Indians were congregated, and encamped on the Verdigris river, near a place called Roe's Fork, from twelve to fifteen miles south of the town of Belmont. I proceeded there without delay. By a census of the tribes taken a few days before my arrival, there was found to be of the Creeks, 3,168; slaves of the Creeks, 53; free negroes, members of the tribe, 38; Seminoles, 777; Quapaws, 136; Cherokees, 50; Chickasaws, 31; some few Kickapoos and other tribes, about 4,500 in all. But the number was being constantly augmented by the daily arrival of other camps and families. . .–A. B. CAMPBELL, surgeon, U.S.A., to James K. Barnes, surgeon, U.S.A., medical director, Department of Kansas, dated Fort Leavenworth, February 5, 1862.

tendance. As soon as possible, cheap blankets[531] were furnished and some condemned army tents. The journey northward had been undertaken in the bitterest of cold weather. With a raw northwest wind beating in their faces,

And over the snow-covered roads, they travelled all night and the next day, without halting to rest. Many of them were on foot, without shoes, and very thinly clad. . . In this condition they had accomplished a journey of about three hundred miles; but quite a number froze to death on the route, and their bodies with a shroud of snow, were left where they fell to feed the hungry wolves. . .

Families who in their country had been wealthy, and who could count their cattle by the thousands and horses by hundreds, and owned large numbers of slaves, and who at home had lived at ease and comfort, were without the necessaries of life.[532]

---

[531] These were purchased by Coffin, acting under the advice of Hunter [Dole to Smith, June 5, 1862, Indian Office, *Report Book*, no. 12, pp. 392-396].

[532] Extracts from Agent Cutler's *Report*, September 30, 1862. Various reports, more or less detailed, descriptive of the intense sufferings of Indian refugees in the first weeks of their sojourn in Kansas may be found in the *Annual Report* of the Commissioner of Indian Affairs for 1862, pp. 135-175. Those of Turner, Campbell, Cutler, and George W. Collamore are particularly good. Some of the reports originally accompanied Dole's *Report* of June 5, 1862 [Indian Office, *Report Book*, no. 12, pp. 392-396; Commissioner of Indian Affairs, *Report*, 1862, pp. 147-149; House *Executive Documents*, 37th congress, second session, vol. x, no. 132], which was prepared in answer to a House resolution, calling for information on the southern refugee Indians.

Collamore's *Report* of April 21, 1862 is to be found in manuscript form in General Files, *Southern Superintendency, 1859-1862*, C1602. Another report, most excellent in character, issued from the pen of special agent, William Kile, February 21, 1862. It is in Land Files, *Southern Superintendency, 1855-1870*, K107. There are also a few good accounts of the Creek exodus of 1861. One of them is a sworn statement, presented by Holmes Colbert in a letter, dated March 25, 1868, and authoritatively cited by Mix in an office letter to Secretary Browning, June 8, 1868 [Indian Office, *Report Book*, no. 17, p. 308].

Another account came from John T. Cox to W. G. Coffin under date of March 18, 1864, and, while not in the least detailed, is worth quoting because of its tribute of respect to the loyal Indians. It runs thus:

Herewith I enclose a map of the route of retreat of the early Loyal Refugee Indians, under Apoth yo-ho-lo, in the Winter of 1861.

With the facilities within my reach, for obtaining facts connected

When, sometime in early December, Commissioner
Dole heard of the resistance that the unionist Creeks
were making to Colonel Cooper, he immediately ap-

with that remarkable exodus, I am fully warrented in saying, that the
history of the War does not furnish a parallel of patriotic devotion to
the Union.

The Rebels had managed so adroitly during the administration of
Buchanan, as to secure the appointment of, or favor of every Government Official, or Employee, within the limits of the South Indian Country, all sources of information were corrupted or poisoned. Postmasters
deplored the fall of the Old Government, as already taken place, Indian
Agents, and all others holding business relations with the several tribes,
used every means in their power to discourage them and destroy their
confidence in the Old Government, resorting to the grossest Misrepresentations, Bribery of Chiefs, Headmen, &c., Malfeasance and Robbery –
Military Posts, Government Stores, Ordnance &c. &c. were surrendered
or abandoned under color of the most dire military necessity, and the apparent tardiness of the Old Government to render them timely assistance,
or in any way counteract those influences, left them without counsel, and
without friends, and implied a total abandonment of the Indians. Yet
under all the discouraging surroundings a large portion of the Creeks,
Cherokees, Seminoles and others maintained their loyalty. The Chickasaws were divided in their Councils, and the Choctaws went over almost entirely to the Rebel Government.

In the month of March 1861, international councils were held, first
at the Creek Agency, next at North Fork, without affecting very materially the fidelity of the Indians. But in the latter part of April, the
Choctaws and Chickasaws gave in full adhesion to the Confederate
Government. The remaining tribes were alternating between the Coun-
sels of Apoth-yo-ho-lo, McDaniel and others on the one hand, and a
swarm of Rebel Commissioners on the other.

The Rebel Government was pushing forward the organization of
Indian Regiments, under the McIntoshes, Stan Watie, Adair, Jumper,
Smith and others, while the Conservative element, forming a Cherokee
Regiment under Col. Drew, for armed neutrality, but in truth loyal to
the Union, while Apoth-yo-ho-lo headed the hostiles, as they were
termed by the Rebels.

In a Report dated Creek Agency C.N. Dec. 16th., 1861, addressed to
the Hon. David Hubbard, Commissioner of Indian Affairs, Richmond,
Va., the Creek Agent, Col. Garrett says, See Copy marked "A" (Garrett's report to Hubbard appears in another connection in the present
work. It seems to have come into the Indian Office from two independ-
dent sources). I have noted this to show the attitude of the several
tribes at the beginning of the Rebellion.

The principal object of this report is to call attention to the real
claims of the Indians upon the Government, not only to sympathy, but

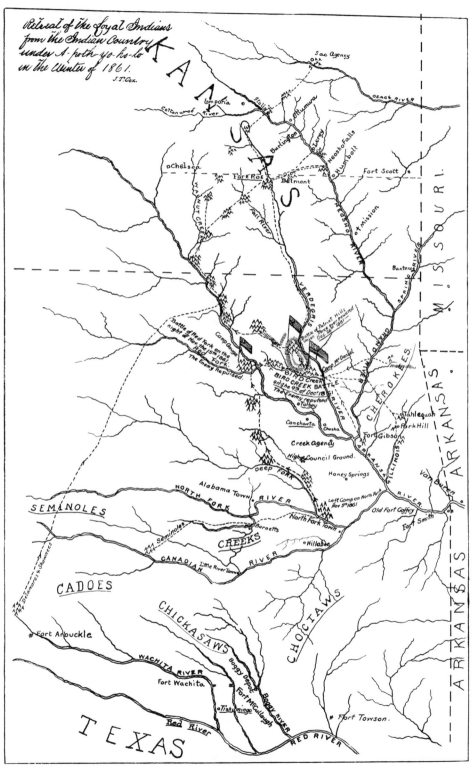

Retreat of the Loyal Indians from the Indian Country under A-poth-yo-ho-lo in the Winter of 1861.

J. T. Cox.

[From Office of Indian Affairs]

plied once more, through the Secretary of the Interior, to the War Department for troops sufficient to assert Federal supremacy south of the Kansas line, his immediate object being, the strengthening of the force then opposed to Cooper. At the moment, Lane's expedition was under consideration, Lane having managed to convince the Washington authorities, both congressional and administrative, that an expedition southward was absolutely necessary [533] for the protection of the frontier.

Somewhat earlier, in fact in the late autumn, the non-secession Indians of various tribes had made their own appeal for help. They had made it to the United States government and also, a little later on, to the Indian tribes of Kansas. Along about the first of November, a mixed delegation [534] of Creeks, Seminoles, and Chick-

compensation for services from the time they abandoned their homes and all they possessed, and took up arms in support of the Government.

Although they claim nothing of the kind, yet the moral effect of such a tangible recognition of their early services, would insure fidelity of all other tribes against any other future rebellion or disaffection against our Government.

The history of their destitution, and terrible sufferings in their pilgrimage of three hundred miles in mid-winter, is familiar to you and not necessary here to relate [General Files, *Southern Superintendency, 1863-1864*, C824].

[533] Others had reached that decision likewise. On the tenth of December, McClellan had written to Halleck, "I shall send troops to Hunter to enable him to move into the Indian Territory west of Arkansas and upon Northern Texas. That movement should relieve you very materially" – *Official Records*, first ser., vol. viii, 419. See also the letter of December 11, 1861 [*ibid.*, 428].

[534] It was to this delegation, I have no doubt, that the Shawnees sent their note of encouragement. It bears date November 15, 1861 and was issued from the Shawnee Agency, Johnson County, Kansas. Its inspiring passages are these:

Brothers, hold fast to the Union! Hold to your treaties! And now call upon the United States government to fulfill their treaty stipulations with you by protecting you in this your time of need, and save your country to you first, and then, by so doing, save the whole of the Indian country to the Union.

. . . And now our advice to you is, go immediately to Washington City, lay your case before President Lincoln, state everything, and we assure you that he will protect you, and that immediately; we think that delay on your part will be ruinous to your people; we believe that

asaws had made its appearance[535] at Leroy and, finding there the United States Creek agent, George A. Cutler, had consulted with him "in reference to the intentions of the Federal government regarding the protection due them under treaty stipulations." Cutler advised the Indians to talk the matter over with Senator Lane and accompanied them to Fort Scott, Lane's headquarters, for the purpose. Arriving there, they learned that Lane had gone to Washington and had left his command in charge of Colonel James Montgomery. Colonel Montgomery counselled with the Indians as Cutler had done and helped them to reach the decision that it would be best to proceed to Washington and lay their complaints before the Commissioner of Indian Affairs. At the same time, Montgomery notified[536] President Lincoln of their intention.

Still accompanied by Agent Cutler, the delegation resumed its journey, going by way of Fort Leavenworth. There they conferred[537] with General Hunter and left greatly strengthened in their resolution of proceeding to Washington; for Hunter, too, thought that such a trip might compel the government to realize the Indian's very real distress and its own obligation to relieve it. We are fain to believe that General Hunter personally believed in the military necessity of securing Indian Territory even though he did do all he could to oppose the project of Senator Lane in the early months of 1862 and even though he did disapprove of the formation of the department of Kansas and his own assign-

your agent ought to conduct you there. Put your confidence only in the Union and you will be safe. . . – Commissioner of Indian Affairs, *Report*, 1861, p. 45.

[535] Report of Agent Cutler, September 30, 1862 [Commissioner of Indian Affairs, *Report*, 1862, p. 138].

[536] Montgomery to Lincoln, November 19, 1861 [*ibid.*, 1861, p. 461].

[537] Hunter to Dole, December 1, 1861 [Commissioner of Indian Affairs, *Report*, 1861, p. 49].

ment to it instead of to that of Missouri, which would have been his preference. If he at any time to date had wavered [538] in his opinion as to the needs of the Indians and their legitimate claim upon the United States government for protection, Carruth's letter of November twenty-sixth ought to have settled the matter, unless, indeed, its rather savage tone had created prejudice instead of working conviction as was intended.

> . . . I have from the first believed it would be good policy to let loose the northern Indians, under the employ of government; it certainly would be better for the border States to have the Indian country for a battle ground than to have it remain a shelter for rebel hordes the coming winter. . .[539]

The visit of the Indians to Washington proved very opportune. By the twenty-seventh of December, they were back at Fort Leavenworth and considerably reassured. Superintendent Coffin had a council with them on the twenty-eighth "at the Fort to good satisfaction." He says of his interview,

> I gave them Presents of Pipes, tobacco, and Sugar, and they went on their way to Fort Scott rejoicing they seem to be in fine Spirits,[540] but are at a Loss what to do for a living til Lanes Army goes down there into the Indian Territory they want very much to get Some of the Funds now due the Creeks. . .[541]

---

[538] Note that Hunter, when writing to McClellan, December 19, 1861 [*Official Records*, first ser., vol. viii, 450], professed that, previous to the receipt of McClellan's letter of the eleventh, he had not known that it was expected of him that he should undertake an expedition for the defense of Indian Territory. He declared that Thomas' communication of November twenty-sixth, touching the matter, had been vague in the extreme.

[539] Extract from letter of Carruth to Hunter, November 26, 1861 [Commissioner of Indian Affairs, *Report*, 1861, p. 49].

[540] It seems a little surprising that they did depart from Fort Leavenworth in such good spirits; for, while there, they surely must have heard rumors of the final attack upon Opoeth-le-yo-ho-la. Agent Cutler tells us that he heard of the exodus a few days after his return to Kansas with the delegation. He had then left Leavenworth, however, for he says farther on in his letter that he went back there to confer with Coffin as to what should be done.

[541] Extract from letter of Coffin to Dole, December 28, 1861 [General Files, *Southern Superintendency, 1859-1862*].

A more pathetic appeal, and one more immediately telling in its effects, was that made to the brother Indians of Kansas. It came direct from Opoeth-le-yo-ho-la and when it reached the Delawares found in them a ready response. It invited their coöperation [542] in the war and asked for men and ammunition. [543] This is the Delaware reply: [544]

We are much rejoiced to receive your letter by James McDaniel [545] and David Balon. Our Agent has sent it to our

[542] See letter of Mix to F. Johnson at the Delaware Agency, Quindaro, Kansas, dated January 22, 1862, acknowledging Johnson's letter of January fourth, which enclosed

A copy of the reply of the Delaware Chiefs in Council to the letter of the Creek Chief O-poeth-lo-yo-ho-la, inviting their coöperation against the rebel States. . . – Indian Office, *Letter Book*, no. 67, pp. 271-272.

[543] On the 1st inst., I mailed you the letter of Opoth-la-yar-ho-la Muscogee Chief to the Delawares asking for men and ammunition. On the 2nd inst. the Delaware chiefs in Council returned the following letter in answer to Opoth-la-ho-la. . . – F. JOHNSON to Dole, dated Quindaro, Kansas, January 4, 1862 [General Files, *Delaware, 1862-1866*, J543].

[544] John Connor, Head Chief, Ne-con-he-con, Sur-cox-ie, Chas. Journeycake, Assistant Chiefs, to Oputh-la-yar-ho-la, Muscogee Chief Warrior and our loyal Grand Children dated Delaware Nation, Kansas Jan, 3rd 1861.

[545] James McDaniel seems to have been a Cherokee. On April 2, 1862, Agent Johnson reported to Dole that forty-one Delaware Indians had returned destitute from the Cherokee country and that he had given them assistance and also "a refugee Cherokee chief, James McDaniel." This idea is further borne out by the following letter:

Office of U.S. Agent for Cherokees
Tahlequah, Ind. Ter. April 7, 1873

HON. H. R. CLUM, Acting Commissioner of Indian Affs

SIR: I beg leave to call your attention to the fact that in the fall and winter of 1861 Opothleyoholo a Creek and James McDaniel a Cherokee placed themselves at the head of the loyal Creeks, Seminoles, Cherokees & others. Unsustained by any U.S. forces they gathered on Bird Creek, in this Nation, to resist rebel conscription into their army. They tried to avoid a fight, to make their way peacably to the union army in Kansas, by a far western route. But Gen. Douglas H. Coopper, & Gen. Stand Watie, with troops from Texas, & Arkansas, & with rebel Cherokees, Creeks, Choctaws &c pressed upon them, & attempted to bring them into subjection to the Southern Confederacy.

great Father, the President, "at Washington," and to Gen. Hunter at "Fort Leavenworth." It gives us great pleasure to hear that you are good and true friends to the President, and to the Government of the United States. We hope you will continue to be their friend. If bad men of the South ask you to go to war against the President, stop your ears, don't listen to them, they are your worst enemies, they are trying to destroy you and the Country.

Grand Children it does our hearts good, we rejoice to hear of the victories you have gained over your enemies of the Government under your brave leader Oputh-la-yar-ho-la.

Grand Children we are ready and willing to help you. Our brave Warriors are ready to spill their Blood for you, and are only waiting to hear from our great Father at Washington, we have asked of him the privaledge of going to your assistance, and hope that our request will be granted, we don't wish to go to War against the wishes of our great Father the President. We have heard that the President will soon have a large Army in

They adhered to their loyalty. Fought the rebel forces in three or four battles. At first vanquishing the rebel forces, but finally were overcome, & compelled to flee to Kansas in mid-winter, with women & children. In Kansas these men were organized into regiments, & on arriving in the Cherokee Nation were largely reinforced by their friends here, & in the Creek & Seminole Nations.

I have made this statement so that you may see the situation in which these men are placed, & judge intelligently.

Now I wish to know if men wounded in those engagements, under Opothleyoholo & James McDaniel, while fighting against the rebels, & the widows of those who were killed, & those who were otherwise disabled in those fights, & in the subsequent flight, are entitled to the benefits of pension laws. Can they be pensioned under existing laws?

If not, can you, through the Secretary of the Interior, prevail on the President to have the matter presented to the next Congress, with a view to having these persons placed on the rolls of the pension office. I need say nothing of the propriety of the Government rewarding as far as possible, such acts of loyalty & voluntary fighting for the Government by full blood Indians — when all the influence & power of faithless Indian Agents, & Superintendants, & the Southern army from Texas & Arkansas, & the more wealthy & educated mixed blood Indians, were arrayed against them. It should be rewarded, as far [as] practicable, as an incentive to like faithfulness in any emergency that may arise in the future. I have the honor to be Very Respectfully Your Obdt. Servant
                    JOHN B. JONES, U.S. Agent for Cherokees

the Indian Country to protect you, that he has ordered Gen. Lane to march to your relief. We are confident that our great Father is able and will protect his red children – Grand Children we pray to the "great spirit" to protect you and keep you out of the hands of the bad men of the South, who are trying to destroy you and the Government – We have no fears as to the result of this war – the President has large Armies in the field that will conquer and punish the Rebels – We are proud of our Muscogee Children.

The United States government had already determined upon an expedition to the Indian country and, yielding to the importunities of Senator Lane, who represented General Hunter as in full accord with himself in the matter, had decided to use the Kansas Indians in the making up of the attacking force. It was well that the Indians had manifested a readiness to fight and that the Delawares, particularly, had overcome their previous aversion. The first official record of the fact that the decision to use the Kansas Indians had been reached appears to be a communication[546] from Assistant Adjutant-general E. D. Townsend to Surgeon-general C. A. Finley, under date of December 31, 1861, notifying him that medical supplies would soon be needed for a force of about twenty-seven thousand men, about four thousand of whom were to be Indians, which was to be concentrated at an early day near Fort Leavenworth. On the third of January, Lane wrote[547] to

---

[546] *Official Records*, first ser., vol. viii, 576.

[547]   WASHINGTON, D.C. January 3, 1862.
MAJOR-GENERAL HUNTER, Commanding Kansas Department:

It is the intention of the Government to order me to report to you for an active winter's campaign. They have ordered General Denver to another department. They have ordered to report to you eight regiments cavalry, three of infantry, and three batteries, in addition to your present force. They have also ordered you, in conjunction with the Indian Department, to organize 4,000 Indians. Mr. Doles, Commissioner, will come out with me.   J. H. LANE.
Official Records, first ser., vol. viii, 482.

Hunter, informing him, as if at first hand and semi-officially, of the new plan. It is not to be wondered at that General Hunter took offence at the officiousness and presumption Lane displayed. In point of fact, it was a clear case of executive interference.

Now that it had, to all appearances, gained a long-desired object, the Indian Office lost no time in lending the War Department its hearty coöperation. Commissioner Dole was especially enthusiastic and, under instructions from Secretary Smith, prepared to go out to Kansas himself to help organize the Indians for army service. He also sent particulars [548] of the new movement to Superintendent Branch and a circular letter [549] to the agents of the central superintendency, detailing the advantages that would accrue to individual Indians should they enlist. Dole wrote these letters on the sixth of January and was then expecting to be in Leavenworth City for the making of final arrangements eight or ten days "hence." He did not manage to get away,

---

[548] It being the intention of the Gov't of the United States to take into its miliary service 4000 Indians from the borders of Kansas and Missouri, to be organized under Major Gen¹ Hunter, you are hereby made acquainted therewith. The different Agents in your superintendency will be instructed direct from this Office to use their best endeavors to engage the above number of Indians, taking care that those so engaged are capable of good service and are well affected towards this Government.

All the operations in this behalf should be conducted with dispatch and as much secrecy as the nature of the measure will admit of.

I understand that the Government proposes to equalize the pay of these Indian volunteers with that of other volunteers, but giving the chiefs an additional compensation. Each man will receive a blanket, and those not having arms of their own will be provided by the Government. Their subsistence will be the same as that provided in Revised Regulations No. 5, Section 39 of this Bureau, or the army subsistence, whatever that may be. Where any of the Indians, thus engaged, shall die or be killed whilst in service, their pay will be given over to their families – Indian Office, *Letter Book*, no. 67, pp. 211-212.

[549] — *Ibid.*, 215-216.

however, quite so soon; but the agents went to work immediately and, even before Dole arrived in Kansas, Agent Farnsworth, who had always been rather too eager for Indian enlistment, was able to report[550] the initial steps taken. By the twenty-first of January,[551] Dole was well on his way west. He reached Kansas in due season and there learned[552] for the first time, that Opoeth-le-yo-ho-la had been completely overwhelmed, that the refugees were on the Verdigris, and that General Hunter was subsisting them. This was doleful news, indeed, and made the project of a southern expedition seem more and more expedient.

General Hunter had done the best he could to relieve the awful sufferings of the refugees; but, on the sixth of February, he was obliged to inform[553] Dole that he could do no more, that he had practically reached the

---

[550] Farnsworth wrote on the 21st, acknowledging Dole's letter of the sixth and saying,

> Its contents has been explained to two trusty Indians, who will keep the matter entirely secret until the time for public action comes. I have sent for the Indians to come in. I think they will all be here by the 30th or 31st of this month. I will enroll them as soon as possible. I think I shall be able to enlist about 150 vigorous warriors. . . – General Files, *Kickapoo, 1855-1862*, F335.

[551] Your communication to this office of the 31st December last has been received enclosing a letter which was brought to you by a messenger from the South, as you were holding a Council with the Delaware Chiefs of your Agency, and which letter you desired to be laid before the President of the United States. Your communication also represented the readiness of the Delawares and all the other Western tribes to engage in military service on the side of the Government against the rebel States.

> With reference to all these Subjects, you will have an opportunity of conferring with the Commissioner of Indian Affairs (who has perused your letter in person) at Leavenworth City, for which destination he left this City on Sunday last on public business. – CHARLES E. MIX, acting commissioner, to F. Johnson, January 21, 1862 [Indian Office, *Letter Book*, no. 67, p. 268].

[552] Commissioner of Indian Affairs, *Report*, 1862, pp. 26, 147-148.

[553] I have the honor to inform you that Capt. J. W. Turner, Chief Commissary of Subsistence of the Department, has just returned from

end of his resources, and that, after the fifteenth of February, the whole responsibility of subsisting the destitute Indians would have to fall upon the Interior Department. Dole was almost at his wits' end. He had no funds that he could use legitimately for the need that had arisen. It was a case of emergency, however, and something certainly had to be done. Before the fifteenth of December arrived, additional reports[554] came

the encampments of the loyal Indians, on the Verdigris river, and in its vicinity. Having made arrangements for subsisting these unfortunate refugees until the 15th day of the present month.

In the neighborhood of Belmont and Roe's Fort, there were, at the time Capt. Turner left, about four thousand five hundred Indians, chiefly Creeks and Seminoles. But their number was being constantly augmented by the arrival of fresh camps, tribes and families.

Their condition is pictured as most wretched – destitute of clothing, shelter, fuel, horses, cooking utensils and food. This last named article was supplied by Capt. Turner in quantities sufficient to last until the 15th instant after which time, I doubt not, you will have made further arrangements for their continued subsistence.

In taking the responsibility of supplying their wants until the Indian Department could make provision for their necessities I but fulfilled a duty due to our common humanity and the cause in which the Indians are suffering. I now trust and have every confidence that under your energetic and judicious arrangements these poor people may be supplied with all they need after the 15th instant, on which day the supplies furnished by Capt. Turner will be exhausted.

I make no doubt that provision should be made for feeding, clothing and sheltering not less than six thousand Indians, and possibly as high as ten thousand, on this point however, you are doubtless better prepared to judge than myself. I only wish to urge upon you the necessity for prompt measures of relief.

P.S. Copies of the reports made by Capt. Turner and Brigade Surgeon Campbell will be furnished to you by tomorrow's post, in view of the urgency of this case, and the fact that these Indians cannot be supplied any further than have been done from the supplies of the army, I send one copy of this letter to Topeka and the other to Leavenworth City. Fearful suffering must ensue amongst the Indians unless the steps necessary are promptly taken.

This letter was forwarded by Edw. Wolcott, at Dole's request, to the Indian Office [General Files, *Southern Superintendency, 1859-1862*, W513].

[554] Coffin to Dole, dated Fort Roe, Verdigris River, Kansas, February 13, 1862 [General Files, *Southern Superintendency, 1859-1862*, C1526]; Snow to Coffin, February 13, 1862 [General Files, *Seminole, 1858-1869*].

in from Superintendent Coffin, detailing distress. Under the circumstances it was necessary to act quickly and without congressional authorization. Dole telegraphed[555] to Secretary Smith,

> Six thousand Indians driven out of Indian territory, naked and starving. General Hunter will only feed them until 15th. Shall I take care of them on the faith of an appropriation?

He received a reply[556] that should have been dictated, not so much in the spirit of generosity, as of simple justice:

> Go on and supply the destitute Indians, Congress will supply the means. War Department will not organize them.

With this approbation in hand, Dole went to work, purchased sufficient supplies on credit, and appointed[557] a special agent, Dr. William Kile of Illinois, who had been commissioned[558] by President Lincoln to act on Lane's staff and was then in Kansas as Lane's brigade quartermaster, to attend to their distribution. Meanwhile, the attention of Congress had been called to the matter and a particularly strong letter of Dole's, describing the utter misery of the exiles, was read in the Senate February 14, in support of a joint resolution for their relief.[559] It was intended originally to apply only to the loyal Creeks, Seminoles, and Chickasaws but had its title changed later so as to make it include the Choctaws. On the third of March, Congress passed[560] an act providing that the annuities of the "hostiles," Creeks, Chickasaws, Seminoles, Wichitas, and Cherokees, should be applied, as might be necessary, to the relief of ref-

---

[555] Commissioner of Indian Affairs, *Report*, 1862, p. 148.

[556] — *Ibid.*

[557] Dole to Dr. Kile, February 10, 1862 [Indian Office, *Letter Book*, no. 67, pp. 450-452].

[558] Commissioner of Indian Affairs, *Report*, 1862, p. 148.

[559] *Congressional Globe*, 37th congress, second session, p. 815.

[560] United States *Statutes at Large*, vol. xiii, 562.

ugees from Indian Territory. It was expressly stipulated in this enactment[561] that the money should not be used for other than Indian Territory tribes.

Secretary Smith's telegram, as the reader has probably already observed, had given to Dole a small piece of information that was not of slight significance, signifying as it did a change of front by the War Department. The War Department had rescinded its former action and had now refused to organize the Indians for service. The objections to Lane's enterprise must have been cumulative. Before the idea of it had embraced the Indians and before it had become so closely identified with Lane's name and personality, in fact, while it was more or less a scheme of McClellan's, Hunter had interposed[562] objections, but purely on military grounds. His force was scarcely equal to a movement southward. Subsequently, Halleck interposed objections likewise and his reasons,[563] whatever his motives may have been, were perfectly sound, indeed, rather alarmingly so, since they broadly hinted at the miserably local interests involved in the war in the west and the gross subordination of military policies to political. Then came

---

[561] It was, however, the beginning of a great deal of graft and misuse of government funds. Citizens of Kansas, otherwise reputable, prepared to reap a rich harvest. and government officials were not at all behindhand in the undertaking. Presumably, immediately upon the departure of Hunter's commissary from Fort Roe, the Indians began to get into the debt of the settlers and the sum of the indebtedness soon mounted up tremendously. Coffin again and again urged payment [Coffin to Dole, May 12, 1862], so did Colonel C. R. Jennison of the Seventh Regiment Kansas Volunteers, and so did General Blunt.

The act of March 3, 1862, reinforced by that of July 5, 1862 [United States *Statutes at Large*, vol. xii, 528] was re-enacted, in whole or in part, each year of the war [Act of March 3, 1863, United States *Statutes at Large*, vol. xii, 793; Act of June 25, 1864, *ibid.*, vol. xiii, 180]. In addition, special appropriations were made, like that of May 3, 1864, for the refugees.

[562] Hunter to Thomas, December 11, 1861 [*Official Records*, first ser., vol. viii, 428]; McClellan to Hunter, December 11, 1861 [*ibid.*].

[563] Halleck to McClellan, January 20, 1862 [*ibid.*, 509-510].

Lane with energy like the whirlwind, a local politician through and through. He had absolutely no respect for official proprieties and the military men, opposed to him, were men of small calibre. He reached Kansas, joyfully intent upon putting into immediate effect the power that Lincoln had conferred upon him, only to find that there stood Hunter, fully prepared to contest authority with him. The Adjutant-general had written [564] Hunter that Lane had not been given a command independent of his own and that, if he so desired, he might conduct the expedition southward in person. In the evening of the twenty-sixth, Lane reached Leavenworth, and the very next day, Hunter issued general orders [565] that he would command in person. Taken aback and excusably indignant, Lane communicated [566] at once with John Covode and requested him to impart the news to the President, to Stanton [567] and the new Secretary of War, and to General McClellan.

Official sensitiveness was unquestionably at the bottom of the whole trouble, yet Lincoln was very largely to blame for having yielded to Lane's importunities. He frankly said that he had wished to keep the affair out of McClellan's hands as far as possible. [568] He hoped to profit by the services of both Hunter and Lane; but, if they could not agree, then Lane must yield the precedence to Hunter. He must report for orders or decline the service. [569] Military men, stationed in the west, and civil officers of Kansas were all prejudiced

[564] Thomas to Hunter, January 24, 1862 [*Official Records*, first ser., vol. viii, 525-526].

[565] — *Ibid.*, 529-530.

[566] — *Ibid.*

[567] Stanton had become Secretary of War, January 15, 1862. On the real reasons for Cameron's retirement, see Welles' *Diary*, vol. i, 57.

[568] Lincoln to Stanton, January 31, 1862 [*Official Records*, first ser., vol. viii, 538].

[569] Lincoln to Hunter and Lane, February 10, 1862 [*ibid.*, 551].

against the "Lane Expedition." [570]   They expected it to be nothing but jayhawking and marauding of the worst description.   The Indians, however, were deeply disappointed [571] when a halt came in the preparations.

[570] Hunter to Halleck, February 8, 1862 [*Official Records*, first ser., vol. viii, 829-831]; Halleck to Hunter, February 13, 1862 [*ibid.*, 554-555]; McClellan to Halleck, February 13, 1862 [*ibid.*, 555].

[571] My object more particularly in writing to you to-night is on account of the orders that we learn here to-night from General Gennison to General Hunter that no Indians are to be mustered into the Service we have taken greate paines and have made flattering progress in enrooling them according to the orders of your Selfe and General Hunter nearly all of them set apart 10 Dollars out of their wages pr month for their families and many that have no families leave it in the hands of the Agents for their benefit after the war is over and they are burning with revenge and spiling for a fight and I have no dout at all but they would doo good Service there are two amongst them at least perhaps many more that I think would make good Commanders Billy Bowlegs & Little Captain the latter a Creek that commands in all the Late Battles and they suposed that he was killed but he got in a few days sinc Billy has also recently arivd I am fully of the opinion that these Indians at least two Thousand of them for such a campaigne as they are designed for or the one is suposed to be that is to go South from here are as well calculated for as any Troops that could be selected and it will make great trouble with them as they have their harts set upon it and will be most cruelly disappointed if not permettd to go and they should be got back as soon as posabl to their homes as the planting season is near and if they do not get there in time for putting in a crop the present Spring it looks like they will have to be suportd by the Government til August 1863 or til a crop can be maturd nex year which could not be sooner than August this would entail a heavy expense upon the Indian department that I would like to be avoidd I have had an Interview with General Gennison and he is very sure that if they would arm these Indians and give him three thousd other Troops he could put those Indians into their homes in time for a crop this year all here are very much disappointed and mortified at the course things are for their families will be no small Item in lessening the expense of Subsisting them which with all the Economy we can use will be very large.– COFFIN to Dole, dated Humboldt, Kansas, February 28, 1862 [General Files, *Southern Superintendency, 1859-1862*, C1541].

    Since writing you from Humboldt Dr. Kile & my selfe have visited Fort Roe to make arrangements for moving the Indians to the Neosho on getting there we found that about 1500 of them had left for this place they left Saturday noon it turned cold Saturday night and com-

Opoeth-le-yo-ho-la personally addressed a communication[572] to Lincoln. He wanted nobody but Lane to command the expedition. Pending a settlement, Dole

menced snowing and snowed hard most of the day Sunday and last night was the coldest of the season the Indians all got to timber Saturday night to camp and remained in camp Sunday but most of them ware on the Road to day tho it was too coald to travel in the fix they are in I saw many of them barefooted and many more that the feett was a small part of them that was bare, these people realy seem to be doomd to suffer for this Loyalty beyond measure, the goods and shoes ordered by Dr. Kile and an order sent by myselfe before Kile's arival have not yet reached here. Kile remained at Fort Roe to Settle and close up business there and assist in the araingements for starting them from there and I came on to se to those on the way and make araengments for taking care of them when they get here I found many of them Sick and not able to leave camp till teams are sent to them to aid them. We find that we cannot move them with less than about three Teams to the Hundred and it may overrun that the weather is moderating now and we shall make a vigorous effort to move them as quick as possible, we find it very dificult to get Teams on government vouchers and may not be able to move them in a reasonable time on that account the funds I brot down three Thousand Dollars was nearly exausted before Kile arived we are now nearly destitute of money if I find it as dificult around here to get teams as I have between here and the fort I shall make an effort to raise some funds for that purpose tomorrow with what success remains to be seen we have kept them pretty well suplied with Something to eat so far but that is all we can bost of, iff we ware to say they ware well clothed there would be ten thousand square ft of nakedness gaping forth its contradiction; they have been out of Tobacco for Several days and I doo think one days experience in camp would convince the most skeptical that with Indians at least the weed is a necessity, the Indians of all tribs held a grand council last Thursday at Fort Roe in regard to the war, at which they determined with great unanimity to gather up and arm as best they could, all there able bodied men and go down with the army on their own hook and aid in driving out the Rebels from their homes in time to plant a crop for this season and then gather all the Ponies they can and they think they can capture enough from the Rebels with what they have to come up for their families. *Cannot the Government aid so Laudible an enterprise as that at least with a few guns and some amunition* they appear to be in good earnest and are feeding up the best of their Ponies for the Trip. . .—COFFIN to Dole, dated Leroy, March 3, 1862 [General Files, *Southern Superintendency, 1859-1862,* C1544].

[572] Letter of January 28, 1861 [*Official Records,* first ser., vol. viii, 534].

ordered[573] Coffin[574] to desist from further enrollment. Secretary Stanton was declared opposed to the use of Indians in civilized warfare.[575] Soon the orders for the expedition were countermanded with the understanding, explicit or implied, that it should later proceed under the personal direction of General Hunter.

The military situation in the middle west and the great desire on the part of the Confederacy to gain Missouri and to complete her secession from the old Union necessitated, at the opening of 1862, a thorough-going reörganization of forces concentrated in that part of the country. Experience had shown that separate and independent commands had a tendency to become too much localized, individual commanders too much inclined to keep within the narrow margin, each of his

---

[573] I have a despatch from Secretary Smith saying that the Secretary of War is opposed to mustering the Indians into the service, and that he would see the President and settle the matter that day (Feb. 6).

This as you will see disarranges all my previous arrangements, and devolves upon me the necessity of revoking my orders to you to proceed with the agents, to organize the loyal Indians in your Superintendency into companies preparatory to their being mustered into the service by Gen. Hunter. I have now to advise that you explain fully to the Chiefs that no authority has yet been received from Washington authorizing their admission into the army of the United States; but I would, at the same time advise that you proceed to ascertain what number are able and willing to join our army, and that you so far prepare them for the service as you can consistently do, without committing the Government to accept them, as I still hope for the power to get these refugees if no others, into the service, it being one, and as I think, the best means of providing for their necessities. . . – DOLE to Coffin, February 11, 1862 [Indian Office, *Letter Book*, no. 67, p. 448].

[574] Coffin had not been written to, Jan. 6, because the original plan did not contemplate the employment of southern Indians. Not until he heard of their presence, as refugees in Kansas, did Dole include them in his list of possible soldiers.

[575] Superintendent Branch may have had something to do with the opposition that grew up in Washington after Dole's departure; for he was there the last days of the month. Lane asked for his immediate return to the west [MIX to Lane, January 27, 1862, Indian Office, *Letter Book*, no. 67, p. 293].

instructions, for the good of the service as a whole to be promoted. It was thought best, therefore, to establish the Trans-Mississippi District of Department No. 2[576] and to place in command of it, Major-general Earl Van Dorn. The district was to comprise all of Louisiana north of the Red River, all of Indian Territory proper, all of Arkansas, and all of Missouri west of the St. Francis. Wise in the main, as the scheme for consolidation unquestionably was, it had its weak points. The unrestricted inclusion of Indian Territory was decidedly a violation of the spirit of the Pike treaties, if not of the actual letter. Under the conditions of their alliance with the Confederacy, the Indian nations were not obliged to render service outside of the limits of their own country; but the Confederacy was obliged, independent of any departmental reörganization or regulations, to furnish them protection.

Almost the first thing that Van Dorn did, after assuming command of the new military district, was to write,[577] from his headquarters at Jacksonport in eastern Arkansas, to Price, advising him that Pike would shortly be ordered to take position in southwestern Missouri, say in Lawrence County near Mt. Vernon, "with instructions to coöperate with you in any emergency." Van Dorn was then laboring under the impression that Pike's force consisted of a majority of white troops, three regiments, he thought, out of a brigade of eight or nine thousand men, whereas there was only one white regiment in the whole Indian department. Colonel Cooper complained[578] that this latter condition was the fact and insisted that it was con-

---

[576] Special Orders, no. 8, Jan. 10, 1862 [*Official Records*, vol. viii, 734].

[577] Van Dorn to Price, February 7, 1862 [*Official Records*, first ser., vol. viii, 749].

[578] Cooper to Pike, February 10, 1862 [*ibid.*, vol. xiii, 896].

FORT McCULLOCH

Choctaw Nation
I.T.

C.P. Kahler Del.

trary to the express promises made, by authority,[579] to the Choctaws and Chickasaws when he had begun his recruiting work among them the previous summer. Had Van Dorn only taken a little trouble to inquire into the real state of affairs among the Indians, he would, instead of ordering Pike to bring the Indian regiments out of Indian Territory, have seen to it that they stayed at home and that danger of civil strife among the Cherokees was prevented by the presence of three white regiments, as originally promised. At this particular time as it happened, Pike was not called upon to move his force; for the order so to move did not reach him until after the Federals, "pursuing General Price, had invaded Arkansas."[580]

It proved, however, to be but a brief stay of execution; for, as soon as Van Dorn learned that Price had fallen back from Springfield, he resolved[581] to form a junction with McCulloch's division in the Boston Mountains and himself take command of all the forces in the field. He estimated[582] that, should Pike be able to join him, with Price's and McCulloch's troops already combined, he would have an army of fully twenty-six thousand men to oppose a Federal force of between thirty-five and forty thousand. Pike was duly informed[583] of the new arrangement and ordered[584] to "hasten up with all possible dispatch and in person direct the march of" his "command, including Stand Watie's, McIntosh's, and Drew's regiments." His men

---

[579] Walker to Cooper, May 13, 1861 [*Official Records*, first ser., vol. iii, 574-575].

[580] Report of Albert Pike, dated Fort McCulloch, May 4, 1862 [*ibid.*, vol. xiii, 819].

[581] Van Dorn, Report to Bragg, March 27, 1862 [*Official Records*, first ser., vol. viii, 283].

[582] Van Dorn to Mackall, February 27, 1862 [*ibid.*, 755].

[583] Maury to Pike, March 3, 1862 [*ibid.*, 763-764].

[584] Maury to Pike, March 3, 1862 [*ibid.*, 764].

were to "march light, ready for immediate action." [585]
The outcome of all these preparations was the Battle of
Pea Ridge [586] and that battle was the consummation, the
culminating point, in fact, of the Indian alliance with
the Southern Confederacy. It was the beginning of
the end. It happened just at the time when the Richmond legislators were organizing [587] the great Arkansas
and Red River superintendency, [588] which was intended
to embrace all the tribes with whom Albert Pike had
made his treaties. Albert Pike retired from Pea Ridge
to his defences at Fort McCulloch, angry and indignant
that the Indians had been taken out of their own country to fight the white man's battles. His displeasure
was serious; for the Indian confidence in the Confederacy depended almost wholly upon the promises and
the assurances of the Arkansas poet.

---

[585] Maury to Drew, McIntosh, and Stand Watie, March 3, 1862 [*Official
Records*, first ser., vol. viii, 764].

[586] This will be discussed fully in a later volume.

[587] *Journal*, vol. i, 640, 743; vol. ii, 19, 20, 51, 52; vol. v, 47, 115, 116, 151,
167, 210.

[588] The act was passed April 8, 1862 [Confederate *Statutes at Large* (edition of 1864), 11-25].

APPENDIX A – FORT SMITH PAPERS

Copy   TAHLEQUAH, January 9th 1857.

SIR: – Some time since I received a letter from you calling for information in reference to the white intruders who were settling upon the Cherokee Neutral Land. I have been creditably (credibly) informed that there are several white families living upon the Neutral Land, some of them are making improvements, others are in the employment of Cherokee Citizens, living on the Neutral Land, from the best information that I can get, most of the intruders are good citizens of the U-States. I have notified them to leave, with the understanding that if they do not leave by spring, they will be removed by the Military. My reason for not removing them at an earlier date is, the weather is so cold and disagreeable that it would be improper to turn women and children out of doors, therefore I will not remove them til the winter breaks it maybe that the Military will have to be employed in their removal: yet I shall make the effort to remove them peacefully and without the military if possible. Very Respectfully, Your ob't, Svt.   (Signed). GEO. BUTLER, Cherokee Agent. Doct. C. W. Dean, Sup't. of Ind. Affs.

Copy   FORT SMITH, ARKANSAS, February 19th, 1859.

SIR: I deem it my duty as an independant citizen to apprize you, as the head of the Indian Bureau, of a recent transaction of the Superintendent of Indian Affairs at this place, and demand of you the proper action the facts may impose.

A contract has been given to an intimate friend and relation of the Superintendent, to feed the Witchita and other Indians inhabiting the country between the 98th and 100th degrees, West Longitude, at a sum pr ration, of one third, perhaps one half, more than other persons would have fed these Indians for; which persons were denied the privilege of contending for the contract, as no puplic notice inviting proposals was made, and the contract was given privately.

I assert this postively, as to the notice for proposals, and enclose you a letter of Capt. J. H. Strain, confirmatory of the fact, that he

was willing to feed the Witchitas, for a sum far less than the records
of your Office must show the government has been pledged to pay
another. The character of this gentleman, who has been for years
Sutler at Fort Arbuckle, if unknown to you, can be avouched by the
U. S. Senators from this State.

The Seminoles are now fed under a contract given in the usual
regular mode of publishing invitations for proposals and awarding the
contract to the lowest bidder, at the sum of about seven cents pr ration. The Witchitas are encamped only forty or fifty miles from the
Seminoles and near the Texas and Chickasaw lines, where corn and
beef are much cheaper and more abundant. In proof of this I refer
you to late contracts for these articles given at Fort Washita and Fort
Arbuckle – the first being near the Witchitas, and the other near the
Seminoles. Captain Strain says he would have fed the Witchitas for
ten cents per ration, and if proposals had been invited, the Contract
would have been taken for a less sum.

There are some seven hundred Indians now fed, and thirteen cents
pr ration is the sum stated as allowed – I believe it is more, but the
Indian Office contains the proof of the exact sum. If the Contract
had been given at nine cents pr ration, it would have been a saving of
twenty eight dollars pr day, over the price said to be now paid, which
would amount to eight hundred and forty dollars pr month, and ten
thousand and eighty dollars a year. This is surprisingly large, for a
small Indian contract, and at a time too when the duty of government
Officers to retrench expenses is so imperiously demanded.

I am opposed to such favoriteism under any circumstances, and particularly so, when the recipient can lay no claim to Democratic support.

I am credibly informed that the number of the Indians fed under
this contract, is rapidly increasing, and that efforts are all the time
made to induce the Texas Reserve Indians to claim relationship with
the Wichitas, and come into their camp and draw rations. One of
the employees under this Contract makes this statement, and says quite
a number have already been induced so to come. If the number is
swelled to two thousand, as conjectured here, the large price now
paid will roll up the sum thus disbursed to the Superintendents fa-
vorite so much that other notice will be taken of it, unless you find it
in your power to interfere.

I am tired of such conduct and such unfairness towards the government, and now make the charge distinctly and demand of you that it be stopped.

Of course I have no desire to withhold my name, and can refer you to Senators Sebastian and Johnson for an endorsement of my character.

Please acknowledge receipt of this. I am most respectfully, Your Obt. Servant, A. G. MAYERS.

Hon. J. W. Denver, Comr. Ind. Affairs,
Washington City, D. C.

P.S. I may add that I am not, nor have I ever been interested in these sort of Contracts, and have no desire to be interested in this one. A.G.M.

FORT SMITH 16th Feby. /59.

DEAR SIR: I am in receipt of yours of the 15th inst. You were correct in understanding me to say, that I was willing to feed the Witchita Indians, near Fort Arbuckle, at ten cents per ration.

Was the contract to be let to the lowest bidder, it would go below what I said I was willing to take it at. Very Respectfully, Your Obt. Servant J. H. STRAIN.

Gen. A. G. Mayers, Ft. Smith, Ark.

DEPARTMENT OF THE INTERIOR. OFFICE INDIAN AFFAIRS,
May 12th 1859.

SIR, For your information and such action as you may deem necessary, I transmit a copy of a letter, and its enclosures, addressed to this Office by A. G. Mayers on the 21st ultimo, and of my reply of the 11th instant. Very respectfully, Your Obt. Servant,

CHARLES E. MIX, Commissioner, ad interim.

E. Rector Esq, Superintendent &c,
Fort Smith, Arkansas.

Copy FORT SMITH, ARKANSAS April 21st 1859

CHAS. E. MIX, Esq, Acting Comr. of Indian Affairs
Washington City D. C.

SIR: — Allow me to ask of you the favor to inform, officially whether the funds provided by the Government for the subsistence of the Wichita Indians has been turned over to the Superintendent of Indian Affairs at this place or any other disbursing offices of the department, to carry out the Contract made by the Supt. with C. B. Johnson for subsisting those Indians after the facts reported by me in regard to the matter, in a letter to the Commissioner of Indian Affairs of date the 19th Feby 59 –.

It has been stated to me that such monies have been so turned over to the Superintendent, and statement has been contracted, I therefore wish to know of you the truth of the matter, and am assured such information will be readily afforded me,

I may add, to strengthen the report of facts formerly made by me in regard to the Wichita Contracts, that the Seminoles, who are subsisted at a sum less than seven cents per ration, under contract given after publication for proposals, are near Fort Arbuckle, and the Wichitas, who are subsisted under private contract at over thirteen cents per ration, are near Fort Washita and within the Chickasaw Nation (much of course to the annoyance of the Chickasaws). Now I ask a reference to the Comparative Contracts to feed the two tribes on file in your office, with the Contract for corn and beef given at the two posts mentioned to supply the Soldiers, on file in the War Office, to convince you that the Witchitas are fed at an exhorbitant cost to the Government.

I also herewith enclose a letter from Mr. Dennis Trammel, who was the Contractor to feed the Seminoles; stating that he was willing, and had so stated it to the Supt, to feed the Wichitas for seven cents pr ration. For Mr Trammel's veracity I can avouch and full endorsement can be given of it from others, if required; as can be done for my own character and standing in this community.–

I intend to follow up this matter to a conclusion, and in so declairing must state that I do it without motive of personal malice and simply as an impartial Citizen and a supporter of the administration – impelled to the duty in view of the universal acclaim throughout the Country for economy in Govt. expenses on account of the depleted state of the Treasury, Otherwise I might have left the unpleasant affair to the proper officers of the Government to find out and determine as they might see proper,

Let me ask; – Is it true that the Supt. has received the Two hundred thousand dollars due the Creeks under the treaty of 1851, without an order from that tribe to the government to send out the money and upon the Supt's own responsibility? – An early reply will greatly oblige me, Very Respectfully Your obt. Svt.　　A. G. MAYERS.

Copy   GREENWOOD ARKANSAS April 18th 1859.

DEAR SIR: I have understood that you was willing to feed the Wichataw Indians at the same price that you received from the Government for feeding the Seminole Indians.

Please state if I am correct in so understanding your propositions Very respectfully Your Obt. Servt.   A. G. MAYERS
Mr Dennis Trammell, at Greenwood Arks.

Copy   BACKBARN Aprial 19. 1859.

DEAR SIR: I recd your note of the 18 instant and state that you are correct, I have stated that I was willing to feed them at the same price 7 cents. I am Yours, &c.   DENNIS TRAMMELL
Genl, A. G. Myers Esq.

Copy   DEPARTMENT OF THE INTERIOR, OFFICE INDIAN AFFAIRS
                                          11th May 1859.

SIR: In reply to your letter of the 21st Ultimo I have the honor to state that a portion of the funds appropriated by Congress towards defraying the expenses of Colonizing the Wichita and other Indians in the western part of the Choctaw and Chickasaw country, including their temporary subsistance, has all along been in the hands of Superintendent Rector, to meet any necessary current expenses connected with said measure.

In regard to the contract made with Mr. C. B. Johnson by Superintendent Rector, for feeding the Witchitas, it was but a temporary measure to meet an emergency, and was fully approved by the late Commissioner of Indian Affairs, under subsequent instructions Supt. Rector, will it is expected, at an early day, make a different arrangement, for furnishing said Indians with such subsistence as must necessarily be supplied to them by advertising for proposals therefor, or by causing it to be purchased and issued to them direct by an agent of the Government, as may be best and most economical.

The money due the Creeks under the Treaty of 1856, to which you refer, was placed in Superintendent Rectors hands to be paid to them, in compliance with the formal and urgent demand of the Council of the tribe. Very respectfully Your Obt Servant
             Signed.   CHAS. E. MIX, Commissioner ad interim.
A. G. Mayers Esq., Fort Smith Arks.

DEPARTMENT OF THE INTERIOR, OFFICE OF INDIAN AFFAIRS,
March 14, 1860.

SIR: Robert J. Cowart, Esq. of Georgia, has been appointed by the President, by and with the advice and consent of the Senate, Agent of the Cherokee Indians in place of George Butler, Esq. whose commission has expired.

He has been directed to report himself to you at Fort Smith for instructions, when you will assign him to duty. His compensation will be at the rate of $1500 per annum, and the time of its commencement will be fixed upon when he arrives in this City, which he has been directed to take in his route to Fort Smith. The sufficiency of his bond will also be made the subject of examination at this Office upon his arrival.

A letter has been written to Mᴿ Butler notifying him of the appointment, and directing him to make up and forward his accounts immediately, and to turn over to Mr. Cowart all moneys, papers, and other property in his hands upon application. Very respectfully, Your obedient servant, A. B. GREENWOOD, Commissioner.
Elias Rector, Esq., Superintendent, &c., Present.

DEPARTMENT OF THE INTERIOR, OFFICE INDIAN AFFAIRS,
April 21, 1860.

SIR: From information that has been received at this Office in regard to certain persons, who are residing within the limits of the Cherokee nation, it is found necessary to call your attention to the propriety of seeing that the provisions of the Intercourse law are observed with respect to them. By reference to the law, you will find that no person can reside within the limits of the country of any Indian nation or tribe without permission, and such must be obtained under certain prescribed rules; and even after permission is given, if the party is found abusing the privilege by acting in violation of any of the provisions of law, or is found unfit to reside in the country whether from example, from the want of moral character, from his interference with the institutions of the tribe, from seditious language and teachings, or from any cause tending to disturb the peace and quiet of the tribe, or tending to alienate their attachment to the Government of the United States, the Superintendent of Indian Affairs, and Indian Agents have authority to remove him; and the President is authorized to direct the Military force to be employed in such removal.

The necessity for such power, and for greater facility in carrying the same into execution, was so apparent, that at the first session of the 35th Congress it was found advisable to legislate further in the matter; and the 3rd Section of the Indian appropriation bill was accordingly passed, which is, "That the Commissioner of Indian Affairs be, and he is hereby, authorized and required, with the approval of the Secretary of the Interior, to remove from any tribal reservation any person found therein without authority of law, or whose presence within the limits of the reservation may, in his judgment, be detrimental to the peace and welfare of the Indians, and to employ for the purpose such force as may be necessary to enable the agent to effect the removal of such person or persons."

As I remarked before, I am induced to believe that the Cherokees have just cause of complaint from the presence of some such persons within their limits, – and it is my desire that you call the attention of the newly appointed Agent particularly to the subject. He should look not only to those cases which are there originally without authority of law, but also to those who, with ostensibly worthy purposes, have received permission, and falsified their pretensions. This is a delicate trust, and should be executed with great caution and discretion, and you cannot enjoin upon the agent too much care and circumspection for although I shall examine carefully the grounds of his charges, yet I must be guided in a great measure by his opinion, and am determined that the law shall be enforced.

You will therefore, so soon as Mr. Cowart shall report to you for duty, communicate to him the contents of this letter, and require him to investigate, as quietly as possible, the cases of all white persons found within the limits of his agency, and report to me, through you, such as are there without the authority of law, and such as may be unworthy longer to remain although they may have originally had permission to enter the country. Very respectfully, Your Obt, Sevt.

A. B. GREENWOOD, Commissioner.
Elias Rector, Esq.; Fort Smith, Arkansas.

DEPARTMENT OF THE INTERIOR, OFFICE INDIAN AFFAIRS,
June 4th 1860.

SIR: The attention of this office has been called to an article which appeared in the Fort Smith Times (which is herewith enclosed) in which it will be seen that a secret organization has been formed in the Cherokee Nation, which is rapidly increasing. The existence of such an organization, the objects of which cannot be misunderstood, has caused in my mind the greatest apprehension as to the future peace and quiet of that country; and, if permitted to mature its plans, will be productive of the worst results. The article alluded to points to the Jones' as being the leaders in this movement, and who have been permitted for a long time to enjoy the privileges of that Nation. It is believed that the ultimate object of this organization is to interfere with the institutions of that people, and that its influences will extend to other tribes upon the Western border of Arkansas.

This scheme must be broken up: for if it is permitted to ripen, that country will, sooner or later, be drenched in blood. You are aware that there is a large slave property in the Cherokee country, and if any steps are taken by which such property will be rendered unsafe, internal war will be the inevitable result, in which the people of the bordering state will be involved. The relations which the Editor of the Times bears to the Cherokees enables him to procure reliable information from that section which is not accessible to all and hence the greater credit is due to his published statements in relation to the affairs of that people. This office is also in possession of private advices from that country, which fully corroborates the statements in the article referred to. This organization and its purposes are no longer left to mere conjecture. In view of these facts I have to direct that in addition to the instructions contained in a letter from this office, of the 21st of April last, the contents of which you were instructed to communicate to Agent Cowart, you will direct him immediately on his arrival at his Agency to cautiously, institute inquiry as to the existence of this secret organization, its objects and purposes; who are the counsellors and advisers of this movement, and proceed at once to break it up; and, if in his investigation he should be satisfied that any white persons residing in the Nation are in any way connected with this organization he will notify such person or persons forthwith to leave the Nation. You will inform Agent Cowart that the Secretary of War will be requested to place such force at his disposal as may be necessary to enforce any order he may deem it his duty to make. You will direct him also to spare neither time or trouble in carrying out these instructions, and that he report direct to this office, advising you in the meantime of his action.

A copy of this letter has been sent direct to Agent Cowart.   Yours Respectfully,   A. B. GREENWOOD, Commissioner.
Elias Rector, Esq., Supt: Ind. Affairs:
   Fort Smith, Arkansas

TROUBLE BREWING AMONG THE CHEROKEES
WHAT DOES IT MEAN?

The Fort Smith (Ark.) *Times* says: We noticed a week or two ago that there was a secret organization going on in the Cherokee Nation, and that it was among the full-blood Indians alone. We are informed by good authority that the organization is growing and extending daily, and that no half or mixed blood Indian is taken into this secret organization. The strictest secrecy is observed, and it is death, by the order, to divulge the object of the Society. They hold meetings in the thickets, and in every secret place, to initiate members. We are told that the mixed-bloods are becoming alarmed, and every attempt to find out the object of this secret cabal has thus far proved abortive. The Joneses are said to be the leaders in the work, and what these things are tending to, no one can predict. We fear that something horrible is to be enacted on the frontier, and that this secret work will not stop among the Cherokees, but will extend to other tribes on this frontier. The Government should examine into this matter, before it becomes too formidable.

CHEROKEE AGENCY. Near Tahleguah C.N.
HON. ELIAS RECTOR, Supt. Ind. Affairs
Fort Smith, Ark.
Sir: Yours of the 15th Inst, is before me, contents closely noted.

In reply I have to state, that I am in receipt of the Instructions of which you write, from the Indian Ag^t

And I now hasten to Lay before you the result of my investigations, thus far in this nation,

Soon after I entered the nation before I had proceeded say half days travel, I was met with complaints against certain persons (white men) who it was said had been enterfearing with the Institution of Slavery – to which I invariably replied to the complainants, bring me the charges – or the witnesses – by whome I can substantiate them, and my duty, will be as pleasant, as promptly fulfilled – *none came*,

In Tahlequah in time of Circuit Court, I made a short speach to the Citizens, in which I told them, that if they, or any of them, knew any thing on the subject – to report forthwith to me,– *and none have reported* and while I have heard much said on the subject – I have not as yet been able to get any thing that would do for proof – that would be reliable. And while I make the above statement I do not entertain a doubt, of the truth of the charges – And being satisfied of the truth of those charges – I shall use evry effort to establish them,

As regards those Secret Societies, I firmly believe, that they are gotten up with a view to aid in coveying those abolition plans of operation, to a successful termination   Allow me to say – that I shall continue to travel in and through the Nation (unless differently instructed) until I establish those charges if it can possible be done,

Mean while, I shall be pleased to recive Instructions and advice from you on the subject, and will keep you advised of my movements, I am Sir with much respect, your obt Servt,

ROBT. J. COWART, U. S. Cherokee Agent

Private

The Second Chief is about to call the Council together to take into consideration the conduct of those white men who are interfearing with the institutions of Slavery – and to devise means by which those Secret Societies may be put down, and when the Council meets, I think we can remidy all those evials –

I find there are many white men in the nation without permits – and one or two English men, these I shall order to leave the nation Instanter,   R. J. COWART

TAHLEQUAH C. N. July 9th 1860

DEAR MAJ RECTOR,   When I reached home I found that Hon. A. B. Greenwood had been here, stayed two days, and a half & left. I am told that he expressed a verry strong desire to see me but had not time to remain here or go to Fort Smith.

He has brought his family home to Ark. to remain as he writes me –

I wish now verry much to see you and Col. Pulliam, of which I have written him, I would go forthwith to see Greenwood but suppose from what he wroat me that he had left, or will have done so before I could get there.   I am with much respect, your friend

R. J. COWART

Hon. Elias Rector Fort Smith, Ark   Tahlequah C.N.

CHEROKEE AGENCY. TAHLEQUAH C. N. August 15th 1860
HON. ELIAS RECTOR, Sup^t Ind Affairs Fort Smith, Arks.

Dear Sir: Tomorrow morning I set out, to the Neutral Lands –

and am advised to take a few men with me which I propos doing,
It may be truely said, that, this Nation is in the midest of a *crises.*

I shall be compelled to call for Military aid – which I expect to
do forthwith –

Immediatly upon my return from the Neutral Lands – I expect
to go to Fort Smith –

Please Remember me kindly to my friend Col Pulliam –

I am very kindly your obt Servt.   R. J. Cowart
Tahlequah C. N.

OFFICE U.S. NEOSHO AGENCY, QUAPAW NATION
Augt 24th 1860

SIR: By refference to my letter of July 11th you will find that I
according to your instructions, gave all the intruders upon the Osage
reservation notice to leave forthwith, or that they would be removed
by Military force. That notice was dated May 22nd 1860, & the
intruders are still there, and I have most respectfully now to suggest,
that in view of the situation of the Neutral land of the Cherokees and
the reserve of the Osages, they, laying adjoining each other, and the
great number of squatters therein, I would advise that at least two
companies of U. S. Dragoons or Cavalry be called for, both to act
together in the removal of the intruders from the Osage and Neutral
lands –

I learn that Major Cowart expects to be at your office in a few
days, in order to make a Requisition upon the Commanding Officer
of Fort Caleb for Troops to remove the intruders from the Neutral
land, and enclosed you will find one from me, which if approved by
you, please forward by the same express, in order that the Troops
may march together, as their destination is about the same –

I would also say that in my opinion, that in order that the removal
should avail anything that all their improvements should be destroyed
by the Troops as they progress –

Your instructions are requested in all this matter. Very Re-
spectfully Your Obt Svt   ANDREW J. DORN, U.S. Neosho Agnt
Major Elias Rector, Supt Indian Affairs
Fort Smith Arkansas.

N.B. Please forward the enclosed letter directed to Capt W. L.
Cabell U.S.A. and much oblige yours truly   A.J.D.

EVANSVILLE, ARKS Sept 6th/60

FRIEND, THAD . . . I wish you woold come up in this part of the country. I am going to start to Campmeeting next Saturday at Cane Hill there was a big Camp meeting a going on when I came here in the nation it was about five miles west of this place. I did not go as I was busy fixing up to work tho if I dont have any bad luck I think I will have a good time at Cane Hill

I think business will be pretty good here from the prospects I think I will spend a couple months at Tahlequah this fall. I want to attend the next council there which will begin in Oct. . . . etc.
Remain your Friend   JNO. C. DICKENSON
Mark,, T,, Tatum, Greenwood, Arks

TAHLEQUAH CHEROKEE NATION, September 8th, 1860.
HON. ELIAS RECTOR, Supt. Indian Affairs, Fort Smith, Arks.

Dear Sir, Enclosed please find Copy of letter from the Secretary of War, to Hon. A. B. Greenwood –

Unofficial   WAR DEPARTMENT June 14th 1860,

DEAR SIR – In answer to your note of the 11th Inst in regard to trouble among the Cherokees, I have to inform you that orders have been given to the Commander of Fort-Cobb, as suggested, Yours &c,   Signed JOHN B. FLOYD.

HON. A. B. GREENWOOD, Commr.– It seems from the above that orders have been given the Commander at Fort Cobb to furnish me Troops to remove intruders from this Nation. I have not heard any thing from Washington since I left Fort Smith.

I would be glad to have the Troops as early as convenient, as I feel that I can do but little more without them.

I this day sent a Notice to John, B. Jones to leave the Nation by the 25th Inst.– which I trust he will do. I am writing to the Department today and giving the facts in refference to this Nation – I have asked for contingent funds, as the requirements of the Department, are, that money appropriated for one purpose, should not be used for another.

Please give me the benefit of any information, you have or may get on the subject of Troops. I am as ever your friend And obedient Servt.   R. J. COWART
Tahlequah C, N,

TAHLEQUAH CHEROKEE NATION, Oct 29th 1860
COL. PULLIAM,

My Dear friend, Will you be so kind as to forward the enclosed Dispatch to Hon A. B. Greenwood Washington D.C. Please Consult Capt. Sturgeons, you may, find it necessary, to change it, if so, please make any alteration, you and the Capt may, think best.

I expect to visit Fort Smith in a few days – when I hope to settle up my accounts, and spend some time with you – I [illegible] say pleasantly.

I Learned from Capt ———, your Recent affliction. Please allow me to tender to you and Especially to Mrs. Pulliam my heart felt Simpathy.

Write me by the barer all the News, I send written to Maj. Rector for two hundred Dollars, please see that the matter is arranged. I am very kindly yours, R. J. COWART
Tahlequah C. N.
Col R. P. Pulliam, Fort Smith Ark.

FORT SMITH A.R.K. Oct 31st 1860.
HON. A. B. GREENWOOD Com. Ind. Affairs, Washington D.C.

Intruders Removed from Neutral land – much desire to confer with you and [illegible] in person with Capt Sturgeons who commanded Troops. R. J. COWART, U.S. Cherokee Agent

SIR: I have received reliable information that Forts Washita, Arbuckle, and Cobb, all in the Choctaw & Chickasaw Nations, and recently abandoned by Federal troops, are now in possession of Texas State troops, and that Texas is now urging at Montgomery, that the Wichita Indians and bands affiliated with them, occupying the district of Country between the 98 and 100 degrees west longitude & between Red River & Canadian leased by the United States from the Choctaws & Chickasaws, for the purpose of Locating said Indians are within the Jurisdiction of this, the Southern Superintendency, and by an examination of the treaty of 1855 made between the U. S and the Choctaws & Chickasaws, you cannot fail to see the impropriety of the Indians occupying said district being attached to the Jurisdiction of Texas. unless she also extends her Jurisdiction over the Choctaws and Chickasaws.– Texas has tried on several occasions heretofore to have those Indians in the Leased district placed under her jurisdiction, but the Indians regard her as their ancient, and present enemy, and will never consent to such arrangement,

I have thought it my duty to call your attention to the subject that you may, if you think it expedient, lay it before your Honorable body for such action as it may think proper in the premises. Very Respectfully Your obt Servt   ELIAS RECTOR, Supt. Ind Affairs. Hon David Walker, President Arks. State Convention.

CHEROKEE AGENCY, May the 15th 1861
To the Superintendent of Indian Affairs
    Fort Smith Arks.
SIR: I have the honor of making the following report have this day taken into my possession as Agent for the Cherokee Indians, the following property as left by late Agent R. J. Corvort (gone) Dwelling house Kitchen and other out houses one office, houses all in bad repair one farm belonging to the Agency, in bad repair one table three desks and papers all in very bad condition one box containing old papers almost distroyed by rats one letter press and Books one Rule one Inkstand and letter Stamp one chair one Iron Safe.   I also have in my possession 14 Bounty Land Warrants received by me from you at office of Superintendency left by R. J. Corvort late Agent and receipted for by me to Superintendant the Book on Treaties as reported to of been, left by R. J. Corvort in office not found by me. Yours Respectifully   JOHN CRAWFORD, U.S. Agent for Cherokees Elias Rector, Superintendant Indian Affairs.

WICHITA AGENCY L.D., June 30-1861
SIR,   Enclosed herewith I have the honor to transmit my quarterly return, for the second quarter of the current year, and with it my operations as a Federal Officer will cease.

The seizure of the mules, wagon etc. by Gen¹ Burrow, rendered it necessary in my judgment, to issue at once to the Indians all the public property, moneys and effects in my hands, intended for their use and benefit by the original U. S. Government; believing as I do, that the moneys and other means which I have held in trust for them, would be as liable to seizure as the mules and wagon were, and result in a loss: the losses sustained by them on the Arkansas River and at Fort Smith by fire of very many of their goods, cause them to be in much need of the goods which I have issued, more particularly as there appears to be no arrangements by which they may expect supplies during the present year. The sudden withdrawal of the troops spread alarm and disquiet through the different settlements or encampments, many of them fled from the L.D. with a hope elsewhere to find security and protection, the remainder would have followed, but for the issue of goods which I made them, and assurances that they would not be molested.

With these remarks submitted, I have the honor to be, sir, Very Respectfully Your Ob't Srv't,   M. Leeper, Ind. Agt.
Major Elias Rector, Supt. Ind. Affairs
Fort Smith, Arks.

ESTIMATE OF FUNDS REQUIRED IN THE OFFICE OF SUPERINTENDENT INDIAN AFFAIRS ARKANSAS SUPURENTENDENCY.

For Salary of Superintendent. for ½ year of 1861. which
    includes 3 & 4th qrs. at $2.000 – per Anum .   . $1000.00
Pay of Clerk ½ year 3 & 4th qrs. at $1.500 – .   .   750.00
" " Interpreter "   " "   400 – .   .   200.00
" " Traveling expences. Contingences of office &c .   500.00

                                            $2.450.00
" Office rent for ½ year 200.00

                                          $2.650 00

ESTIMATE OF FUNDS NECESSARY FOR DISBURSMENT TO SEMINOLE INDIANS UP TO 30TH DECEMBER 1861 AS PROVIDED FOR BY TREATY OF 7TH AUGUST 1856

To provide for the Support of Schools for ten years the
    sum of $3000 – per Annun. from 7th August, 1856
    to 30th December 1861. .   .   .   . $16.000.00
For agricultural assistance. from 30th December 1859
    to 30th December 1861. at $2000 – per Annm .   4.000 00
For the Support of Smiths & Smith Shops from 30th
    December 1859. to 30th Decr. 1861. at $2.200 per
    Annum 4.400.00
Interest on $500.000 – invested at 5 per Centum from
    30th Decr 1860 to 30th Decr 1861.   .   . 25.000.00

                                          $49.400 00

Pay of Agent for year 1861　.　　.　　.　　.　1.500.00
"　" Interpreter for year 1861　　.　　.　　.　400.00
Contingent expenses of Office　.　　.　　.　　.　300.00
Provisions for Indians attending payments of annuities &
　visiting Agency on business　.　　.　　.　　.　300 00

$2.500 00

Amount invested by Old U S government for Seminoles as per treaty 7th August 1856 at 5 per centum. $500.000 – This amount has never been invested in State bonds but held by the Government.

ESTIMATE OF FUNDS NECESSARY FOR DISBURSMENT TO CREEK INDIANS FROM 30TH JUNE TO 31ST DECEMBER 1861. AND BALANCES DUE THEM BY THE OLD U. S. GOVERNMENT. UP TO 30TH JUNE 1861.

Permanent provisions for Blacksmiths　for ½ year 1861.　1.680.00
"　　　"　　" Iron & Steel　" " "　540.00
"　　　"　　" Wheelwrights　" " "　300.00
"　　　"　　" Wagon Makers " " "　300.00
"　　　"　　" Agricultural assistance for ½
　　　　　year　.　　.　　.　1.000.00
Interest on $200.000 – at 5 per Centum. for purposes of
　Education. from 30th June 1860 to 30th June 1861.　10.000.00
Interest on same from 30th June to 30th December　"　5 000 00
Unexpended balances Interest due on same. up to 30th
　June 1860 which has never been paid　.　　.　15.000 00

$33.820 00

Pay of Agent for 3 & 4 qrs 1861　.　　.　　.　750.00
"　" Interpreter 3 & 4 qrs 1861　.　　.　　.　200.00
Contingent Expences "　"　"　"　.　　.　　.　150.00
Provisions for Indians at payment of Annuities .　.　150.00

$35.070.00

AMOUNT OF MONEY DUE CREEK INDIANS ANNUAL-LY UNDER TREATY 7TH AUGUST 1856

Permanent Annuity	$24 500.00
Permanent provisions for Blacksmiths . . .	3.360 00
" " " Iron & Steel . . .	540.00
" " " Wheelwrights . .	600 00
" " " Wagonmakers . .	600 00
Assistance in Agriculture. . . .	2.000.00
Interest on $200.00. at 5 per centum for purposes of Education	10.000.00
	$41.600.00

Amounts due Creek Indians for amounts invested by Treaty 7th August 1856.		
For purposes of Education . .	$200 000	
Creek Orphan fund . . .	200 741	
	$400.741	

CREEK ORPHAN FUND INVESTED AS FOLLOWS

In Bonds of State of Kentucky at 5pr Cent, .	$1.000 00
" " " " " Missouri " 5½ " .	28.000 00
" " " " " " " 6 " .	28.000.00
" " " " " Tennessee " 5 " .	20.000.00
" " " " " Virginia " 6 " .	73 800 00
United States " 6 " .	49 941 00
	$200.741.00

NORTH FORK OF CANADIAN RIVER, 5th July 1861

SIR: On receipt of this you will please effect a continuance, on behalf of the Confederate States of America, with Mr. Charles B. Johnson of Fort Smith, of the contract existing up to 30th June last between the United States of America and himself, for feeding the Wichitas, Caddoes, and other kindred and other bands of Indians now settled in the country leased from the Choctaws and Chickasaws.

If no more favorable terms can be effected, you are authorized to adopt those of the former contract, with its conditions and stipulations in all respects.

You will provide that the contract shall end, at the pleasure of the

Commissioner of Indian Affairs, on the 31st day of December 1861, and not sooner; and that it shall be at his option to continue it for such further term as he may please, upon the same terms in all respects.

You will provide that the contract shall relate to, and take effect as of the first day of July 1861: and you will receive bond, in form used by the United States, but to the Confederate States, with sufficient sureties, and in such sum as you may consider sufficient to ensure faithful performance. I have the honor to be, Sir

ALBERT PIKE, Commissioner of the Conf.
States to Indian Tribes West of Arkansas.

Elias Rector Esq, Superintendent Ind. Affairs,
Arkansas Superintendency.

Agreement made and entered into, this 14th day of August 1861, at the Wichita Agency, between Albert Pike, Commissioner of the Confederate States of America to the Indians west of Arkansas, of the one part, and Charles B. Johnson of the County of Sebastian and State of Arkansas, of the other part.

This agreement witnesseth, that the said Albert Pike, Commissioner as aforesaid, for and on behalf of the Confederate States of America and the said Charles B. Johnson, his heirs executors and administrators, have covenanted and agreed, and by these presents do covenant mutually and agree to and with each other as follows to wit:

That the said Charles B. Johnson, his heirs, executors and administrators, shall and will supply and issue or cause to be issued and supplied at such times and places in the Leased District west of the 98th degree of west longitude as the Wichita Agent may direct, daily rations to the several Tribes and Bands of Comanches, Wichitas and other Indians that now are or may hereafter during the continuance of the present contract be settled in the said Leased District, for and during the term of one full year, commencing with the sixteenth day of August instant, at the price of sixteen cents for each complete ration issued as aforesaid: which rations shall be issued, one for each individual in all of said Tribes and Bands and shall consist of one pound of fresh beef or fresh pork, and three quarters of a quart of corn or corn meal or one pound of flour to every ration, with four quarts of salt, three pounds of coffee, six pounds of sugar, two quarts of vinegar, one and a half pounds of tallow and three pounds of soap to every hundred rations.

Payment shall be made quarterly for the rations furnished under this contract, but in the event of the Commissioner of Indian Affairs being without funds for such purposes, the payment to be made as soon thereafter as funds are provided for such purposes.

This contract may be terminated in whole or in any part at any time by the Commissioner of Indian Affairs, upon equitable terms and conditions whenever it shall be deemed expedient to do so upon giving thirty days' notice of such intention.

Witness our hands and seals the day and year first above written. Signed and Sealed in triplicate

ALBERT PIKE, Commissioner of the Confederate States
Signed and Sealed in our presence.

WM QUESENBURY   CHARLES. B. JOHNSON.
W WARREN JOHNSON

NORTH FORK OF THE CANADIAN RIVER, 5th July 1861

SIR: I have sent a Special Messenger to the Wichita and other Indians on the Reserve in the Country leased from the Choctaws and Chickasaws, requesting Black Beaver, and other Captains and Chiefs to meet me at the Seminole Agency on the 22nd instant, in order to hear a talk from me and enter into a Treaty. If they should not do so, I shall go from the Seminole Agency to the Reserve for that purpose.

As it was through your instrumentality these Bands were settled on the Reserve, and the promises made them were made through you, and as you are favorably known to them for these reasons, and as the Head of the Superintendency of Indian Affairs in which they are included, your presence and cooperation with me, in negotiating with them, will, I am very sure, be of great service.

I therefore request, that, if your health and other duties permit, you will be present with me at the Seminole Agency on the 22nd, and accompany me, if necessary, to the Reserve.

I shall leave this place about the 9th, and at furtherst by the 10th, and go round by Forts Washita and Arbuckle. I shall be gratified if you can so time your movements as to overtake me on the way.

I wish also to suggest that the presence of the Agent, Mr. Leeper, will be indispensable, and to desire you to direct him to accompany you, that he may as soon as possible repair to his Agency. I have the honor to be With deep regards your obt Svt

ALBERT PIKE, Commissioner of the Confederate
States to Indian Tribes west of Arkansas.
Elias Rector, Esq, Superintendent Ind. Aff. Arkansas Superintendency.

Confederate

THE ~~UNITED~~ STATES,

TO Elias Rector   DR.

Date.		Dolls.	Cts.
1861 August 24	For Services rendered assisting Comr. Pike in making treaties with Seminole, Wichita And Commanche Indians under orders so to do, by Comr. Pike, from 10th July to 24th August 1861 inclusive 45 days at $5.00 pr day .	225	00
	For hire of Bugg. horses & driver for same length of time at $5— per day	225	00
	For hire of wagon team & driver for same service & same time, to Transport tent Baggage provisions &c. at $5 per day	225	00
	Forrage for 4 horses for same length of time and for same service 50 cents per day each horse . . .	90	00
		$765	00
	Paid ferrage Crossing streams . .	8	00
		$773	00

Received at   185   , of ELIAS RECTOR,
Superintendent of Indian Affairs for the Southern Superintendency,
Dollars in full of this account

$

(Triplicate.)

I CERTIFY, on honor, that the above account is correct and just, and that I have actually, this   day of   185   , paid the amount thereof.   Sup't Indian Affairs.

WICHITA AGENCY L. D. Sept. 15th 1861

SIR; A considerable amount of intermittent fever has made its appearance at this place, supposed to be occasioned by an unusual degree of dampness produced by the most luxuriant growth of vegetation I ever knew, and the recent heavy rains which have been almost incessant for many days past, it gives us just cause of alarm as we are entirely out of medicines of almost every kind and placed at so remote a distance from the settlements, that none can be procured short of a visit to Fort Smith; I had a slight attack of fever myself and luckily for me, Dr. Shirley discovered a small portion of Quinine which I partly consumed, and which had escaped the vigilant search of the so called Texas Troops at the time they took from him his medicines and medical books, and transferred them to parts unknown. These causes in addition to some information in reference to Indians which I will impart, I hope will be considered an ample apology for incuring the expenses of an Express, I have employed a man at $3.00 per day, he bears his own expense, and runs the risk of meeting with wild Indians and land Sharks by the way.

The renowned Indian warrior and Chief Buffalo Hump has made his appearance with fifteen or sixteen followers, the remainder of the Indians and the principal part of his own party, he says are encamped on the Canadian and head waters of the Washita, he called on me the second day after his arrival, and told me that he was now old and desirous of abandoning the war path, and spending his latter days in quietness and peace with all men, but said the winter would soon be at hand, and that he would require a much better house than any he saw at the Comanche Camp, that he thought if he had a house, such as the Agency building, that he would be warm in cold weather, and that he would be content to live in it, and pursue the walks of white men, I replied to him that I knew he was a great man and had an immense amount of influence with the wild tribes, and that the Confederate States had also heard of him, and that if he thought proper to bring in his people and settle down in good faith on the Reserve, quit stealing and depredating upon the country, that they would give him all that had been promised, and that he might calculate, that if houses were built for him, that they would not be as good as those at the Comanche Camp, that several of those houses were more extensive and expensive, than would be deemed necessary in future, that he might only look for small cabins, and perhaps only receive assistance in their erection, that it was the object of the Confederate States to learn the Indians to work and support themselves, not to work for them and support them; that upon those terms if he were disposed to settle I would be glad to receive him, if not, it mattered but little, that he was at liberty to pursue just such course as suited him best. The next day he called again his tone and bearing was altogether changed, professed to be satisfied and said at the falling of the leaves, the time appointed for settlement and consumating the Treaty with Capt. Pike, he would be here with his people. He gave it as his opinion that the others who had a conference with Capt. Pike would not come in or settle; but I learn from Py-oh who went out with those Chiefs and returned with Buffalo Hump that their respective bands are divided in sentiment, that about half of each band will come in and settle, and that the others will probably remain on the prairies, they have large bands of stolen horses and mules, and he thinks they are afraid to bring them in, lest they should be taken away from them.

Jim Ned and the other Delawares with the exception of one family left the Reserve without any cause, he returned from his first encampment and attempted to persuade Jim Pock Marked to leave with his people, by telling him that he would be assailed by the Texans before long, and if not by them, most certainly by the northern Troops, and that he had better leave at once, and save the lives of his women and children. Jim Ned is a most unmitigated scoundrel, and I have no doubt that most if not all the disquiet heretofore produced among the Reserve Indians might be traced to him, and I think it very fortunate that he has abandoned the Reserve, by doing so, he has forfeited his right of citizenship upon it, and the protection which the Confederate States had guaranteed to him.

I learn from an Indian Mexican and a half breed Delaware Indian who have recently returned from Santa Fe, that all the northern Indians who visit that part of the country are amply armed and equiped by the Federalists, and sent in every direction over the plains as spy Companies, that propositions of the like character, had been made to the Southern Indians, but not accepted, they are now regarded as enemies, and have retracted farther South, not being permitted to inhabit the country or travel as far north as heretofore; Py-oh remarked that they were herded in by Texas and Mr. Lincoln's government like a band of horses or cattle.

Please forward by my Expressman, blank forms of every description, and ask Mr. Johnson to forward blank forms for provision checks; you will also oblige me by making an application for the Indian mules taken by Burrow, and by aiding the bearer to procure the public wagon and my harness which were loaned to Algernon Cabell.

You are aware that I cannot close my returns without funds for

the purpose, when shall I look for them? Very Respectfully Your
obt. Srvt.   M. LEEPER, Ind. Agent
Elias Rector Esqr., Supt. Ind. Affairs
    Fort Smith Arks.

                                CREEK AGENCY, Sept 30th 1861
    SIR: I have the honor to hand you herewith the Bond License,
and Invoices of John Barnwell of the Creek Nation
    Very Respectfully Your Obt Servant
                        W. H. GARRETT, C.S. Agent for Creeks
Maj Elias Rector, Superintendent C. A.
    Fort Smith, Ar

                        TAHLEQUAH C. N. October the 10th 1861
MAJ ELIAS RECTOR, Superintendant of Indian Affairs,
    Fort Smith, Ark.
    Dear Sir: I have the honor of transmitting through your office
to the Commissioner of Indian Affairs at Richmond a requisition for
the Annuities School and Orphan funds due the Cherokee Indian on
Stock invested up to July 1861. I send two copies. If it is not necessary to send but on[e] you can arrange that in regard to the leave of
Asence that I wished you to grant me I will not ask for owing to the
Governor declaring my seat vacant in the Legislator and ordering an
election though I am under many obligations to you for your willingness to grant me leave the Treaty will be ratified today. Every thing
going on well the Texas Troops passed through on Wednesday the
Creek excitement turned out to be nothing I shall be anxious to hear
from you at any time on all subjects I have the honor Sir to be
your most obedient Servnt
                        JOHN CRAWFORD Agent Cherokees, C.S.A.
Hon. E. Rector, Superintendant Indian Affairs

                        TAHLEQUAH, C. N. October 10th, 1861
DAVID HUBBARD Commissioner of Indian Affairs, Richmond, Va.
    Dear Sir: I have the honor to make out and transmit to you a
requisition for the Annuities due the Cherokee Indians for the year
1860 and 1861
For the installments of interest on the permanent General fund as
estimated for July 1860 and January and July 1861 forty three Thousand and three hundred and Seventy two dollars and thirty six Cents
                                              $43 372 36

For the installments of interest on the permanent Orphan fund as estimated and uninvested for July 1860 and January and July 1861 four thousand and five hundred dollars $4.500
For the installment of interest on the permanent School fund as estimated for July 1860 and January and July 1861 Seventeen thousand Seven hundred and Seventy two dollars $17.772.
Total Amount due the Cherokees on Stock invested Sixty five Thousand Six hundred and forty four dollars and thirty Six Cents

$65.644.36

One half years pay of Agent	.	.	.	750 00
Contingent expenses, ½ year	.	.	.	75 00
pay of interpreter ½ year	.	.	.	200.00

$66.669.36

Sir the Statement as made out is correct to the best of my judgment I have been acting as Agent for the Cherokee Indians Since the 22nd day of April 1861 Came by request of Hon R. W. Johnson of Arkansas. received a letter from the Hon David Hubbard Commissioner of Indian Affairs dated 12 June 1861 requesting me to try and get along as Agent of the Cherokees the best that I Could which I have done to the best advantage and evry thing here is working well for the South I have not received any moneys from the Lincoln govenment Since I have been acting as Agent for the Cherokee Indians Your most obedient Servt   JOHN CRAWFORD,
        Agent for the Cherokee Indians West of Arkansas, C.S.A.
David Hubbard, Commissioner of Indian Affairs
    Richmond, Va

WICHITA AGENCY L.D. Oct. 21st 1861

SIR: Five weeks ago I despatched a messenger to Fort Smith with a report to you, and for medicines for the Agency and Indians; since which time I have heard nothing either from the report or messenger, sufficient time has elapsed for the man to have made two trips. In the report of that date I apprised you of the sickness which had and still prevails here to a considerable extent, and that we are destitute of medicines: Dr. Shirley's supplies having been forcibly taken from him by persons from Texas, claiming to act as a military posse from that State. You are aware that we are entirely cut off from mail facilities, and from an opportunity of procuring medicines of any description short of Fort Smith, the want of which has been excessively annoying, and perhaps the occasion of several deaths; this report will be handed you by a second messenger, whom I hope you will furnish with a supply of Quinine, Calomel and blue mass if nothing more.

On friday last a man was shot at by an Indian in company with six others within a mile of the late Fort Cobb; on the next day two Indians arrived as messengers on the part of the Kiowas and all the Southern bands of Comanches, who are said to be encamped on the North Canadian within four days ride of this place; they say that their intention is to be here at the falling of the leaves, to conclude a treaty with Capt. Pike. The Kiowas inform us that they received the white beads and tobacco from Capt. Pike, and that they desire to be on terms of friendship with us, that it is the wish of the whole band, with the exception of one bad man and fifteen or twenty followers, whom they cannot control, and that they desire us to kill them, that if it is not done, they will surely commit serious depredations, and that they believe they are now in this vicinity.

The Indians at present on the Canadian are supposed to number Seven or eight thousand, and if they should come here as is anticipated, they will require a large amount of provision, I would therefore respectfully suggest the propriety of your notifying the Contractor of the fact, that he may not be taken on Surprise: you will also perceive the necessity of Capt. Pike or some other duly authorized person, to be here at the appointed time to consummate treaties with them; they say that no further depredations will be committed on Texas, provided the twenty men above described are killed.

It is impossible for me to keep you advised of the affairs of this reserve without some kind of mail facilities, therefore, I hope you will unhesitatingly employ some one to carry the mail once in two weeks at least, until such time as the Government shall have made permanent arrangements, it is not more strange than true, that I have not since my arrival here on the Sixth of August, received a solitary news paper or any other item of news, except such as can be gathered from an occasional stragling teamster, and that is the most reliable information that I have in reference to the battle at Springfield, the particulars of which I know very little.

When Capt. Pike left here it was his intention to have the place garrisoned in the shortest time practicable, he left authority with Jno. Jones to enlist thirty Indians to act as a protection to the Agency, and as a spy company in its vicinity, Jno. Jones could only enlist Seventeen, all Comanches, those and the few employees on the reserve are the only protection we have, and I would not give a fig for the security the Indians would afford me in a case of actual danger, they might be useful however in giving information of the approach of an enemy: I shall feel obliged if you will inform me of the time the troops may be expected, if the day is far distant, I shall deem it my indispensable duty to select some place of security and safety for my family, if it is the intention or wish of the Confederate Government to leave this place ungarrisoned, I am willing to risk the consequences myself, but I am unwilling to detain my family, where they are in danger of being destroyed by savages: it is also apparent that no Agent can exercise the control necessary to fill the expectations of the Government, without the means placed within his reach of doing so; without troops the most flagrant violations of the Intercourse Laws might be practiced every day with impugnity; and without funds to meet the expenses incident to the Agency, the employees cannot be retained a great while. Those Indians who expect to treat with Capt. Pike expect also supplies of blankets and clothing, and white men to instruct them in the erection of houses for the winter.

Please advise me by the return of my messenger, when troops may be expected, at what time the Commissioner will be here, and funds to enable me to forward my accounts. The Estimates submitted in August, in addition to the more liberal allowances of Capt. Pike in his recent treaty with the Indians, I hope will be all that is required on my part at present.

One of the Articles in Capt. Pike's late treaty, appears to be an offense to the people of Texas, and I think it very doubtful whether any assistance could be derived from that quarter, if we were threatened with the most iminent danger: with these remarks submitted, I have the honor to be, Very Respectfully Your Obt. Servt.

M. LEEPER, Indian Agent

Elias Rector Esq, Supt. Ind. Affairs
Fort Smith Arks

FORT SMITH ARKANSAS, Nov. 7th 1861

MAJOR ELIAS RECTOR, Superintendent of Indian affairs

Sir: As you intemated to me a few days since you ware going to Richmond, and would do me a favor if it Laid in your Power

I ask you for the appointment of Forage Master at Fort Smith and The Authority of Selling off all condemd Goverment Property belonging to the confederate Stats at Fort Smith vanburen and Fayetteville, you can Sir do me this favour, I am also a good judge of Stock capable of receiving and receipting for any property belonging belonging to the quarter masters department,, Such as horses mules oxen and Waggens

I want this appointment for The, Sole purpose of keeping yenkee Edwards, from dying with a very common Disease in the Garrison cald the Big head   I am Sir with much Respect your Obt, Servent

THOS. MCCARRON

P.,S if you do me this favour I will discharge the duties with Honour to you, and credit to Myself   T.M.C

RICHMOND 21″ November 1861.

SIR: The Commissioner of Indian Affairs has caused to be transmitted to New Orleans the sum of twenty five thousand dollars, to be used in purchasing the articles that are to be supplied to the Comanches and other Reserve Indians.   As soon as you arrive here the money will be placed at your disposal.

As soon as possible after receipt of this letter, you will please send a proper person to the Wichita Agency, and let the Comanches who it is said are encamped, waiting for the leaves to fall, that they may come in and settle, that I have been delayed, by circumstances that I could not control, so as not to be able to meet them as soon as I intended; but that you will bring or send up their goods, and I will meet them during the winter.   It is important that this should be told them at once.   It would be better, if Col. Pulliam *can* go there himself, that he should do so.   I do not know who else would answer.

Orders go by the messenger who takes this, from the Acting Commissioner to Agent Leeper, directing him to use all the government laborers in putting up houses for the Comanches who are coming in, and not to use them for any other purpose.   If it is possible to send up additional laborers, it had better be done.   I am very respectfully yours   ALBERT PIKE, Commissioner of the Confederate
                    States to the Indian tribes West of Arkansas
Major Elias Rector, Superintendent of Ind. Affairs.

FORT SMITH, Novr. 22d 1861.

DR MAJOR.   I send you the enclosed document from the Acting Comr. Ind Affairs. recd here today.   As I cannot respond to it for you as you are there on the ground – I send it to you for you to make such reply as you think proper, in the premises.

We have just recd authentic information from the armies above,, the federals have left Springfield and are making their way towards St. Louis. for what cause is not certainly known but it is thought that their army have become demoralized by the displacing of Fremont and the appointment of Hunter to the Command. Genl Price broke up his encampment at Pineville at day light on Saturday last. and at last accounts was at Sarcoxie. making his way towards the Mo. River it is thought he is pursuing Hunter. you will see by an examination of the map that he will cut of a considerable distance by that route. Coming into the road Hunter will have to travel at Bolivar. or Warsaw. On the same day, (Saturday last) Genl McColloch took four hundred picked men from each of his Mounted Regiments making 2000 men with ten days provisions and started in the direction of Prices army. his destination however is not known. it is supposed however that he & Price are going to throw their Cavalry forward to attack & cut off, or hold until their Infantry can be brought up., Hunters army. Whether these conjectures are true or not time will tell. Cooper is on the march after Opothleyohola. who it is said has taken Maj Emorys trail through Kansas towards Leavenworth,

Small Pox still raging Mrs Nowland lost a negro to day. I saw your boy Henry to day he says your family are all well.

My kind regards to Pike. Also to Mr Scott. Your friend &c
R. P. PULLIAM

The above war news is reliable. and you can give the information to the papers if you wish.   P

I write this in Suttons Store, he says the above contains all the news we have. all of which is confirmed by Messengers and private letters. Consequently he will not write as he promised until something further turns up   P

TISHOMINGO C.N., Nov. 26, 1861

GEN. A. G. MAYERS

Sir: Having appointed as a Delegate from this Nation to the Southern Congress, am at a loss when the Congress does meet. I have all along understood from newspaper accounts that it was to be on the 22d of February but some seems to think it is sooner. Will you please inform me at your earliest convenience at what time the S. Congress does meet. Your attention to the above is respectfully requested I am yours very Respectfully   JAMES GAMBLE

P.S. Please continue to send me the Parallel. I will make it all right with you when on my way to Va.   J.G.

OFFICE SUPT. IND. AFFAIRS FORT SMITH, Decr. 1861
MR. JESSE CHISHOLM

Dear Sir: I have just returned from Richmond where I have been to see the President on Indian business. I wish you to go out immediately and see the bands of Comanches that are encamped above Fort Cobb and tell them that it is the wish of their great father at Richmond that they come in at once and settle on the reserve, that so soon as they do so they will be furnished with Beef – Flour, Salt, Sugar & Coffee. And that the great father says that all the goods & things that Commissioner Pike promised them will be furnished and given to them. That the Arkansas River has now too little water in it for Steam Boats to come up from the big Cities to bring goods, but as soon as the big water comes in the River and Boats come up their great father will send up to them many large wagons filled with nice goods that I want them to send four or five of their Chiefs and head men to Genl. Pikes head quarters, near Fort Gibson where he and myself will meet them and talk with them and give them a great many presents and satisfy them that the government will do all that Commissioner Pike promised them. I wish Buffalo Hump and his band now on the reserve to be told this, and for him and four or five of his principal men to come also,. I will direct the Contractor at the Wichita Agency to furnish them with Rations to bring them over and I will furnish them with Rations to return home, tell them to bring, in all about twenty pack horses to carry back their presents. I want them to meet us at Genl Pikes Camp or head quarters near Fort Gibson, on the first of February if possible I have written a letter to T Caraway inviting him to come with some three or four of his men and I wish you to urge him to come, Commissioner Pike is now in Richmond with their great father making arrangements to get their goods and to do much for them he would have been up to see them at the falling of the leaves but he has been very sick and could not travel he is now well and will be here soon and will go from here to his head quarters.   [ELIAS RECTOR]

CONFEDERATE STATES OF AMERICA, WAR DEPARTMENT,
            Office of Indian Affairs, Richmond, Dec 2d, 1861.
MAJOR ELIAS RECTOR, Superintendent of Indian Affairs.

Sir: I am instructed by the Secretary of War to say that three requisitions have been drawn by him on the Secretary of the Treasury in your favor, as Superintendent of Indian Affairs &c.,– One for nine thousand, six hundred and fifty dollars, dated Dec. 4th 1861, one for two thousand, one hundred and four dollars and fifty cents, dated December 5th 1861, and the other for thirty thousand dollars, dated December 6th 1861.

With the money received by you upon the first named requisition, you will pay Charles B. Johnson, the amount of his account against the Confederate States for Beef furnished certain Bands of Reserve Indians, from July 1st to August 16th under a verbal contract made by him with Albert Pike, Commissioner, &c., and also pay the mounted escort of Creeks and Seminoles, engaged by General Pike to accompany him to the Comanche Country, &c. In regard to this escort General Pike, in a letter to the War Department, of the 14th October, says that he had muster rolls regularly made out, and gave pay accounts to the officers, and slips showing the amount due each of the men.

With the money received by you upon the second named requisition you will pay Charles B. Johnson the balance due him by the old United States Government prior to the 30th June, 1861, and which General Pike, at the time of making the verbal contract hereinbefore mentioned, agreed to pay or have paid him.

And with the money received by you upon the third named requisition, you will pay such expenses of the Superintendency and different Agencies, as may be necessary, proper and legitimate. The balance of this money can be applied to the purchase of suitable clothing, if it can be bought at fair prices, for the Reserve Indians, which Commissioner Pike, in the Treaty of the 12th August, 1861, agreed should be speedily furnished them.

You will forward a statement as to the disbursement of these several sums of money with the proper voucher, &c. Very respectfully,

S. S. Scott, Act'g Commr. of Indian Affairs.

Treasury Department, C.S.A., Second Auditor's Office
Richmond, Va, Dec 7th – 1861.

Sir: The Treasurer of the Confederate States will remit to you the sum of Thirty two thousand one hundred & four 50/100 dollars ————— —————, being the amount of Requisition No. 1889 & 1890 issued in your favor on the 6th Inst –, with which you are charged on the Books of this Office, on account of the following Appropriation, to wit:

"To meet the Incidental Expenses of the Public service within the Indian Tribes," as per Act May 21, 1861, No. 232.

Requisition No. 1889. ——— ——— .　.　. $2,104.50
Req. ——— " 1890, Same as above ——— .　. 30.000. "

$32.104.50

The Treasurer will advise you when the same will be remitted for which you will please forward a Receipt to this Office, specifying therein the date, number and amount of said Requisition. I am, very respectfully, Your Ob't Serv't　　　　AUDITOR.
To Elias Rector, Esq, Supt. Ind. Affairs, Present

WICHITA AGENCY L. D., Decr. 12th 1861.

SIR: In all my official relations I have endeavored to be governed strictly by the instructions of my superior officers, and in reference to the alledged real or imaginary impropriety of my course towards Buffalo Hump in your letter of the 12th Oct. last, I must plead my instructions in mitigation which I followed strictly, not being in possession of any, except the verbal instructions of Commissioner Hubbard, which was in effect to exercise my best judgment in the management of the affairs of the Reserve, but in all things to be governed by strict rules of economy. In my report to you of the 12th Augst. I solicited written instructions, a copy of the Intercourse Laws and of the Contract for furnishing supplies for the Indians, but as yet, have not received even a reply to my communication. There is no Indian with whose character and habits I am more familiar than with Buffalo Humps; he is a fugitive from the Texas Agency of which I was placed in charge; the late Superintendent of that State worried with him for three years before he could induce him to settle, he would come in and make promises to do so, and the Superintendent would load him with presents, he would return to the prairies depredate upon the country until his blankets were worn out, then return with a plausible excuse for not coming in with his people, receive other presents return again to the prairies and repeat the same thing over again until the Superintendents patience became exhausted, and informed Buffalo Hump that he would not submit to any further trifling on the subject, that he had nothing more for him, but as he had come in peace, he might return in peace, but that afterwards he would pursue and hunt him down with the troops; Buffalo Hump then changed his tone, begged to be permitted to have a certain length of time allowed him to bring in his people without renumeration or presents, at that time it was granted, and at the appointed time he brought in his people and settled on the Reserve, where he remained until a feud took place between him and the Chief of the band located previously, which caused him to abandon the Reserve and pursue his former predatory habits. I induced him to come in this time, in addition to the other wild chiefs, who met Commissioner Pike in Augst. last, and entered into an informal treaty with them, it was the result of a years negotiation, which was carried on by means of messengers from this Reserve; it was attempted years ago by Judge Rollins, one of the ablest Indian Agents perhaps the U.S. ever had, who spent eighteen months in attempting to accomplish the object; Agent Stemm lost his life in efforts of the kind; Major Neighbors a very ingenious and competent Agent exerted his influence for six or seven years to no purpose: — Dr. Hill, a most popular Indian Agent and influential man, labored four years without effect, and Capt. Ross' influence was equally ineffectual, yet I am informed in your letter of the 12th Oct. that both yourself and Commissioner Pike regret much that I did not hold out all the inducements which were in my power, and use all the forces and means at my command to provide him with such houses as were contemplated and provided by Commissioner Pike for the comfort of those Indians. In this matter I appear to be peculiarly unfortunate. You are fully aware that I have not received any means for the erection of houses or for any other purpose, and that the few employees who were induced to engage in the work with a hope of renumeration hereafter were all sick, which fact I made known in my report of the 15th Septr. last, therefore it will be perceived that I had no means in my power to build houses or any thing else, nor would I have employed them in building houses for Buffalo Hump in advance of his settlement, if I had possessed ever so much in the absence of positive instructions to that effect. The course I pursued with him induced him to come in with his people a week in advance of the time promised and settle, he has given me no further trouble, tells me he intends to remain here for life, that he does not wish houses built until such times as he can select a suitable place on the Reserve for his future home, and has employed as spies for me two of his sons who are with the wild tribes watching their movements and those of the northern troops, to give immediate notice in case of an advanced demonstration upon this part of the country.

During a period of more than twenty years public service, I have received two rebukes only from my superior officers on account of my official conduct, yours in reference to Buffalo Hump and from the late Superintendent in Texas for failing to insert at the close of one of my official letters "your obt. Srvt."

I infer from your letter of the 30th of Octr. that you conclude, I am disposed to interfere with your appointment of Commissary, I can assure you that such was not nor never has been my intention to disturb or meddle in the slightest degree with the appointment of Commissary or any other which it may be your pleasure to make; sending Sturm as messenger was a matter of necessity not of choice, I apprised you by him that I was not only sick myself, but that my family and almost every one on the Reserve were sick and without medicine, Sturm although sick, was the only person I could obtain as messenger who was willing to make the trip alone, and with the confident hope that by sending him I would obtain medicines which would afford my family relief; I was induced to do so with an understanding that he was to receive pay not only as Commissary during the time of his absence, but three dollars per day also for his services as messenger and I procured the assistance gratuitously of Mr Bickel one of the interpreters to act as Commissary during his absence, whose name appears on the prevision checks for that quarter merely to prevent confusion of the accounts, but my most sanguine hopes were disappointed for the messenger returned without medicines, and my son has not recovered yet. Whilst upon this subject allow me most respectfully to direct your attention to the fact, and through you the Department, that the office of Commissary is a sinecure, and expense which is utterly useless to the Government and an injury to the public Service, the duty of Commissary simply being an impartial weigher and witness to the delivery of supplies agreably to the terms of the Contract; I, hold it to be the duty of the Agent where issues are made at the Agency to be present, and represent the interest of the Indians, and the Interpreters who are required to be present to witness the issues, such has been the case heretofore, no Commissary has ever been employed at other Agencies, except where issues were made at remote places or where it was impracticable for the Agent to be present; the Commissary is employed perhaps half a day once a week, the remainder of the time is spent in utter idleness, and in gossiping with the employees and Indians on the Reserve.

I received a recent visit from the Chiefs who met Comr. Pike in Augst. last, after preparing to hold a Council or talk with them, their first demand was whiskey, they said they could not talk without having whiskey first, after a length of time however, I convinced them that I had no whiskey, and that whiskey was not allowed on the Reserve, they then informed me that they had approached this place at the appointed time "the falling of the leaves" and ascertained that the Commissioner was not here nor the presents agreably to promise, that now they were here long after the time and still there are no presents or Commissioner, I explained to them that the Comr. had delegated to me his authority for the time being, and that he was now purchasing goods to issue in accordance with his promise as soon as they would comply with their part of the agreement and settle with their people on the Reserve, that they would have the privilege of settling on any part of the Leased District that suited them best, and that I would issue provisions to them until such time as the goods would arrive, they informed me that they had been lied to a good deal, and that they wanted some greater and further evidence now of the sincerity of the Government, that as the goods were not here, which were intended for them, that they would take a few that the trader had, and be satisfied with those, until such time as the others would be forthcoming, and probably settle at the time the grass rises in the Spring, I told them that the traders goods did not belong to me or to the Government, and that I was consequently unauthorized to issue them, they then instantly rose up and told me they were going, I called back a Kioway Chief and told him as it was his first visit, that I would make him a present of some blankets, paint and tobacco, that I was glad to see him, that the Government desired to be on friendly terms with him and his people, and that if he thought proper to come here with his people and settle, that he could do so on the same terms as the others, he informed me that that was the object of his visit, that he would return and consult on the subject and at no distant day would make me another visit, and apprise me of the result of their deliberations; in the mean time the others returned in a better humor, and I told them that upon my own responsibility, I would make them a few little presents, of blankets, paints, &c. which appeared to satisfy them, and when they finally left, declared their friendly intentions, and said they would ultimately settle here in compliance with the treaty.

In compliance with your letter of instructions of the 25th of Octr
last, I have rendered H. L. Rodgers all the assistance in my power
in the way of his building operations. Very Respectfully. Your
obt. Servt.   M. LEEPER, Ind. Agt. C.S.A.
Elias Rector Esq., Supt. Indian Affairs.
   Fort Smith, Arks.

FORT SMITH, ARK., Dec. 27th, 1861.

   SIR: Owing to the continued excitement in the Creek and Seminole Nations, and the dangers necessarily to be encountered by persons
either residing in or travelling through the Indian Country, my
return to the Agency has been delayed longer than I expected. Taking
into consideration all the circumstances of the case I deemed it best
and most prudent to await your return from Richmond and submit
a report of the case to you. When I left the Agency early in November
there seemed a unity of opinion and general profession of Loyalty to
the Southern Confederacy; but since then there has been much disaffection and increase of excitement. The consequence has been that
some of the Traders residing among the upper Creeks have left —
narrowly escaping with their lives. Others are, as I learn, preparing
to leave. Since my departure from the Agency there has been two
engagements between the Confederate forces under command of Col.
Cooper and the followers of Hopothleyoholo, in both engagements
Col. Cooper was victorious. This, however, has only increased the
vindictiveness of Hopothleyoholos Party and, consequently, magnified
the dangers attendant on travelling through or residing in the Nation.
My Agency is, as you are aware, situated two hundred miles west of
this place, and wholy unprotected and exposed to depredation, it is
very insecure. Parscofer and others as stated in my report to the
Department as heading the disaffected party, were leaders, in the
recent battles, on side of the enemy. But I am pleased to be able
to state that Jumper, Short Bird, Cloud and Holatut Fixico were
found with Col. Cooper doing their duty as faithful and Loyal allies.
It will, probably, not be a great while before the excitement may
subside, rendering travel and residence there more secure. When
you deem it necessary and safe for me to return I will be ready. I
await your orders on the subject. I am very Respectfully Your
obt. Servt.   SAM'L M. RUTHERFORD, C.S. Agent for Seminoles.
Maj. E. Rector, Sup. Ind. Affairs, C.S.A.,
   Fort Smith, Ark.

RICHMOND, VA., 29th December, 1861.

SIR: I send herewith, to your care, by a Special Messenger, packages for the Principal Chiefs of the Cherokee, Creek, Seminole, Choctaw and Chickasaw Nations, which please forward to each immediately by express.

Also a talk for the Comanches and Caiawas, which, if they are still near Fort Cobb, I wish sent to them by express. There is a letter to Chisholm, and it would perhaps be well to send the talk to him and get him to go up and see them.

Also a letter for Major Dorn and one to his Indians. I want them to come down to Head Quarters and receive what is to be given them. I do not know how you will get his letter to him.

The Treaties are all ratified, with two or three amendments that will cut no great figure. As to the *money* part, nothing has changed. Congress appropriated $681,000 and over, under the Treaties, including Charley Johnson's money up to middle of February, of the whole sum, $265,000 and odd is to be paid in specie. I shall get the Treasury notes to-morrow, and the Specie in New Orleans, and shall bring it all to you. The Secretary agreed, indeed proposed, to send it out by me.

Among them, they fixed my compensation at $3,750.

I mean to be at Head Quarters by the 25th of January. I hope the different Tribes will ratify the amendments, so that you can pay them pretty soon after that time.

I think you had better buy all the goods, of Cochran and others, for the Comanches, that you can. I want them to meet me at Head Quarters, and it will be necessary to have *some* goods for them. Congress would not agree to give them any arms.

I hope when we pay the Indians their money, and I get some white troops in the Country, we shall settle the difficulties there. God knows.

Give my kind regards to Mrs. Rector and the children. Always yours.　　　　　　　　　　　　　　　　　　　ALBERT PIKE.

I send Dr. Duval's appointment, and Mr. Sandals', by the Messenger.

CONFEDERATE STATES OF AMERICA, WAR DEPARTMENT
Office of Indian Affairs, Richmond, December 30th, 1861.

MAJOR ELIAS RECTOR, Superintendent of Indian Affairs,
　　　Fort Smith, Arkansas.

Sir: The first session of the Congress of the Confederate States will be held on the 18th February next; and it is important that the Report, from this Bureau, in regard to Indian Affairs, for the benefit of that Body, should be as full as possible. That this may be so, it is essential that information should be sent here, at least by the 15th of that month, of the true condition of affairs, in each of the several Agencies under your supervision.

You will, therefore, write to all of the Agents, and state to them these facts. Advise them also to give you *full reports* of all matters connected with their respective charges, and forward them, when received to this office. Very respectfully,

S. S. Scott, Act'g Commr. of Ind. Affairs.

CONFEDERATE STATES OF AMERICA, WAR DEPARTMENT
Office of Indian Affairs, Richmond, Jany. 1st, 1862.
MAJOR ELIAS RECTOR, Superintendent of Indian Affairs,
Fort Smith, Arkansas.

Sir: An Act was recently passed by the Congress of the Confederate States, and approved December 26th, 1861, "making appropriations to comply, in part, with Treaty stipulations made with certain Indian Tribes." The whole amount appropriated by this Act was six hundred and eighty one thousand, eight hundred and sixty nine dollars, and fifteen cents.

By sundry requisitions of the Secretary of War upon the Secretary of the Treasury, this sum has been placed in the hands of General Albert Pike, for delivery to you, as Superintendent of Indian Affairs.

Herewith you will receive Tabular Statements, marked Numbers (1) and (2) for your information and guidance, as to the times manner, &c., that this money is to be disbursed.

You will perceive from these statements, that one hundred and nineteen thousand, three hundred and forty dollars can be used, for the purposes indicated immediately, or, whenever, it may be deemed essential by you; while the residue, amounting to five hundred and sixty two thousand, five hundred and twenty nine dollars and fifteen cents, is dependent, for its dusbursement, upon the ratification of the Treaties, as amended by the several Indian Tribes. Very respectfully, S. S. Scott, Act'g Commr. of Indian Affairs.

TREASURY DEPARTMENT, C.S.A., SECOND AUDITOR'S OFFICE,
Richmond, Va. Dec 31st 1861.
SIR – The Treasurer of the Confederate States will remit to you the sum of six hundred and eighty one thousand, eight hundred &

sixty nine 15/100 dollars –, being the amount of Requisitions Nos.
2175-76-77-78-79-80-81-82-83 & 84 issued in your favor on the 20th
Instant –, with which you are charged on the Books of this Office, on
account of the following Appropriation, to wit:
"An Act making Appropriations to comply in part with Treaty
Stipulations made with certain Indian Tribes," as per Act

Requisition No. 2175	For Contingencies of superintending & Agencies	$	3,500.00
Do " 2176	" Sundry Appropriations for Cherokee Indians		237,944.36
" " 2177	" Do Do " Seminole Indians		61,050.00
" " 2178	" " " " Choctaw & Chickasaws	.	115,126.89
" " 2179	" " " " Creek Indians		72,950.00
" " 2180	" " " " Comanches .	.	64,862.00
" " 2181	" " " " Reserve Indians		82,905.00
" " 2182	" " " " Seneca Indians		11,962.46
" " 2183	" " " " Quapaw Indians		9,000.00
" " 2184	" " " " Osage Indians		22,568.44

Total $681,869.15

The Treasurer will advise you when the same has been placed to
your credit on his Books, or hand you a Draft – for which you will
please forward a Receipt to this Office, specifying therein the date,
number and amount of said Requisition. I am, very respectfully,
your ob't serv't,   W. H. S. Taylor, Auditor.
To Genl Albert Pike, Agent for the War Department for delivery
of the above funds to Elias Rector, Supt. Ind. Affairs, now in
Richmond, Va.

Confederate States of America, Treasurer's Office,
Richmond, Va., Jany 23
Elias Rector, Fort Smith, Ark.
Sir, I have this day placed to your credit 3,000 Dollars, amount
of Warrant No. 23 Issued in your favor by War Department.
Your checks on the Treasurer of the Confederate States will be
honoured for that amount. Please acknowledge the receipt of this
Notification, and enclose your official signature. Very Respectfully,
E. C. Elmore, Treasurer C.S.

CONFEDERATE STATES OF AMERICA, WAR DEPARTMENT,
Office of Indian Affairs, Richmond Jany 23d 1862.
MAJ. E. RECTOR, Superintendent &c, Fort Smith, Arkansas.

SIR: General Pike of date Dec. 30th 1861, writes to this Bureau, as follows:

> In order to obtain the ratification, by the several Indian Tribes, of the amendments made by Congress to the Indian Treaties negotiated by me, and to effect a Treaty with the Caiowas, I have sent messages to the Creeks, Seminoles, Cherokees, Choctaws and Chickasaws, requesting that their national Councils may be convened; and to the Chiefs of the Osages, Quapaws, Senecas, Senecas and Shawnes, Comanches, Reserve Indians and Caiowas, requesting them to meet me at my head Quarters.
>
> It will be necessary to furnish provisions to the Creek and Seminole Councils, and to feed the more uncivilized Chiefs, while in Council, and on their return, and also perhaps to make some presents; for which purposes no funds are in the hands of the Superintendent or myself.

In accordance with these suggestions and at the request of this Bureau a requisition was drawn by the Secretary of War, a few days ago, for the sum of three thousand dollars, which is to be placed to your credit in the Treasury.

You will please use this money, or so much of it, as may be necessary, for the purposes, and in the manner, above indicated. Very respectfully,　　　　S. S. SCOTT, Act'g Commr. of Ind. Affairs.

LITTLE ROCK, ARK., 28th January, 1862.

DEAR RECTOR: I will leave here on Friday morning. It will take me, I suppose, six days to reach Fort Smith with the money. This will bring me to the 5th, 6th or 7th of February.

I have $265.927.50 in specie, all in gold except $65.000 in silver. Of course I must stay with it. I think I can make the journey, though in six days.

I think you had better go up to my head Quarters immediately, and arrange to feed the Comanches and others if they come there; and keep them there until I reach the place. I can take the money there, and send by the same messenger who takes this, to Colonel Cooper for an escort.

The Treasurer of the Choctaws means to sell the coin his people get, buy Confederate paper, and put the difference in his pocket. We must stop that. I think the best way will be for you to notify the Chief, Hudson, the amount to be paid in coin, and that you will pay it to the Treasurer only in the presence of three Commissioners appointed by himself.

If you *can* pay the Choctaws and Chickasaws at my Head Quarters, it will of course be much better.

I have had to ask the *immediate* removal of Leeper, and the appointment of Col. Pulliam in his place. This I have done to-day, sending extracts from your letter, Charley Johnson's and Quesenbury's.

The Secretary is also advised, now, of Garrett's continual [illegible].

Why do you not demand his removal, and name a person for his place?

I don't believe Col. Cooper will be removed. The President said in my presence, "Now that the Choctaws have a Delegate in Congress, what need of an Agent?"

About 150 gamblers are here, following up the Indian moneys. I enclose an order requiring passports, that will keep them out of the Nation.

I have the $150.000 advance for the Cherokees, the $12.000 due the Nation, and the $10.300 due the Treaty party or Stand Watie's, – all in paper. Also the $50.000 advance for the Choctaws. In paper and specie, I have for you $631.000 and over.

Have you received the money, (some $3.000) that I asked should be sent you to pay expenses of the new Indian Councils?

If you *cannot* go to Head Quarters immediately, you will have to send some one, and let him and Colonel Cooper keep the Indians contented. Always yours, ALBERT PIKE.
Maj. E. Rector.

OFFICE SUPT. IND. AFFAIRS, Fort Smith, Feby 1st, 1862.
SIR: I have the honor to transmit herewith the Reports of Agents Leeper, Cooper, Rutherford and Crawford. No report has been received from Agent Dorn.

Business of importance requires me to leave here to-day for Fort Gibson and the Creek Agency, it is important for me to take charge of the public property at the Creek Agency which I shall do on my arrival there and I will turn the same over to R P Pulliam who I have appointed Agent to act until the Department may make a permanent appointment and I hope Mr Pulliam may be the person appointed. I have also appointed to meet a delegation of Comanches and Kiawas at Fort Gibson where I expect Genl Pike and myself will effect treaties with them. I have sent a lot of goods to make some presents to them and to the wild bands with whom Genl Pike made treaties last fall and to whom he promised some goods; after meeting these delegation and ascertaining what can be effected with them I will make out and forward to you a report of Indian matters generally in this superintendency which I hope will reach you in time to be of some service to the Department. I could not, until after I meet those Indians and ascertain the condition of the Creek Agency, make a full and satisfactory report.

In regard to Agent Crawfords report I must here state, that from the best information I can obtain of the condition of affairs among the Cherokees, I cannot concur with him, but I will inform myself fully in this regard during my present visit among them and will furnish my views fully in my report, Very Respectfully Your Obt. Servt.   E. RECTOR, Supt. Ind. Affairs
S. S. SCOTT Esq Acting Comr. Ind. Affairs
Richmond, Va

OFFICE SUPT IND AFFAIR, Fort Smith Feby 1st 1862
SIR: Genl. Pike is here with $50.000 Dollars in Gold and Silver for the Choctaws, and as I am compelled to accompany him on important business to Fort Gibson, I have determined to take the above money with me to that place and pay it out there, which will be as convenent for you as to pay it here, and as Col Cooper will have to be present at the payment, it is necessary to make the payment when he can attend. I will be ready to pay over to your Treasurer the above money at Fort Gibson in   days from this date, and I wish you to send with your Treasurer a delegation of three responsible persons to be selected by you to witness the payment. This I require, as it is a special case with our government to pay out Coins to the Indian tribes at this time, and to insure the payment by the Treasurer of the same funds to your people, that he receives from me. Our government is determined to use all precautions to prevent speculations out of the funds sent out to pay to Indian tribes. Very Respectfully Your Obt Servt.   E. RECTOR, Supt Ind Affrs
Hon Hudson, Chief Choctaw Nation.

CONFEDERATE STATES OF AMERICA, WAR DEPARTMENT
Office of Indian Affairs, Richmond, Feby 7th 1862.
MAJOR E. RECTOR, Superintendent of Ind. Affairs.

Fort Smith, Arkansas.

Sir: Your two letters, dated January 9th & 10th, have been received. The former gave a brief statement of the facts, in relation to the arrest, by Agent Leeper, of one Meyer, supposed to be a spy, with $6.455.70, in Drafts and Specie upon his person, and enclosed copies of letters from Messrs Leeper and Shirley, bearing upon same subject. The latter simply covered the Affidavit of a Mr. Barnes, claiming the Drafts referred to, followed by affidavits of Meyer and one Jacob Mariner intended to substantiate it.

The questions presented in this case should properly be investigated by Brig. Genl. Pike, who has command of the Department of the Indian Territory, where this person was arrested; and a letter has therefore been written to him from this Bureau, for the purpose of calling his attention to the fact.

You will take the necessary steps to have the man Meyer turned over to him. Very respectfully,

S. S. SCOTT, Act'g Comr. of Ind. Affairs.

FORT SMITH, 16th Feby 1862
ELIAS RECTOR Esq, Superintendent of Ind. Affairs

Sir: As to the case of Fredrick Meyer, arrested as a spy, there is nothing beyond suspicion against him, except his possession of certain drafts drawn by a U. S. Quartermaster on the Assistant Treasurer at New York, and the Statements of Comanche Indians, who are not competent witnesses.

I decline to place him in custody as a spy or to order a Miltary Court to try him. I cannot order his discharge or the return of the drafts and money taken from him, because the Military power is silent, within the limits of Arkansas, in the presence of the Court power, as to reports that may be asserted and remedies that may be pursued, in the Courts. If I had the power, I should make the order.

If you continue to hold the property in question, or to detain the party, you will please consider that you do it on your own authority. I am very respectfully yours,

ALBERT PIKE, Brig. Genl. Commr. Ind. Dept.

MOUTH OF CANADIAN, 23d Febr. 1862.

MAJOR: I reached this place last night, and leave this morning. The teams furnished me at Fort Smith are hardly able to go further, and our progress must be slow. I shall hardly reach Spaniard's Creek before tomorrow night, and wish you to meet me there. I did think of sending the money, at least the specie, direct from this point to North Fork, but have determined to keep it with me until I meet you. If you will meet me at Spaniard's Creek, we can then determine what disposition to make of it.

Gen. Price is at Walnut Grove, eight miles south of Fayetteville; will take position near Cane Hill, and means to attack as soon as he gets 5,000. men in addition to his present force. McCulloch is on the telegraph road, to his right. *They are not acting in harmony,* Col. Gatewood says.

Our forces in Kentucky and Tennesse have had to fall back before 70,000 of the enemy. The new position, it is expected, will be at Stevenson and Charleston road. When the enemy took Fort Donelson, both Bowling Green and Columbus became of value to us. Each position was carried. But we have only taken a new position, losing no battle. The fort surrendered. Columbus is or will be evacuated and Nashville surrendered.

There are no means of crossing the Arkansas here, except one boat, that must have a bottom put in it. I must bring at least part of the Choctaws to Gibson, to cross the river and move towards Cane Hill, and in order to be able to do it as soon as possible I wish to turn over the money to you. Truly yours ALBERT PIKE Major Elias Rector.

OFFICE SUP'T IND. AFF'RS, Fort Smith, Feb'y 28th, 1862.

SIR: I have the honor to acknowledge the receipt of your letter of 23d ultimo notifying me that the sum of $3,000 – had been placed to my credit in the Treasury on Requisition No. 23 from the War Department subject to my Draft and request my official signature which is hereto affixed. Very Respectfully your Ob't Serv't.

E. RECTOR, Sup't Ind. Aff'rs.

E. C. Elmore Esq., Treasurer of the Confederate States
    Richmond, Va.

OFFICE SUP'T IND. AFFAIRS, Fort Smith, Feb'y 28th, 1862.

SIR: I have the honor to acknowledge the receipt of your letter of Jany 1st accompanying Tabular Statements sent out by Gen'l Pike. On his arrival here I was absent in the Indian Country where I had been ordered by him to meet a Delegation of wild Comanches and Kiawas. Genl P— did not leave the money here to be paid over to me but tuck it in the Indian Country to his head quarters, where he will I presume pay it out to the Indians himself. Very Respectfully, your ob't Serv't.   E. RECTOR, Sup't Ind Affairs. S. S. SCOTT Esq. Acting Com'r Ind. Affairs, Richmond, Va.

[Rector to Scott]

OFFICE SUPT IND. AFFAIRS, March 4th, 1862.

SIR: I deem it my duty, in justice to myself, as well as my duty to the government to notify you that Gen'l Pike has been paying over certain of the funds sent out by him to the Indians, one payment which he has made, I wish here to enter my protest against as not meeting with my approbation, it was in paying over to Agent A. J. Dorn the specie sent out for the Indians in his Agency. My objections to said payment are these: Agent Dorn has never executed a Bond to the Confederate government for the faithful accounting for of funds placed in his hands, and I should certainly not turn over large amounts of government funds to any Agent in my Department until he first gave a good and sufficient Bond and next; the Agency which Mr. Dorn fills is in the limits of the State of Kansas and has been in the possession of the Federals for six or seven months, Dorn cannot even get to it, he has no fixed locality for his Agency sometimes he is with the army, at others in the State and is now here at this place and has with him the money.

I am clearly of the opinion that this money should have been kept in some safe place in this State until after our present troubles are over. The Federal army is now invading within fifty miles of this place and between him and the Indians for whom Dorn is Agent, which makes it impossible for him to pay it to them if he so intends.

None of the Agents in this Superintendency have entered into Bond. Nor do I know whether they intend to do so except Agent Rutherford he came here from his Agency a few days since for the purpose of giving his Bond but is now on a bead of sickness from which it is doubtful if he ever recovers. . .   ELIAS RECTOR.[589]

---

[589] The writer of this letter was evidently Elias Rector, although the document from which this copy was made is in the handwriting of Albert Pike.

APPENDIX B - THE LEEPER[590] OR WICHITA AGENCY PAPERS

Office Supt. Indian Affairs, Fort Smith, Oct. 12th, 1861.

Sir: I have to acknowledge the receipt of your letter of 15th

[590] The history of the collection that I have designated for convenience of reference, the *Leeper Papers*, is outlined in the following letter from F. Johnson, Delaware Indian Agent, to Dole, January 20, 1863 [Indian Office, General Files, *Wichita, 1862-1871*, J62].

On or about the first of September last a company of Delaware & Shawnee Indians numbering ninety-six, seventy Delawares and twenty-six Shawnees, left Kansas on an expedition southwest from Kansas under the leadership of Ben Simon a Delaware Indian.

He reports that the expedition traveled to the Neosho River in southern Kansas where they halted a few days. From thence they marched in a southwest direction seventeen days to the leased district in Texas, they then traveled up the Wichita River, one day to the neighbourhood of the Wichita Agency. Simon then sent Spies and Scouts to the Agency who reported two hundred Indians well armed at the Agency in the Service of the Southern Confederacy. On receiving this intelligence the Delawares & Shawnees immediately proceded to the Agency which they reached about sundown. On arriving at the Agency they surrounded the buildings when the Agent a man large sized with black hair came out of the house and asked them what was wanting. Simon replied to him that he was his prisoner. At the same instant the Indians rushed into the house when one of the Delawares was shot dead and a Shawnee wounded – there was four white men at the Agency; when the Indians saw their comrades killed and wounded they killed the three men in the House and Agent Leeper who Simon had hold of at the door – the Indians then took possession of the Property and papers belonging to the Agency and burned the buildings. On the next morning they found the trail of the Indians who had escaped from the Agency and followed it to a grove of timber and found as they supposed about one hundred & fifty Indians a part of whom was women and children whom they attacked and report they killed about one hundred the Ballance making their escape. The Delawares and Shawnees then turned homewards with their Booty which consisted of about One hundred Ponies Twelve hundred Dollars in Confederate Money, the papers correspondence etc. which is wrapped in a rebel Flag taken at the Agency Among the papers taken I would respectfully call your attention to the treaties in

inst. by Expressman Sturm [591] at Tahlequah C.N. while on public business at that place on the 2nd inst and in answer must say.

Your requisition for Medicine I cannot comply with. I have no Medicines on hand for the Indian Service. Neither have I been instructed to furnish either Medicines or Medical assistance to the Indians, and if I were disposed to take the responsibility and advance the funds to purchase Medicines they could not be procured at this place.

I am pleased to learn that Buffalo Hump came in to see you, but both myself & Com^r. Pike regret that you did not hold out to him all the inducements which were in your power, and use all the forces and means at your command to provide him with such houses as were contemplated and promised by Com^r. Pike for the comfort of those Indians and to make them satisfied and anxious to come in.

The Com^r. has issued an order prohibiting Jim Ned from returning to or ever occupying any portion of the Leased District again, this order you will see carried out. He has also ordered the Military to kill Ned should they find him.

No blanks have been furnished to the office as yet. Nor have even forms been purchased for the vouchers, abstracts etc. You must rule and arrange your papers as best you can for the present as I have to do myself.

I have turned over to Mr. Sturm four mules turned over to me as mules taken from you by Genl Burrow. I obtained them with great difficulty in bad condition, nearly on the lift. I have had them three or four weeks, these were all I could find and do not know whether they are all that were taken from you or not.

---

manuscript entered into between Albert Pike Commissioner on the part of the Confederate States and the diferent Tribes of Southern Indians as also the commission of Mathew Leeper Indian Agent from James Buchanan President of the United States dated 1st of February 1861.

These Indians few in numbers marching upon a point more than five hundred miles distant furnishing their own transportation forage and provisions without cost to the Government certainly exhibits a great degree of Loyalty daring and hardihood.

591 J. J. Stürm, commissary for the Indians of the Leased District [Rector to Stürm, July 1, 1861]. On Oct. 3, 1861, Stürm reported to Leeper:

I arrived here over a week ago, and have been waiting for Maj. Rector, who is absent making a Treaty with the Cherokees, and other Tribes at Telequa. . . No talk of anything but war here. Price has taken Lexington, Mo., he took and killed over four thousand of Abe's men, with a great deal of war material. . .

As stated above I have received no funds for the Indian Service from the Confederacy, in fact there has been no Indian Department organized consequently no appropriation has been made nor will any Indian business be done in the War Department until after the late Treaties are submitted and approved.

I shall leave here in a short time for Richmond for the purpose of organizing the business of the Superintendency, procuring funds, goods etc. for the Indians in compliance with the Stipulations of the late Treaties.

C. B. Johnson is absent at New Orleans and is expected back in a few days.

Enclosed you will find Sutton & Springs receipt for $200.

Owing to Creek difficulties I send Mr. Sturm back by direct route for his safety and the safety of your property. Very Respectfully Your Ob't. Servant   E. RECTOR, Supt. Ind. Affairs. Col. M. Leeper, Ind. Agent, Wichita Agency, L.D.

OFFICE SUPT. IND. AFFAIRS, FORT SMITH, ARKS.
Oct. 30th, 1861.

SIR: I have to acknowledge the receipt of your letter of the 21st inst. by Expressman.

On the 12th Inst, I wrote you by your expressman Mr. Sturm and as then, state I have no funds in my hands for the purchase of Medicines or for any other purpose for the Indian Service. Nor have I been authorized to provide the Indians with Medicines or Medical assistance; there has been no Indian Department regularly organized as yet, by our Government, nor will there be until after the Treaties lately made by Comr Pike are laid before the President and approved.

I have purchased for you on your own account, all the medicines I can purchase in this place that would be useful to the Indians. I send them by your Expressman with the bills, you can charge the Government with them in your account.

I am pleased to learn that the Kiowa Indians are likely to come in and make a treaty. Comr Pike cannot possibly be there to treat with them for some months to come, the treaties made by him with the Comanches places all of those Indians who may hereafter come in on the same footing with those who entered into treaty stipulations, and I hereby authorize you, as I have authority to do from Comr Pike, to make the same treaties and hold out the same inducements to the Kiowas as were made by him with the Comanches, do not, however, promise them blankets this winter as it would be impossible to procure them, the Government cannot procure a sufficiency of them for the Soldiers, not even at the most exorbitant prices. Agents are traveling over the States purchasing second hand blankets from families who take them off their beds to accomodate the Soldiers in the field.

H. L. Rogers is now on his way to your agency with hands to build houses for the Indians, he is sent out by Com^r. P'ike on his responsibility. I wrote you by him.

Gen'l Pike will have command of the Military Department of the Indian Country. He is now on his way to Richmond Va., when he will [return] I am not advised, it will be with him to direct what military force will be placed at Fort Cobb for the protection of your agency, when that protection will be furnished I am unable to advise you, of the importance of an efficient force being stationed there at an early day there can be no doubt.

In regard to the Mail or Express arrangements you speak of, I must say I have neither power, authority, or means to establish mail or express routes to your agency or elsewhere. Our State and other States are suffering greatly for want of mail facilities, and I cannot involve myself pecuniarily in the matter, this matter must be brought regularly before the Department and its action had.

In regard to the time when you may expect funds to close your accounts I can only say that you need not expect funds until after the treaties recently made are ratified and appropriations made in accordance with your estimates furnished Com^r Pike, the Government will not, of course, send out funds for Indians until it is advised that it has some treaty relations with them, I will leave here on the 7th day of next month for Richmond for the purpose of assisting in the organization of our Indian business, and for the procurement of funds, goods, etc, to carry out the provisions of the late treaties, on my return you will be advised of the result of my mission.

I learn from Mr. C. B. Johnson that you had advised him that Mr. Beckle is acting as Commissary, this is wrong and is calculated to produce confusion in the accounts. Mr. Sturm is the recognized commissary regularly appointed by me, he should not be sent away from his regular duties on any other business and I so informed him while here and notified him that his absence from his regular duties on another occasion would be sufficient cause for me to remove him and appoint his successor, the appointment of commissary belongs exclusively to me, and you are well aware of the importance of his being constantly at his post, as he is the check on the contractor in filling the requisitions of the agent. In future I hope he will not be detailed for any other duties. Mr. Sturm is and will continue to be Commissary until removed by me either upon charges or such cause as I may think requires his removal. Very respectfully, Your Ob't. Serv't, E. RECTOR, Supt. Ind. Affairs. Col. M. Leeper, Indian Agent, Wichita Agency, L.D.

The bearer of this letter, Capt. H. L. Rogers, has been employed and empowered by Genl Pike Commissioner with plenary powers, to proceed to the Wichita Agency, with hands, to erect buildings necessary for the Commissary and cabins for the Indians, Commissioner Pike becomes responsible for the work. . . – RECTOR to Leeper, dated Fort Smith, October 25, 1861.

SUBPOENA [592]

Confederate States vs. Matthew Leeper, Indian Agt, Comanche, et al. State of Arkansas, The Confederate States of America.

To J. J. Sturm — Greeting. You are hereby commanded, that laying all manner of excuses aside, you be and appear before the undersigned, special commissioner of C.S.A. at the Law Office of James P. Spring, in the City of Fort Smith, in the County of Sebastian, and State of Arkansas, on the 10th day of January, 1862. Then and there to testify and the truth to speak in a certain matter before said Commissioner pending, wherein The Confederate States of America prefers certain charges against Matthew Leeper, Indian Agent of Comanche and other reserved Indians west of the State of Arkansas, and on behalf of the C.S.A.

Herein fail not at your peril.

In testimony whereof I, James P. Spring, Commissioner of Exami-

---

[592] These two brief communications have a bearing upon Leeper's case:

You are hereby ordered to remain at Fort Smith Arkansas from 10th. January 1862 untill further ordered by the undersigned, as a witness in the case of the Confederate States of America against M. Leeper, Ind. Agt. on certain charges preferred. – JAMES P. SPRING, commissioner, to J. J. Stürm, dated Fort Smith, Ark., December 22, 1861.

Spring may not be able to begin on Leeper's case before Jan. 20– Is obliged to leave city. If Leeper wants while Spring is away, [to go] to Fayetteville, he may & Spring will telegraph him upon his return. – SPRING to Leeper, dated Fort Smith, Ark., December 23, 1861.

nation, have hereunto set my hand and affixed my private seal [there being no public seal for such purposes provided] in the City of Fort Smith, this 12th. day of November, 1861.

JAMES P. SPRING, [Seal], Commissioner of Examination, C.S.A.

QUESENBURY [593] TO LEEPER

Gen. Pike is now in Richmond. I am engaged in building winter-quarters for his Brigade. The General will probably return about the 10th of December.

I hope you will honour my requisitions for forage for the animals of the expedition for the blankets at Mr. Shirley's. The trip will be a hard one, and I fear a long one.

There is no news of import from my quarter. There was something of an occurrance in the Ho-poieth-le Yohola imbroglio the other day. Mr. Scrimpsher can give you the current particulars. . .

FORT SMITH, Dec 4, 1861.

DR. SIR: — We have no late news of importance. The Federal troops 30000 strong came as far as Springfield and fearing to advance further returned to St. Louis & Kansas; the Kansas party took from the vicinity of Springfield 600 negroes from Union men as well as Secessionists.

A heavy battle was fought in Mo. opposite Columbus a few days since. Pillow commanded the Confederate forces 2500 strong, the Federals came down in their gun-boats 7000 strong & landed. The fight lasted 4 hours with heavy losses on both sides. Pillow was then reinforced and drove the Federals back to their boats making a perfect slaughter of the Yankees. Our victory was complete and a very important one it was. Price has gone back to the Mo. River, McCulloch is bringing his army down here to go into winter quarters on the Arks. River.

Hardin is marching on Louisville, Ky., with from 80 to 100,000 Confederate troops. We are expecting to hear of his having possession of that city soon.

McClellan is said to be advancing slowly and continuously on Johnson and Boregard. They are anxious for him to pay them a visit.

Our legislature has elected Bob Johnson & Chas. Mitchell Senators, the Washington County District elected Batson over

---

[593] William Quesenbury to Leeper, dated Fort Gibson, C. N., Nov. 28, 1861.

Thomason to Congress. G. D. Royston is elected in this District and Judge Hanley in the Helena District.

Can't think of anything else that would interest you. Your friend in haste, R. P. PULLIAM.
Col. M. Leeper.

OFFICE SUPT. IND. AFFAIRS, FORT SMITH, Dec. 4th, '61.
SIR: I enclose herewith a Copy of a letter from Albert Pike Comr. etc. to Elias Rector, Supt. Ind. Aff., of date 21st. ultimo also two official letters.

That portion of Comr. Pike's letter relating to inviting the Indians to settle on the Reserve was anticipated by Supt. Rector's letter of instructions to you of the 30th October last.

The messages which Comr. Pike wishes given to the Indians you will, of course, deliver to them.

Maj. Rector left here for Richmond about ten days ago. When he will return I am unable to say, as it seems from Pike's letter he has to purchase and bring on the Indian goods. Very respectfully, R. P. PULLIAM, Clk.
Col. M. Leeper, Wichita Agent.

WICHITAW FED [FEED] HOUSE, December 10th 1861
DEAR CONL. From what I can asertain the Dutchman supposed to be a spy is one of the party who of ten, (five Mexicans & five whites) who prevented the wild Comanchees from coming in by telling them that we were fixing a *trap* to destroy the last one of them. when we got them here, and as an indusement to dispose of their Buffalo Robes this party told the Indians that we would take the last Robe from them with our troops.

The [above] I was informed of by the Comanche Cheves several days ago Very truly J. SHIRLEY
Col M. Leeper, Wichitaw Agency.

WICHITA AGENCY L.D., Decr 10th 1861
A memorandum of moneys and effects found on the person of a german who says his name is Frederick Myer, arrested and detained here, he being suspected of being a spy on the part of the United States in opposition to the Confederate States of America. The individual together with the moneys and property found upon his person

is intended to be forwarded to the Superintendent of Indian Affairs
Fort Smith at as early a day as practicable

Four drafts on the U. S. Asst. Treasurer New York, dated at
Santa Fe N. M. Sept. 17th 1861 and drawn by Jno P. Hatch Capt.
Rm R. Actg C. S. in favor John Dold transferred to Frederick
Myer, viz. –

   No 103.   Twelve Hundred & fifty dollars
   "   104.   Twelve Hundred & fifty dollars
   "   105.   Four Hundred & Eighty four dollars
   "   106.   Two Hundred & nineteen 50/100 dollars.

Also five other drafts as above described dated on the 19th Sept.
1861. viz ; –

   No. 112.   Six Hundred dollars
   "   113.   Five Hundred dollars.
   "   114.   Four Hundred dollars
   "   115.   Three Hundred dollars
   "   116.   Two Hundred dollars.

One draft dated Sept. 18th 1861 drawn by J L Donnevhen P. M.
favor Stephen Bryce or order transferred to Frederick Myer

   No 1669.   Nine Hundred & eighty three 25/100 dollars.

   Also in Gold One Hundred & fifty five dollars
       Silver Seventy cents

One Colts Revolver, belt & Scabbard
One large Pocket Knife
Also found in his possission two ponies one gray and one sorrel
Four letters addressed as follows,

   Mr. J. W. Gregory   Santa Fe N. M.
   Mr B Seligman   "   "
   Mr. Geo. T. Madison   "   "
   Mr W. W. Griffin   "   "

Received Wichita Agency L. D. Decr. 15 1861, all the above articles
moneys &c. excepting the two ponies bridle and saddle and saddle
bags, large knife and ten dollars in gold which were forwarded by
H. L. Rodgers accompanying the prisioner, all of which balance in
my possession to be delivered to the Superintendent of Indian Affairs Fort Smith Arks.   M. Grimes

Received Fort Smith Dec. 9th 1861 from M Grimes the above monies
& Pistol as per his Recpt to Col Leeper

                           E. Rector, Supt. Indian Affrs

WICHITA AGENCY S.D., Decr. 12th 1861

SIR: I forward to your charge by H. L. Rodgers, a german by the name of Frederick Myer, whom I arrested as a spy or smugler in behalf of the United States, and upon whose person was found Six Thousand three hundred dollars in drafts upon the Assistant Treasurer New York, one hundred and fifty five dollars in gold and seventy cents in silver, four private letters of unimportant import, two ponies and revolver pistol No 72,942 belt and hoster, one riding saddle, one pack saddle and one pair saddle bags, all of which will be forwarded to you by Mr Marshall Grimes, with the exception of the two ponies bridle and saddle and saddle bags and ten dollars in gold, which I have placed in charge of Mr H. L. Rodgers and will accompany the prisoner.

The principal evidence against Frederick Myer, was derived from the Trader Mr. John Shirley, whose written statement is herewith enclosed. Very Respectfully Your obt. sert.

M. LEEPER, Ind. Agt. C.S.A.

Elias Rector Esq, Supt. Ind. Affrs,
Fort Smith Arks.

WICHITA AGENCY, L.D. December 15th 1861

To JOHN JUMPER, and our brothers in the Seminole Nation,

We have nothing particular to write you, we are all well and doing well here

Since we had the talk we have *understood* that you had some difficulty among your people, but that does not have any bad effect upon us as we are friends the same as at the time we made the treaties – Our brothers the Comanches, and all the other tribes, are still friends with you, and are all very sorry that you are fighting one against another, brothers against brothers, and friends against friends. When Mode Cunard and you were here and had the talk with Genl Pike – we still hold to the talk we made with Genl Pike, and are keeping the treaty in good faith, and are looking for him back again soon.

We look to you and Mode Cunard and Genl Pike as brothers – General Pike told us at the council that, there were but few of us here, and if anything turned up to make it necessary he would protect them. We are just as we were when Genl Pike was up here and keeping the treaty made with him – Our brothers the wild Comanches have been in and are friendly with us.

All the indians here have but one heart — our brothers, the Texans, and the indians are away fighting the cold weather people we do not intend to go North to fight them but if they come down here, we will all unite to drive them away – Some of my people are one eyed and a little Crippled, but if the enemy comes here they will all jump out to fight him – Also that Pea-o-popicult has recently the principal Kiowa Chief has recently visited the reserve, and has expressed friendly intentions, and has gone back to consult the rest of his people and designs returning

HOSEEA MARIA   BUFFALO HUMP
KI-KAD-A-WAH
            Chiefs of the Comanches
TE-NAH   JIM POCKMARK.
GEO WASHINGTON

The Confederate States of America
To M. GRIMES   Dr.

1861: Nov 30   For Services rendered of negro man
                 Guss as Laborer from 1st Oct. to
                 30th Nov 1861, inclusive, 2 mos.
                 at $300.00 pr. an.   .   . $ 50.00

Received at Wichita Agency L.D. Decr 31st 1861, of M. Leeper Ind. Agt. C.S.A.   Fifty dollars in full of the above account.
$50.00   M. GRIMES.

I certify on honor that the above account is correct and just, and that I have actually this 31st day of Decr. 1861, paid the amount thereof.   IND. AGT. C.S.A
[Triplicates]

The Confederate States of America
To A. OUTZEN   Dr.

1861: Decr 31   For Services rendered as Wheel-
                 wright etc. at Wichita Agency,
                 L.D. from 1st Oct. to 31st Decr.
                 1861 inclusive, 3 months at
                 $600.00 pr an .   .   . $ 150.00

Received at Wichita Agency L.D. Decr 31st 1861 of M. Leeper, Indian Agent, C.S.A. One Hundred & fifty 00/100
$150.00   A. OUTZEN Wheelwright.

I certify on honor that the above account is correct and just, and that

I have actually this 31st day of Decr 1861, paid the amount thereof,
[Triplicates]   IND. AGT. C.S.A.

The Confederate States of America
                    To J. B. BEVELL   Dr.
1861: Decr 31   For Services rendered as Laborer at
                     Wichita Agency L.D. June 1
                     Oct. to 15th Nov 1861 – inclusive
                     1 mo & 15 days at $300.00 pr an $ 37.50
                     And as Farmer from 16 Nov to 31
                     Decr 1861 inclusive 1 mo & 15
                     days at $600.00 pr an   .   .   75.00
                                                         ─────────
                                                         $ 112.50

Received at Wichita Agency L.D. Decr 31st 1861 of M. Leeper
    Ind. Agt. C.S.A. One Hundred & twelve 50/100 Dollars in full
    of the above account.
$112.50.   JOHN BEVELL Farmer

I certify on honor that the above account is correct and just, and that
I have actually this 31st day of Decr 1861, paid the amount thereof,
[Triplicates]   IND. AGT., C.S.A.

The Confederate States of America
                    To D. SEALS   Dr.
1861: Decr. 31   For Services rendered as Farmer at
                     Wichita Agency L.D. from 1st
                     Oct. to 31st Decr. 1861 inclusive,
                     3 months at $600.00 per an   . $ 150.00

Received at Wichita Agency L.D. Decr. 31st 1861 of M Leeper In-
    dian Agent C.S.A. One Hundred & fifty 00/100 Dollars in full
    of the above account.
$150.00   DAVID SEALS, Farmer

I certify that the above account is correct and just, and that I have
actually this 31 day of Decr 1861, paid the amount thereof,
[Triplicates]   IND. AGT. C.S.A.

                    FORT SMITH, January 13th, 1862.
     SIR: In compliance with your letter of instruction of the 10th
inst. I have the honor to present in detail the condition of affairs con-

nected with the Wichita Agency. In thus presenting my report I shall attempt to be governed by as much brevity as possible.

In detailing the affairs of the people in my charge and of my action in reference to them it will become necessary to refer not only to the present but to their past history in Texas. There was a time in Texas when these people were in a prosperous and happy condition, and they advanced as rapidly in the arts of civilization during that time, perhaps, as any people ever did. But evil disposed persons in their vicinity and those not far distant on the frontiers of Texas became dissatisfied with their locality and determined to disperse and break them up. They continued their work of desolation until the indians were compelled to abandon their homes and seek a refuge west of the Chickasaw and Choctaw Nations on the Leased District. In doing so they suffered many and very severe losses and privations. Numbers of their horses and cattle were driven off by their enemies and many things useful to them, were necessarily abandoned. Estimates were prepared of the amount of damage and submitted to the original United States Government but before any action was taken, the government dissolved and their just claims consequently failed. Therefore permit me most respectfully to suggest the propriety of immediately calling the attention of our Government and of the proper Department to the fact, in order that these people may obtain adequate remuneration. In reference to their habitations, they have nothing to claim. They have more and better houses than they had in Texas. The Commanches have eight or ten neatly hewn log cabins with good chimneys. Three double log hewn houses with good chimneys, to each room for the chief's in addition to a number of warm comfortable picket houses which they partly built themselves and covered with grass.

In Texas they had but one house which belonged to the Chief, in the scramble for the spoils at the time of the abandonment of Fort Cobb by the federal troops they were not altogether behind for I have observed among them several new Sibley tents and a number of new common tents. The Tonkahwas have warm comfortable houses made of poles and grass such as they had in Texas. And for the chief I built a good double log house with chimneys to each room and a hall or passage in the centre, in which he now lives.

The Anahdahkoes have quite a number of comfortable houses consisting of four double houses with chimneys to each room, passages in the centre and to some of them shed rooms attached. The remainder consist of hewn log cabins and Picket houses such as they had in Texas covered with grass. The Caddoes also have quite a number of houses consisting of various double houses, single houses and picket houses.

The Witchitas have no houses except such as they have built for themselves consisting of a net work of sticks and grass but they are warm and comfortable. They are not decided upon a permanent location and consequently refuse to have houses built. The Tahwac-carroes, Wacoes, Ionies and Kechies inhabit the same kind of houses as the Witchitas and like them have not decided upon a permanent location. The Shawnees and Delawares all have good comfortable cabins.

In February last whilst at Washington I closed all my former accounts with the department of the Interior of the United States Government and estimated for the first and second quarter of 1861 which estimates amounted to 13899 dollars and eighty-five cents. On my way to the Agency in the Indian Country prepared to carry out the designs and expectations of the government I was arrested by one Burrow who represented himself to be a general on the part of the State of Arkansas, who examined my papers and took from me one wagon four set of harness, one horse and seven mules, property which had been purchased by the United States government for the use and benefit of the Indians in my charge, all of which has been subsequently returned with the exception of two of the mules. After the wagon and mules were taken I hired transportation and proceeded to the Agency where I found the Indians in a high state of excitement and alarm; their fears having been excited by a Delaware Indian by the name of Jim Ned and other evil disposed persons, tattlers and tale bearers who are apt to be found loitering about Indian Reserves.

In reference to the people of Texas, I succeeded in satisfying them that their apprehensions were groundless, let several contracts for breaking prairie and commenced to work generally in accordance with my estimates and the wishes of the Department. But soon afterwards my state (Texas) seceded from the Union and I determined no longer to act as a federal officer, and having no authority to act for the Confederate States, I delivered to the indians all the property in my possession which was held in trust for their benefit with the exception of two wagons which were used in my transportation, which together with one which had previously been loaned to the Commissary are now reported on my property rolls. With a hope to satisfy the indians until an agent should be appointed by the Confederate States (which I assured them would soon take place) I expended the remainder of the money's in my hands for blankets tobacco and clothing for them, they being in a destitute condition, occasioned principally on account of losses sustained by their goods being sunk in the Arkansas River and by the fire at Fort Smith. The goods were intended to be duplicated and money's had been promised for that purpose in advance of their regular supply of goods of which the indians were apprised.

Upon the withdrawal of Texas from the Union, they again became apprehensive of danger from the people of that State. I reminded them that I was a Texan, and in order that they might have a positive guaranty of safety, that they should have Texas troops to defend them. I made the application and Capt. Diamond's company arrived on the day of my departure.

During the whole course of my operations as Commanche Agent, and more particularly the past year, my best efforts have been employed with a hope to induce all the southern bands of Comanches to abandon their wandering habits become colonized and settle, that being the most effectual means, and by far the least expensive mode of checking their depredations on Texas, and finally by means of messengers and messages I induced them to come in on the first of August last and enter into treaty stipulations with Commissioner Pike. A train of untoward circumstances prevented the commissioner from complying strictly with his agreements with them which have cast a shade of discontent upon their minds, and they say that it is the cause of the non-compliance on their part, which was to settle on the reserve last fall and abandon their roving habits. This however I do not believe: if the commissioner had met them at the time appointed (the falling of the leaves) with all the goods promised I am of opinion they would have received the goods – made some excuse, and returned again to the prairies. Such has been the case of the other Comanches who have settled for several years and I think they would have done so too. Perhaps their stealing operations would not have been so extensive; but they say that that practice shall cease at any rate as long as they are friends with us.

In November last I received a visit from a Kiowa chief by the name of "Big-head" who made many fine promises and agreed to settle on the reserve with his people, but in this I place but little reliance. The Kiowa's are a very numerous band. They are northern indians and their principal range is from the sources of the Arkansas River to Bents Fort. Their principal chief originally contemptiously spoke of the United States government and troops, notwithstanding he annually received a large amount of presents from that government, consisting of blankets, clothing, tobacco, rifles, powder and lead, etc. They now have a federal agent at Bent's Fort.

During the past six months, but little has been done on the reserve – I have had no means to accomplish much. The employees who have been engaged have suffered considerably with sickness during the months of September and October last. They have built a very comfortable double log house with a gallery in front and a stable which is partly finished to which a room is attached for the benefit of employees. Without such protection and security there is no safety for the public animals necessary to carry on the farming operations of the reserve.

No troops being stationed on the Leased District I have been unable to exercise the necessary control. The indians have been kept in a constant state of turmoil by false representations both in reference to myself and things affecting their individual interest. No indian reserve can be conducted in a satisfactory manner either to the government or indians without the coöperation of troops to enable the Agent to enforce the intercourse laws and eject disorderly persons from amongst them.

No funds as yet have been received to meet the current expenses of the Agency, nor has any forage been furnished except twenty four bushels of corn and twelve of oats, which were received from Commissioner Pike. The remainder of the forage which was used in sustaining two government animals and four private animals employed in the public service from the first of August until the last of October and from that time till the 31st of December four additional public animals, was gathered up at the different corn houses which had been abandoned and were going to destruction at Fort Cobb, and a small amount purchased on my own responsibility from the contractor for supplying the indians.

It is deemed useless to suggest additional plans of retrenchment and economy to the government as I am not advised as to the extent and nature of the design of its future operations in reference to the affairs of the reserve. With these facts submitted I have the honor to be Sir very respectfully Your obedient Servant   [M. LEEPER.]
E. Rector, Superintendent of Indian Affairs, Southern Superintendency

WITCHITA AGENCY, Jan. 31st., 1862.

BRIG. GEN'L A. PIKE, Com'd'y Indian Territory.

Sir: – Enclosed please find muster roll of Reserve Indians enlisted in the services of the Confederate Government under your authority of the 30th Aug't, 1861 to M. Leeper, Indian Agent, to act as spies and for the protection of the Agency until relieved by Confederate forces.

You will perceive that I enlisted them on the 9th Sept. last and have made up the roll to the 9th Feb'y, 1862, at which time I would respectfully suggest the disbandment of them as they have already served three months longer than they anticipated at the time of their enlistment and they are anxious to be disbanded at the expiration of this month.

As much doubt has been expressed by the other Indians not enlisted, of these ever receiving pay for their services, I believe if they were paid off [it] would at once convince them of the integrity and honor of the Confederate Government and should any emergency hereafter arise they will more readily flock to the standard of our country.

Having received special instructions from M. Leeper, Indian Agent, to remain at my post during his absence, I therefore forward these papers by Mr. John Shirley and authorize him to act for me in this matter.

MUSTER ROLL OF RESERVE INDIANS MUSTERED INTO THE CONFEDERATE STATES OF AMERICA UNDER COMMAND OF LIEUT. GEN'L H. P. JONES, SEPT. 9, 1861.

	HORSE	BRIDLE & SADDLE	RIFLE	BOW, ETC.
1. Pinahontsama, Sergt.	$60.	$5.00	$25.	$5.00
2. Pive-ahope Corpl.	$60.00	$5.00	do.	5.00
3. Chick-a-poo	30.00	5.00	25.00	5.00
4. Charley Chickapoo	30.00	5.00	25.00	5.00
5. Somo	40.00	5.00	10.00	5.00
6. Boo-y-wy-sis-ka	50.00	5.00	25.00	5.00
7. Cu-be-ra-wipo	50.00	5.00	25.00	5.00
8. Ca-na-with	40.00	5.00	25.00	5.00
9. A-ri-ka-pap	55.00	5.00	25.00	5.00
10. Pith-pa-wah	50.00	5.00		5.00
11. Pe-ah-ko-roh	35.00	5.00	35.00	5.00

	HORSE	BRIDLE & SADDLE	RIFLE	BOW, ETC.
12. Jim Chickapoo	65.00	5.00 six shooter 25.00		5.00
13. Na-na-quathteh	40.00	5.00		5.00
14. To-no-kah	80.00	5.00	25.00	5.00
15. Ath-pah	25.00	5.00 Pistol #5.00		5.00
16. Pe-ba-rah	30.00	5.00	25.00	5.00
17. Cur-su-ah	45.00	5.00	10.00	5.00
18. Cow-ah-dan Sept.23d. $60.		5.00	15.00	5.00

Signed Sealed & delivered in the presence of David Seals & Dr. Bucket, Sept. 9, 1861.

WICHITA AGENCY L. D. Feby the 9th 1862

I certify on honor that I have received from Messrs Johnson & Grimes Seventeen hundred and fifty-four rations of Beef, Flour, Coffee, Sugar, Soap, and Salt for the use of my Spy Company raised for the protection of the Wichita Agency by authority of Commissioner A. Pike as per letter dated Augt. 30th 1861 to M. Leeper Indian Agent   H. P. JONES, Lt. Com'd'y. and Act'g C. of S.

HEAD QUARTERS DEP'T OF IND'N TERRITORY,
FORT McCULLOCH, 23rd April 1862.

SPECIAL ORDERS, No. –

Lieut. Col. Harris, Commanding Chickasaw Battalion, will station four companies instead of two, of his Battalion, at Camp McIntosh, and two only at Fort Arbuckle. He will consult with the Agent for the Reserve Indians, Col. Matthew Leeper, and do everything in his power to protect the Agency and the *peaceful* Indians on the Reserve, placing, if necessary his troops at or near the Agency, and controlling the unruly Indians, by force of arms, if it becomes necessary. By order of Brig. Gen'l Com'd'g

FAYETTE HEWITT A. A. General

[Copy]   May 7, 1862.

Hon. Comr. Indian Affairs, enclosing copies from Gen'l Pike.

WASHITA AGENCY, L.D. May 7, 1862.

SIR: Enclosed herewith I have the honor to transmit for the information of the Department the copy of a letter addressed to Gen'l Pike on the 13th April last, and his reply thereto; the troops promised by the General have not arrived nor have I any tidings from them.

There can be no question, if the Confederate States desire to keep up this Agency and to continue their friendly relations with the Indians adjacent to the Reserve, that a strong garrison is necessary. The appearance of friendship could be maintained perhaps without it, but to put an entire stop to the depredations upon Texas, cannot be accomplished without the restraining influence of a military force; a small force at all times here is necessary to enable the Agent to enforce the Intercourse Laws, and to expell from the Reserve, disorderly persons and idlers, hovering around the Indian Camps without any legitimate business or employment. I would further respectfully suggest with all due deference to the military skill of Gen. Pike, that white troops would be infinitely better and far more available in every particular than Indians. It is well known that the people of Texas adjacent to the Reserve have no very kind feelings for Indians generally, and if it should become necessary to exercise military authority over a Texan no matter who he is or however worthless he might be, if it was done by Indian soldiers, it would engender deep-rooted malice in the minds of very many of the Texan people against the troops, which, in all probability would militate largely against the interest of the Government. White troops have a greater influence upon the Indians than Indian troops would have, and understand more perfectly the obligations of enlisted men.

In my letter to Gen. Pike, I gave it as an opinion that it would be better to either drive the Indians off, who are not located, or to require them to settle on the Reserve. Various conversations had with them since that time has been the means of changing my opinion; I think by continuing the practice of giving them provisions and more supplies of presents when they visit the Agency will perhaps induce them to remain quiet and not disturb Texas, particularly if we present an array of troops sufficiently strong to chastise them in the event of their forfeiting their promises and acting a faithless part. To-day I held a Council with some of the wild chiefs, they made fair promises, and promised to bring to the Agency on the 20th of June next, the other wild chiefs who have never visited this place, for the purpose of entering into a general treaty of peace, and they say they will use all their influence with the Kioways to restore the horses lately stolen from the Reserve Indians and cause those to treat likewise. If it should be the desire of the Government for me to have them sign the Treaty with such amendments or alterations as may be suggested, there would not be the slightest difficulty in the way, it can be accomplished without any further parade or expense, except the ordinary supply of provision and a few small presents in the way of goods.

Allow me to direct the attention of the Department to the fact that the present Contract for furnishing rations to the Indians will expire, I am told, on the 16th August next, (I have never been furnished with a copy) and that it will be necessary in order to give satisfaction to the public to give at least a month's notice of the time and place, a new one will be let and having been informed that the next Contract would be let at this agency, and that the local agent would be charged with the duty, I deem it necessary immediately to repair to Fort Smith to await instructions and other necessary papers in reference to my official station and to receive funds for the present and to forward an estimate for the ensuing fiscal year.

May 8th.

To-day I was visited by quite a number of chiefs belonging to the wild Comanches who have never been here before. They say they are desirous of making a perpetual and ever-lasting peace with the Southern people, the fourth of July is appointed for a general gathering in Council of all the Chiefs and principal men belonging to the Comanches for the purpose of entering into a general and lasting peace upon the same terms and conditions which are offered those already settled. I appointed the 4th of July that I might have an opportunity in the mean time of consulting with and ascertaining the pleasure of the Government in reference to them. I am of the opinion that three or four thousand dollars worth of goods furnished upon that occasion and distributed to them as presents would have a beneficial effect.

I learn from them that four white men and four Indians were recently killed on the Llano, Texas that the Indians were returning from Mexico & without knowing anything of the friendly relations which now exist between our people and theirs, they stopped as usual, stole a parcel of horses, were pursued and the killing aforementioned was the consequence, they assert that they will control their people hereafter from depredating upon Texas, and that if any of their bad men should cross Red River that they will give immediate notice of the fact that they may be overtaken and killed, and if they should escape notice steal horses and return they will immediately take them from them, deliver them to the Agent with information in reference to the place from which they were taken, so the owners can recover them again.

With these facts submitted, I have the honor to be very respectfully, Your Obedient Servant

(Sgd.) M. Leeper, Indian Agent, C.S.A.

COPY TO BRIG. GEN'L A. PIKE, APR. 13, 1862. IN REF-
ERENCE TO THE CONDUCTING OF THE RESERVE
COMANCHES AND WILD BANDS OF COMANCHES, AL-
SO REQUESTING A MILITARY FORCE TO BE STA-
TIONED ON THE RESERVE

WASHITA AGENCY, L.D. April 13, 1862.
BRIG. GEN'L A. PIKE, Com'd'g of Indian Terr'y

Sir: It becomes my duty under official instructions to keep you
advised of the feelings and bearings of the Indians on the Reserve
and more particularly of the wild bands adjacent to it who profess
friendship for us. The recent friendly relations which have been
professed on the part of the Indians and attempted to be cultivated
on our part have produced an opposite result upon the Comanche
Reserve Indians from that which was anticipated, boys who have been
partly reared upon the Reserve and who hitherto have conducted
themselves with the greatest propriety are now unruly and are subject
to the most unbridled passions and unheard of improprieties, they
have destroyed pretty much all the poultry belonging to Dr. Shirley,
have shot arrows into his milk cows, killed several of the beeves belonging to the contractor. They are in the habit of shooting beeves
full of arrows in the beef pen before they are issued, killing some
of them and rendering others unable to be driven to the different Indian encampments, this practice was repeated on yesterday in the
presence of the chiefs, when one of the interpreters, Mr. H. P. Jones,
admonished Buffalo Hump to check such outrages and reprove the
boys for such improprieties, but was fiercely turned upon by the old
Indian and abused in the most unmeasured terms, the boys then rode
to the Agency, approached the horse lot and one of them was just in
the act of shooting a horse, I succeeded in preventing him from doing
so myself.

Those wild fellows come in, hold war dances and scalp dances,
speak of their agility in stealing horses and of their prowess in taking
scalps of white men and Mexicans, and of the rapture with which
they are received and amorous embraces of the young damsels on their
return until the young men heretofore inclined to lead an idle but
civil life on the Reserve are driven mad with excitement, some of
them have left, others are going today with the wild Indians for the
ostensible purpose I am told of depredating upon Mexico, but really,
in my opinion upon Texas, many depredations have recently been com-

mitted upon that frontier, and lately an Anahdahko Indian and a
negro belonging to that band crossed Red River, stole five horses,
killed three of them and returned home on the other two, they alledge
that it would not have taken place, but for the want of the restraining
influence of the Chief who was absent at Fort Davis for presents
(this is a mere subterfuge of course).

The wild Indians are principally located within two days ride of
this place and I suppose could muster two thousand warriors, when
they come here they are rather impudent and insolent in their demands
and upon one occasion threatened to force the doors of the Commissary and help themselves. A few days since three of their young men
forcibly opened one of the doors of Dr. Shirley's house and attempted
to enter his wife's bed chamber. They were met by the doctor at
the door who, after a scuffle and slight altercation with one of them
caused them to desist.

Many horses have recently been stolen from the Reserve Indians,
some of which are known to have been taken by the bands professing
friendship, who promised to restore them.

I am clearly of the opinion that this Reserve cannot be sustained
without a strong military force, and that it would be much better to
require those wild fellows either to settle on the Reserve or quit the
country, at present they appear to make it a place of convenience, to
rest, feed and recruit themselves, on their return from a stealing expedition, and to procure provisions and a suitable outfit, the better to
enable them to prosecute their fiendish designs. Therefore permit me
respectfully to solicit you to furnish at the shortest practicable period
a strong mounted force, say one Regiment at least to be situated here
to act in concert with the Civil Authorities in holding those Indians
in check, preventing the forays in Texas and in regulating the affairs
of the Reserve. I would also with due deference suggest the name
of Col. Alexander of Sherman, as a gentleman eminently qualified
for the service. Texas troops would be more available here at present
than any others, for the Indians have an instinctive dread of them.

In the event that it should become absolutely necessary in the
absence of suitable protection to abandon the Reserve, a suggestion
from you in reference to the proper course to be taken would be acceptable, my notion is to fall back upon Red River or into Texas
with all the Indians who are true to the South and if overtaken by
the way, defend to the last extremity.

All my official correspondence I report to the Department but before I could get an expression of opinion from that source, it would probably be too late to avail anything. I shall feel obliged for a reply by the messenger. Very respectfully, Your obedient servant.

[M. LEEPER]

JONES [594] TO PIKE

I have the honor to inform you that the reserve Comanche indians enlisted in the service of the Confederate States by your authority of the 30th August 1861 were on the 9th April last disbanded with the consent and knowledge of Col. M. Leeper indian agent The reason for so doing was that latterly they would not remain at their encampment and their horses were never at hand when wanted.

JONES [595] TO PIKE

The indians placed in my charge by your order for the protection of this agency finally proved uncontrollable and utterly useless, and were therefore with the knowledge and consent of the Agent discharged on the 13th of April last. . .

[On the 11th of August, 1862, Agent S. G. Colley transmitted to Dole from Fort Larned two documents,[596] one of which he thought reflected upon the loyalty or honesty of Capt. Whittenhall, formerly commanding at Fort Larned.]

(A)   I have this day received of Lone Wolf a chief Kiowas a paper from Albert Pike of the so-called S.C. which I will give to him again and another to the said Albert Pike after the Indian agent shall distribute the goods to the Indians.

D. S. WHITTENHALL, Capt. Com'd'g Post.
July 22, 1862
[Endorsement] A true copy.

J. H. LEAVENWORTH, Col. 2nd Reg't C.V.

(B)   WICHITA AGENCY L.D., May 31st, 1862.
The bearer E-sa-sem-mus Kiowa Chief has visited and promised on the part of their tribe to be friendly with the people of Texas and

---

594 H. P. Jones, late lieutenant-commanding to Brigadier-general A. Pike, commanding Indian Territory, dated Washita Agency L.D., May 8, 1862.

595 H. P. Jones to Pike, dated Washita Agency, May 8, 1862.

596 Indian Office, Land Files, *Upper Arkansas, 1855-1865*, C1749.

ourselves it is hoped that so long as they carry out that promise they will be treated kindly. M. LEEPER, Ind. Agt. C.S.A.
per C. A. ZICHEL

[Endorsement] A true copy.
J. H. LEAVENWORTH Col. 2nd Reg't C.V.

LEEPER TO PIKE

WASHITA AGENCY, L.D., June 26, 1862.
BRIG. GEN'L A. PIKE, Com'd'y Ind. Terr'y and Act'g Superintendent.

Sir: Being desirous of keeping you advised of all my official operations, enclosed herewith you will please find a copy of requests made by Capts. Hart & James. I found those officers courteous and prompt, and manifesting an unreserved degree of willingness to aid me in carrying out the designs of the Confederate States of America in sustaining the Reserve and giving satisfaction to the Indians located thereon.

I learn that an annual festival or dance of the Kioways and the wild Comanche bands is expected to be held about this time, which may detain them beyond the 4th of July, and with a view to have reliable information in reference to the matter and ascertain the precise time they may be expected here, three or four days since I dispatched To-sha-hua and Pinahontsama to visit their encampments for the purpose; they will return in about six days. Upon the arrival of the Kioway Chiefs here, I shall have your excellent address carefully interpreted to them and get them to sign the Treaty. If it should be your pleasure they should do so, I apprehend that I can take all the Comanche Chiefs and the Kioway Chiefs to your Head Quarters, which I will cheerfully do, in that event however they would naturally expect in addition to their daily supply of food a few presents in the way of clothing and tobacco.

The present fiscal year is now within a few days of being closed, the employees on the Reserve and the trader from whom small presents have been purchased for the Indians are unpaid, no funds have been furnished for the purpose except fifteen hundred dollars which was handed me by the late Superintendent and was in part used in liquidation of my own Salary and the remainder, say six or seven hundred dollars, in the payment of employees, for the want of funds I have been unable to close my account, they will all be ready, however, on the first of July, and if you should be in possession of funds for the purpose, after the anticipated meeting of the Indians here, if it should meet your approbation, I will take the accounts to your Head Quarters and submit them to your inspection in order that they may be closed, provided it is inconvenient for you to transmit the money to me.

I desire to call your attention particularly to the fact that the present Contract for supplying the Indians with rations on the Reserve will terminate I am told (I have never been favored with a copy) on the 16th of August next, and it therefore would seem proper that a new contract should be let in time for the Contractor to have his supplies in readiness for delivery at that time, and it is but justice to Mr. Chas. B. Johnson, the present Contractor to say that he has complied with his Contract to the entire satisfaction of all concerned, kept ample supplies at all times on hand, and disposed to be pleasant and obliging not only to the Indians, but to all other persons with whom he has had business to transact.

When the Kioways arrive I apprehend they will have many horses and mules in their possession which will be identified by the Texas people here as the property of people living in Texas; the friendly relations and recent social intercourse of these Indians with those of the wild bands has been the cause of introducing here several horses and mules of that description already. My original instructions under the United States Government was to take possession of all such property and have them delivered to their proper owners, but if a course of that kind was now pursued it would at once defeat the Treaty with the wild bands and cause them to recommence their depredations with increased violence and renewed vigor. The 10th Article of the recent Treaty reads thus:

> It is distinctly understood by the said four bands of the Ne-um, the State of Texas is one of the Confederate States, and joins in this Convention, and signs it when the Commissioner signs it, and is bound by it; and that all hostilities and enmities between it and them are now ended, and are to be forgotten and forgiven forever on both sides.

Also the 19th Article commencing at the 15th line reads thus:

> And the same things in all respects are also hereby offered to the Kioways and agreed to be given them, if they will settle in said Country, atone for the murders and robberies they have lately committed and show a resolution to lead an honest life; to which end the Confederate States send the Kioways with this talk, the wampum of peace and the bullet of war, for them to take their choice, now and for all time to come.

But the Treaty is silent in reference to the manner in which the owners of property lost in that manner are to be remunerated.

In a consultation which I held with Capts Hart and James we determined to take proof in reference to the ownership of the property, place a fair valuation upon it and submit it to the Confederate Government for their approbation, approval, and allowance, provided, however, that it should meet your approbation in the first place.

A short time since a delegation from all the tribes here except the Tonkahwas and Comanches visited the Kioways to obtain from them their horses which were stolen by the Kioways, one of the Waco Chiefs has returned and says they delivered to him ten of the stolen horses, were disposed to be friendly and said all of them should be given up, but after he left a Wichita stole from the Kioways twenty-one horses and a Caddo four and have brought them to the Reserve. I held a consultation with the Chiefs in reference to the matter in which it was determined that the horses should be taken from those who stole them and returned to the Kioways immediately after the return of the Wichita Chief La-sa-di-wah, who will report the facts as they are.

In all my official relations I have avoided, as far as possible, incurring useless or unnecessary expenses, and now the troubled condition of the country would seem to render it doubly necessary, allow me therefore to suggest that the office of Commissiary is a sinecure, a useless expenditure of public money to the Government and an injury to the public service, it has never been allowed before at an Agency where an agent could be present and witness the issues himself, the Interpreters necessarily have to be present, and heretofore have witnessed the issues, the Commissary merely being an impartial weigher between the Contractor and the Indians which can be done just as well by one of the Interpreters without incurring any additional expense to the Government.

One of the greatest injuries which I have met with during a term of more than five years service, has been experienced from officious meddlers, idlers and tale-bearers who are apt to hover round Indian encampments, and I have never found one more so than the present Commissary. J. J. Sturm who spends the principal part of his time at the Indian encampments pretends to know more than anyone else, palpably neglects the instructions given him and has produced more disquiet on the Reserve than has been produced from all other causes, he would have been suspended and reported long since, but I was apprehensive that it might be supposed that I was actuated from vindictive feelings towards him on account of an injury which he attempted to inflict upon me. At the close of the present Contract if you should deem it necessary to continue such an office, I hope a more suitable man will be appointed.

At the close of the present fiscal year I shall report in detail everything connected with the Reserve and the Indians thereon, the expenses thereof and the reasons and necessities for so doing. I am sir, Very respectfully, Your obt. servant. [M. LEEPER]

LEEPER TO PIKE

Copy to Brig. Gen'l Albert Pike, Acting Supt., Comr., Etc., in reference to making a treaty with the Kioway Indians and the signing of the amendments of Congress.

WASHITA AGENCY, L.D., July 11, 1862.

BRIG. GEN'L ALBERT PIKE, & Act'g Superintendent, Commissioner, etc.,

Sir: In compliance with your instructions and authority, I have this day entered into Treaty stipulations with the Kioway Indians and all the wild Comanche bands with the exception of the Kua-ha-ra-tet-sa-co-no who inhabit the western portion of the "Staked Plains," and with those I am negotiating and shall probably conclude a treaty of peace in September or October next. Those who treated in August last have also signed and adopted amendments of Congress.

They retired well satisfied with themselves, and with the action of the Confederate Government, consequently peace and quietness may be expected to prevail in future upon the frontier of Texas, provided, however, that a band of fugitives from the various clans who have congregated on the Pecos, numbering it is said one hundred and fifty or two hundred, governed by no law and disposed to spread desolation wherever they go, are destroyed or our troops can receive aid from the bands who have treated in hunting down and destroying those "fellows". I am sir, Very respectfully, Your obt. ser't

[M. LEEPER] Ind. Agency, C.S.A.

NOTICE

As Agent and Acting Commissioner on the part of the Confederate States of America, I have entered into Solemn Treaty stipulations of perpetual friendship and peace with the Kioway Indians and wild bands of Comanches except the Kna-ha-ra-tet-sa-co-no whose habitations are on the Western extremity of the "Staked Plains" and with those I am negotiating and will probably conclude a treaty some time in September next.

Therefore perfect peace and quietness may soon be expected to prevail on the Texas frontier.

In order to convince the Indians of our sincerity and punctuality, it is necessary to comply strictly with the Treaty, and to do that, the Government expects me to employ four or five farmers and twenty laborers which I desire to do; farmers with families would be preferred, to whom fifty dollars per month and rations will be given, and to laborers twenty-five dollars per month and rations, negro men would be preferred.

At present there is not the slightest danger there, the agency is one of the most quiet and peaceful places within the limits of the Confederate Government.

Apply to the undersigned who will remain a few days in Sherman and afterward at the Washita Agency.

July 21st 1862.

LEEPER [?] TO PARKS

SHERMAN, TEXAS, July 28th, 1862.

MR. ROBERT W. PARKS,

Sir, – Enclosed you will please find the copy of a letter of instructions to me from Gen'l Pike the Acting Superintendent of Indian Affairs (addressed to you) in reference to fifteen thousand dollars appropriated by the Government to purchase farming utensils, oxen, wagons and stock animals for Indians located on the Washita Reserve, which fund was handed to you. The direction of the expenditures of the fund legitimately belongs to the local Agent who is alone supposed to know the amount and description of articles necessary to be purchased for the Indians, hence Gen'l Pike's letter. Before making any of the purchases indicated it would be well to see me in order to ascertain the amount and description required, the Indians already have been furnished with a few wagons, oxen and farming utensils, in fact in reference to farming implements they are well enough supplied with the exception of weeding hoes and axes; and in reference to the stock animals to be purchased I would like to have a distinct understanding with regard to the quality and the price; a responsible gentleman whom I met here is willing to furnish cows and calves, the cows not to exceed six years old delivered at the agency at sixteen dollars; therefore I should be unwilling to receive on the part of the Government animals of that description at a higher price in the absence of positive instructions to that effect; the quantity also to be purchased is an important item.

If you will take the trouble to visit the Agency, I will give you an exact description of the articles necessary to be purchased and will give you the preference as a contractor for furnishing the same.

A copy of this letter will be furnished the Acting Superintendent Gen'l Pike, and the Department. Very respectfully, Your obt sevt.

[M. LEEPER]

WASH., ARK., Aug. 19, 1862.

COLONEL: I have forwarded you letters to the Commissioner of Indian Affairs. Having resigned and been deprived of command in the Indian Country, I am also relieved of duty as Acting Superintendent, for which crowning mercy, God be thanked.

Mr. Parks returned on receiving your letter and refunded me $15,000 placed in his hands, except $200, paid for a mowing machine. I have deposited the residue, with all other Indian moneys, (Coin and paper), in a safe place, and so advised the Commissioner. As soon as a new Superintendent is appointed, I hope to get rid of it all.

If you had written me, *before*, what you write now, in regard to McKusken[?], you would not have had to complain that I frustrated your efforts. You sent him to me it is true, but with no such charges, and consequently left me bound to pay him off. I had employed him, and no showing was made to me that he did not deserve his pay. I hear the charges *now* for the first time.

As to the corn at Cobb, I think you are misinformed. When I returned there last fall I found it difficult to get a small quantity, because the officer in Command said they needed it all; although the troops were on the point of leaving. I know it had been so wasted that there was not much left and what *was* left, you needed, as you had none. I wonder you did not send your wagons and get it, as soon as the troops left, if there was any remaining, and account for it.

I *was* sorry to hear that you had made unkind remarks in regard to myself, and though apparently my friend, were secretly my enemy – and I am truly glad to receive your flat contradiction. I have *never* had any unkind feelings towards you, and was glad to believe after meeting you this Summer, that you had none towards me. For any imputations against yourself in your official capacity, you are indebted in chief measure to Major Rector who made them openly, anywhere, and in the presence of many. What Mr. Sturm said was not said willingly, but drawn from him. He showed a great disinclination to say anything against you.

Believe me, I would now, as always for years past, rather serve than injure you. And I sincerely hope our friendly relations may continue. I expect to settle not far from you and will always gladly aid in cultivating friendship with the Indians and enabling you to succeed with them. I am very truly yours ALBERT PIKE Col. M. Leeper C.S. Agent Etc.

DESHLER [597] TO LEEPER

Gen. Holmes in reply to your letter of 17th inst. just received, instructs me to say, that Gen. Hindman is going to take command of all the troops in the Indian country, he starts in a day or two. Col. W. P. Lane's Reg't has been ordered to Fort Arbuckle. The gen. com'd'g thinks these measures will be sufficient to insure quiet in your region, but instructs me to say that if he knew of any available force in Texas he would have no objection to sending 5 or 6 Companies to you, but there are no troops available other than Col. Lane's Reg't already ordered to Arbuckle.

---

[597] James Deshler to Leeper, dated Little Rock, Sept. 28, 1862.

SELECTED BIBLIOGRAPHY

I. GENERAL ACCOUNT OF DOCUMENTARY SOURCES.

The material for this book has been drawn almost entirely from documentary sources and, in a very large measure, from unpublished documentary sources; namely, the manuscript records of the United States Indian Office. Those records to-day are in a very disorganized state, largely due to change of system and to the many removals to which they have been subjected within the last few years. At the time when they were examined for the purposes of the present work, such of them as were not included in *Registers, Letter Books*, and *Report Books* were classified as *Land Files, General Files, Special Files, Emigration Files, Miscellaneous Files, Star Files*, and the like, the basis of classification being, convenience in the current and routine work of the office. The individual files were arranged according to tribe, agency, or superintendency and every incoming letter had its own file mark. It had a letter to designate the transmitter, that letter being the initial of the transmitter's surname or of the office he represented, and it had a number to indicate its rank in a series, all the papers of which bore the same initial letter and had been received in the same given year. Finally, it was rated as belonging to a particular tribe, agency, or superintendency and to a particular file.

In the autumn of 1911, an attempt was made to consolidate the old *Land* and *General Files* with the result that now they are no longer distinct from each other; but it has seemed best not to change the reference in the citations. The year, the letter, and the number are permanent indices and, with them at hand, there ought to be no difficulty in the locating of a paper, except for the fact that nearly everything in the United States Indian Office seems, just now, rather transitory and chaotic. Had the inaugural ball for 1913 not been dispensed with, the plan was, to use the records as the base for the band-stand, a decidedly interesting reflection, one must admit, upon the popular notion of the value of the national archives.

Among the manuscripts used in the preparation of the present work, were two collections of papers that came into the United States Indian Office out of the regular course of its official business. In the citations, one is noted as *Leeper Papers*, and the other as *Fort Smith Papers.* Their history, since they came into the Indian Office, proves how urgent is the need for a Hall of Records. Inasmuch as these papers were not required for the every-day business of the office, they were packed away, years and years ago, along with a lot of other commercially useless papers, in huge boxes and stored in the attic of the old Post-office Building. There they were left to be forgotten. In the course of time, the Office of Indian Affairs was moved from the old Post-office Building to the Pension Building; but the packing-boxes in the attic were inadvertently left behind. One day, however, the writer discovered that papers, found at the Wichita Agency at the time Agent Leeper was killed, October, 1862, had really come into the Indian Office; but the question was, where were they? A search high and low was totally without success until it developed that the packing-boxes in the attic were supposed to contain "useless" papers and were still in the old Post-office Building. Permission was obtained to have them examined and, for this purpose, they were transferred to the Pension Building. Among their contents was found a number of interesting and valuable documents which very likely would soon have been lost forever, destroyed by the General Land Office because abandoned by the Indian. The contents included, besides the *Leeper Papers* for which the search had been especially conducted, letter-books of Michigan territorial governors, file-boxes of all sorts, and a mass of Confederate stuff, brought from Fort Smith. The last-named proved a veritable mine of wealth. It comprised the occasional correspondence of Cooper, Cowart, Crawford, Drew, Dean, Rector, Pike, and many others whose official life had brought them into contact with the Indians. It was all very suggestive and remunerative.

To supplement the manuscripts an exhaustive search of the *Official Records of the War of the Rebellion* has been made and with good results. It is a pity that the material in the *Official Records* is so badly arranged and so much of it duplicated and often triplicated. Had it been better edited and better indexed, the danger of over-looking important documents would have been minimized a hundred-fold. The volumes found particularly useful for Indian participation in the Civil War were the following:

First Series, vols. i; iii; iv; viii; ix; xiii; xxii, parts 1 and 2;

xxvi, parts 1 and 2; xxxiv, parts 1, 2, and 3; xli, parts 1, 2, 3, and 4;
xlviii, parts 1 and 2; liii, supplement.
Third Series, vols. i; ii; iii.
Fourth Series, vols. i; ii; iii.

II. ALPHABETICAL LIST OF SOURCES

AMERICAN ANNUAL CYCLOPEDIA, 1861-1865, inclusive (New
York).

ARKANSAS. Journal of the House of Representatives for the
Thirteenth Session of the General Assembly, November 5, 1860 –
January 21, 1861 (Little Rock, 1861).

—— Journal of the Convention, 1861.

—— Messages of the Governors.

BUCHANAN, JAMES. Works, collected and edited by John Basset
Moore (Philadelphia, 1908-1911), 12 vols.

CAIRNES, J. E. Slave Power: its character, career, and probable
designs (New York, 1863), pamphlet.

CONFEDERATE STATES OF AMERICA. Journal of the Congress, 1861-
1865. (United States Senate *Executive Documents*, 58th congress, second session, no. 234).

—— Provisional and permanent constitutions; and acts and resolutions of the first session of the Provisional Congress (Richmond,
1861).

—— Special orders of the adjutant and inspector general's office,
1862 (Richmond, 1862).

CONNELLEY, WILLIAM E., editor. Provisional government of Nebraska Territory and the Journals of William Walker [Lincoln,
Nebraska, 1899].

DEAN, CHARLES W. Letter Book, May 26, 1855 to December 31,
1856 (Manuscript in United States Indian Office).

DREW, THOMAS S. Letter Book, June 1, 1853 to June 1, 1854
(Manuscript in United States Indian Office).

FORT SMITH PAPERS. A miscellaneous collection of manuscript
materials, transmitted from Fort Smith, Arkansas, at the close of
the Civil War. Among them is the fragment of one of Elias
Rector's *Letter Books*.

—— Minutes of the private meetings of the commissioners, 1865
(Land Files, Indian Talks, Councils, etc., Box 4).

HAGOOD, JOHNSON. Memoirs of the War of Secession from the
original manuscripts of Johnson Hagood (Columbia, S.C., 1912).

KAPPLER, CHARLES J., compiler and editor. Indian affairs: Laws and Treaties (United States Senate Documents, 58th congress, Second session, no. 319), 2 vols.

LEEPER PAPERS. Manuscripts, chiefly letters written or received by Matthew Leeper, successively United States and Confederate States Indian Agent, brought from the Wichita Agency after the massacre of October, 1862.

LINCOLN, ABRAHAM. Writings, edited by A. B. Lapsley (New York, 1905-1906), 8 vols.

—— Complete Works, edited by John G. Nicolay and John Hay (New York, 1894), 2 vols.

McPHERSON, EDWARD. Political history of the United States of America during the Great Rebellion (Washington, 1864).

MASON, EMILY V. Southern poems of the war (Baltimore, 1867).

MATTHEWS, JAMES M., editor. Statutes at Large of the Confederate States of America from February 8, 1861 to February 18, 1862, together with the constitution of the provisional government and the permanent constitution of the Confederate States, and the treaties concluded by the Confederate States with the Indian tribes (Richmond, 1864).

—— Statutes at Large of the first congress of the Confederate States of America (Richmond, 1862), pamphlet.

—— Statutes at Large of the Confederate States of America, commencing the first session of the first congress and including the first session of the second congress (Richmond, 1864).

MISSOURI. Adjutant-general's report of the Missouri State Militia for 1861 (St. Louis, 1862).

MOORE, FRANK, editor. Diary, or Rebellion record (New York, 1868), 11 vols. and a supplementary volume for 1861-1864.

NEWSPAPERS. Arkansas Baptist (Little Rock).
Arkansas Gazette (Little Rock).
Arkansas Intelligencer (Van Buren).
Arkansas True Democrat (Little Rock).
Chronicle, The (Little Rock).
Daily National Democrat (Little Rock).
Daily State Journal (Little Rock).
National Democrat (Little Rock).
State Rights Democrat, The (Little Rock).
Unconditional Union (Little Rock).
Weekly Arkansas Gazette (Little Rock).

PHISTERER, FREDERICK. Statistical record of the armies of the United States (New York, 1890).
Supplementary volume to the Campaigns of the Civil War Series.

PIKE, ALBERT. Poems, edited by his daughter, Mrs. Lillian Pike Roome (Little Rock, 1900).

RAINES, C. W., editor. Six decades in Texas, or the memoirs of F. R. Lubbock (Austin, 1890).

RECTOR, ELIAS. Letter Book.
A Fragment. Ms. in United States Indian Office among the Fort Smith Papers. Many of the letters have been almost obliterated by exposure.

RICHARDSON, JAMES D., editor. Compilation of the messages and papers of the Confederacy, including the diplomatic correspondence (Nashville, 1905), 2 vols.

—— Compilation of the messages and papers of the presidents, 1789-1897 (Washington, 1896-1899), 10 vols.

SEWARD, WILLIAM H. Works, edited by G. E. Baker (New York, 1853-1884), 5 vols.

SMITH, WILLIAM R. History and debates of the convention of the people of Alabama, January 7, 1861 (Montgomery, 1861).

TEXAS. Ordinances and resolutions of the convention held in the city of Austin, January 28, 1861, to February 24, 1861 (Austin, 1861).

UNITED STATES OF AMERICA. Attorney-general, opinions, 1791-1908 (Washington, 1852 –).

—— Report of Covode committee, 1860 (House *Reports*, 36th congress, first session, no. 648).

—— Report of select committee to investigate abstraction of bonds held in trust by the United States government for the Indian tribes (House *Reports*, 36th congress, second session, no. 78).

—— Department of the Interior, Reports of the Secretary, 1861-1865, inclusive.

—— Office of Indian Affairs, Land Files, General Files, Miscellaneous Files, and Special Files.

—— Office of Indian Affairs, Letter Books [letters sent]:
No. 50, August 28, 1854 to February 20, 1855.
" 51, February 21, 1855 to June 12, 1855.
" 52, June 13, 1855 to October 27, 1855.
" 53, October 29, 1855 to March 19, 1856.
" 54, March 20, 1856 to July 30, 1856.
" 55, July 31, 1856 to December 31, 1856.
" 56, January 2, 1857 to May 25, 1857.
" 57, May 26, 1857 to October 31, 1857.

" 58, November 2, 1857 to April 30, 1858.
" 59 May 1, 1858 to October 23, 1858.
" 60, October 25, 1858 to April 29, 1859.
" 61, April 30, 1859 to August 23, 1859.
" 62, August 24, 1859 to February 9, 1860.
" 63, February 10, 1860 to June 26, 1860.
" 64, June 27, 1860 to December 7, 1860.
" 65, December 8, 1860 to June 1, 1861.
" 66, June 3, 1861 to October 23, 1861.
" 67, October 24, 1861 to March 25, 1862.
" 68, March 26, 1862 to August 7, 1862.
" 69, August 8, 1862 to January 20, 1863.
" 70, January 20, 1863 to June 5, 1863.
" 71, June 5, 1863 to October 14, 1863.
" 72, October 15, 1863 to January 8, 1864.
" 73, January 9, 1864 to April 23, 1864.
" 74, April 25, 1864 to July 28, 1864.
" 75, July 28, 1864 to December 7, 1864.
" 76, December 8, 1864 to April 4, 1865.
" 77, April 4, 1865 to August 3, 1865.
" 78, August 3, 1865 to December 8, 1865.

UNITED STATES OF AMERICA. Office of Indian Affairs, Registers (letters received):

No. 44, January 4, 1855 to July 31, 1855.
" 45, August 1, 1855 to December 31, 1855.
" 46, January 1, 1856 to June 30, 1856.
" 47, July 1, 1856 to December 31, 1856.
" 48, January 1, 1857 to June 30, 1857.
" 49, July 1, 1857 to December 31, 1857.
" 50, January 1, 1858 to June 25, 1858.
" 51, June 25, 1858 to December 29, 1858.
" 52, December 30, 1858 to June 27, 1859.
" 53, June 28, 1859 to December 31, 1859.
" 54, January 1, 1860 to June 1, 1860.
" 55, June 1, 1860 to December 31, 1860.
" 56, January 1, 1861 to June 30, 1861.
" 57, July 1, 1861 to December 31, 1861.
" 58, January 1, 1862 to July 1, 1862.
" 59, July 1, 1862 to December 31, 1862.
" 60, January 1, 1863 to June 30, 1863.
" 61, July 1, 1863 to January 2, 1864.
" 62, January 2, 1864 to May 30, 1864.
" 63, June 1, 1864 to December 31, 1864.
" 64, January 1, 1865 to June 30, 1865.
" 65, July 1, 1865 to December 29, 1865.

UNITED STATES OF AMERICA. Office of Indian Affairs, Report Books:

No. 8, May 1, 1854 to August 9, 1855.
" 9, August 10, 1855 to December 31, 1856.
" 10, January 1, 1857 to March 31, 1858.
" 11, April 1, 1858 to September 2, 1860.
" 12, September 3, 1860 to December 9, 1862.
" 13, December 12, 1862 to August 19, 1864.
" 14, August 20, 1864 to December 12, 1865.

—— Department of War, Reports of the Secretary, 1861-1865, inclusive.

—— Statutes at Large (Boston, 1850 –).

WAR OF THE REBELLION. Compilation of the official records of the Union and Confederate armies (Washington), 129 serial volumes and an index volume.

WELLES, GIDEON. Diary (Boston, 1911), 3 vols.

III. ALPHABETICAL LIST OF AUTHORITIES

ABBOTT, LUTHER J. History and Civics of Oklahoma (Boston, 1910).

ABEL, ANNIE HELOISE. Indians in the Civil War (*American Historical Review*, vol. xv, 281-296).

—— Indian reservations in Kansas and the extinguishment of their titles (Kansas Historical Society, *Collections*, vol. viii, 72-109).

—— History of events resulting in Indian consolidation west of the Mississippi River (American Historical Association, *Report*, 1906).

—— Proposals for an Indian State in the Union, 1778-1878 (American Historical Association, *Report*, 1907, vol. i, 89-102).

ADAMS, RICHARD C. Brief history of the Delaware Indians (Senate *Documents*, 59th congress, first session, no. 501).

ALEXANDER, GROSS. History of the Methodist Church South (New York, 1894).

BANCROFT, FREDERIC. Life of William H. Seward (New York, 1900), 2 vols.

BAPTIST HOME MISSIONS in North America, 1832-1882.
    Published by the American Baptist Home Missionary Society, New York, 1883.

BISHOP, ALBERT WEBB. Loyalty on the frontier, or sketches of union men of the southwest (St. Louis, 1863).

BOUDINOT, ELIAS C. Speech delivered before the House Committee on Territories, February 7, 1872 (Washington, 1872), pamphlet.
—— Oklahoma, an argument before the House Committee on Territories, January 29, 1878 (Alexandria, 1878), pamphlet.

BREWERTON, G. DOUGLAS. War in Kansas (New York, 1856).

BRIGHAM, JOHNSON. James Harlan (Iowa City, Ia., 1913).

BRITTON, WILEY. Memoirs of the rebellion on the border, 1863 (Chicago, 1882).
—— Civil War on the border, 1861-1862 (New York, 1891).

BROUGH, CHARLES HILLMAN. Historic battlefields (Arkansas Historical Society, *Publications*, vol. i, 278-285).

BROWN, GEORGE W. Reminiscences of Governor R. J. Walker, with the true story of the rescue of Kansas from slavery (Rockford, Ill., 1902).

BRUCE, HENRY. Life of General Houston (New York, 1891).

CALLAHAN, JAMES MORTON. Diplomatic history of the southern confederacy (Baltimore, 1901).

CHEROKEE INDIANS. Memorial of the delegates of the Cherokee Nation to the president and congress of the United States (Washington *Chronicle Print*, 1886).

CHESHIRE, JOSEPH BLUNT. Church in the Confederate States (New York, 1912).

CONNELLEY, WILLIAM ELSEY. James Henry Lane (Topeka, 1899).
—— Quantrill and the border wars (Cedar Rapids, 1910).

CORDLEY, RICHARD. History of Lawrence (Lawrence, 1895).

DAVIS, JEFFERSON. Rise and fall of the Confederate government (New York, 1881), 2 vols.

DELAWARE INDIANS. Report on the military service (United States Senate *Documents*, 61st congress, first session, no. 134).

DRAPER, J. W. History of the American Civil War (New York, 1867-1870), 3 vols.

EVANS, GENERAL CLEMENT A., editor. Confederate military history (Atlanta, 1899), 10 vols.

FITE, EMERSON DAVID. Presidential campaign of 1860 (New York, 1911).

FLEMING, WALTER L. Civil War and Reconstruction in Alabama (New York, 1905).

FOULKE, WILLIAM DUDLEY. Life of Oliver P. Morton (Indianapolis, 1899), 8 vols.

GARRISON, W. P. and F. J. GARRISON. William Lloyd Garrison, 1805-1879 (Boston, 1894), 4 vols.

GIHON, JOHN H. Geary and Kansas (Philadelphia, 1866).

GOODLANDER, C. W. Memoirs and recollections of the early days of Fort Scott (Fort Scott, Kans., 1899).

GREELEY, HORACE. American Conflict (Hartford, 1864-1867), 2 vols.

HALLUM, JOHN. Biographical and pictorial history of Arkansas (Albany, 1887).

HILL, LUTHER B. History of the state of Oklahoma (Chicago, 1908), 8 vols.

HODDER, FRANK HEYWOOD. The Genesis of the Kansas-Nebraska Act (Wisconsin State Historical Society, *Proceedings for 1912*, pp. 69-86), (Madison, 1913), pamphlet.

HOLLOWAY, JOHN N. History of Kansas to 1861 (Lafayette, Ind., 1868).

HOLST, HERMANN VON. Constitutional and political history of the United States (Chicago, 1876-1892), 7 vols.

JOHNSON, ALLEN. Stephen A. Douglas (New York, 1908).

JOHNSON, THOMAS CARY. History of the Southern Presbyterian Church (New York, 1894). American Church History Series, vol. xi.

KAUFMAN, WILHELM. Sigel und Halleck (*Deutsch-Am. Geschichtsblätter*, Band x, 210-216).

MARTIN, GEORGE W. First two years of Kansas (Topeka, 1907), pamphlet.

MEIGS, W. M. Life of Thomas Hart Benton (Philadelphia, 1904).

NORTH, THOMAS. Five years in Texas, 1861-1865 (Cincinnati, 1871).

PARKER, THOMAS VALENTINE. Cherokee Indians (New York, 1907).

PAXTON, WILLIAM M. Annals of Platte County, Missouri (Kansas City, Mo., 1897).

PHILLIPS, ULRICH. Georgia and state rights (Washington, 1902).
—— The life of Robert Toombs (New York, 1913).

RAMSDELL, CHARLES WM. Reconstruction in Texas (Columbia University *Studies in History, Economics, and Public Law*, vol. xxxvi, no. 1).

RAY, P. ORMAN. Repeal of the Missouri Compromise, its origin and authorship (Cleveland, 1909).

REYNOLDS, JOHN H. Makers of Arkansas (Story of the States series), (New York, 1905).

RHODES, JAMES FORD. History of the United States from the Compromise of 1850 (New York, 1893-1906), 7 vols.

ROBINSON, CHARLES. Kansas Conflict (Lawrence, 1898).

ROBLEY, T. F. History of Bourbon County, Kansas, to the close of 1865 (Fort Scott, 1894).

ROSS, D. H. and others. Reply of the delegates of the Cherokee Nation to the demands of the commissioner of Indian affairs, May, 1866 (Washington, 1866), pamphlet.
    Land Files, Treaties, Box 3, M392.

ROSS, MRS. WM. P. Life and times of William P. Ross (Fort Smith, 1893).

SCHOULER, JAMES. History of the United States under the Constitution (New York, 1899), 6 vols.

SCHWAB, JOHN CHRISTOPHER. Confederate States of America, 1861-1865 (New York, 1901).

SHINN, JOSIAH. Pioneers and makers of Arkansas (Little Rock, 1908).

SPECK, FRANK G. Creeks of Taskigi Town. American Anthropological Association *Publications*, vol. ii, part 2.

SPEER, JOHN. Life of James H. Lane (Garden City, Kans., 1897).

SPRING, LEVERETT W. Kansas: the prelude to the War for the Union (American Commonwealth series), (Boston, 1885).

STEPHENS, ALEXANDER H. Constitutional view of the late War between the States (Philadelphia, 1870), 2 vols.

STOVALL, PLEASANT A. Robert Toombs (New York, 1892).

TENNEY, W. J. Military and naval history of the rebellion in the United States (New York, 1866).

THOMPSON, ROBERT ELLIS. History of the Presbyterian Churches in the United States (American Church History series, vol. vi), (New York, 1893).

VAN DEVENTER, HORACE. Albert Pike, 1809-1891 (Knoxville, 1910).

VILLARD, OSWALD GARRISON. John Brown, 1800-1859; biography fifty years after (Boston, 1910).

WALKER, WILLISTON. History of the Congregational Churches in the United States (American Church History series, vol. iii), (New York, 1894).

WILDER, D. W. Annals of Kansas (Topeka, 1875, 1885).

WILSON, HENRY. Rise and fall of the slave power in America (Boston, 1872-1877), 3 vols.

WOOTEN, DUDLEY G. Comprehensive history of Texas (Dallas, 1898), 2 vols.

INDEX

ABBOTT, J. B: 245, *footnote*

Abel, Annie Heloise: work cited, 71, *footnote*, 191, *footnote*

Abolitionists: Indians' slaves enticed away, 23; charges against Calhoun, 30; Quantrill in league with, 48; desire Indian lands, 76, 118; among Cherokees, 132; Cherokees repudiate idea that they are, 225; charges against, 291-294

Adair, W. P: 219, *footnote*

Address: of John Ross at Cherokee mass-meeting, 220

Agency system: under Confederacy, 179

Alabama: Creeks, Choctaws, and Chickasaws from, 20, 193, *footnote*; Choctaws in, 20, *footnote*; David Hubbard, commissioner from, 108

Alliance: Indians given political position in return for, 17; reasons for southern Indians entering into, with Confederacy, 18; Confederate State Department to effect, 140, *footnote*; failure of Pike to effect, with Cherokees, 156; Choctaw General Council authorizes negotiation of treaty of, 156; Confederacy paid dearly for its Indian, 177; nature of Seminole, with Confederacy, 197; principles of active, inserted by Pike into treaties, 212; McCulloch to accept Drew's regiment of Home Guards as soon as treaty of, be consummated, 227; conditions of, between the Indians and Confederacy, 280; result of Battle of Pea Ridge on Indian, 284

Allies: Indian, 17; hope of finding in Cherokees, 125

Allotment in severalty: suggested to Creeks, Choctaws, and Chickasaws, 58

American Baptist Missionary Union: 38

American Board of Commissioners for Foreign Missions: work among Cherokees and Choctaws, 39; records of, 40, *footnote*; missionaries among Choctaws remove themselves from patronage, 41, 42, 43, *footnote*

American Civil War: [See Civil War]

American Historical Association: *Report*, 20, *footnote*

American Revolution: effect upon Cherokee emigration to Texas, 20, *footnote*; work of Committees of Correspondence in connection with, 83

Amnesty: provided for, 176

Annuities: negro and Indian halfbreeds share Indian, 23, *footnote*; Choctaw, distinct from Chickasaw, 34, *footnote*; Indian, declared forfeited by Lincoln government, 145; John Ross considers Indian, safe, 147; payment of Indian, assumed by Confederacy, 163; Indian, diverted from regular channels, 170; to use, of hostile Indians, 274; Crawford makes requisition for Cherokee, 307

Antelope Hills: 55, 136, *footnote*

Apucks-hu-nubbe: district of, 34, *footnote*

Arbuckle, General: 193, *footnote*

Arkansas: Choctaws and Cherokees tarry in, 19, *footnote*; Indian Territory annexed to, for judicial purposes, 23, *footnote*; and Indian patronage, 59; and Indian participa-

tion for the opening up of, 28; compared with Choctaw country, 31, *footnote*; suggested organization causes excitement among Indians, 33-34; citizens encroach upon Cherokee Neutral Lands, 46; drouth in, 58; political status of tribes in, 62, *footnote*; and Cherokee Outlet, 64; Elder, citizen of, 186; Pike desires to raise Indian battalion, 207; Indians wish to fight, 227, *footnote*

Kansas Historical Society: *Collections*, 19, *footnote*, 34, *footnote*

Kansas-Nebraska Bill: effect upon Indian interests, 29, 35; settlers demand Indians to vacate territory covered by, 36; Seward's speech on, 58-59

Kansas Territory: first districting illegally included Indian lands, 35; free-state settlers charge Buchanan government with bad faith, 37

Kappler, C. J: work cited, 20, *footnote*, 34, *footnote*, 49, *footnote*, 50, *footnote*, 52, *footnote*

Kaskaskias: from Illinois, 19

Keitt, Lawrence M: 127, 129

Kennedy, John C: 211, *footnote*

Kickapoos: from Indiana, 19; tarry in Missouri, 19, *footnote*; denominationalism among, 37, *footnote*; refugees, 56, *footnote*; Leeper to communicate with, in name of Albert Pike, 181, *footnote*; Pike hopes to meet, 189, *footnote*

Kile, William: 261, *footnote*, 274

Kingsbury, Rev. Cyrus: 40, and *footnote*, 43, *footnote*, 76

Kingsbury Jr., Cyrus: 79

Kiowas: 52; Texans reported tampering with, 210, *footnote*; messengers from, 309; talk for, 320; treaty with, to be effected, 323, 331; delegation of, 324; Big-head, chief of, 342; Lone Wolf, chief of, 350; E-sasem-mus, chief of, 350; annual festival of, 351; treaty with, 354

Knights of Golden Circle: probable influence with Arkansas Legislature, 68, *footnote*; evidence of activity among Indians, 68; halfbreeds belong to, 86, *footnote*

Koonsha Female Seminary: 40, *footnote*

LANDS: plot to dispossess Indian of, 18; pledged by U.S. government as Indian possession in perpetuity, 18, 28; of Cherokees extended north of thirty-seventh parallel, 21; of Indians coveted by Forty-niners, 28; of Indians in Kansas excluded from local governmental control, 35; allotment in severalty proposed to Creeks, Choctaws, and Chickasaws, 58; violation of treaties to cost Indians their, 86, *footnote*; property rights of Indians guaranteed by Confederacy, 161 *et seq.*; Indians to have right to dispose of by will, 172; Cherokee halfbreeds fear designs upon Indian, 216

Lane, James H: 125, 229, 231, *footnote*, 233, 242, 251 and *footnote*, 265, 270, 276, 278

Lane, W. P: 357

Laughinghouse, G. W: 120

Leased District: 52 and *footnote*, 54, 56, 57, *footnote*, 63, 67, 96, 179, 199, 297, 340, 349

Lee, Robert E: 88, *footnote*, 98, *footnote*, 99

Lee, S. Orlando: letter, 75-79, 197, *footnote*

Leeper, Matthew: 57 and *footnote*, 82 and *footnote*, 96, 98 and *footnote*, 99, 180, *footnote*, 199, *footnote*, 303, 304-307, 311, 315-319; removal of, asked for by Rector, 323; death of, 329, *footnote*; charges against, 333

Leeper Papers: cited, 57, *footnote*, 99, *footnote*, 102, *footnote*, 181, *footnote*, 186, *footnote*, 199, *footnote*, 200, *footnote*, 201, *footnote*, 329-357